Thunderbolt to the Rebels

The United States Sharpshooters in the Civil War

Darin Wipperman

STACKPOLE
BOOKS

Essex, Connecticut
Blue Ridge Summit, Pennsylvania

STACKPOLE BOOKS
An imprint of The Globe Pequot Publishing Group, Inc.
64 S. Main Street
Essex, CT 06246
www.globepequot.com

Distributed by NATIONAL BOOK NETWORK

British Library Cataloguing in Publication Information available

Library of Congress Cataloging-in-Publication Data available

978-0-8117-7568-7 (cloth)
978-0-8117-7569-4 (electronic)

∞™ The paper used in this publication meets the minimum requirements of American National Standard for Information Sciences—Permanence of Paper for Printed Library Materials, ANSI/NISO Z39.48-1992.

To the expert marksmen of the United States Sharpshooters

Men must understand each other, or they will always war.

—John Monahan, Company F,
1st United States Sharpshooters, 1863

Contents

List of Maps

Acknowledgments

My wife Jan has played a key role in all three of my Civil War books. She was a great researcher and proofreader again, immeasurably helping me tell anew the story of the United States Sharpshooters. She also volunteered to create the bibliography, a work taking many hours. Jan did a brilliant job on that necessary part of the book, saving me much time. Her work and support will forever be appreciated.

I must profusely thank two excellent scholars who read my entire manuscript. I met Dr. Zack Fry when we both gave presentations at the 2023 Spring Symposium of the Antietam Institute. He quickly agreed to assist me, which led to numerous improvements to my finished product. Dr. Tim Orr, who has researched and written a great deal about the USSS, provided many cogent ideas, leading to very positive changes. Both Zack and Tim helped me greatly with their time, knowledge, and kindness.

As my work on this manuscript wound down, I had e-mail exchanges with John J. Hennessy, a highly respected historian who worked for many years at the National Park Service. John provided me several digital files with Sharpshooters' letters that I had not found in my research, especially important because they added perspectives from New York and Michigan marksmen, relatively underrepresented companies in surviving sources. I very much appreciate John's interest in sharing information with me. His wonderful history of Second Manassas, *Return to Bull Run,* remains my all-time favorite Civil War campaign history. John's eager assistance honored me greatly.

Dave Reisch at Stackpole Books has shown great faith in me for several years now. I appreciate his guidance and expertise. Across the years several other Stackpole staff have worked really well with me in turning a manuscript into a finished product.

Superb maps can improve any Civil War book. Once again, Hal Jesperson provided his cartographic images to make a story of mine better. Hal works incredibly well with authors. I thank him for a third time for his map-making acumen. May Hal live a very long life and never retire.

The public servants and others who make old books, newspapers, and manuscripts easily available through the Internet save countless hours for authors. Fruitful visits to several libraries to review manuscript collections and books also made my story about the USSS possible. Civil War historians and readers should be forever grateful for the diligent work of those preserving and providing access to records of the conflict.

Because so many dedicated people post tidbits about individuals on FindaGrave.com, I often used the site, which can include extensive details about Sharpshooters, including letters and obituaries. I thank the wonderful people I will never know who helped me along on this endeavor through their electronic postings.

Two FindaGrave users deserve special mention. The book's cover photograph appears courtesy of Jade Schmitt Wanger, a very diligent genealogist and FindaGrave veteran. I grew fascinated with the three Tarbell brothers in the picture, Jade's great uncles four generations previous. Thomas, James, and Abner served together in Company E, 2nd Regiment. Brian White's fine work over the years includes the posting of many USSS photographs. I thank Jade and Brian for allowing me to publish from their personal collections.

Nothing illustrates the trauma experienced in the USSS better than the words of the marksmen themselves. The soldiers' perspectives crafted this book far more than my efforts at researching, writing, and editing. The warriors in green have my infinite respect. I dedicate the finished product to all those who served in the USSS.

Although assisted greatly by many, I alone hold responsibility for any errors herein.

Preface

Born eighteen months apart in the early 1840s, Silas Howard and Robert Twombly learned to shoot well. When their country called during the Civil War, the superb marksmanship of Howard, Twombly, and hundreds of others accrued to the Union's benefit through their enlistment in the 1st or 2nd United States Sharpshooters (USSS). Howard and Twombly mustered into the 2nd Sharpshooters, with Howard, who was born in New York, part of a Vermont company, and Twombly joining from his native New Hampshire. West of Antietam Creek on September 17, 1862, both men sustained wounds on what would be the bloodiest day in the history of the United States and the second deadliest for the 2nd Sharpshooters. Not yet twenty years old, Twombly suffered a fatal headshot "while pulling down the Rebel flag" along the Hagerstown Pike. Howard's multiple injuries nearly added him to the list of the slain. Instead, the tough Yankee breathed his last in October 1928, one week short of his eighty-seventh birthday, nearly two-thirds of a century after his Antietam wounds.[1]

The word "sharpshooter" finds frequent use in contemporary and modern sources pertaining to the Civil War. Several companies or regiments had "Sharpshooter" in their names. Although any skilled rifleman could lay claim to the title of sharpshooter, this book focuses only on the 1st or 2nd United States Sharpshooters, often referred to as Berdan's Sharpshooters. The 1st Sharpshooters included ten companies from five states, while the 2nd enrolled eight companies from six states. With less than ten companies, the 2nd Sharpshooters served as a battalion, but, like other authors, I will refer to the unit as a regiment for the sake of simplicity.

Like regiments in their nation's professional army, the USSS had "United States" in their name. Nonetheless, the Sharpshooters were not Regular Army soldiers. Some sources erroneously list the marksmen as professional troops.

Instead, USSS members enlisted as volunteers through their respective states, like most of their infantry comrades.

Because much has been written about the United States Sharpshooters, some may doubt the utility of a new extended treatment. After conducting a research project to identify members of the USSS who died from battle wounds, I discovered that much new could be told about their field service. The content of many fine books and articles detail Hiram Berdan—the founding father of the Sharpshooters—their Camp of Instruction early in the war, the soldiers' excellent Sharps Rifle, and unique green uniforms. All of these important topics receive their due in the forthcoming pages, but this book focuses on the two regiments' very difficult thirty-four months of combat operations starting with the 1st USSS at Yorktown in April 1862.

I tell this story of the Sharpshooters thanks to a wide range of primary sources, several untapped in previous USSS histories or articles. Light gets shed—and some men gain a spotlight after being rarely if ever mentioned before—when certain letters, diaries, and memoirs gain a wider audience. No author can use every possible source, but I wished to present more of the Sharpshooters' own words to illustrate how they felt, lived, and died.

As part of the Army of the Potomac, the USSS won extensive laurels. For all the glamour of their status as elite warriors, the Sharpshooters faced many obstacles and endured immense trials just like those in the less exalted infantry regiments. Although envisioned with a distinct role, the Sharpshooters often did not feel special. They echoed many of the complaints of infantrymen. USSS companies often charged like infantry, rather than their expected role of concealing themselves to target cannoneers and enemy officers. Sharpshooters were not spared from fatigue duty either, frequently spending days gathering wood, building roads, or constructing entrenchments.

Problems existed in the USSS for a variety of reasons. The men rightly lacked faith in Berdan's leadership, while some adapted poorly to the rigors and hierarchy of military life. Also, many Sharpshooters grew distraught about the pace and course of the war. In addition to not keeping several promises to the Sharpshooters, the army failed to create a formal tactical doctrine for the USSS, another blow for men who expected a lofty place in the war's story.

The army's neglect of the USSS as a special line of service constitutes the defining aspect of the eighteen companies' shared history. Inconsistent implementation of a proper vision of how best to deploy the Sharpshooters brought great frustration to the green-clad warriors. Moreover, the heavy toll taken by disease and battle losses laid bare the problem of insufficient USSS recruitment. Many companies dissolved after completion of three years of service, with the remainder broken up two months before the war ended. Clearly, the army failed to protect the marksmen from a steady decline in numbers to the point of oblivion.

Even with their waning fortunes, the Sharpshooters were deemed two of the "300 Fighting Regiments" across the Union's armies. William Fox, creator of the list in the late nineteenth century after his exhaustive study of casualty records, counted 278 killed or mortally wounded in the USSS, slightly more than 10 percent of all enlistees. This book lowers that number to 260 after the use of existing sources to confirm those Sharpshooters with a fatal battle wound. Such a downward revision is common when comparing Fox's numbers to extant data for many infantry regiments. Still, when adding deaths from disease and other non-battle causes, one in five Sharpshooters would not survive their war experience.

Casualty data can vary by source. Per a state roster, one Michigan company in the 1st Sharpshooters listed six more members killed in action or mortally wounded than Fox's total. In several other companies, Fox may have added to his tally a missing soldier without a confirmed death, a common mistake. Contrary to conventional wisdom, many missing men returned to their companies or survived as prisoners. Fox may have also counted as killed a wounded marksman without surviving evidence confirming death from a combat injury. Even accepting the variance that exists in the historical record, this book includes the names of all Sharpshooters who I confirmed through existing sources as having lost their lives to battle wounds. The appendix details the steps taken to identify the names of those fallen patriots.

The first year of battle for the USSS led to less than seventy combat fatalities, with nearly 30 percent of those in the 2nd Regiment at Antietam. After hard duty at Chancellorsville and Gettysburg in 1863, life grew much worse. More than one in four Sharpshooters who lost their lives from Confederate bullets or shells fell during an eight-day stretch in May 1864. Surviving primary sources are not as numerous for the last year in the field compared to earlier months. Nonetheless, much can and must be told about the Sharpshooters at the battle of the Wilderness and later due to the epic harm those months wrought.

Fox may have correctly opined that the USSS were "the best known of any regiments in the Army."[2] Nonetheless, many perspectives from their own words can still be presented to expand our understanding of the Sharpshooters as men and soldiers. No historian can tell the complete or perfect story of a Civil War battle or unit. A new book continues, rather than closes, the perpetual march of history. At the very least, through an intensive examination of source material, I hope to present a more complete picture of the individuals bravely serving and dying as United States Sharpshooters.

Introduction: Recruitment and the Camp of Instruction

Humanity's first highly skilled users of ranged weapons prowled battlefields millennia before the United States Sharpshooters in the 1860s. Two leading characteristics of human history—the drive to advance societal goals through technology and end lives through warfare—led to development of better weaponry and enhancement of warriors' skill sets across the generations.

Long before the invention of gunpowder, soldiers of the Roman Empire sometimes found themselves on the losing end of military advancements. A nineteenth-century historian described the utter destruction of a Roman army in 217 BCE at Lake Trasimene in central Italy. The Roman right flank became "overwhelmed by a storm of javelins and arrows." If this was not damaging enough, slingers added "ponderous stones" capable of crushing shields, helmets, and the hopes of Rome's military leaders. One modern author suggested the best "sharpshooters" in ancient times could hit a target more than one thousand feet away.[1]

In later centuries, inventive minds brought forth more ways to kill efficiently. Simply cutting grooves down the barrel of a long firearm, a process known as rifling, brought a sea change to warfare. A rifled barrel increased a round's speed and accuracy, leading to dramatically greater potency for any line or group of soldiers, especially troops possessing enhanced shooting skill.

The American Revolution proved the usefulness of dedicated and skilled riflemen. Early in their war against the mighty British, the Second Continental Congress envisioned excellent American shots with rifles obliterating lines of King George's Redcoats. The world's first battalion of riflemen, generally from the mid-Atlantic states, resulted from the vision of the Congress, with Daniel Morgan's troops earning a special place in the annals of American war.[2]

Hiram Berdan, a New York inventor and marksman, took the initiative to call for recruits into what would become the United States Sharpshooters. LIBRARY OF CONGRESS

The Civil War occurred during an era of fascinating technological change. With an inquisitive mind tailor-made for the times and the steady hand of a brilliant shot, inventor Hiram Berdan seemed destined to play a notable role in America's deadliest conflict. A New Yorker born in 1824, Berdan's creations assisted gold miners, sailors, telegraphers, and other groups. From a young age, Berdan found time to shoot as well as invent. He was likely the most famous marksman in the United States a decade before the Civil War without ever serving in the military. Berdan's talents offered his country seemingly limitless potential.

Northern interest in forming a group of sharpshooters began soon after the Confederate States of America bombarded Fort Sumter, South Carolina, in April 1861. With many individuals who knew Berdan's accomplishments, the inventor-marksman received suggestions to make real the idea of a group of skilled shooters with excellent rifles on the hunt for Confederate troops. One of Berdan's associates was Henry Albertson Van Zo Post, a young and skilled engineer destined to lead the 2nd USSS, if only for a short time.[3]

Busying himself with newspaper announcements and letters to state and national officials, Berdan sought to organize a band of expert riflemen. On May 31, the *New York Herald* published Berdan's call of the previous day to "The Sharpshooters of the North." Already, Berdan proclaimed, interested individuals inquired about the possibility of joining a sharpshooter regiment. Therefore,

> *I propose that all gentleman who have made themselves good shots at long distance, who are willing to place their skill in this way at the service of our country in this her great struggle, should send their names to me, with an affidavit showing the best shooting they have done at two hundred yards, or more. . . . No application will be considered in which the average of ten consecutive shots exceeds five inches from the centre of the target to the centre of the ball at two hundred yards.*[4]

A prewar associate of Berdan, Henry A. V. Post would take command of the 2nd USSS. Nearly eight full years younger than Berdan, Post took to his task as regimental commander with a focus on discipline without losing the respect of his men. A wound would require Post to end his military service far too soon, with his very appreciative eight companies of marksmen remembering his great courage and leadership.LIBRARY OF CONGRESS

Other Northern editors helped get the word out. A Vermonter, rightly suggesting the state "abounds in sharp-shooters," called on a new generation of Green Mountain Men to try out for Berdan's force. Much to the chagrin of many future members of the USSS, the exuberant newspaperman proved incorrect with part of his analysis when he predicted Berdan's men would "be devoted to *sharp-shooting, and nothing else.*"[5]

Less than two weeks after Berdan's letter to the North's marksmen, the *New York Herald* editorialized, "We hope that every sharpshooter in the country will report himself without delay, properly armed and equipped." The *Herald*'s suggestion for sharpshooters to bring their own weapons looked prophetic because U.S. Secretary of War Simon Cameron flatly declared the government would not foot the bill. After Berdan gained the approbation of President Abraham Lincoln and Winfield Scott, the army's general-in-chief, Cameron swiftly authorized the formation of a sharpshooter regiment. However, the secretary concluded his June 15 missive by declaring the regiment could not be armed at the expense of the government.[6]

Determined and resourceful men organizing companies (about one hundred soldiers each) constituted the most important development in the early history of what would soon be known as the United States Sharpshooters. Caspar Trepp, a New Yorker and citizen of Switzerland with experience leading marksmen in Europe, sought a meeting with Berdan after hearing about plans for a sharpshooter regiment. Trepp then assisted with organizing what became Company A, 1st USSS. Most of the men passing the marksmanship test and enlisting in the company were natives of either the German states or Trepp's home country. A proud New York journalist labeled Company A's men as professionals who were "almost unerring in their aim."[7]

Dozens more Empire State residents eagerly tried to join Berdan's elite organization. New York would contribute three additional companies to the 1st Regiment: B, D, and H. Southeast of Rochester in Yates County, orderly sergeant John Smith Brown visited the town of Penn Yan, enlisting Lt. William Elmendorf and others. Elmendorf remained as a recruiting officer for what would become Company B. A local newspaper ebulliently noted the prowess of those earning their place in the company's budding ranks. Confederate troops would "stand clear when these boys get a crack at them," the reporter promised.[8]

George Hastings, an affluent Yale graduate, established a recruiting office in Brooklyn, with the goal of raising a company for Berdan. With a target range nearby and travel from Albany through Long Island, Hastings established credentials as a motivated and dependable leader. He served as the original captain of Company H.[9]

Marksmanship tests close to the urban environments of New York's cities could attract large crowds. In July, hundreds of interested Albany residents saw Berdan and some dignitaries preside over a shooting audition as dozens attempted to meet the USSS standard. Only six applicants satisfied the shooting requirement that day, although a newspaper reported the sessions would continue for a few days to attract more Sharpshooters. Albany's leading citizens, the paper added, wished the city "to be fully represented in this greatest of all regiments." Ads for new recruits would run in an Albany newspaper into 1862.[10]

On August 17, several men tried out in Brooklyn. As in Albany the month before, many of those looking to make the cut failed the test. Determination to help fill a select unit burned bright for those not accurate enough, with "most of them saying they would practice until they could be admitted into the regiment." Another round of marksmanship tests was slated for the 19th, offering the rejected patriots a chance to erase their disappointment.[11]

Great pride accompanied the new enlistees, with many immigrants feeling intense emotions. Rudolf Aschmann, only twenty years old, viewed the war as necessary for the betterment of the United States, because slavery was contrary to his new nation's ideals. A degree of hesitancy cast some doubt over Aschmann's decision to fight. He wondered if someone could hold such strong feelings for two countries, his native Switzerland and the United States. Those philosophical musings encumbered Aschmann for only a short time. He concluded all men should feel bound to fight for freedom.[12]

On August 7, a newspaper suggested fifteen total companies would be raised in states outside New York, only one more than reality by the end of the year. Nonetheless, states such as Missouri and Kentucky promised companies that never mustered in. New York's governor envisioned an entire ten-company regiment of Empire State Sharpshooters for Berdan, six short of what would actually happen.[13] Optimism failing to pan out became something USSS members would experience across the war.

In communities throughout several states, Sharpshooters meeting the marksmanship test began their journey to destiny. In mid-August, eight recruits departed Hillsdale, Michigan. Showing deep appreciation for the patriot marksmen, a large crowd gave three cheers as the train started south for Detroit, where the first of Michigan's four USSS companies would be organized. As a newspaper reported, "the boys responded from the platform of the rear car, with three cheers for Hillsdale." The story continued, "Those who have joined the company from this place are not only sharp shooters, but active and energetic young men." Less than a year later, two of the eight Hillsdale warriors would be out of the army, discharged for disability. Another duo in the brave group would die before the war ended.[14]

Weehawken, New Jersey, served as the initial training site for organized companies of the 1st Sharpshooters. The New Yorkers quickly formed at the regiment's Garden State camp, finding good comradery and plentiful food. George Hastings oversaw additional recruitment efforts at Weehawken, with New Yorkers invited to take the 42nd Street ferry across the Hudson if they wished to try out as a Sharpshooter.[15]

Shooting practice at Weehawken served as an obvious way for USSS members to display their skills. On August 13, forty-eight marksmen each fired a single shot at a target six hundred feet away. As a reporter described,

> *The target consisted of a painted figure of a man attached to an upright board . . . of the forty-eight balls fired, forty four pierced the target so near the line that they could all be covered by an eight inch circle of pasteboard. One of the others was aimed at the head, and passed through the forehead of the image, and the remaining three were put through the left arm about three inches from the heart spot.*[16]

Jocular marksmen shooting at a man-shaped target may have facilitated the primary goal of organizing the USSS. Modern studies suggest soldiers become more likely to develop a "killer instinct" during training when firing at human images compared to the traditional bull's-eye. This "conditional technique" can help someone become a dependable soldier.[17] The psychological dynamics of turning a fine squirrel hunter into a triumphant USSS member present complexities beyond the scope of this book. Nonetheless, any fun found during practice against human targets may very well have begun a mental transition for USSS members that would make them legendary warriors for the Union.

Men from northern New England, Michigan, and Wisconsin took longer to organize in their home states; they would spend little or no time in Weehawken before Berdan's soldiers set up a new camp and training ground in Washington, D.C., by late September. The site, a bit over a mile north of downtown Washington, would be called the Camp of Instruction, sometimes labeled Camp Burnside.[18]

The first New Hampshire company included men who all performed quite well in their shooting tryouts. A historian noted an impressive range of seven to thirty inches as the total distance from the center of the bull's-eye for each individual's ten shots. Thus, the worst marksman in the company missed the middle of a ten-inch target by only three inches in an average shot. The precise Granite Staters, under the command of twenty-three-year-old Dartmouth College graduate Capt. Amos Jones, would constitute Company E, 1st USSS.[19]

As a means to garner new recruits, newspapers helped Jones get the message out. A September call for more Sharpshooters noted the work of recruiter Horace Scales, a member of Company E, who had an office at a rifle factory in the town of Fremont. With the accuracy requirement Berdan established printed in an advertisement, readers were asked to, "Come early and join the best Regiment in the service."[20]

Vermonters answered the call early in Berdan's recruitment process. What would become Company F started under the command of Capt. Edmund Weston Jr., a thirty-one-year-old dentist. After a rendezvous in the town of Randolph, 113 enlisted men quickly proceeded to Weehawken. Berdan appreciated the state's work to raise a large number of excellent marksmen. His hopes would exceed reality, however. Berdan opined to the Green Mountain governor of his intention to fill an entire regiment (ten companies) with Vermonters.[21]

Like those in Company F, Wisconsin marksmen departed their home state in September. Under the original command of Capt. William Alexander, deemed "one of the best rifle shots in the world," the Badger State recruits learned about soldiering and what would be expected of them. Even prior to their departure from home, soldiers showed much respect for Alexander. One Sharpshooter wrote of the captain, "he can't be beat not only at shooting, but in good nature or anything else."

Company G started with 106 men. "You sent me a splendid Co[mpany]," Colonel Berdan wrote Captain Alexander, who was still in Wisconsin looking for more recruits. The colonel added, "They are making great progress in drill." Alexander remained home for months in an effort to send more qualified Sharpshooters to the Camp of Instruction.[22]

Organizing a Second Regiment

Berdan happily wrote Secretary Cameron in late September, noting the assembly of ten companies. Some of the men had already gone on a short expedition at the request of Maj. Gen. George McClellan, commander of Union forces around Washington known as the Army of the Potomac. Berdan's letter mentioned his goal of more than one additional regiment in the USSS, but he would only receive eight more companies. These units would become the 2nd USSS, pursuant to Cameron's October 3 authorization. Table I.1 lists the state of origin for each of the eighteen companies in the two USSS regiments.[23]

As during the organization of the 1st Regiment, enterprising men had been seeking sharpshooters, working with agents who spanned out across several states. After permission from the governor, Vermonter Homer Stoughton labored throughout autumn to augment the ranks of the USSS. He wrote letters from "Headquarters, 2nd Company, Vermont Sharpshooters" in West Randolph. In one missive, he promised the position of First Corporal, "or possibly a Sergeant" to one of his recruiters. Although interested in as many sharpshooters as possible, Captain Stoughton established, "No person of Intemperate habits will be accepted."[24]

Francis Peteler, original captain of Company A, labored to organize the westernmost outfit in the USSS. His Minnesotans journeyed to Washington in early autumn. With ranks rapidly filled, the company arrived at the Camp of Instruction on the morning of October 10, 1861. A resident of Minnesota serving in Berdan's Wisconsin company described Peteler's band as "Stalwart, hardy looking boys" after the wearying train ride. Peteler updated newspaper readers by declaring, "Our company attracted much attention. . . . We are all well satisfied with our reception." At the time, Company A included ninety-one officers and men.[25]

Michigan's fourth unit of Sharpshooters became Company B, 2nd USSS. Theodore Preston noted some positives and negatives in camp. "My health is good and has been all the while so far," Preston wrote, "The health of the Company has generally been good, not more than three or four boys having been dangerously sick. Two of the boys will be sent home on account of ill health." He added news of a comrade who, while wrestling the evening prior, sustained an

Table I.1. States of Origin for USSS Companies

1st United States Sharpshooters	
Company	**State**
A	New York
B	New York
C	Michigan
D	New York
E	New Hampshire
F	Vermont
G	Wisconsin
H	New York
I	Michigan
K	Michigan
2nd United States Sharpshooters	
Company	**State**
A	Minnesota
B	Michigan
C	Pennsylvania
D	Maine
E	Vermont
F	New Hampshire
G	New Hampshire
H	Vermont

injury when his elbow went out of joint. The energetic albeit battered marksman seemed better the following morning.[26]

Michigan's Company B illustrated what would become a defining aspect of the USSS, a frequent change in leadership. The three highest ranking members of the company, Capt. Andrew Stuart, 1st Lt. John Whitman, and 2nd Lt. Darius Calkins, would be gone from the command in under a year, two from resignation and one from a mortal wound.[27]

Pennsylvania's sole USSS company arrived in Washington with barely seventy members. Difficulties in recruiting would plague Company C across its years of service. A sergeant setting up a recruiting office in the state later in

1861 advertised a need for forty more members of the company. Individuals joining the company mustered in starting in September. Samuel Lattimer stood with his fellow Keystone Sharpshooters. Born in 1833 and a Pennsylvania native, Lattimer had married in 1856. His sister wed the brother of Lattimer's bride at the same service, certainly a memorable moment for the family. Sadly, Samuel departed for war a year after a tragedy. His young son had died in 1860.[28]

After spending much time in 1861 recruiting a Sharpshooter company, Vermonter Homer Stoughton logged an extended period of field service in the 2nd USSS before being captured in 1864. LIBRARY OF CONGRESS

Berdan sensibly considered Maine a great state from which to recruit avid hunters and those quite familiar with rifles. From Weehawken he wrote Maine officials, requesting the rapid organization of another component of the USSS. James Fessenden, son of William Pitt Fessenden, a U.S. Senator since 1854, would be a leading figure in the early history of Company D, 2nd Regiment. Men from across Maine became members, including Washington and Wellington Tucker, twin brothers from Cherryfield, in the southeast part of the Pine Tree State.[29]

Jacob McClure, who traveled widely in Maine to find recruits, expressed some frustration with the process. Fortunately, he continued to enlist qualified men in small groups across several months, writing state authorities about his time in Cherryfield, where he possibly oversaw the tryout of the Tucker twins. "I have done all that can be done without going as far east as Calais," on the Canadian border, McClure wrote in mid-October. "What men I have recruited more than fills my expectations," with McClure suggesting the men could become New England's best company of the war.[30]

Riflemen,
ATTENTION!

A COMPANY OF ONE HUNDRED MEN to be selected from the

BEST RIFLE SHOTS,

In the State, is to be raised to act as a COMPANY OF SHARP SHOOTERS through the War. Each man will be entitled to

A BOUNTY OF $22,00,

When mustered into the service of the United States, and

100,00 DOLLARS

at the close of the War, in addition to his regular pay.

No man will be accepted or mustered into service who is not an active and able bodied man, and who cannot when firing at a rest at a distance of two hundred yards, put ten consecutive shots into a target the average distance not to exceed five inches from the centre of the bull's eye to the centre of the ball; and all candidates will have to pass such an examination as to satisfy the recruiting officer of their fitness for enlistment in this corps.

Recruits having Rifles to which they are accustomed are requested to bring them to the place of rendezvous.

Recruits will be received by JAMES D. FESSENDEN,

Adams Block, No. 23, Market Square, PORTLAND, Maine.

Sept. 16, 1861.

Bridgton Reporter Press,—S. H. Noyes, Printer.

A Maine advertisement promoting USSS recruitment. LIBRARY OF CONGRESS

Maine's Adjutant General John Hodsdon ensured energetic work occurred to fill Company D. Back in the late summer of 1861 he declared, "The utmost dispatch in filling up this Company is required." The noble service of the Maine marksmen began with transport to Washington in mid-November, with initial duty including three consecutive days of drill at the Camp of Instruction starting on the 18th of the month.[31]

Already represented in the 1st Regiment, New Hampshire (Companies F and G) and Vermont (E and H) bolstered the 2nd USSS. With his work to raise another Green Mountain company, Homer Stoughton gained the leadership of Company E. Three officers and eighty-eight enlisted men mustered in on November 9, with a departure for Washington on the 21st. Company H would depart Vermont on the last day of the year, with nearly 20 percent of enlistees staying behind due to a measles outbreak, an early problem wherever USSS recruits camped.[32]

With nearly one hundred men each, New Hampshire sent their new USSS members to the Camp of Instruction by late autumn. The original captains were Henry Caldwell (F) and William McPherson (G), neither of whom would remain before the end of 1862.[33]

Early December started a highly unsatisfying military career for William B. Greene, Company G, who rapidly developed an aversion to soldiering. Family members appeared surprised to learn from one of Greene's December letters that he had joined the army. His mother, with observation skills of a great parent, told William on December 29, "You seem to write in pretty good spirits, but I think I can see through it."[34]

The Necessity of Training

Although each person entering the USSS proved highly accomplished with a rifle, much work remained to turn a shooter into a soldier. Like the infantrymen flocking to Washington camps as part of the Union army, USSS members could not escape repetitious drills and military discipline. Through their compulsory training, the men learned intently. Boring days without the action so many Sharpshooters craved had the purpose of instilling the tedious though vital actions and expert movements Berdan had in mind when envisioning a band of great marksmen.

Berdan had some sense of his own limitations as a military leader. Months before all eighteen companies of the USSS assembled in Washington, Berdan requested a training officer capable of turning raw marksmen into confident and dependable troops. The Sharpshooters soon gained the dedicated service of Frederick Mears, who had been born in early 1836. He became a respected

USSS member at a crucial time of learning for the command. Mears was in the 9th U.S. Infantry at the start of the Civil War, moving from lieutenant in the Regulars to lieutenant colonel in the 1st USSS. His teaching acumen helped regiments across the capital region. Prior to a return to the Regular Army and a post to the Pacific Northwest in early 1862, Mears trained about fourteen thousand volunteer soldiers around the national capital.[35]

Sharing an understanding of the importance of discipline in a military organization, Mears and Caspar Trepp formed a good team at the Camp of Instruction. Both earned the respect of the common soldier while also ensuring the men understood the rigors of military life and the basic maneuvers they would be expected to complete in stressful battlefield situations.[36]

Summing up his first few months in the army, 2nd Lt. Frederick Peet, Company H, 1st USSS, remembered, "Our life at Washington was a round of drills and instruction." Reality struck home plainly in an early edict. Pursuant to Regimental Order #5, issued on September 25, 1861, the command's regular post-breakfast exercises "will be devoted to company movements." Drill later in the day focused on skirmishing, the expected primary function for the USSS in the field.[37]

Learning to fan out, work independently, use cover, and quickly move were the hallmarks of what the Sharpshooters had to grasp as part of skirmish drill. Skirmishing was to be conducted by a single soldier, small group, or line of men in advance of the rest of the army. A skirmisher's role included early engagement with the opposing front line, keeping an eye on the enemy's movements, and targeting cannoneers or Confederate officers. Vermonter William Ripley, destined to rise to lieutenant colonel, 1st USSS, wrote of the "particular attention being paid to the skirmish drill, in which the men became wonderfully proficient." Even without the availability of arms across most companies, Ripley opined that USSS skirmishers "were excelled by few volunteer regiments in the service."[38]

How were the rookie soldiers to receive orders when dispersed? Bugles became the means for the USSS to act in concert even when not concentrated like a line of infantry. Turning orders into music offered the means to communicate with soldiers in camp, on training grounds, or on a battlefield. Each regiment had a Chief Bugler who worked with two men in every company to ensure musical sound fulfilled its vital purpose. To maintain sufficient backups in case of wounds, some officers attended bugle practices in addition to their regular duties, as Frederick Peet explained to his mother in a November letter.[39]

In early November, Sharpshooters celebrated news of George McClellan's promotion to general in chief, the highest position in the army. Minnesotan Joseph Dickey grew enthralled with the festivities marking McClellan's new position. "There was the greatest display of fire works that I ever saw," he penned. Dickey estimated some rockets burst two hundred feet in the air. The pleasant weather added to the memorable autumn day. Even without signs of engaging Confederates in battle, Dickey enjoyed camp. "There is something interesting taking place every few days," the Midwesterner wrote.[40]

A dispute between Berdan and Mears led to the younger officer's decision to leave the Sharpshooters in November 1861. Shortly before departing, Mears penned a note expressing optimism for the future of the USSS. The expert trainer "congratulates the Officers and men of this command on the assurances he continues to receive, public and private, of the rapid improvement and soldierly efficiency this command has attained in less than six weeks." With their devotion and growing expertise, Mears expected the men will "fight bravely" and, if necessary, "die nobly."[41]

Schedules for several months show some diversity in exercises. By early 1862, the soldiers completed different kinds of drill across the five weekdays, including field duty lasting six hours on Tuesday and Friday. The men sometimes performed battalion drill, which involved a group of multiple companies training together. Saturday included "general policing and cleaning of quarters and equipments."[42]

Regardless of the repetitive nature of their life as soldiers in training, military regimen did not sink in for many members of the USSS. Court-martial activity proved quite regular, with an assortment of punishments handed down. The prewar independent life of shooting and being free from restraint failed to translate well for dozens who buckled under their regimented U.S. Army life.

Disciplinary problems justifying court-martial began early in the Sharpshooters' experience. Fines of a month's pay resulted from several cases, while a private in Company A, 1st USSS was sentenced to fifteen days of hard labor and loss of two months' pay after an October incident. A month later, another Company A man had to wear a ball and chain in addition to forfeiting pay.[43]

A 2nd USSS soldier found himself in trouble amounting to three charges from an episode of misbehavior in early January 1862. He stood accused of referring to Colonel Berdan as a "God dammed old liar and a damned old fool," in addition to allegations the commanding officer was stealing money from his men. With conduct "prejudicial to good order and military discipline," the soldier hopefully learned a valuable lesson after the loss of a month's pay, reduction in rank, and placement on a bread and water diet for a week.

Later in the winter, four members of the 2nd USSS each faced a $5 fine and "severe reprimand" after not taking their duties as sentries seriously enough. An officer inspecting the line found the group "engaged in singing and conversation," obviously not paying sufficient attention to their task. In early March, another group of Sharpshooters faced justice after failures related to an inspection of their belongings. A corporal was to "be detailed for ten days extra guard duty for not having his knapsack properly packed and for giving as an excuse that he 'did not want to lug his clothes out in his knapsack.'"[44] Being an expert shot did not automatically make one a diligent and deferential soldier.

Even with the discipline problems, the Camp of Instruction instilled many positive memories. President Lincoln's visit to a shooting demonstration included practice by the chief executive himself. Berdan also showed his prowess with the rifle while Lincoln watched. As other Sharpshooters joined in, a distant effigy of Confederate President Jefferson Davis took a large number of hits, hilarious visual proof that the USSS meant business.[45]

Large crowds often visited Berdan's camp to see some of the best marksmen in the country as they trained. Friendly rivalry worked wonders, focusing the new soldiers on becoming even better. Most men continued using their own rifles from home; the government's issuance of weapons across all companies was months away. William Ripley remembered, "Under the stimulus of competition and organized practice, great improvement was noted in marksmanship, even among those who had been considered almost perfect marksmen before."[46]

"Special Pets of the Government"

Details related to equipping his command had been occupying Berdan since June. The inventive and analytical New Yorker had to change his thinking on a variety of important matters, including weaponry and the uniform for his men. At first, Berdan believed individuals' own target rifles provided a way to arm the Sharpshooters while being true to Cameron's dictate of no cost to the government. Target rifles made a poor choice, however, due primarily to their weight, with some exceeding thirty pounds. Even half that heft would be difficult to wield for a rapidly maneuverable force of stealthy marksmen. Some Sharpshooters suggested the target rifle's telescopic sight failed to offer a consistent ultra-accurate shot worth the trouble and extra weight.[47]

The government's concern about not incurring costs to arm the USSS soon disappeared from correspondence, alleviating one headache for Berdan. Perhaps Secretary Cameron gave up on the matter when told of the undesirability of cheaper muzzleloaders or the limits of target rifles in the field. Or, new Secretary of War Edwin Stanton, on the job in early 1862, may not have retained Cameron's stingy approach.

Differing thoughts about the best uniform for the USSS prevailed for a time. The idea of a green outfit, great especially during the warmer months so the men could blend in with leaves and grass, led to the ultimate resolution of the question. The USSS were not history's first soldiers to don green uniforms, but they looked exceptional compared to the blue of most infantry regiments. For months, Berdan viewed the distinctive color as vital to morale. In an August letter to the Governor of New York, Berdan suggested his soldiers would not accept a uniform that made them look like infantrymen.[48]

Berdan correctly ascertained the Sharpshooters' sense of their place in the war. Vermonter Curtis Abbott remembered how recruiters and state officials wished to inculcate a tremendous sense of pride in those meeting the marksmanship test. Looking back in his excellent memoir, Abbott rightly mocked the grandiloquence of bureaucrats, suggesting the government hoodwinked the USSS and many other Union soldiers.

> *Among the inducements held out to recruits, was a special line of service, with many immunities from the drudgery of the infantry soldier, and a rifle exceeding any firearm then in use. . . . Inducements, fascinating in themselves, and made doubly so by being passed from tongue to tongue, were held out to decoy young recruits, till the too credulous of this, as of other organizations among the thousands then hurrying south, believed themselves sorted out as the special pets of the government.*[49]

The pressing matter of the Sharpshooters' exact weapon created much expectation in budding company ranks. The unarmed "special pets" grew intensely frustrated as weeks passed. Early on, Berdan thought the standard muzzleloading infantry rifle manufactured in Springfield, Massachusetts, would suffice. He quickly changed his mind. A Sharpshooter could not effectively fulfill his role using a weapon with a slow rate of fire that would be difficult to load while prone, a likely position for USSS members in battle.

The Spencer repeating rifle, used in limited practice shooting in Washington, earned a place in some Sharpshooters' hopes. Also, a five-shot revolving rifle from Colt gained a level of respect from the men. Colt produced the weapon in sufficient quantities, which led Berdan to gravitate in that direction. Theodore Preston, Company B, 2nd USSS, referred to the revolving rifle as "a splendid looking gun" in a November 13 letter. However, he added, "but I think I should not like it as well as a Sharps Rifle."[50]

Many passing the marksmanship test and joining companies deemed themselves all but entitled to the Sharps, a single-shot breechloader capable of rapid fire, perhaps three times the rate of an infantryman's muzzleloader. Under development since the 1840s, the weapon's trigger guard and breech block provided the unique firing mechanism capable of nearly ten shots a minute. After firing, the shooter pushed the guard forward, opening the breech. Loading the round followed by the closing of the guard cut the back of the paper cartridge, exposing the powder and making the Sharps rifle ready to fire.

Double triggers were another development helping USSS members. In a hurried situation, the rear trigger could be pulled to fire. Or, the front trigger could be pressed, which made a "hair trigger" out of the rear lever. The only weakness of the weapon was a limitation of the times. Using black powder cartridges meant the Sharps rifle created smoke, potentially disclosing a hidden position or clouding vision while seeking a new target.

Private Truman Head, perhaps the most colorful and eccentric member in USSS history, had purchased a Sharps Rifle with his own funds. The weapon had Head's fellow Sharpshooters quickly enthralled. Unfortunately, Christian Sharps and his company, busy with prior government contracts, did not have the ability to produce the large number of arms the USSS needed. Berdan's order of the Colt revolving rifle seemed a necessary act on his part, even as New Hampshire marksman Darius Starr deemed the revolving rifle "not fit for sharp-shooters."[51]

One reason the marksmen preferred the Sharps pertained to safety. Some men firing Colt's revolving rifle suffered serious injuries from exploding cylinders or shards of metal flying into the face or hands. A justifiable lack of faith in the weapon soon developed. As Theodore Preston described one early 1862 incident, a Badger "was firing one when three barrels went off at once cutting away his forefinger and thumb." Concerns about Colt's gun led to Berdan's effigy being blown up at the Camp of Instruction.[52]

"The Thanks of the Unfortunate"

Like so many other soldiers during the Civil War, Curtis Abbott used humor to conquer the disappointments of military life. He referred to the Sharpshooters' early time in the National Capital as "anything but a camp of instruction" due to the lack of weaponry. Abbott proclaimed, "This camp, within sight of the capital, was the most cheerless" the USSS would ever occupy.[53]

Disenchantment with the slow pace of arming the regiment likely contributed to some carelessness among those who used training rifles for practice early in the Camp of Instruction. On October 9, Berdan replied to a concern from army headquarters about rounds falling beyond the limits of the Sharpshooters' camp. Although Berdan doubted USSS companies were always responsible when errant rounds hit private buildings, he replied, "I have given orders to cease firing until I can select grounds for target practice more remote from the city." Safety of others served as the guiding standard for his marksmen in training, Berdan pledged.[54]

Some Sharpshooters expressed happiness with their lot, at least early in their camp experience. A Wisconsin soldier used an October letter to inform people back home of the company's blank list of sick men. The Badgers "flourish" in the army, readers were informed. With Captain Alexander busy in Wisconsin on recruiting duties, Edward Drew commanded Company G. Respected, even though an outsider, Drew added to the good times for Wisconsin members of the USSS.[55]

Benjamin Calef wrote home, "How pleasantly we are situated," with camp "on a hill opposite the first Regt." With a staff assignment, Calef enjoyed some luxuries not afforded to many marksmen. He shared a double tent with a comrade. The front tent served as an office and dining room, with beds and a sitting area in back. Additionally, the digs were "nicely floored and furnished," much to Calef's delight. Although happy, Calef longed for home. "I wish I could be with you on Christmas Day," he wrote.[56]

Missing family and friends occupied the minds of other green-clad troops, adding to sad feelings across Berdan's companies. One Sharpshooter wrote two interesting sentences on the subject with a philosophical air. "I have heard the remark many times since being here that our friends back home missed us men more than we did them," Wolverine Gardner Clark mused, "It is hard for me to understand as much."[57]

William Ripley detected a dour mindset in his wife when reading her letters. "I dread the effect of my absence upon your health more than anything else," the proud marksman officer wrote. He suggested she maintain a "cheerful heart" as a means to conquer sad feelings.[58]

Camp activities, however routine, offered opportunities for men to cheer up. Competitions provided one way for the men to gain respect for each other and add some frivolity to their lives. Games that took place on Thanksgiving proved a boon to morale. William Ripley recalled one Michigan comrade's feat in early December. While using a target rifle "off hand," or without any supports, from six hundred feet, the Wolverine missed the center of a bull's-eye by a combined six inches with three shots.[59]

Newspaper reporters spent time around the Sharpshooters, perhaps attracted to the distinctive attire and skill on display. One report from early December described the prowess evident. "The riddled appearance of a target . . . struck at a distance of 150 yards substantiated the accounts we had heard of the wonderful proficiency in the use of the rifle exhibited by these men," a Michigan reporter exclaimed.[60]

Lack of preferred weaponry and the dearth of action against the enemy still prevailed. In a November letter, a Vermonter suggested his state had done so much from early in the war, well out of proportion to its small population. Yet, "the high expectations of our efficiency entertained by the public have not as yet been realized." Training and comradery might help soldiers develop skills and confidence, but a lack of a great weapon across the companies seemed quite embarrassing. "Unless energetic measures are adopted," the distressed Sharpshooter concluded, "we may remain for some time yet unable to face the enemy."[61]

Although Berdan worked hard to transform enlistees into equipped and ready soldiers, he did not have a winning personality or the natural qualities of military genius. He failed to place his ego aside at key moments, which damaged Berdan's reputation with the marksmen, as well as his place in history. He faced numerous credibility problems outside of the slow pace of arming his soldiers.[62]

Anger at Berdan's leadership spilled out in letters. In early January 1862, company commander James Fessenden informed his superiors in Maine, "It is very evident to me, and to every man in this camp, that this Berdan arrangement is a humbug by reason of the selfishness and incompetency of the individual at the head of it." The disgusted captain added his hope that the government will "place over this really splendid body of men some officer of experience who would make of the sharpshooters what they ought to be." Fessenden suggested the USSS would not see any service under Berdan. Instead, the Sharpshooters seemed destined to remain "a useless tax upon this overburdened country."[63]

Pictured later in the war as a general, James Fessenden, son of a U.S. Senator, began his Civil War service leading Maine's Company D, 2nd USSS. MAINE STATE ARCHIVES

Members of the 2nd USSS had much more faith in their leader, Henry A. V. Post. Younger than Berdan, Post possibly related to his men better. He did not seem overwhelmed with ego and delusions about what was owed to him. Even as a president of some courts-martial, Post, a stickler for military protocol, did not lose respect across his companies. As Curtis Abbott explained, Post's "method of teaching, which is usually called discipline, was retained in the regiment until its final muster-out."[64]

Soon after the departure of Lt. Col. Frederick Mears, Maj. William Rowland resigned from the USSS due to problems with Berdan. Unlike Mears, Rowland did not seem to possess great talents or the ability to inspire rookie soldiers to become better. Nonetheless, disputes between senior USSS officers brought further schisms while hindering efficient operations, further lag to the hope of quickly turning the Sharpshooters into the "special line of service" many envisioned.[65]

Many men in camp had far more serious concerns than strife between officers. On the last day of 1861, Sgt. George Marden, a New Hampshire enlistee holding a staff position at Berdan's headquarters, sadly wrote, "The sick are fearfully plenty. Three men died yesterday, two of them from N.H." In additional letters written in the first week of the new year, the disturbing news continued. "The sick list is tremendous," Marden penned, "One company turned out only Eleven files to dress parade." The next day, he added, "The prevailing disease is measles which are followed by something else." Perhaps disappointment with their war life so far contributed to the Sharpshooters' health woes. As Marden suggested, "Many of the men are discouraged and thus are more affected by disease than if they were in good spirits."[66]

Minnesotan Joseph Dickey deemed his own health subpar, but he suffered less than average. Two days before Christmas he counted more than forty men far worse off. "Most of them have measles," Dickey wrote, "ain't I lucky." By the second week of January, he questioned the army's purpose. "It seems to me," the disgruntled Minnesotan averred, "that it is *genuine murder* to keep this army until spring without accomplishing *anything*." He wished Congress "would present a few more bills" pertaining to "the disposition of the nigger, and *adjourn*," then let the two sides settle the dispute on the battlefield.[67]

Through personal experience, New Yorker Harrison De Long wrote, "It is no child's play for one to have the measles in camp." The sick Empire Stater praised Lt. William Elmendorf, who "looked after me, as he does all of his men, with great care, for which he has the thanks of the unfortunate." Adding commentary about the army, De Long had limited faith in several others of higher rank around Washington. He concluded, "I am convinced that many of the officers in the army are serving more for the emoluments of office and the pecuniary benefits than through patriotic motives."[68]

In a January 15 letter, Granite Stater Henry Campbell could at least begin, "I am yet alive." He had been confined to a tent for days with the measles, which did not seem to bother him horribly. Seventeen comrades were in the large tent suffering from the same condition. Campbell then noted how one Sharpshooter recently died of diphtheria. Even with threats to life from disease, Campbell concluded with a concern common among Civil War soldiers. "I can write often," he declared, but "I have not heard from home since I left."[69]

On the same day as Campbell's letter, a New York newspaper scathingly commented on the state of the USSS. The article found that the high level of sickness and demoralization plagued the marksmen, with the lack of arms a notable disgrace. Recruited for service relying on their skills as great shots, the Sharpshooters demanded the right to be armed appropriately. As expected, the men declared the muzzleloading Springfield rifle an infantryman's weapon, unworthy of use in the USSS.[70]

The medical director of McClellan's army also found much to criticize. With more than two hundred of the 1,465 Sharpshooters listed as sick, the early 1862 report found the USSS "in a bad sanitary condition," which had not been improving. Because of inadequate drainage, the physician deemed as "decidedly necessary" a change to "a fresh and dry camp." Unfortunately, an update later in the winter found the USSS "still severely affected" with measles cases. No change occurred to the location of the Sharpshooters' temporary home.[71]

Death stalked each company before either regiment lost a man to Confederate fire. In less than two weeks on either side of the New Year, Pvt. Rufus Chilson and Corp. Andrew Newman, Company C, 2nd USSS, lost their lives from unrecorded sickness.

Nagging and ultimately fatal health problems plagued some Sharpshooters who appeared well enough to visitors. Jerome Fountain, a Company C man in the 1st USSS, had complained of some sickness for a while. After visiting the ailing marksman, a family member wrote his sister about Jerome looking thin, although he did not seem sick. Fountain had not had a fever or other persistent problem for several days as of the January 31 letter. Alas, the unfortunate USSS member died of disease on February 10.[72]

Fountain's company, which would suffer the second most killed in action or mortally wounded in the entire USSS, endured tragic loss from disease before they faced the Confederates in their first campaign. A state roster published after the war lists Fountain and four other Company C men dying of disease prior to field service, with sixteen discharged for disability.[73] Bacteria and viruses cared not how distinguished the USSS appeared.

Data from the New Hampshire companies illustrate the wicked impact disease had on the USSS. The three units enlisted 294 marksmen at the start of their service. By the end of March 1862, one of every seven was gone, thirty having been discharged for disability, with twelve dying from sickness. A day short of his twenty-third birthday, Sgt. Franklin C. Wadsworth, Company E, 1st USSS, lost his life back home. He had departed Washington with a medical discharge earlier in the winter.[74]

Even though he did not fire a shot at the enemy, Wadsworth earned the tributes mentioned at his funeral, which took place in the town of Franklin on March 23. The pastor lamented "the foul treason that blackens the land, and sends mourning for the slain into so many of our homes." He praised Wadsworth's interest in seeking God, rather than worldly honors. During his final illness, the mourners heard, Wadsworth "felt ready and willing to die." By knowing the deceased, Wadsworth's comrades could be ennobled, while his memory will "fortify the patriotism and piety of multitudes here and in communities of the land."[75]

Dreary Weeks before Spring

Sharpshooters lucky enough to dodge serious ailments filled their minds with hopes for the future and thoughts of home. In a very interesting letter on January 29, Frank L. Smith from Wisconsin covered a wide range of topics. Limited news from family stood as a leading complaint. With good enough health, Smith grumbled far less about the idle winter in camp than sadness about those apparently unconcerned about him. "I have begun to feel uneasy about you on account of receiving no answer to my letters," he complained, "If all are well I wish you would at least send me a card with 'well' written on it." Perhaps Smith's personal disappointment contributed to his rebellious mindset. Without his promised rifle, he noted men in the company planned to protest by not going on guard duty.[76]

Insubordinate activity from some marksmen perhaps added to court-martial activity, but no severe uprising occurred. Still, Sharpshooters remained glum. George Marden grew more distressed as winter rolled on. "I have found nearly every day like every other day," he suggested in January, "and thus anything like chronological order seems nearly useless." These words remained true as weeks passed. Ubiquitous mud became a bitter enemy at the Camp of Instruction, making normal activities outside a tent difficult. Perhaps the laziness bearing down across the monotonous season had one positive. Marden noted he was six pounds heavier, meaning, "I am in no sort of danger of starving."[77]

Two dedicated New Hampshire family men wrote to their hometown in late January with concerns about their loved ones. John Robinson and Orin West hoped the selectmen in the town of Epping could ensure their families had some money and enough to eat. The two marksmen must have received letters from home expressing concerns about basic life necessities. The visions of home some Sharpshooters informed loved ones about did not always include pleasant thoughts, but rather concern that their families lacked the ability to support themselves with breadwinners away at war.[78]

A 2nd Regiment Vermonter wrote a gloomy letter on February 5. "We are still here in the mud, in common with all soldiers," the perturbed marksman declared. With drill sometimes canceled due to poor conditions, company members had not advanced in skill much since leaving home. Classroom instruction, a reminder of youthful and peaceful days, helped, "But how different is the problem to be solved now. Instead of learning the rudiments of some useful science, we are now being taught the *real art* of war." With measles on the decline, at least some optimism could be felt, even with eighteen company members on the sick list. The soldier suggested the changeable weather likely accounted for the problems with sickness in his outfit since arriving in Washington. With many still lacking a weapon to call their own, another Vermont editorialist wondered if the USSS was being used properly.[79]

In the other USSS regiment, Lt. Col. William Ripley bristled under Berdan. "I have no confidence in his military skill at all," Ripley wrote home on February 8. Later in the month, the chagrined Vermonter added, "I wish I could go home," although he found positives in his new horse, even if the equine did not hear well. "I think I shall like him for all that," Ripley wrote.[80]

Some enlistees respected the work Berdan logged to arm the marksmen. A Wisconsinite suggested that "the machinations of certain persons not very well disposed toward our Colonel, and consequently ourselves" prevented the orders that would have fully armed the USSS weeks before. Although the stiff winds of bureaucracy may have delayed the final outfitting of Berdan's companies, an anti-USSS conspiracy failed to materialize to the extent suggested in the Badger's letter. After all, senior officials all the way up to President Lincoln respected the potential and dedication of the marksmen. The upset Sharpshooter could at least write of the strong leadership in the company, and the many honed shots ready for their first campaign.[81]

Marksmen on recruiting duty back home shared the winter doldrums evident to many at the Camp of Instruction. When writing to his sister, Thomas Connington, Company K, 1st USSS, wondered if the future would be better. Justifying his lack of contact, the Michigan marksman began, "It has been a long time since I have written to you and I hardly know how to excuse myself, but the fact of it is, I have not felt much like writing." With his effort at recruiting not being that fruitful—and feeling deceived into joining Berdan's organization—Connington added, "I am pretty much disgusted with everything."[82]

Another Wolverine, one of the greatest leaders the USSS would ever know, also spent part of his winter back in Michigan on recruiting duty. First Lt. James

H. Baker gave an update about USSS life in general to a newspaper in his state's capital. With progress made on arming all companies and improved health conditions by February, Baker expressed satisfaction with the government's support of the USSS.[83] His thoughts on life as a Sharpshooter provide a very interesting contrast to his Michigan comrade Connington.

From the Camp of Instruction in early March, Corp. Owen Evans, destined to serve as the last captain of Minnesota's company, wrote of the likely march to battle. He optimistically suggested the conflict with the South would be over by August 1. Still, the lack of weaponry in most USSS companies made Evans conclude, "We are very much mortified" at potentially not becoming part of the war.[84]

Lieutenant Colonel Ripley had worried about much more personal matters a few days before. "I was regularly homesick for two or three days last week," the officer wrote, "but I feel better now." He then quickly added, "not that I do not think often & fondly of you & my dear children & all the loved ones at home." Even a high-ranking officer could feel "no heart for my business when such thoughts possess me." Ripley also echoed other marksmen who pleaded for letters from home as a way to improve soldierly motivation. One letter could work miracles as the Vermont officer worried about the mud and lack of weaponry.[85]

Army leader Maj. Gen. George McClellan spent the season planning extensively. Under orders to begin a campaign in February, some rigorous movements were required. After finding the Confederates had vacated their position near Manassas in March, McClellan shelved one plan, an advance on Richmond after landing on the Rappahannock River near Urbanna. He then selected a more southerly point to launch the campaign he believed would close out the war. The effort would start to the southeast of the Confederate capital, then move up the Peninsula between the James and York Rivers.[86]

Not in the know about the deep strategic questions, the Sharpshooters remained in camp well into March. As Frederick Peet remembered, "Waiting in Washington was tedious." In a letter to his father on March 15, Peet described the intense labor some Sharpshooters completed the day before to ensure an adequate supply of firewood at the Camp of Instruction.

> *Yesterday, the day was not clear, nor yet rainy, it was one of those brown days (peculiar to the climate). I was detailed to superintend the wood cutting. As all the men have stoves or fireplaces, much wood is consumed; the amount given by Uncle Sam is not generally enough, so once or twice a week five or ten men are detailed from each company to go back into the country, generally near a fort, where the trees are already cut down, and there cut or split.*

Further details about the woodwork illustrated how, early in their experience, USSS members likely did not feel like "distinct" troops with an elevated position in the army. Peet's detail of thirty-five men had to walk five miles to commence biomass processing near Fort Saratoga, northeast of the Camp of Instruction.[87]

Many marksmen became bored. Quartermaster Benjamin Calef wrote regimental headquarters with a severe problem on March 14.

> *I have again to report to you the inefficiency and gross negligence of duty on the part of the sentinels posted to guard the stores belonging to my department. Last night a case of stockings was opened, also one of shoes, and the articles were scattered outside. In consideration that I am charged with and personally responsible for every article in store I have the honor to request that you will take such measures as you think best to insure us against further loss and bring the offenders to justice.*

The reply to Calef promised toughness. Stern measures would be taken to protect regimental supplies. "Stealing in camp will promptly be met with punishment by death or prosecution by law," Calef read. Negligent sentinels would be deemed "equally guilty with the thief."[88]

More active service beckoned before anyone could be executed for stealing government property. Theodore Preston witnessed signs of an advance while on guard duty in March. "It is a rainy day but my post is under cover," the Wolverine declared, "I saw two regts. marching over for Dixie. There has been a continual string of troops going over the river for the last week or so."[89]

A displeased Green Mountain Sharpshooter, identified in the letter as W. W., also witnessed signs of activity. "The weather for two or three days has been like June," he wrote, "The parade ground has got quite dry, and the mud is fast disappearing." Three different battalion drills occurred daily, another portent of an active campaign season. "I hope the cause will not suffer for want of our services while we are waiting for arms," W. W. concluded.[90] He and his comrades had plenty of tough times ahead. Two hundred sixty green-clad marksmen would sustain fatal battle wounds in less than three years.

Part One

"We have no reason to think him alive," March 1862–April 1863

Going in different directions at the start of McClellan's Peninsula campaign, ten months would pass before the two USSS regiments reunited at the same camp. Their differing experiences offered much education to the soldiers across the eighteen companies. In a variety of forms, danger beckoned.

The 2nd Sharpshooters departed the Camp of Instruction first. Colonel Henry Post's eight companies formed on the morning of March 19, 1862. By 2:30 p.m., the men headed south, crossing the Long Bridge over the Potomac, and thus into Virginia. The march to Alexandria amounted to just under ten miles, far from a dizzying pace for Civil War troops, but conditions proved difficult. Extensive amounts of gear fell along the road as Sharpshooters looked to lighten their burdens. Wyman White remembered nearly passing out from the enervation, made worse when rain fell as they approached Alexandria. Curtis Abbott remembered the day "sorely tested the capacity of the men, especially those convalescing from the sickbed." Sharpshooters might not have said much on the march, Abbott concluded, but "their haggard faces told how their strength was being tried."[1]

Drenching rains and a concomitant lack of tents during the night added to the miserable experience across the 2nd Regiment. Adaptive soldiers become quite inventive. Men worked to tie rubber blankets together, which created a makeshift tent, as Benjamin Calef discussed in a March 23 letter from Camp Williams, two miles west of the Potomac. Still on the regimental staff, Calef retained his own government-issued tent.[2]

Eager for his first campaign but outlining a tale of woe, Wolverine Theodore Preston wrote his father after his initial saunter as a soldier in the field. "The march that far was very pleasant and exciting," the rookie marksman proclaimed, "the boys were all in good spirits and full of fun." With roads in fine condition, Preston found "the only inconvenience was the weight in the knapsack." The unfortunate Sharpshooter would never get a chance to shoot at the enemy. The coming weeks would drain his health, confining him to a hospital for many weeks. He would die in Alexandria in early September.[3]

Serving as acting captain, 1st Lt. Jacob McClure wrote home later in March to announce the departure of James Fessenden from Company D. Taking a staff assignment outside of McClellan's army, Fessenden would never lead his Maine Sharpshooters in battle. McClure's letter noted Colonel Post's interest in introducing officers outside of company ranks to fill vacancies, something the Maine men might dislike. McClure remained as acting company commander until the patient marksman received his promotion to captain six months later.[4]

No longer camping with their USSS comrades in the 1st Regiment, Post's companies joined the First Brigade, First Division of Irvin McDowell's First Corps. At Camp Williams, Vermonter Henry Campbell spoke with men from the 22nd and 30th New York Infantry, part of the new brigade. Expectations included a boat ride as part of McClellan's force heading to the Peninsula. "We may go tonight," Campbell surmised.[5]

Captain Andrew Stuart, Company B, also expected the 2nd Sharpshooters to soon be on the way to the Peninsula. Very eager for the start of field service, Stuart wrote with great anticipation about heading into action. "God speed the day that shall bring us face to face with the men that have torn down the old flag of the Union and sought to erect another in its stead," Stuart proclaimed.[6]

Fate had a different role in mind. The Lincoln administration detached McDowell's entire corps from the Army of the Potomac at the start of McClellan's Peninsula endeavor, a fact that infuriated the general. Staying at Camp Williams until April 4, Post's men went south on an overland route to Falmouth, across the Rappahannock River from Fredericksburg. On the rainy journey of nearly fifty miles, Post's men often marched in front of their corps, as expected. Joseph Dickey proudly wrote about leading the journey to Falmouth as skirmishers. He mentioned a general, perhaps brigade commander Christopher Augur, commenting on how the Sharpshooters "advanced as though we were going to church" when on the lookout for the enemy.[7]

Not destined for immediate action, hundreds of Sharpshooters would garrison Falmouth through mid-August. Relative quiet prevailed. Darius Starr still recorded, "we are kept very busy" with picket duty and basic tasks. Henry Post continued to lead the 2nd Regiment, with Minnesota's Francis Peteler promoted to lieutenant colonel. Another original captain, Amos Jones, rose to major.[8]

To Yorktown

Unlike the 2nd USSS, intense combat and wearying marches would be the 1st Regiment's fate for weeks across the spring and beyond. Shortly after leaving the Camp of Instruction on March 20, the ten companies encountered rain and mud on the way to Alexandria. The regiment joined the division of Brig. Gen. Fitz John Porter, in the Third Corps, Army of the Potomac. Soon, the regiment boarded vessels taking them on their first campaign. By the 25th, the 1st USSS camped near others in Porter's command around Hampton, Virginia, on the eastern end of the Peninsula. They rested nearly seventy miles from the Confederate capital of Richmond. Fine weather, with plentiful food ranging from strawberries to oysters, awaited McClellan's army.[9]

As Post's boys marched south toward Falmouth, the 1st Regiment—with Col. Hiram Berdan, Lt. Col. William Ripley, and Maj. Caspar Trepp—had a key role in the advance away from Hampton. Shaking off the winter doldrums, the entire Union force spread out across several miles, with Berdan's men in the front of Porter's division, near the right of the army. Sharpshooters on picket seized some Confederate prisoners as early as March 25. Two days later, skirmishing activity while around Big Bethel added to the stress of the moment and the excitement the Sharpshooters felt. Most companies used the Colt revolving rifle.[10]

Brigadier General George Morell, commanding a brigade under Porter, wrote of the problems advancing toward Yorktown. "The rain commenced falling," Morell wrote, causing the roads to turn "exceedingly heavy," another reference to Virginia's unyielding mud. Mother Nature made McClellan likely regret the comment to his superiors earlier in the year. The army commander suggested the Peninsula's roads would be passable at any time of year.[11]

Mother Nature likely contributed to McClellan's penchant to plan extensively before launching major combat operations, such as the effort to occupy Yorktown. William Ripley informed his wife on April 2 of the generally idle nature of the previous two weeks, a fascinating insight due to the skirmish duty, marching, and preparations always part of a campaign. "We have a large force here," the Vermont officer continued, even as the Sharpshooters lacked enough Colt rifles to arm all men in the ten companies.[12]

Hot action awaited the 1st USSS on April 5, their first notable confrontation with Confederates. As William Ripley wrote a Vermont newspaper,

> *The Sharps-Shooters were immediately pushed to the front, where we engaged the enemy as skirmishers. . . . We were opposed to long ranges of rifle pits and strong forts, on which we kept up a constant fire all day, and they*

> *returned it briskly. . . . We kept the large fort silent for two hours, when our artillery having obtained all the information they wanted withdrew. . . . The men behaved splendidly, and the whole army rings with their praises. . . . The fight has not yet really commenced, though there is more or less firing going on all the time.*[13]

The USSS faced danger in the lead of Porter's division, which advanced near the York River. Even without a major engagement on April 5, the Sharpshooters lost three lives due to wounds. John Ide, Company E, and David Phelps, Company H, became the first two members of either USSS regiment to die in action. Ide fell with a bullet to the head. A bursting shell took the life of Phelps. Frederick Peet deeply felt the loss. In a letter to his own father, Peet described Phelps as "one of the best men we had. He was always a still quiet fellow, never troubling any one, and always doing his duty."[14]

Daniel Painter's fatal injury also occurred on April 5. The valiant New Yorker died twelve days later. He was laid to rest at Yorktown National Cemetery.[15]

Corporal Charles Peck, twenty-one years old in Vermont's Company F, also sustained a wound on April 5. Like so many casualties during the Civil War, Peck's fate included months of medical care, followed by a discharge. He mustered out due to disability on November 26, 1862, seven-and-a-half months after his Yorktown injury. He lived until 1916.[16]

General Porter quickly learned of the value of the USSS. Division headquarters expressed approbation to Colonel Berdan on April 6. Of the Confederates the missive suggested, "They begin to fear your sharpshooters," and were made to "bite the dust" thanks to the rapid and accurate fire of the USSS. General Porter concluded of Berdan's men, "when their trusty rifles are pointed at the foe, there will be one rebel less at every discharge."[17]

Captain George Hastings did not seem that enthused. "Berdan's vanity now knows no bounds," the captain suggested. Berdan looked to tell as many stories as possible about his unit, which was easy enough due to the reporters who advanced with the army. Hastings believed Berdan grew a bit tyrannical with his troops, especially officers. Instead of ensuring the men had tents or baggage, Hastings found Berdan too worried about advancing his own reputation.[18] With Sharpshooters expecting much from their leader, Hastings's words offer an initial glimpse of the disappointment many would feel in Berdan.

"Uncle Head"

Berdan's egotism and the determination of the 1st USSS could not alter the situation along the Warwick River, which separated the two armies at Yorktown. McClellan lacked the boldness of an intrepid general, settling into a siege that would occupy four weeks. As a tense status quo began, the siege offered a perfect opportunity for the Sharpshooters to bolster their reputation. Isolated men, whether a single soldier or a small group, possessed a heightened chance to silence Confederate cannons, or decrease the threat to Northern comrades from Confederate infantry. Yet, like so much of Sharpshooter history, negatives remained. On April 9, the Sharpshooters slept in the open air; their tents had yet to make the move up the Peninsula from their camp in Hampton.[19]

Truman Head, often called "California Joe," engrained his immortal place in USSS lore at Yorktown. Declaring an occupation of "hunter" when he enlisted as a Sharpshooter, Head, considerably older than the average marksman, used the Sharps Rifle bought with his own funds as if he was still targeting grizzly bears on the West Coast.[20]

George Marden would never forget Head's determination. Writing on April 17, Marden noted "one continuous roar" of fire along Union lines. As expected, Head instilled "great havoc among the rebels" during such tense moments. Referring to his Michigan comrade as "Uncle Head," Marden reported a hit Head's rifle took, with part of the round grazing the older Sharpshooter's cheek. Head "said he didn't care about his face but he was afraid" the Confederate warrior had wounded the Sharps Rifle. "Amid a crowd of admiring comrades" later that evening, Head regaled fellow Sharpshooters about the harrowing day.[21]

As April continued, a key aspect of the 1st Regiment's service included sixty men assigned each day to picket duty near the front line. "Every day they do something good," happy William Ripley informed his wife in a letter on the 18th. Adding that the USSS served as "the pride of the whole army," the officer hoped the Sharpshooters could "sustain their reputation." With continued worry about his lonely spouse one thousand miles away, Ripley continued, "I am never so unhappy as when I think of your unhappiness."[22]

A Confederate shell on April 22 nearly cost the lives of several Wisconsin Sharpshooters, including Lt. Frank Marble. George Lewis informed his sister, the "shell struck within 6 feet of myself and 3 other men from my company" without bursting while the men worked the picket line. He remarked that the incident, "made my hair stand straight on my head." Lewis still informed his sibling that he was "enjoying myself," even "considering where I am and what I have to do." What Charles Stevens called a "fiery shower" regularly landed near Sharpshooters at Yorktown, a sign of the determination among Southerners to target their marksmen foes.[23]

Improved Confederate earthworks made Union soldiers consider the advantages of McClellan's slow approach to capturing Yorktown. Martin Van Buren

Bronson, a Vermont lieutenant, suggested the army commander had a good plan as he looked across the wasteland toward Southern positions. "McClellan intends to siege Yorktown rather than storm it. I think that is a wise plan," surmised the officer who turned twenty-six years old that month. Counting thirteen Confederate forts with impressive artillery positions, Bronson hoped for a way to win the day without the company's first fatality.[24]

Sharpshooters did their best to inhibit Confederate construction of protective features. Colonel Robert McAllister, who would eventually command a brigade that would include USSS companies, respected the work of the 1st Sharpshooters during the siege. He noted the dangerous duty of the marksmen, as well as how their work protected Union artillerists and others from enemy fire.[25]

Hard times without a rifle in their hands defined some tough hours for USSS members later in April. One marksman wrote a New York newspaper about fatigue duty improving the protective features around a Union artillery battery. "The spades, picks and shovels were soon clicking briskly," the Sharpshooter wrote, "We were just in the edge of some woods, so our labors were not visible to the enemy." Part of the day's work included digging trenches to connect different batteries.[26] However important, this intense labor was not what USSS recruits signed up to do.

Abounding danger each day did not equate to every second being tense at Yorktown. George Marden wrote of two weeks passing with "very little excitement" while the Sharpshooters alternated between duty on the firing line and time resting. At Camp Winfield Scott, the Granite Stater detailed his lunch on April 30,

> *The bill of fare was roast mutton, green corn, green peas, Irish stew, potatoes, bread and butter and baked beans. Whiskey and water for those who chose to partake. . . . Today we had shell sauce. . . . The rebels threw some half dozen at our gunboats just out on the river, and we could hear their whistling along and bursting generally just before they struck.*[27]

Across the siege of Yorktown, two other 1st USSS soldiers would lose their lives to battle wounds. On April 25, Anton Sauer, a native of Germany, become the first Company A man to receive a fatal round. Sad over the loss of another comrade, George Marden noted Sauer's horrible head wound. The devoted American soldier left a wife and four children. Many members of the regiment contributed funds to assist Sauer's family.[28]

Joseph Durkee, Company G, became the fifth and final 1st Regiment man killed by Confederate fire at Yorktown. Protecting a detail that worked to

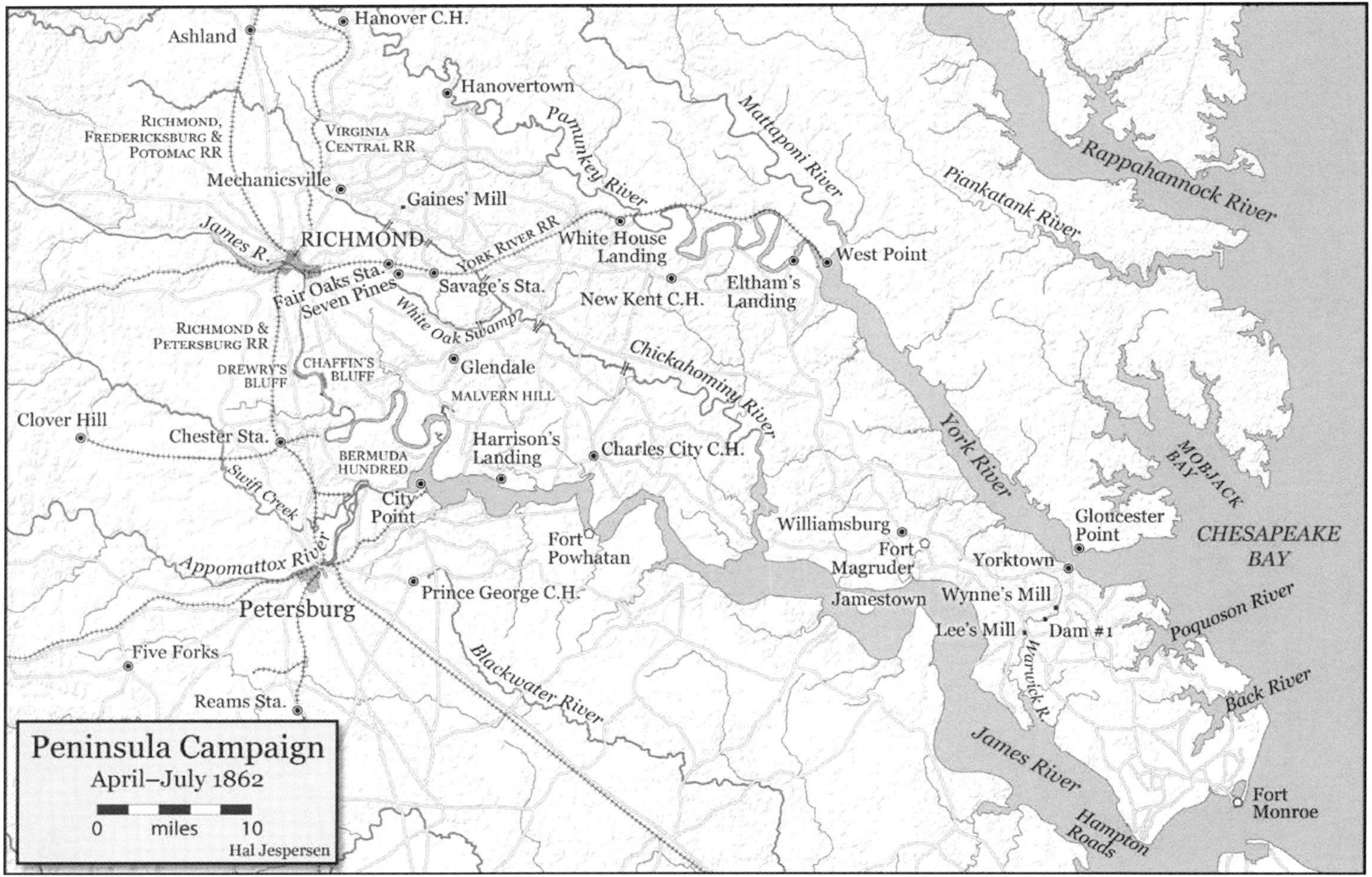

Peninsula Campaign
April–July 1862
0 miles 10
Hal Jespersen
Ashland
Hanover C.H.
Hanovertown
Richmond, Fredericksburg & Potomac RR
Virginia Central RR
Mechanicsville
Gaines' Mill
Pamunkey River
Mattaponi River
Rappahannock River
Piankatank River
James R.
RICHMOND
York River RR
White House Landing
West Point
Fair Oaks Sta.
Seven Pines
Savage's Sta.
New Kent C.H.
Eltham's Landing
White Oak Swamp
Richmond & Petersburg RR
Chickahominy River
Drewry's Bluff
Chaffin's Bluff
Glendale
Malvern Hill
Clover Hill
Chester Sta.
Harrison's Landing
Charles City C.H.
York River
Mobjack Bay
Bermuda Hundred
Swift Creek
City Point
Williamsburg
Gloucester Point
Chesapeake Bay
Fort Powhatan
Fort Magruder
Yorktown
Appomattox River
Prince George C.H.
Jamestown
Wynne's Mill
Petersburg
Lee's Mill
Dam #1
Poquoson River
Five Forks
Warwick R.
Blackwater River
Back River
Reams Sta.
James River
Fort Monroe
Hampton Roads

construct lines closer to the enemy on May 1, Durkee, deemed "fearless" to the point of "sheer recklessness" by the regiment's original historian, fell only about forty yards from his Southern antagonist. Lt. Frank Marble, perhaps knowing his subordinate's penchant for risk, had cautioned Durkee about the dangers he accepted so willingly. The fallen Badger's body would not be recovered until the Confederate evacuation of Yorktown. Durkee was buried at the site of his last bold work. His son, born in early 1862, lived until 1948.[29]

The close proximity of the opposing pickets, all too real for those wounded and killed USSS members, gained notice in the letters of a staff officer in one of Porter's brigades. Richard Auchmuty informed his parents in late April of the nearly personal nature of the rifle fire. "In the trenches we are very near them," Auchmuty noted, "I have been near enough to talk had I wanted to."[30]

"Such a Cheer I Never Heard"

On their first campaign for only a month, the stress and difficulties of military life caused myriad problems for Sharpshooters who endured enemy bullets and shells without a wound. Henry Harrington, Company D, reported that he had lost twenty pounds since leaving Cherry Valley, New York. "I am getting better, though weak," the Sharpshooter added.[31]

The fatigue and sickness in Union ranks did not stop the tide. Confederates knew of their inability to hold their Yorktown lines for long. On May 4, Union troops moved up to occupy the town. Writing to a newspaper, a Vermonter mentioned Sharpshooters were the first Union troops into the Confederate works. Enemy flags and a wide range of personal items from Confederates fell into Sharpshooter hands. "The rebels seem to have left in a hurry," penned the Green Mountain marksman. Bugles and bands played in Yorktown later in the day, contributing to the positive feeling of finally taking the city.[32]

George Lewis quickly wrote his sister of his generally positive circumstances after taking Yorktown. "I am still alive & well and enjoying myself very well," the Badger proclaimed. Yet, weather continued to batter the Sharpshooters. Lewis dourly added, "We have had very unpleasant weather here for the last week but I am in hopes it will soon be pleasant again for I do not like so much rain at one time."[33]

Captain George Hastings took a bullet to the fleshy area around the knee on the 4th, which, although far from serious, sent him home for a time. On a steamer about to head north, Hastings concluded, "I am not suffering" while being treated well. Hastings would be gone from his company for nearly seven weeks.[34]

The men felt exhilaration with the conquest of Yorktown, the pleasing result of their first month of field service. The moment instilled many impressions into Vermonter Jacob Bailey, who wrote home on May 5. After study of the Confederate fortifications, Bailey seemed happy that the enemy had withdrawn. Formidable protective structures combined with the large number of cannons the Confederates abandoned would have led to great loss for a Union assault force, he suggested. With the enemy on the run, Bailey predicted, "Many of the boys think they will get home to celebrate the 4th of July."

The Vermonter also shared the sentiments of one of his enemies, evidence of Confederate determination that would prolong the war far longer than Bailey envisioned. The Confederate had scrawled a note shortly before falling back. He warned his Northern foes to not believe the South was giving up on the war because of Yorktown's evacuation. The determined Rebel signed off, "Your enemy until death."[35]

The most welcome news after the victory was the provision of Sharp Rifles to Berdan's entire regiment. As he looked over the ten boxes that would arm dozens of Sharpshooters, George Marden called the fantastic guns "as fine a set of death dealing weapons as there ever was in the world anywhere." When groups handed in their Colt for the Sharps, Marden added, "such a cheer I never heard from the throats of men."[36]

Berdan would write Colt's treasurer in the spring of 1862 about the decision to scrap the company's revolving weapon. Perhaps with an eye on postwar business interests, Berdan clearly exaggerated the Colt's performance and utility.

> *We are today exchanging our Colts Revolving Rifles for Sharpes Rifles and it occurs to me that to do this without explanation may be a cause of great injustice to your valuable arms. The change is made in accordance with a promise made to the men when they were enlisted that they should have the Sharpes Rifles. All our reputation thus far has been made with the Colts and the target Rifles and the former have found themselves a very superior weapon especially for skirmishers.*[37]

Whatever the Colt's faults, the guns facilitated the initial reputation of the USSS in battle. Based on input from Confederate deserters or prisoners, Frederick Peet likely felt justice for his departed comrade Joseph Durkee. "The Sharp Shooters are regarded with the utmost fear & horror," he claimed. In addition to the enemy's retreat, Peet ecstatically observed the wonderful weather, "a more beautiful day I never saw."[38]

McClellan promised a rapid pursuit. A major engagement involving other divisions occurred near Williamsburg on May 5, about ten miles beyond Yorktown. Companies A and C, 1st USSS, had gone ahead with the advance that day. McClellan also sent a division up the York River. These men, under William Franklin, had been released from McDowell's force while the 2nd USSS and other units remained around Falmouth.

After departing Camp Scott on May 8, the 1st USSS camped near West Point Landing—where the York meets the Pamunkey and Mattaponi Rivers. Some days of rest for the bulk of the Sharpshooters seemed like a sufficient reward for their distinguished Yorktown service. Quiet prevailed until May 13, when Berdan's men marched to Cumberland Landing on the Pamunkey, west of West Point. William Ripley remembered the day's trek as a weary one due to scarcity of water, extensive dust, and warm weather. At least the enemy was nowhere in sight.[39]

George Marden hoped for an improvement in available food, as he wrote in a May 19 letter from Cumberland Landing. He found the lack of bread and meat troublesome, even with the available jellies, fruit, and ginger snaps. "I revel in lemonade," the staff officer from New Hampshire added.[40]

A review by Secretary of State William Seward offered the Sharpshooters visual contact with a central adviser to President Lincoln. General McClellan accompanied the secretary, although the soldiers might have questioned the wisdom of the moment due to poor weather. Frederick Peet summed up Seward's review by writing, "we were obliged to turn out, went half an hour, got wet, gave three cheers and double quick back to camp."[41]

After more soggy marching, the Sharpshooters helped occupy White House Landing, only twenty miles northeast of the desk of Confederate President Jefferson Davis. The Unionists thus gained access to a railroad that buttressed supply options as the army trekked westward.

Joe Johnston, leading Confederate forces east of Richmond, made the sound decision to withdraw his army closer to the capital. President Davis grew frustrated with the continued retrograde, but Johnston rightly knew he had better defensive prospects if the Chickahominy River did not divide his lines or flow behind his army. McClellan's pace since Williamsburg gave the Confederates time to prepare for the onslaught. The advancing Northerners started to reach the Chickahominy on May 21, with Granite Stater Charles Shepard informing his parents of the effort "to keep up with the flying rebels." Even with precipitation creating misery across the army, Shepard noted how intense sunlight changed his features. Freckles "make me look like a leopard," the young USSS member added, while peeling skin on some comrades made them appear decades older.[42]

Astride the unpredictable river, the tactical reality would prove highly detrimental to McClellan's precious plans. His concerns about the army's right flank dictated a move by Fitz John Porter, now in command of the Fifth Corps, created in mid-May. Berdan's marksmen became part of the new organization. For the trip north to the area near Hanover Court House, another company temporarily joined Berdan's regiment. Officially named the Second Company, Minnesota Sharpshooters, the unit was deemed Company L, 1st USSS. Having departed home in April, they slowly journeyed to the Peninsula, then trained with the Sharpshooters in mid-May, seemingly destined for permanent attachment to the regiment. However, Company L would quickly depart the 1st Sharpshooters.[43]

The Trying Day of May 27

McClellan's efforts to extend his army to the north had multiple justifications, including the possibility of reinforcements from Falmouth. The Lincoln administration's promise of releasing all of McDowell's men to join the Army of the Potomac would have reunited the two USSS regiments. Rising concerns about the safety of Washington kept most of McDowell's large force away from the Peninsula, although another division would go to McClellan from Fredericksburg. At the very least, control of Hanover Court House offered greater security for McClellan's advance to Richmond.[44]

The day's difficulty became evident before daylight. As officer Charles Stevens remembered, "the Sharpshooters rolled out of their tents and fell into line, the rain falling fast." The precipitation continued for the hours of marching. A Company L man then described the wicked advance north, "We travelled eighteen miles in the mud and arrived just in time." Three days later, he informed a sister of a narrow escape when Confederate cannoneers fired a shot "at me much closer than is agreeable." The round knocked two men in the company out of action, the same number of casualties, both nonfatal, the Minnesotans endured that day.[45]

In his first major work as a corps commander, Porter labored under a dearth of information about the enemy's position. Berdan's regiment reached the field at the head of George Morell's First Division. On the right front of the line, the USSS joined other troops under Porter heading toward the courthouse, in response to some firing. Sensible enough at the time, this continued trek left a small but not insignificant Confederate force to the left rear of Porter's advance. As Frederick Peet remembered, the USSS double-quicked back to the crossroads they had moved beyond earlier. Three Union regiments had been holding off the enemy advance, with Peet suggesting the musketry "was like a roll of thunder." The Sharpshooters became engaged, with Berdan having two horses shot under him.[46]

A Wisconsin soldier who had just turned twenty years old proved especially brave during the day. In an advanced position with a comrade, Benjamin

Atwell looked back to see three Confederate artillerists completely oblivious to the presence of any Union soldiers in the area. Rushing forward, Atwell and his fellow Sharpshooter demanded and received the surrender of the startled trio, including a lieutenant.[47]

Confederate forces were not prepared for the wallop the bulk of a Union corps could provide after Porter moved back to the south. As one Union eyewitness suggested, the enemy force was "entirely routed and scattered and driven in every direction." A large number of knapsacks fell into Porter's hands, as well as many prisoners. William Ripley wrote his wife that the captured Confederates seemed "glad enough to be taken."[48]

Always looking for dramatic words to boost the administration's view of his army, McClellan informed Secretary Stanton that Porter won "truly a glorious victory. . . . The rout of the rebels was complete."[49] Unfortunately, the Confederate force Porter defeated stood much farther from Richmond than the bulk of Johnston's troops defending their capital. The rest of the Union army manned too poor a position for the cautious McClellan to make much use of the rest of his army nearer the Confederate capital.

The 1st USSS lost their sixth man to a mortal wound on May 27, Vermonter William Dawson, who died on June 1 from a musket ball to the neck. The fighting at Hanover Court House inflicted nonfatal wounds on six others in Berdan's regiment, providing more examples of soldiers discharged long after a disabling injury. Company B's James Drake, who had enlisted in October 1861, would gain a medical discharge on Christmas Eve, seven months after the battle.[50]

Capture of a USSS surgeon proved an unfortunate development. After setting up a small hospital near the start of the main engagement later in the day southwest of the courthouse, Guy Marshall fell into Confederate hands. Lieutenant Colonel Ripley called Marshall's unfortunate fate "a great loss." Devoted to treating his fellow captives at Libby Prison in Richmond, Marshall soon died, "as truly the death of a hero as though he had fallen at the head of some gallant charge."[51]

May 27 had the Sharpshooters on their feet while marching or fighting from before dawn into the evening. The USSS did not play a major role in the day's outcome, but they certainly proved themselves fine team players in addition to soldiers with the fortitude to endure the very long and hazardous ordeal. The night grew especially difficult due to limited supplies, although captured Confederate goods assuaged some anguish. As Frederick Peet wrote, "We slept at night on secesh blankets which the 'Butternuts' had thrown away . . . in their efforts to skedaddle." After more than a day of rest, the 1st USSS returned to their camp north of the Chickahominy on May 29. They then rested at a fateful location near Gaines Mill.[52]

Due to a very unfortunate circumstance, Jacob Bachmann, another Swiss member of Company A, fell unnoticed into a very intractable mud hole on the return march to Gaines Mill. Stuck in the cold goo until rescued the following morning, Bachmann arrived at the 1st Regiment's camp on a stretcher. He required extended medical treatment, needing weeks to regain much use of his limbs. In his early forties, Bachmann would gain a medical discharge in November.[53]

The Travails of the 2nd Sharpshooters

Life had not proven nearly as arduous for Post's 2nd Regiment. As Irvin McDowell parceled out units, moved men in response to rumors, and wondered about the fate of his command, the 2nd USSS attempted to make the most of their experience. In their retreat from the Union advance in April, Confederates had burned bridges across the Rappahannock. Thus, McDowell faced little to no risk at Falmouth as the river separated his men from the enemy to the south.

"We live very well here," Benjamin Calef wrote home on May 12. As a quartermaster, Calef had the opportunity to get to know other officers. His bond with 2nd USSS Adjutant Lewis Parmelee proved especially memorable. "I like him much," Calef penned, "both as a comrade and as a good friend." Many others had great respect for the young adjutant, deemed the "beau ideal of a soldier" by Curtis Abbott.[54]

Lack of blankets plagued Post's Sharpshooters in May. Henry Campbell also hoped to have his overcoat, but an inefficient supply system made the 2nd Sharpshooters understand the limits of army logistics. In a May 18 letter to his mother, Campbell focused on money, a matter vitally important to soldiers and their families. Even with inconsistent paydays, he still sent $25 home, then promised more. From the Camp of Instruction, soldiers still kept the needs of their families in mind.[55]

Curtis Abbott recorded several elements of life around Falmouth in his memoir. Although relatively inactive themselves, 2nd USSS morale seemed good due to McClellan's early successes east of Richmond, as well as news from other theaters of the war. The soldiers passed the time

> *in a delightful camp. Wood and water were plentiful, and by the amenities of military discipline some traffic with the townspeople was carried on. A slight addition was made to the variety of their food. They bathed in the Rappahannock and brought flowers from the opposite bank. They felt a renewal of love for the sunny south, such as had not warmed their hearts since they left home.*[56]

Supplements to regular army fare some friendly civilians offered came with extortionist prices. William Greene detailed several different items in a letter to his concerned mother. A sack of salt costing 25 cents in New Hampshire could be had for $15. Several other items seemed extremely expensive, except for an undesirable critter around camp. Copperhead snakes were plentiful and free, Greene said. Accurate marksmen looked to rid the area of the repugnant reptile.[57]

Sickness staggered the 2nd USSS during these months, as evidenced by the seven companies with published rosters. The regiment lost more men to death or disability discharges from April through July 1862 than at the Camp of Instruction, which had featured illness as a major fact of life. Company D had an astounding twenty marksmen either leave due to disability or die from disease in four months. Vermonters in Company E lost nineteen men to disability discharges or deaths from disease in the four months starting in April. From the same causes, eleven more Green Mountain men in Company H departed the regiment. The two New Hampshire companies experienced horrendous culling from non-battle ailments, losing a combined thirty-eight men to discharge or deaths from disease in the same period. The Minnesota roster lists seven men gone during these slow four months, while Michigan's Company B lost fourteen. The costly period amounted to nearly a 15 percent decrease in the regiment's present soldiers, with none suffering a battle wound.[58]

Henry Caldwell, captain of Company F since the Camp of Instruction, would be the regiment's highest-ranking death around Falmouth. An early summer victim of typhoid fever, a common and dangerous affliction in the Civil War, Caldwell lacked the respect of many. Wyman White remembered Caldwell's "overbearing manner." When the company escorted their departed leader's body to the train station for the return home, Wyman saw no man in tears. Caldwell, not yet twenty-three years old, rests at Dunbarton Center Cemetery in his home state.[59]

Two cousins from the Giddings family were part of the toll in the middle months of 1862. Henry was another to die from typhoid. Benjamin gave out during the mid-May effort to augment McClellan, which ended eight miles south of the Rappahannock, when McDowell's force turned back to Falmouth. "I became disabled by rupture on this hard march," the hard-luck Sharpshooter wrote. Benjamin's days as a Sharpshooter trading coffee for flour with the residents of Fredericksburg thus ended.[60]

Losing comrades to germs and exhaustion added to the woes of 2nd Regiment marksmen more than ready to take battle to the enemy. Shortly before heading back north, Walter Smith wrote on May 27 of the anticipation of reaching McClellan's main force. Sensing the budding esprit de corps growing with

Maine marksman Frederick Coffin would be one of dozens of USSS members discharged for disability in 1862. MAINE STATE ARCHIVES

An unidentified member of the 2nd USSS. LIBRARY OF CONGRESS

their infantrymen comrades in the First Corps, Smith concluded, "Our Brigade is spoiling for a fight but I guess we shall get enough of it before we get through."[61]

Soon after being called away from their march to Richmond, a train ride added to the star-crossed early experience of the 2nd Sharpshooters. Post's regiment, part of Rufus King's Division, boarded the rails at Catlett's Station on May 31 as part of an effort to supplement Union forces stymied by Thomas "Stonewall" Jackson's Confederates in the Shenandoah Valley. After a break at Manassas, the ride continued, with a serious accident occurring early on June 1. The Sharpshooters' train, stalled a short distance beyond White Plains, was hit by an engine and cars moving at a steady speed. Some marksmen, riding in an open car, saw the train to the rear about to hit their own. Many jumped, avoiding the worst of the impact. The accident took the life of Maine Sharpshooter Sanford Bartlett, with several survivors in Company D suffering greatly.

The move north proved stillborn, just like McDowell's previous calls to join McClellan. Camped around Haymarket for several days with about four hundred men fit for duty, the regiment's marksmen slowly made their way back to Falmouth, arriving in the middle of the month. Even though the Vermonters of Company H avoided the worst from the train accident, Curtis Abbott still recorded thirteen fewer men in his unit compared to the end of May. The men occupied daily hours with regular drill, in preparation for the combat that seemed so distant. "We have been particularly unfortunate," Darius Starr suggested. "Our regiment cannot last much longer unless it is recruited."[62]

Schisms among officers developed in the days following the train accident. Colonel Post displayed a sense of great disappointment with Capt. William McPherson, who had been leading Company G since September. The company commander faced two charges related to an incident on June 10 where he allegedly gave orders to a bugler contrary to Post's wishes. The following week, McPherson informed Post of his intent to resign, although a court-martial found him not guilty. He suggested Post acted "in an ungovernable passion and rage" because of "a very trivial offence." Serving under what he deemed "your especial dislike," McPherson's days were numbered. He would depart the regiment later in the year.[63]

Regimental Chaplain Lorenzo Barber brought good news after the return to Falmouth. Curtis Abbott recorded a chapel's construction below the branches of "a large and thrifty oak." Thanks to help from the regiment, the seating area witnessed services each Sunday, and some evenings during the week. Barber earned the Sharpshooters' respect with a devotion to their welfare, the sharing of privations, and the steady hand of a fine shot. Deemed the "Fighting Parson," Barber took to the war like an Old Testament prophet.[64]

By late June, McDowell gained command of a new corps in an army formed to better coordinate Union forces from Fredericksburg to the Shenandoah. Major General John Pope commanded the force, the Army of Virginia, with the 2nd USSS part of McDowell's Third Corps. Post's men remained in Augur's First Brigade, First Division. Falmouth remained the 2nd Regiment's home well into the summer.[65]

"We Shall Have to Get an Ark Built"

Slightly more than fifty miles south of Falmouth, events in June along the Chickahominy bristled with unknowns while instilling the accurate sense of an inevitable major fight. The 1st USSS stood prepared as a respected part of Fitz John Porter's Fifth Corps.

Vermonters Brigham Buswell and William Ripley wrote of little occurring for weeks after the short but difficult Hanover Court House ordeal. Both armies remained on edge, especially after a large battle occurred on May 31 and June 1 near Seven Pines, across the Chickahominy from the Sharpshooters. With the continued rain, Northern soldiers had to ponder the fate of bridges linking the

Army of the Potomac, as new Confederate commander Robert E. Lee looked to wreck McClellan's strategy of slow strangulation of the Southern capital. Taking command of Confederate forces from the injured Joseph Johnston, Lee began to visualize an attack to destabilize the Union right, potentially destroying Porter's corps in the process.[66]

As McClellan's best friend in the army, Porter ranked high in his commander's esteem. With the bulk of McClellan's men south of the Chickahominy by mid-June, Porter's force, the largest corps under McClellan, held a vital position north of the river. The 1st USSS and their corps comrades protected the army's right, served as the closest link to the two divisions of McDowell, and guarded the supply line running from the White House on the Pamunkey. Berdan's regiment performed a variety of duties—including regular service as pickets on the lookout for Confederates—without participating in a major battle through most of the month.[67]

An unidentified New Yorker, apparently an infantryman, praised the USSS for their work in early June. "Berdan's Sharpshooters are keeping up a lively fright among the rebel gunners," he proclaimed, "picking them off when they show themselves." The correspondent also recorded data based on a shooting demonstration four companies of marksmen completed. A total of four thousand shots from one-eighth of a mile averaged only two and five-eighths inches from the center of a bull's-eye.[68]

Rain remained a defining feature of life. Sick lists worried members of the 1st USSS as the conditions and swampy ground made good water difficult to find. Fifth Corps staff officer Stephen Weld summed up the problem on June 4, "I begin to think we shall have to get an ark built if the rain continues." William Ripley informed his wife three days later, "heavy rains have raised the river till it is a lake." The horridly wet month seemed unending. Later, Ripley wrote, "This country is more subject to *sudden changes of weather* than any country I was ever in and it tells upon the health of the men severely."[69] Once again, the special soldiers could not dodge disease.

New Hampshire marksman John Carr summarized his experience of spending time in a White House Landing hospital for weeks. Sick for much of the campaign, he wrote a cousin on June 3.

> *I have been troubled with the diarea most of the time since we came to Yorktown; but I kept on duty most of the time until about two weeks ago, my health has improved a good deal since I came here; I hope to be able to join my regiment in a few days. There is quite a large camp of hospital tents here.*

There are about twelve hundred sick and wounded here; but few wounded are here; many of them have been sent north.[70]

Simon Danner, Company I, had a rare arrangement. He wrote home about a side job he had working for the sutler whose shop stood near USSS headquarters. Sutlers often did not possess the respect of many soldiers, due to the prevailing view of the shops selling lower quality food and other items for high prices. Danner appears to have worked for the sutler while still assigned to duties as a soldier. He wrote of his efforts to send money home, another Sharpshooter keenly aware of the war's burdens on families. Like many Sharpshooters, sickness cut Danner's service short. He would head home later in the summer, never to wear green under fire again.[71]

Keeping an eye on the river, the 1st USSS divided into several groups on June 6. The troops performed skirmish duty at picket posts, augmenting the eyes and ears of multiple division commanders. The role perfectly aligned with the expectations of a force of marksmen in isolated groups potentially inflicting loss with accurate shooting from long distance. Lt. Frederick Peet wrote of officers, including himself, wearing the uniforms of enlisted men to not attract attention from Confederate marksmen, trained, like the USSS, to shoot enemy officers.[72]

Companies A and I served on the opposite side of the Union line at Fort Davidson. Major Caspar Trepp commanded this two-company detail, which furnished some men for picket duty in and near the fort. Artillery blasts were regularly heard, with enemy troops about 150 yards away.[73]

Companies C and G stood in support of Sixth Corps division commander Henry Slocum. For a time, these men served as pickets south of the river. After some long days of duty, one Wisconsin man enjoyed "lounging in the thickest shade" south of the river, then an inspection of the Seven Pines area. While attending to their duties, the men received news of the loss of a comrade at a hospital nearby. One Badger wrote about the death from sickness of Gideon Jones, described as "so true a friend" and "able a soldier." Unwell for weeks, Jones stood

determined to push on with his Company as long as possible, rather than be left behind. . . . He had been failing for a day or two past, and although at times quite cheerful, yet it was evident from his actions at intervals, that his recovery was doubtful. . . . I need not say how deeply we deplore the loss of poor Gideon. His noble heart and manly feelings indeared him to all who became associated with him . . . all were his friends.

Along the front of Slocum's command, pickets from both armies met to talk and exchange goods on some occasions. One Badger wrote of some men being arrested for talking to Confederate pickets. Army leadership grew concerned about the practice because the effort to exchange newspapers during the meeting of pickets could lead Lee's army to learn of the Union's war planning or troop movements along the Chickahominy.[74]

Opening the Seven Days

Whatever he might have learned from enemy newspapers, General Lee had been targeting the land north of the Chickahominy. After an indecisive battle at Oak Grove, south of the river and west of Seven Pines, Lee worried about the possibility of an assault on Richmond from Union positions below the river. Nonetheless, the bold Confederate commander, sensing McClellan's caution, continued with his main goal: attacking Porter's troops. With Stonewall Jackson's men marching hard from the Shenandoah, Lee was prepared to assail the Union right with the goal of blasting McClellan's larger army back down the Peninsula.[75]

With an excellent defensive position at Mechanicsville on June 26, brigades of Pennsylvanians under Porter held the Confederates at bay. Later gaining reinforcements, which included elements of the 1st USSS, Unionists made General Lee pay for his boldness. Nearly four Confederates fell that day for every Northerner.

Berdan's regiment lost the life of one man on June 26. Company C soldier John Cole died that evening after being wounded as part of the force bolstering the Pennsylvanians. An ardent patriot in his mid-twenties who signed up for the USSS in the summer of 1861, Cole would become one Sharpshooter whose story seems lost to history beyond basic facts.[76] He was the seventh member of his regiment to lose his life to battle wounds. So far, each of the lost lives represented a different company.

Sharpshooter William Kent remembered the period to dawn on June 27 as a night that seemed to never end. General McClellan ordered Porter to abandon the line his men easily defended on the 26th. Sensing great danger and believing himself heavily outnumbered, McClellan focused on saving his supply line. He would do so by what he deemed a "change of base," a pithy way to describe a retreat that would doom his chance of taking Richmond. Porter's corps would fight nearly alone on the following day, while the bulk of the Army of the Potomac worked to begin the retreat, with the James River selected as the army's supply lifeline.

Porter's retrograde brought the USSS back to a familiar campsite near Gaines Mill. Obvious plans to retreat, including the burning of some supplies and the hustling of cattle south of the Chickahominy, greeted the marksmen after a tramp of about four miles. The site offered phenomenal defensive ground for Porter's entire corps. The swamps and topography certainly appeared like a natural spot for the Sharpshooters. With limited support from the rest of the army, the 1st USSS and the rest of the Fifth Corps would perform magnificently at what would be the costliest battle of the Seven Days.[77]

Assigned to lead a patrol to the front right of Porter's line, Sgt. John Hetherington took ten Sharpshooters on the scouting mission. They ran into part of Stonewall Jackson's command who were heading toward White House Landing. The diminutive group from the USSS sustained some casualties but served an important role in locating a large number of enemy troops. Hetherington's excellent leadership would bless the USSS for more than two additional years.[78]

Early work as skirmishers for some companies in the USSS on June 27 provided a textbook example of what the marksmen had been recruited to do. With cover from trees but not much undergrowth in the woods down the slope from Porter's main line, the Sharpshooters had bountiful chances to make an impact. Some of the men did their deadly work with canteens full of whiskey, leftovers taken from the camp stores not yet burned. Unfortunately, food would become quite scarce for the USSS.[79]

The North Carolinians who endured the whirlwind at Hanover Court House found more trouble from the Fifth Corps a month later at Gaines Mill. Undoubtedly facing Sharpshooters also engaged in skirmish duty, an officer in the 7th North Carolina mentioned two of his companies contending "with such stout resistance." The advanced Confederates sustained a "frightful loss." The duel seemed intense to William Ripley, who viewed the fighting down the slope between isolated skirmishers as more like a brawl between much larger lines of battle.[80]

Caught between opposing lines of infantry, Sharpshooters down the slope had to worry about Confederates moving ahead with fixed bayonets and their own comrades up the hill aiming for the charging enemy. Deafening blasts from cannons added to the horrendous din during the difficult moment. Looking back decades later, with more than a quarter century of life left, Brigham Buswell considered the skirmishers' escape miraculous.[81]

Confederate communication problems worked to the Union's advantage at Gaines Mill. Jackson's advance from the north, a grave threat to Porter's right flank, ran well behind schedule, which brought an uncoordinated opening infantry attack on the afternoon of June 27. Tangling with U.S. Regular troops to their left, a brigade of South Carolinians, destined to lose more than eight hundred men on the day, bristled against the tide, including many Sharps Rifle rounds from the USSS. As one Southern warrior remembered, "Suddenly a volley from the whole Federal line burst upon us. It seemed to sweep the earth." A North Carolina regimental historian added, "Again and again was that position assailed, and again and again we were repulsed by vastly superior numbers."[82]

At the point of the attack, the Tar Heel correctly diagnosed the problem of more Northerners than Confederates. However, the totality of Lee's force severely outnumbered Porter at Gaines Mill as the sun dipped lower. A major attack to the left of the Sharpshooters penetrated the Fifth Corps line, forcing the retreat McClellan envisioned as inevitable anyway.[83]

With their devoted service, the 1st USSS somehow recorded only four killed or mortally wounded as a result of Gaines Mill. Levi Leet, Benajah Jordan, and James Mathews, each representing a different company, suffered fatal wounds on the 27th, with James Read receiving a mortal injury on the following day as part of the Fifth Corps retreat. History records very little about the four heroes. Leet, a native of Quebec, Canada, died in his twenty-eighth year.

Of those suffering nonfatal injuries, Pvt. Edward Himes, Company F, became another seriously injured Sharpshooter who suffered for months in hospitals before a discharge. New Yorker James Winchell had an arm amputated, costing him his career as a soldier. The Rebel bullet shattered Winchell's left arm halfway between his elbow and shoulder. Eventually spending time at a Philadelphia hospital, which he described in unflattering terms, Winchell lived more than a half-century after that fateful day near Gaines Mill.[84]

A New York infantryman who fought near the Sharpshooters correctly deemed the June 27 fight "an awful thing . . . I've seen our boys drop like sheep not only our Regt but different ones. I didn't expect to get across alive."[85] At an enormous cost, the Northern work on June 27 served the purpose McClellan envisioned. Union soldiers gained a strong head start on their disorganized and badly damaged pursuers, with the Fifth Corps destroying Chickahominy bridges after crossing the accursed river. Yet, only three of the Seven Days had ended when the "change of base" started with an earnestness driven by the seemingly unstoppable Confederates.

Six Badgers Gone

Trepp's two-company band, south of the river during Gaines Mill, performed important service on the 27th, taking shots at Confederates near Fort Davidson. The Sharpshooters assisted in the area by targeting both enemy infantry and cannoneers. In his report, brigade commander Winfield Scott Hancock praised Trepp's men while the USSS members teamed up with New Jersey skirmishers.

The Sharpshooters "performed excellent service during the contest," Hancock wrote.[86]

Hunger started to hinder the men as the necessity of retreat refused to abate. William Kent wrote of receiving three days rations on June 25 without being issued more until along the James on July 4. William Ripley labeled the Sharpshooters as "tired, hungry and disheartened" after Gaines Mill. Finding provisions and good water proved quite difficult on the gloomy trek south. With men on edge throughout the army, the slightest unexpected noise could create a devastating panic.[87]

The retreat required the disgraceful abandonment of more than two thousand wounded and sick Northerners near Savage Station. Fighting for the next two days did not change much strategically, even as the dash to the James became encumbered by the large number of men and wagons moving south. Groups of skirmishing Sharpshooters worked hard at different places, with much danger and doubt in the air. Another defensive stand seemed inevitable on June 30 as the Confederate horde stood powerful and impending.[88]

General Lee's problems with army coordination likely saved the day for the Union cause. Although Southerners would get dangerously close to cutting McClellan's army in half at Glendale, the costly battle did not halt the retreat to a measurable degree on June 30. During the fight, Companies C and G, which added up to less than one hundred men, teamed up with another unit armed with Sharps Rifles, the 13th Pennsylvania Reserves. In the seesaw combat, men in both armies staggered under the deadly vortex. Six Badger Sharpshooters would lose their lives to battle wounds, one of the highest losses in any USSS company on one day for the whole war. As a member of the company wrote of the battle, "We drove the rebels first, and then they drove us. It was at this time that they cut our company so bad."

Shot in the head, Cpt. Edward Drew fell early in the fight, as did Sgts. Joel Parker and James Staples. In the early wave of close combat, some men in the company suffered bayonet wounds, while William Clark, barely twenty years old, fell with a wound to the side. He would be captured, and then die a prisoner the following day. He rests at Richmond National Cemetery, far from his native Badger State.[89]

With the Wisconsinites falling back some, Bugler Lyman Thompson fell dead shortly before the company fired about thirty shots from a second line. "George Lanning was killed here," one Sharpshooter added about the new position. "All the boys fought first rate." Lanning, a native of England, became the third member of the USSS since the start of April to lose his life in battle while trying to save his adoptive country.

Sergeant Staples had developed an excellent reputation back home. A Madison newspaper announcing his death declared him "well known to the people of this city," due to his work as a clerk in a boot and shoe store. Deemed "honest and faithful in all things" Staples enjoyed "a large circle of friends in this vicinity, who will deeply lament his fall."[90]

Enduring a head wound at Glendale, Badger warrior Jonas Shepard, a New Yorker born in 1828, would recover and live a long life. He would father children late in the century while living until 1907. Shepard's youngest daughter lived until 1984.[91]

Due to combat deaths, wounds, and capture, the two USSS companies engaged at Glendale were dramatically smaller as July dawned. Temporarily in charge of the USSS men fighting next to him on June 30, Maj. Roy Stone of the 13th Reserves recorded numbers in Berdan's duo of companies. Five officers and eighty-four marksmen lined up with Stone early in the day. Only three officers and twenty-eight USSS members with Stone could answer roll call the following morning.[92]

Sharpshooters at other key points had dangerous roles to play as the army tried to save itself. Frederick Peet, Company H would never return to the Sharpshooters due to a wound sustained on June 30. Thought mortally injured near White Oak Swamp, Peet's devoted comrades did not wish to leave his side. Peet begged for their move to the south with the rest of the army. Captain George Hastings, very impressed with the wounded man's courage and grim acceptance of his fate, suggested to Peet's brother, "I cannot say that there is not great danger that his wound was mortal, a musket ball entered at the shoulder and lodged in his lungs."[93] All involved, including Peet himself no doubt, would be amazed at how many more decades the young officer had left on earth.

Redemption at Malvern Hill

Mother Nature prepared a rude roadblock to Confederate hopes of cutting off or destroying the Army of the Potomac north of the James. A sanctuary Union troops started to occupy on June 30, Malvern Hill gradually rises between Glendale and the river. Planning to make the most of the wonderful defensive position, the Union created an impressive line of infantry and artillery to serve as the rally point for those units still filing down the road to safety.[94] For some reason, the Confederates elected to attack the hill on July 1, once again without solid communication between the tired Southern divisions.

The morning started early for many Sharpshooters, some able to enjoy coffee and sugar, even if food supplies left much to be desired. Boiled apples, William Ripley remembered, became a "fairly palatable" breakfast. Some

Sharpshooters who still had the hill to climb admired the fine defensive position General Porter dominated with troops and big guns. Major confusion defined the morning, however, because some Sharpshooters did not know their exact location. Because the men had marched, fought, and countermarched in so many different directions, William Kent's compass served its purpose.[95]

Multiple USSS companies passed the battle in reserve, but some Sharpshooters made grand use of the hill. One New Yorker wrote of the thousands of Confederates advancing against the Union position. "The sun soon came out and it was one of the hottest days I have seen this summer," he continued. Concealment among high wheat stacks allowed the green-clad warriors to pepper artillerists and advancing infantry. As the enemy pressed on, the Empire State warrior penned, "We immediately commenced firing on them, and at the same time our batteries opened. Hundreds of them must have been killed by this first discharge." As at Gaines Mill, the Sharpshooters damaged the Confederates early on, then retreated closer to the main line higher in elevation. Danger from friendly fire retained its status as a discouraging but inevitable reality for the army's most famous skirmishers.[96]

General Lee had another difficult day, although Porter worried about the fate of his line on July 1, especially the left flank. Solid reserves made the position far less dangerous than Gaines Mill, with the belching Union cannons leaving indelible memories. Union gunboats, key to the defense of the army in McClellan's mind, performed far less service than expected, proving a danger to friendly troops. Brigham Buswell bemoaned the "sad havoc" the naval ordnance created among McClellan's troops. Nonetheless, Buswell seemed saddened by how his Confederate enemies became fodder for the Northern men blasting away so efficiently. To the left of the Sharpshooters for a time during the day's worst, a member of the 4th Michigan Infantry remembered Malvern Hill by writing, "Such a seething hell will never be again enacted on this continent."[97]

No longer stuck on recruiting duty in Michigan, Thomas Connington witnessed the devastation Porter's line inflicted.

> *The Rebels loss was almost 3 to our one for they came at us in great numbers and fell by the thousand. They fought like drunken men going in with all their might. With regard to position, I saw one whole Brigade make a charge on one of our batteries. The Brigade was in the shape of a V, the lower point toward the Battery. When the Infantry poured into their left and the Battery into the center, it looked as if half of the whole Brigade fell.*[98]

Confederates pressed on against the leaden tide. Strong leadership during a time of worry about the Union left brought a Medal of Honor to Lt. Col. William Ripley. "At a critical moment," his citation for the military's highest award declared, Ripley "brought up two regiments, which he led against the enemy himself, being severely wounded."[99]

A small group of Sharpshooters performed important work on the hill. Taking advantage of topography to conceal their mission, Sgt. Richard Tyler recalled his small band blasting part of the attacking force. "From this position," he wrote, "our fire was at short range and most deadly." Information from Tyler guided Union cannoneers as they pummeled the Confederates. Seemingly stranded at first, Tyler skillfully led his men out of the danger zone.[100]

Abram Swits, Company K, lost his life during the battle. New Hampshire men suffered the three other USSS fatalities from the defense of Malvern Hill. Made a prisoner and then exchanged, 1st Lt. Cyrus Jones died of his injury in a New York City hospital. The battle also cost the lives of Corp. Thomas Ward and George Scales. Ward, an English native, died in his mid-thirties, with Jones and Scales more than a decade younger.

Leroy Greenwood, proving as hardy as the granite of his native state, sustained a serious nonfatal injury. While in a Philadelphia hospital, he received a medical discharge nearly six months after Malvern Hill. He would recover well enough to enlist in a New Hampshire infantry regiment later in the war, living until 1913.[101]

Wounded men sometimes felt lucky, because an injury barely missed being far more serious. Brigham Buswell took a bullet to the left arm, near the elbow. The Confederate round also hit his side. Buswell wrote that the second wound nearly left him with a shattered hip. Early 1863 arrived before the Wolverine received a medical discharge.[102]

Problems for Berdan

Col. Hiram Berdan summed up the Seven Days by reporting, "My men have all been in several engagements and are almost worn-out, but are in good spirits." This sentence accurately summed up the conduct of the 1st USSS. However, George Morell, Fifth Corps division commander, excoriated Berdan when the colonel outlined his supposedly heroic action during the retreat at Gaines Mill, trying to quell the chaos at a crucial moment. "Colonel Berdan was not in the fight," Morell flatly declared. Of Berdan's elevated view of his contributions that day, Morell suggested the colonel's "statement is highly exaggerated."

In a July 25 letter disagreeing with a story published earlier in the month, Morell expressed further doubts. The reporter had suggested Morell thanked

Berdan for the colonel's stabilizing presence a mile south of the battle. "Doing so would have been impossible," Morell retorted because Berdan's actions did not amount to nearly as much as first published. The reporter's efforts "to puff a favorite at the expense of the army" cannot be justified, Morell concluded.[103]

Berdan seemed in more trouble with his own men. Many Sharpshooters lost whatever respect they had for Berdan. Soon after Malvern Hill, five officers lodged a formal complaint against the founding father of the Sharpshooters. On July 4, the officers noted Berdan absented himself from Yorktown through the Seven Days, prompting questions about the colonel's fitness for leadership. Although the strongly worded diatribe would be retracted later in the month, the doubts junior officers had likely prompted Major General Porter to withdraw previous praise of Berdan.[104] With William Ripley, their highly regarded lieutenant colonel out with his serious Malvern Hill wound, soldiers across the 1st USSS pondered their future under Berdan, a colonel they did not respect.

Because of inquiries from superiors about the colonel's whereabouts during the Seven Days and problems within the ranks of his regiment, Berdan wrote William Ripley on July 14. The wounded and heroic officer had already returned to Vermont to rest and heal. Berdan suspected that Ripley had criticized his immediate superior in the presence of others during the Seven Days. In particular, Berdan demanded to know of Ripley's answers to a Fifth Corps staff officer who had asked about the 1st USSS leader's whereabouts during the retreat from Malvern Hill. One week after Berdan's letter, Ripley replied, using language that must have increased Berdan's concerns.

> *I replied perhaps with some degree of bitterness, that I had not seen you since morning, that you left the Regt, as soon as the men were posted, on some errand & had not returned during the day to my knowledge.*
>
> *I say that I said this with some bitterness—I had bitter feelings in my heart . . . I remember also how when the Regt was [at] Mechanicsville, I being absent at the time, you, after accompanying the Regt part way, suddenly remembered business of the most pressing nature at the camp, business which it would seem that the Q[ua]r[ter] Mas[ter] (who was at that time present) might have managed without the aid of his Col.*

Ripley added that his wound would prevent walking without a crutch for at least two months. As a result, he intended to resign his commission. The maimed Ripley never returned to the USSS.[105]

The USSS at Harrison's Landing

The final insult of the Seven Days became the horrible mud badgering the USSS as they retreated from Malvern Hill. After the trek south, which finished not far from the James River, the mud seemed able to swallow up overwhelmed soldiers. A battered Badger looked on the bright side that night because the 1st USSS had a soft bed of mud, which produced some very sound sleep for some of the marksmen.[106]

Soon after arrival at Harrison's Landing on the James, Sharpshooters viewed their resting place as a salvation from the woe of the previous three months. New Yorker Harrison De Long wrote home on July 5 with news of his survival. "Those who are yet alive and have been in the recent scenes of licensed bloodshed, and escaped without a scratch, think themselves providentially favored," he mused.[107]

Resting near the river, only 436 men were deemed fit for duty in the 1st USSS. Many in the ranks might not have been able to complete a short march due to sickness and utter fatigue, according to George Marden. "I am sick of war, especially in the summer," Marden exclaimed on July 8.[108]

Luther Frink, Company K, grew quite accustomed to the necessities of war due to the hard weeks of fighting and marching on the Peninsula. In an early July letter, he informed a Michigan newspaper,

> *War certainly tends to harden a man's conscience and benumb his feelings. The battlefield has no terrors for me now; I think no more of marching to fight that I once did of going fishing, and can shoot a rebel with as little compunction of conscience as I ever did a deer or a muskrat.*[109]

McClellan's army accomplished little across July. Disease festered at Harrison's Landing, adding to the ghastly toll nonbattle causes inflicted on the USSS. The vexing problem cost Company G the services of all three brothers of the Melvin family. Earlier in the campaign, Taylor Melvin died at the Gaines Mill hospital. His brother Shepard, ten years older, lost his life to disease on July 16. By the end of August, the last of the trio, Elihu, received a medical discharge.[110]

Seeing the toll sickness inflicted, one Wisconsin Sharpshooter expressed scorn in a letter home. "Somebody is to blame for the suffering here, and some of these Surgeons will have a tuff account to settle with some of the men if they don't die." The flustered soldier also wrote of his dislike of abolitionists, those in favor of ending slavery as a war aim.

> *One thing I think is certain, and that is if we only had all the nigger lovers of the North here we would soon come home, for then we could lick secesh like thunder, by putting them in the front rank and pushing them forward with the bayonet, and as fast as they fall use them for a breastwork.*[111]

Some Sharpshooters wondered about the viability of the organization after the campaign, with hot and humid conditions prevailing. After leaving Wisconsin with 116 men, one Badger wrote in July, less than thirty were fit for duty along the James. The writer complained about several problems, such as the requirement for many sick men to march with their regiments. He also opposed McClellan's penchant for using soldiers to guard the private property of Virginians. Without more common sense from Union leaders, the Sharpshooter suggested, the Confederates could carry on the war for twenty years.[112]

One Sharpshooter declared "playing cards and killing body lice" constituted the major pastimes for McClellan's inert army. With enough downtime, soldiers often grabbed pencils to inform friends and loved ones of army happenings. On July 14, New Hampshire Sharpshooter Joseph Rolfe wrote Charles Shepard, a company comrade in a Washington hospital after a wound received at Malvern Hill. Rolfe noted the ongoing strife between the regiment's officers. He also provided updates on some Company E soldiers. "The boys say keep up good spirits and we will come out all right yet," Rolfe suggested, "Accept the best wishes for your speedy recovery, from your true friend." In the autumn, Shepard headed home with a disability discharge. Both he and his good friend Rolfe would enjoy very long lives.[113]

A member of McClellan's staff summed up the conditions at Harrison's Landing in a July 10 letter, "The heat is awful." Rudolf Aschmann also remembered the high temperatures and flies. The Sharpshooters' camp had some shade, while access to the river had obvious advantages for cooling off and bathing. Cooking became a hobby for some marksmen, a pastime helped along by the improved supply situation. Aschmann detailed the toll sickness played along the James, particularly remembering Christian Schiffman, a company friend who lost his life to typhoid fever on July 29.[114]

Company F lost their original captain, Edmund Weston, who submitted his resignation in late July. "Rheumatic gout," which had plagued Weston, had become more problematic. To emphasize the condition's hold over Weston, the captain "respectfully and urgently" asked Colonel Berdan to grant "immediate and unconditional acceptance" of the request. Weston received his honorable discharge on August 2.[115]

Thomas Connington, Company K, suggested some men faked illness to receive a discharge. He grew upset at the idea of Union forces losing strength because some soldiers could not handle what they should have known would be a dangerous and prolonged task. "I am ashamed of them," the Wolverine wrote, "for no man ought to have come here" if they expected "boys play." In a lighter part of the letter, Connington replied to the sentiment of a female pen pal after the young lady complained about one aspect of the war. "You speak of the last call for volunteers and think as most of the girls do about taking all the merry young men," Connington wrote. "But I will tell you," he sternly replied, "the more and faster they come into the field the quicker this trouble will be settled and all of us get home."[116]

Some decided to depart without authority. Benjamin Morrison seemed envious of his discharged friend Charles Shepard. "I would have one good old time, I bet," Morrison claimed to Shepard if he was also home. Without using specific words, the unmotivated soldier appeared to outline his future plan through repeated references to being back in the Granite State. About to head to Washington due to sickness, Morrison would desert from a hospital on September 1. He then disappears into history, so we do not know how much of a good time he had at home while absent without leave. No record exists of Morrison's return to the army.[117]

USSS members stuck along the James could not avoid typical work. Company drill was scheduled for one hour in the morning, with battalion drill for one hour starting at 5:30 p.m. Supply matters, including an effort to keep the Sharpshooters properly clothed, demonstrated the wear and tear the Peninsula campaign inflicted across McClellan's army. An order from 1st Regiment headquarters showed that Colonel Berdan continued to hold high expectations for his troops. Sharpshooters "will not be allowed to drill without blouses, or in their bare feet," the missive read. Moreover, "All soldiers are required to bathe at least three times a week."[118]

The pleasant surprise of missing men returning to companies made Sharpshooters feel better. One Badger wrote home in August when he saw several comrades, including one missing for almost eight weeks. The good news counters a common conclusion of some historians who label a missing man as killed in action. Often, these soldiers had been taken prisoner, and then paroled by the enemy. The Wisconsin marksman added, "it won't take long to whip out secesh if we have men enough here."[119]

Such hopeful sentiments meshed with McClellan's desire to try for Richmond again. One could not fault the Lincoln administration for having lost faith in their army leader, who was much farther from Richmond than before the

Seven Days. Concerns about Pope's Army of Virginia being attacked played into the thinking of new general-in-chief Henry Halleck, who ordered McClellan's army off the Peninsula in early August. The strategic recalibration would drive the 1st USSS to the same battlefield as Post's 2nd Regiment by the end of the month.[120]

Quiet Weeks around Falmouth

About seventy-five miles north of Harrison's Landing, the 2nd USSS continued weeks of relative inactivity, sickness, and discontent in the summer sizzle. A variety of minor events took place, with food central to Sharpshooters' considerations. Like other soldiers in the war, inventive men augmented their rations by claiming the creatures from central Virginia. As Company F's Amos Abbott wrote on July 22, "[William] Beard killed a rattlesnake—had a duck for supper—it went tiptop." On days earlier in the month, Abbott recorded other activities, such as patrolling along the Rappahannock, trying to beat the heat, and enjoying letters from home. Expounding on his avocation as a chef, he added, "got some Grapes and made a lot of sauce" on July 16.[121]

Still an isolated command around Fredericksburg, the USSS and Rufus King's Division, performed scouting and foraging work. Lincoln administration officials and army leadership wished for soldiers to keep an eye on Rappahannock River fords to the west. Probes and short marches provided information for leaders to study strategic possibilities that might help crush the Southern cause.

To that end, Companies A and C of the 2nd USSS departed later in July for a march that would total about forty miles across four days. Lt. Col. Francis Peteler commanded the Sharpshooter contingent. The trek approached the area of Orange Court House, south of the Rapidan River on the Orange and Alexandria Railroad. Startled by Confederate cavalry, the Union expedition faced some danger, but the Sharpshooters performed well, killing some members of the enemy force. The two USSS companies then protected the rear of the column as the troops marched back to Falmouth. The trip augmented the supply situation for the marksmen, with livestock confiscated from the countryside.[122]

A similar effort took Sharpshooter companies on another Virginia foray in early August. Netting more supplies, the effort ended at Spotsylvania Court House, well northwest of Falmouth. Excused from the march for apparently health reasons, unmotivated soldier William Greene expressed pleasure at avoiding the heat and dust his comrades endured. Uninterested in becoming a great soldier, Greene missed out on the encomiums given to a Sharpshooter company leading the march. As a newspaper reported, the USSS members, in front of the division with some Badgers in the state's 2nd Infantry, "Troops never marched better or behaved more gallantly in anticipation of a battle."[123]

A major dispute at the top of regimental leadership occurred soon after Peteler's excursion to Orange Court House. Colonel Post wrote of the incident,

> *I placed Lt. Col. Peteler under arrest for ungentlemanly, disrespectful and contemptuous language to me in the presence of his men. I very much regret that I was obliged to do so but as the privation and disappointment incident to a soldier's life have had the effect to make him think such language and want of respect for my feelings "not a just cause" for arrest, I have the honor but to ask that his resignation will be accepted.*

In response, Peteler wrote Post, "Believing that the mutual confidence and harmony so essential to the good of the service between Field Officers of the same Regt, cannot as formerly exist between us, since my arrest by you without just cause. And desirous to serve my country where my services may be of some value, I therefore tender my Resignation as Lieut. Col. of the 2nd Regt. U.S. Sharp Shooters." He would soon return home to assist with efforts to quell a Sioux uprising.[124]

Back at the Falmouth camp, an interesting discussion group formed, with many Sharpshooters participating, including Colonel Post. Meetings took place at the oak chapel Chaplain Barber constructed with the help of others in the regiment. Curtis Abbott referred to the organization as a "lyceum," with members talking over issues and debating matters of national interest. Post grew impressed by his soldiers' ability to ponder and talk through questions, with the colonel issuing a congratulatory order for the regiment's dedication. Meetings of the group did not seem to last for an extended period, because the men had to prepare for a new campaign.[125]

Signs of efforts to unite scattered Union forces became evident to Minnesotan Joseph Dickey, who recorded the arrival of troops under Ambrose Burnside at Falmouth in early August. These men, organized as the Union's Ninth Corps, had relaxed some on the Peninsula after successful months along the coasts of North and South Carolina. McClellan hoped Burnside's nineteen regiments would be assigned to his command at Harrison's Landing for another shot at Richmond, an idea the army commander's superiors rejected.[126]

General Lee turned his strategic focus to the north. Pope's isolated position in central Virginia offered the Confederates a chance to damage those Northerners before McClellan's force arrived to save the day. With McClellan's army still along the James, Lee moved part of his command toward the Rapidan River, on a collision course with Pope. The 2nd Sharpshooters finally seemed destined for battle.

Signs of movement arrived with marching orders issued on August 9. For his last evening meal at Falmouth, Amos Abbot recorded, "Potatoes, Eggs, Beets and Salt horse." The march the following morning began at a difficult time for other elements of the Army of Virginia, who fought Stonewall Jackson's force at Cedar Mountain, northwest of Falmouth. Jackson retreated after the engagement, but Pope's army sustained far more casualties. Beset by poor judgment and doubt, a defensive mindset overcame Pope for the rest of the disastrous month.[127]

Shots along the Rappahannock

The 2nd Regiment's march beginning on August 10 set a fast pace, with Culpeper reached late on the 11th, a total distance of forty-six miles in thirty-one hours according to the computations of a Maine historian. Curtis Abbott recorded the crossing of the Rappahannock at Ellis Ford near the end of the first day's march. "The depth, strength of current, and treacherous footing rendered the crossing difficult," the Green Mountain man remembered. The next morning, reveille blew at 2 a.m., without much time to eat. The 2nd Regiment had about twenty-eight miles to go before their day ended.[128]

Days of rest bolstered Post's eight companies after the exhausting march, with whiskey rations given out about midday after a quiet start to August 12. Chaplain Barber used the downtime to visit the Cedar Mountain battlefield, noting a wide range of appalling sights. Even though Union troops suffered more than Confederates, Barber witnessed lines of dead Rebels still on the battlefield after Jackson's retreat. The kind-hearted warrior and religious servant of man lingered to talk with and care for some of the wounded.[129]

The 2nd USSS remained in Culpeper until August 16, when they crossed the Rapidan River to the south, finding a short-term camp near Cedar Mountain on what Darius Starr deemed a "short but disagreeable" march. Jacob McClure's August 18 letter to Maine's governor noted a sergeant's effort back home to recruit more Maine marksmen. The work to bring in additional men would continue, and become more pressing.[130]

The time south of the Rapidan did not last long for the 2nd Sharpshooters. Unsure of Confederate numbers and intentions, Pope's orders led the army back north to a line along the Rappahannock, with Sharpshooters at their new location on August 21. Slow due to crowded roads, the retreat still went well. Lee's attempt to strike Pope's army had been foiled for now. As he prepared for the next phase of the campaign, Pope had about forty-five thousand present for duty prior to the arrival of Porter's Fifth Corps, including the 1st USSS.[131]

Danger from work along the Rappahannock ended the lives of the first three members of the 2nd Regiment to die in action. Confederate shelling, which began at about 10 a.m. on August 21, posed a great hazard to those on picket duty or in full line of battle. Shooting took place across much of the next three days, with mortal injuries claiming one member of the 2nd USSS each day. The first killed in action was John D. Skinner from Michigan, followed the next day by a Company H man, Corp. Warren Stevens. Then, during intense shelling on the 23rd, Company D lost Washington Tucker, one of the twins recruited from Cherryfield, Maine. Tucker lingered for two months, dying at a Maryland hospital on October 17.[132]

The final day along the Rappahannock line started with sunrise shelling from the Confederates south of the river. Amos Abbott counted about thirty shell bursts, each with the potential to inflict harm. Fortunately, only a few wounds were added to the Sharpshooters' toll.[133]

A newspaper account credited Post's men with the killing of forty Confederates on August 23. Such kill ratios might have been possible in some engagements, but the writer likely exaggerated USSS accomplishments. Confederates were still able to target the units with extensive amounts of lead. Generally, artillery made for a poor means to suppress the fire of a line of infantry, especially USSS members who would have been in scattered groups. However, the relatively short distance between the antagonists likely contributed to the fine showing from the Southern artillerists. Accurate bombardment against the lines of McDowell's Corps assisted Lee as his next big plan unfolded, a move around the right of Pope's army. In the immediate term, the Confederate boldness threatened Pope's supply line.[134]

Porter Joins Pope's Army

As Post's men endured their first intense combat, the 1st USSS and Porter's Fifth Corps started moving to assist the Army of Virginia. Lieutenant John Smith Brown, adjutant of Berdan's Regiment, wrote of his happiness at leaving their feckless home. "We were not sorry to go. Harrison's Landing has no pleasant memories for us." The future could do what it will, he exclaimed, "Here, days passed wearily, without a single cheering episode."[135]

Porter's corps departed the James on the morning of August 14. The quick pace remained a major memory for many Sharpshooters. They once again saw the Chickahominy and Williamsburg on the way toward Fort Monroe. They reached Hampton, at the terminus of the Peninsula, on the 18th. One Badger wrote home, "We are beginning to be quite tired from our long marches; but we got through all safe and sound." Another Wisconsin marksman suggested the march to Yorktown had amounted to "the longest twelve miles we ever saw."[136]

The rate of march for the Fifth Corps seems impressive when reviewing Sharpshooter comments about their last days on the Peninsula. However, a week passed from leaving Harrison's Landing to embarkation at Newport News for the boat ride to Aquia Creek, six miles northeast of Falmouth. The men still had quite a trip to join Pope's army. The 1st USSS departed Falmouth with their corps comrades on August 22, then marched to the Rappahannock like Post's men had done earlier in the month. Scarcity of drinking water constituted a primary challenge of the trek to the northwest.[137]

Porter's men guarded fords for a short time after reaching the river. Confusion prevailed due to a lack of updates from Pope; senior officers in the Fifth Corps seemed quite surprised to find the Army of Virginia no longer guarding the river. Resuming the march without clear instructions, the 1st USSS and the Fifth Corps covered ground quickly while moving northeast along the Orange and Alexandria Railroad. Berdan's regiment was afforded a short break from marching, an appreciated respite after the rapid pace since leaving Falmouth.[138]

A shortage of information about the enemy plagued Pope and his force. Confederates continued working around the Union right flank, a great threat to Pope's lines of communication and supply. McDowell's men headed north, with the destination of Warrenton, slightly more than fifteen miles west of the infamous battlefield of Manassas, the site of a major Confederate victory in July 1861. Firing along the road north helped remind Sharpshooters of the danger they continued to face.[139]

August 25 was especially noisy as the 2nd Regiment trekked to White Sulphur Springs, five miles southwest of Warrenton. Amos Abbott recorded cannon fire lasting much of the day. "We were thrown out as scirmishers and went down to the river and let the rebels have it," the New Hampshire marksman recorded. Both Colonel Post and Lieutenant Colonel Peteler (close to his resignation) took enemy fire during the engagement. On the next day, Daniel Willis, Company H, the fourth member of Post's unit to die in action, met his demise. As the Sharpshooters unloaded an intense fire, Willis sustained a fatal headshot. Curtis Abbott referred to Willis as "a man of modest stillness and humility." The company grew especially animated in their firing after Willis fell. Falling back from the front line later in the day, the Vermonters interred Willis, then rested near the spot of their buried comrade.[140]

A modern biographer of John Pope considers August 26 a key day in what would be the Second Bull Run campaign. Movements of the Union's Army of Virginia seemed to align with where Confederates had once been, or where Pope hoped they would be. Rather than using good intelligence to formulate plans, Pope lacked solid information about what to do. Elements of McClellan's Sixth Corps and a part of Joseph Hooker's Third Corps division engaged enemy forces in small fights to the northeast. To make matters worse, Jackson's men were able to ransack the impressive Northern supply depot of Manassas Junction before moving north to an exceptional defensive position west of the First Bull Run battlefield.[141]

The two USSS regiments marched toward battle on different roads. McDowell's Third Corps, Army of Virginia, went northeast on the Warrenton Turnpike while Porter's troops moved up the railroad to witness the burned remnants of Manassas Junction. Late in the afternoon of August 28, the 2nd USSS and other elements of King's Division walked along the Turnpike just south of Jackson's hidden position. An intense battle between six Union regiments and most of Jackson's troops proved enervating and disappointing for the Confederates. The Sharpshooters did not take part in the fight, often called the battle of Brawner Farm.[142]

Having already marched beyond Brawner Farm before the fighting started, Colonel Post and the 2nd USSS camped for a short time east of the unexpected battlefield, with some companies out on picket. General King elected to withdraw early on the 29th, attempting to unite his brigades. Later in the day, the 1st USSS marched with Porter's men northwest from Manassas Junction on the Gainesville Road. They formed along Dawkins Branch, slightly beyond Bethlehem Church. Fighting separately when in action at Second Bull Run, both the 1st and 2nd USSS would lose men to Confederate fire over the next two days.[143]

General Pope's confusion about Confederate intentions continued as his army and supporting units from McClellan coalesced on both sides of the Warrenton Turnpike. Confident the battle of the night before meant Stonewall Jackson could be defeated, Pope neglected to prevent the arrival of Gen. James Longstreet's wing of Lee's Southern army, which lined up south of Jackson. Menaced by his own failures, Pope and his army faced extreme danger. Porter and other senior officers understood the situation better. While in the isolated position south of Dawkins Branch, the Fifth Corps commander witnessed evidence of Longstreet's arrival.[144]

The bulk of the day's fighting occurred north of the Warrenton Turnpike as elements of Pope's force made uncoordinated attacks against Jackson's strong line. The remote nature of Porter's position compared to the rest of the Union's army confined the 1st USSS to a supporting role during the day. In contrast to the regiment at Yorktown or the 2nd USSS along the Rappahannock, sources do not paint a picture of heavily engaged marksmen along Dawkins Branch. One

Sharpshooter wrote of some Confederate artillerists who "blazed away at us with shell and solid shot," which added to the dangers of the regiment's limited skirmish duty. The day proved frustrating due to the lack of progress and very confusing messages from General Pope. Porter's main line remained south of Dawkins Branch due to Longstreet's presence, a fact that doomed Porter's career after Pope filed charges generally divorced from reality.[145]

More than forty years later, Sgt. Edwin Wilson, a Michigan marksman serving as 1st USSS color bearer, favored Porter's arrest for his failures on August 29. Wishing for more action along Dawkins Branch, Wilson criticized Porter for not accomplishing much after the arrival of Longstreet. Wilson, who would rise to lieutenant and suffer two combat wounds as a Sharpshooter, suggested his corps commander lacked the drive to assist the Army of Virginia. "Then commenced the work of McClellan's officers to beat Pope," Wilson opined. Although an interesting perspective, Wilson had an unrealistic expectation of what the isolated Fifth Corps could accomplish.[146]

With skirmishing far less damaging than the attack Wilson suggested, August 29 added two men to the combat death toll of the 1st Regiment: Sgt. William McLean and Norman Wilson. Twenty-eight years old, McLean—who lived for two weeks after his wounding—was the first Company D man to die in action. Like McLean, Wilson died in a Washington hospital.[147]

"I Bade Him Lay Down with My Rifle"

After the overnight retrograde away from Brawner Farm toward Manassas Junction, the 2nd USSS and the rest of their division returned north on the morning of August 29. They lacked much of a role in the fighting against Jackson beyond the Warrenton Turnpike. Pope's mistakes on the day were many, the most damaging of which was a false perception that Stonewall Jackson was retreating. Pope visualized a major charge along the turnpike that could join with Porter to crush Jackson. Brigadier General John Hatch, taking over King's division, was ordered to move west along the road to intercept the "retreating" Rebels. A sizable and excellent group of Confederate troops marched east at the same time. Colonel Post and his marksmen led the advance of the Union division which was in for a major surprise.[148]

Sharing Pope's belief that the Confederates were retreating, corps commander McDowell thought Hatch's advance could seriously damage the enemy. One Pennsylvania infantryman heard McDowell suggest the capture of Confederate prisoners served as the main goal of the late-day advance. When ordered, the Sharpshooters moved at double-quick just as the darkness made the advance especially dangerous.[149]

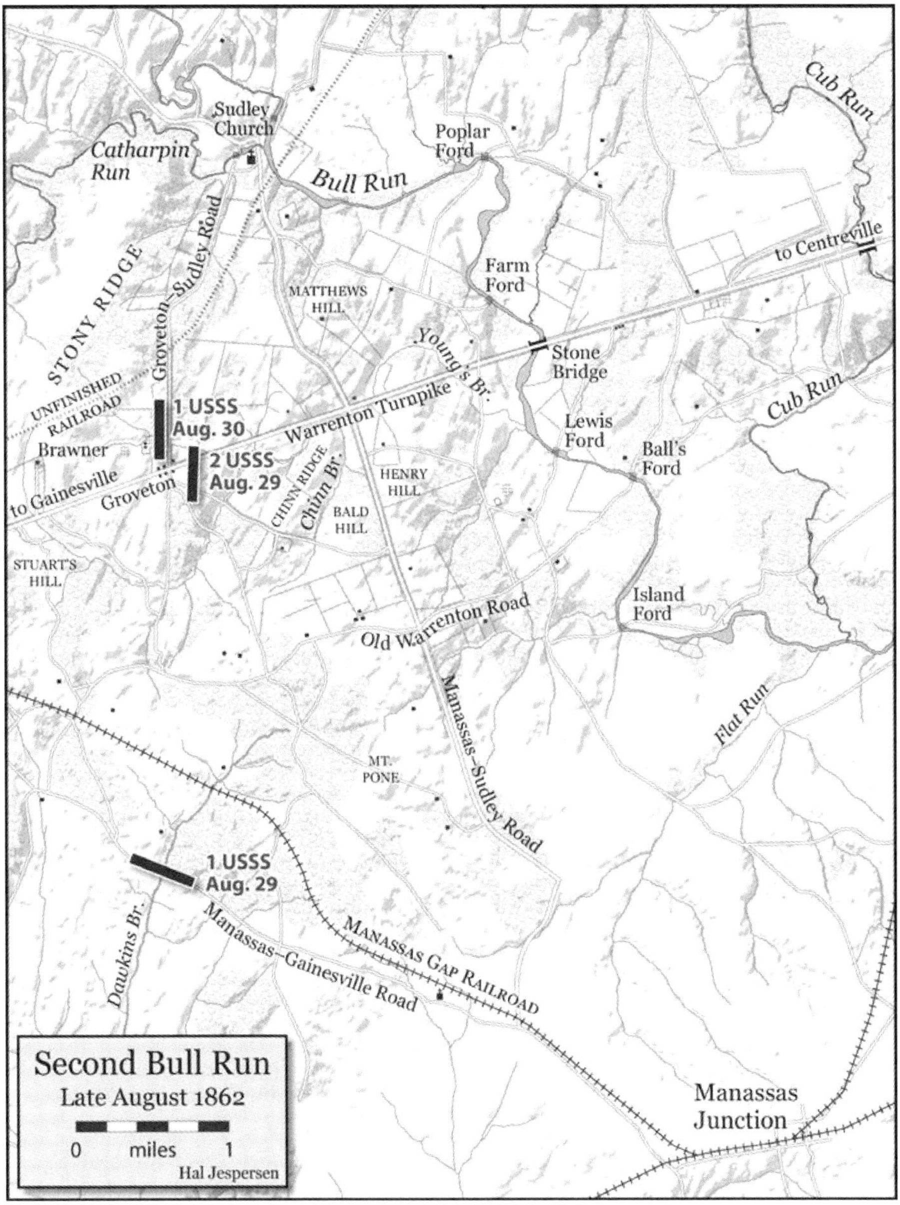

Sudley Church
Catharpin Run
Poplar Ford
Bull Run
Cub Run
Groveton–Sudley Road
STONY RIDGE
to Centreville
Farm Ford
MATTHEWS HILL
Young's Br.
Stone Bridge
UNFINISHED RAILROAD
1 USSS Aug. 30
Warrenton Turnpike
Cub Run
Lewis Ford
Brawner
2 USSS Aug. 29
Ball's Ford
to Gainesville
Groveton
CHINN RIDGE
Chinn Br.
HENRY HILL
BALD HILL
STUART'S HILL
Island Ford
Old Warrenton Road
Manassas–Sudley Road
Flat Run
MT. PONE
1 USSS Aug. 29
Dawkins Br.
Manassas–Gainesville Road
MANASSAS GAP RAILROAD
Second Bull Run
Late August 1862
0 miles 1
Hal Jespersen
Manassas Junction

With John Gibbon's men on detached service, Hatch took three brigades and a few artillery pieces on the mission west. Initial firing from Union skirmishers, including 2nd USSS men, preceded the placement of Hatch's cannons. Curtis Abbott remembered four companies of Post's outfit to the right of the Warrenton Turnpike during the opening stages of the engagement. A staff officer under Brig. Gen. Abner Doubleday witnessed the fine work Hatch's front did early in the encounter, with the Sharpshooters playing their part. Post's divided regiment crept "cautiously forward, peering into wood and glen, every man ready on the instant to bring down a skulking foe or develop a hostile force hiding in ambuscade."[150]

The Northerners found far more resistance than expected, with multiple Confederate brigades involved, including the truculent troops under John Bell Hood, who had smashed Porter's left at Gaines Mill. Pressure on the right flank led many Sharpshooters to see the hopelessness of the evening. Leading the 95th Pennsylvania Infantry as part of Hatch's advance, Maj. Edward Pye summed up the surprise and intense enemy resolve. "A deadly fire from three sides welcomed and drove us back," he reported. General Hood, always proud to extol his soldiers, wrote, "Onward they charged, driving the foe through field and forest," forcing Hatch back down the Warrenton Turnpike.[151]

"The struggle," Hatch reported, "lasting some three-quarters of an hour, was a desperate one, being in many instances a hand-to-hand conflict," something the Sharpshooters never expected. Some Confederates did not receive the chance to confront a Sharpshooter up close. As Henry Campbell remembered, one Confederate "was only about 15 yards from me with fixed bayonet . . . so I bade him lay down with my Rifle and he did so without delay."

Stunned by the Confederate pressure as darkness quickly ruled, Hatch's retreat ended the engagement. In the wake of the short yet wicked fight, seven Company A men were captured, including 2nd Lt. James Doughty. The officer would spend eight months away from the regiment until being exchanged.[152]

Certainly not the finest hour of the war for the 2nd USSS, their leader at least proved his great bravery, earning enduring fame. Colonel Post, who had been leading the four companies on the left of the turnpike, noticed that the 24th New York Infantry had their colors captured during the confused fight. Charging ahead, Post snatched the flag from the Southern victors without sustaining a wound. Boldness at a defining moment made Post a hero, not just a respected leader of men in battle.[153]

Hood's advance inflicted well over one hundred casualties on Hatch's division, including five 2nd USSS members killed. The lost Sharpshooters represented four states, John Jordan of Maine, Charles Jacobs and Francis Storrs of Minnesota, Charles Keith of Vermont, and Granite Stater Benjamin Graham.[154]

John Jordan's case demonstrates the horrible unknowns family members faced in a world without rapid communications. Lack of contact from the beloved soldier created intense doubt and great sadness back home. Nearly two months after Jordan's death, his guardian wrote the state,

> *Will you please inform me whither John Jordan is dead, sick, or wounded. He enlisted about a year ago in the Second Regt USSS, was injured in a Rail Road accident. I have not heard of his recovery or anything from him for over 2 months. He was a very steady young man & constant to write to me till of late.*[155]

An older Sharpshooter sustained a disabling wound in the night fight. Charles Thayer, who enlisted in his late thirties the year before, had a ball pass across the back of his neck in the confusion. Assigned to the Veteran Reserve Corps, Thayer, who does not appear to have rejoined his marksmen comrades, left the army in late 1864.[156]

The Disaster of August 30

New orders, necessary due to the morass Pope had created through his poor understanding of the battlefield, withdrew the Fifth Corps and some supporting elements of McDowell's command from the Dawkins Branch line. Moving before dawn on August 30, Porter failed to ensure his entire corps marched to the same location. The misguided troops, about 2,500 of them, failed to make a turn, a tremendous oversight keeping them away from the battle later in the day. The 1st USSS made the correct left on the Sudley Road, which led to the main concentration of Union forces along the Warrenton Turnpike. Berdan's regiment rested near where the 2nd USSS tangled with Hood the night before.[157]

On a day that would close catastrophically for Pope's army, the 1st USSS deployed in their new position with textbook skirmishing opportunities. Even with a smaller command due to the incompetence that sent a large number of troops down the wrong road, Porter still needed a wide front. Some of the Sharpshooters served as flankers during the day, guardians of the side of Porter's command, not just the front. Brig. Gen. Dan Butterfield, in charge of one of Porter's divisions, placed Berdan's men at the heart of his line of troops. The 25th New York Infantry's skirmishers stood to the right of the USSS, with the 3rd U.S. Infantry on Berdan's left. The left of the skirmish line reached the intersection of the Warrenton Turnpike and Lewis Lane.[158]

Porter stood for hours with a very uncomfortable status quo prevailing. Confederate skirmishers eventually gave way to the USSS, which advanced across the Groveton-Sudley Road, north of the turnpike. A Badger wrote of Confederate fire being quite heavy even in the early part of the advance, when the USSS had the benefit of woody protection. After arriving at some relatively open ground, Berdan found a more significant force of the enemy. He also grew concerned about the lack of Union troops on his right. Meanwhile, Porter's additional men filled in behind the skirmishers, with supporting troops under McDowell filling in the right of the Fifth Corps to address Berdan's concern.[159]

William Ripley's history of Company F grimly painted the moment when the 1st USSS "suddenly passed from the comparative shelter of the woods into an open field directly in the face of Jackson's corps strongly posted." The impressive defensive works Stonewall held then became the Sharpshooters' most notable problem as they rested along a small stream, today known as Schoolhouse Branch. The ability to conquer the hill and railroad cut seemed doubtful. Of the approximately two hours firing at the Rebels and using the creek bed for protection, a marksman wrote, "It was sharp work, I tell you."[160]

Porter's main attack did not begin until mid-afternoon, which left the men much time to ponder the difficulty ahead. As a New York infantryman described the down time before the order to assault Jackson's main force, "It seemed that every square foot of ground was cut with a bullet, not to speak of shells from four batteries."[161]

With about 250 men in battle line, the 1st Sharpshooters essentially became infantry, rather than small groups of skirmishers, when Porter's line moved forward. One Michigan infantry officer recorded General Butterfield cheering on his troops as the advance began. Like their corps comrades, Berdan's warriors faced a line of experienced and expertly deployed troops on strong defensive ground. Berdan had his men move slightly to the right during the attack to offer some protection for the marksmen, who fired between forty and sixty rounds according to the colonel's report.

Berdan wrote of an order for his men to lie down for a time during the main attack, a point confirmed in other sources. The amount of fire made one Wisconsin man realize how intense the war had become. "*My God,* how they did give it to us," he averred. "The boys say the grape, cannister and shell flew a great deal thicker than in any battle they were in on the Peninsula." The day would go down in Confederate lore for the excellent positions of Southern artillerists, revenge perhaps, for Malvern Hill. In contrast, a Sharpshooter deemed Porter's effort as "badly managed," especially because Union artillery seemed unable to match enemy cannoneers. Porter's attack quickly withered.[162]

After a severe wound at Second Bull Run, Capt. William Austin, Company E, 1st USSS, received a medical discharge the following spring. U.S. ARMY HERITAGE AND EDUCATION CENTER

Granite Staters lost their captain to a severe arm wound during the battle. William Austin showed obvious leadership abilities, taking less than five months to rise from private to company commander. Austin received a medical discharge in May 1863. The unfortunate loss took another strong leader away from the Sharpshooters.[163]

Intrepid Sgt. Richard Tyler, Company K, took a bullet to the leg during the August 30 attack. He would soon be back with his men. Other wounded Sharpshooters demonstrated amazing toughness at Second Bull Run. The story of Robert Casey, Company G, illustrated the vim commonplace across both sides of the war. A comrade recorded Casey as "shot in the neck just below the windpipe." Surprisingly not mortally wounded, Casey grew very aggravated.

[He] jumped to his feet, and swinging his rifle at the enemy in an excitable manner, made use of some rather harsh language for their benefit, until the blood in his throat and mouth prevented farther speech. Then, after firing off what cartridges he had left, standing up in full view utterly reckless and determined, the last shot being fired at a hog running along at the foot of the embankment, no rebels at that particular moment being seen, and which he laid out, this gritty soldier walked coolly off the field singing a peculiar tune of his own, completely heedless of the bullet or shell flying thickly about him. He was discharged after much suffering and a struggle for life.[164]

The vicious cost of the August 30 attack—labeled "the most satisfactory battle I've ever been engaged in" by a Confederate division commander—amounted to wounds for one-third of Porter's force.[165] Eleven Sharpshooter lives ended, most of them likely lost during the main attack of the Fifth Corps. As illustrated in Table 1.1, the killed or mortally wounded represented six companies of the 1st USSS.

Rudolf Aschmann witnessed the death of his company commander, Capt. Adolph Sennhauser. The two soldiers had known each other in Switzerland for several years. Shots to the right hip and back led to the officer's fall. Unable to help, Aschmann penned notes of unyielding emotional turmoil from the loss of a great friend. Although knowing his duty as a soldier to press on with the attacking force, Aschmann admitted to staying by Sennhauser's corpse for a few minutes.[166]

Table 1.1. Members of the 1st USSS Killed or Mortally Wounded, August 30, 1862

Company	Killed or Mortally Wounded
A	Charles Bieler Frederick Dittert Adolph Sennhauser
B	Philander Austin George Downing
C	John Schoonover Orson Sturtevant Peter Van Etten
E	Charles Brown
G	George Hartley
K	Sidney Race

Sidney Race's two brothers in his Michigan company survived the war. Several of the mortally wounded men lived for weeks in hospitals. George Downing and Frederick Dittert were examples of men buried in the Washington region, far away from the homes they departed to serve their country.[167]

A memorable poem, etched in the tombstone of New Hampshire's twenty-eight-year-old Charles Brown, could mark the resting place of many a Union soldier in the war.

Mid the battle's roar
With his comrades
True and brave
And his noble form we
Shall see no more
It rests in a hero's grave
Where the rebel foe in his
Might came forth
With all his power and
Pride
And our gallant men from
The rugged north
Like patriots fought and
Died.[168]

The USSS had eighteen killed or mortally wounded across both regiments on August 29 and 30. The costliest battle of the war so far for the Sharpshooters also led to lost time in the field for brave wounded men like John Hetherington, Company D, 1st Regiment. The disaster of Porter's attack at least did not mean the extinction of Pope's army after Longstreet launched one of the great flank attacks of the war following the repulse of the Fifth Corps. A strong defensive stand on both sides of the Warrenton Turnpike helped most Union troops escape to excellent fortifications in Centreville, five miles east. Pope himself, with the failure his fault, never again led Union forces against the Confederates. Like Lieutenant Colonel Peteler, Pope would go to Minnesota in an effort to subdue the Sioux uprising. The failure also cost Irvin McDowell his command. Like Pope, he never held Civil War field leadership again.[169]

Finding some nourishment, rather than dwelling on the fate of senior officers, became a priority for USSS members on their way to Centreville. Curtis Abbott recalled the poor timing of a large Virginia hog that milled about in the vicinity of hungry Sharpshooters. The doomed animal even attempted to stick his nose in Colonel Post's haversack. As Abbott wrote, "The tables were promptly turned on him," with the pig ending up on many bayonet points of Company H, 2nd USSS.[170]

Chaos did not rule the night as Pope's army moved east. In addition to the protective structures at Centreville, troops from McClellan's Second and Sixth Corps added to the security of the Union position. With many comrades gone due to disease and battle, the Sharpshooters required a great deal of fortitude to conquer the severe headwinds battering their lives since Yorktown. Although the 1st USSS had sustained far more loss from Confederate fire, the five months and ten days since leaving the Camp of Instruction withered the 2nd Regiment. Colonel Post reported more than six hundred men at roll call on August 10. At Alexandria, Virginia on September 2, during a short period of rest before heading into Maryland, the 2nd USSS counted 127 fit for duty.[171]

Wyman White, Company F, was one of Post's men absent in early September. The previous few weeks simply zapped the energy and health of the Granite Stater. Gone from the regiment for weeks, White remained active, even if not fit for field service. He found work at a hospital and convalescent camp in Alexandria. In the same company, Darius Starr would also miss the looming campaign due to health problems. After Second Bull Run, Starr wrote home in September, "I called the roll of our company, and only 16 men answered."[172]

Weary warriors looked back on August with great sorrow. Amos Abbott summed up his experience in a September 2 diary entry from the vicinity of Fort Buffalo, near Falls Church. "Our Division is very badly used up, not only in numbers, but in every other respect, being all wore out," he lamented. Counting days of fighting along the Rappahannock, "we have had a very hard time having been in seven battles in the last fortnight and marched 50 miles."[173]

The survivors of both regiments found the means to persevere. The Sharpshooters enlisted for the purpose of saving a united country, a goal which offered great motivation to rise above the summer's suffering. Henry Richards, a 2nd USSS warrior from New Hampshire, suggested the Confederates would not fare as well closer to Washington. "I still think that before cold weather, if our troops come in promptly," the soldier opined, "we can strike some heavy blows, because they are now at our doors." Richards eagerly went forward in the new campaign with the goal "to whip the rebels."[174]

William Ripley pithily described the level of fortitude among the USSS even with "sadly thinned" ranks. "They were not the stuff that wilts and shrivels under an adverse fortune," the Medal of Honor winner declared. Like so many Northerners throughout the horrific conflict, the Sharpshooters stood ready to serve, regardless of cost. When describing reorganization of the armies in the aftermath of Second Bull Run, Curtis Abbott added, "The changes went on, however, while disaster followed disaster. The loyal North bore the test."[175]

Berdan Loses More Respect

Colonel Berdan's reputation among his men took a hit as a result of Second Bull Run, for multiple reasons. First, he exaggerated the extent of a wound he received on August 30. Berdan listed himself as injured in the fight, but many Sharpshooters harbored doubts. While spending much time talking about the specifics of Sharpshooters' injuries, the regiment's first historian only wrote a short sentence to note the colonel's very minor wound from a spent shell. Berdan likely wished his friends in New York City to see him as suffering as much as his men, although that was not the case. Berdan did not endure anything close to death, or a horrible wound like Robert Casey's. The stalwart marksman somehow survived a bullet to the throat.[176]

Contempt toward some of his soldiers cost Berdan a great deal, as well. The colonel confronted an officer who had been part of a two-company force that did not move to the spot Berdan preferred during the August 30 fight. He claimed the two companies (B and G) essentially disappeared from the battle. In a discussion about the issue Lt. William Nash, Company B, attempted to correct Berdan's view of the matter. Then, according to a Badger Sharpshooter, Berdan declared,

> *he did not care a damn for what both companies said, and that a man was not fit to command a company who got so excited as not to understand his Colonel's orders, which was giving Lieut. Nash and the two companies the lie right out and insulting them in the bargain. There is not a man in the whole army, I believe, who is cooler in a fight and knows what he is about better than Nash, and if I was to tell the truth, he knows more military in one hour than the Col. does in a year and is more fit to command a brigade than the Col. is to command a company.*[177]

Interestingly, Berdan had healed enough from his putative wound to question the judgment of Nash and the two companies in person the following day. Pictures of Berdan shortly after Second Bull Run also bring into doubt the colonel's status as a wounded member of the 1st USSS. For someone granted sick leave, Berdan stands tall and looks quite vigorous.

Major General Porter approved Berdan's request for additional leave to recruit new Sharpshooters. The colonel did not seem to make such a trip. Instead, a surgeon in Washington reported Berdan as under his medical care on

September 15. A week later, Porter requested Berdan be dropped from the muster rolls for failing to report his status for service or location. Captain John Isler, the regiment's highest-ranking officer in September because of Caspar Trepp's sick leave, also reported his confusion about why Berdan was not with the regiment. By the 26th, Porter wrote to acknowledge the extension to Berdan's leave army headquarters had granted. Wherever he stayed during the month, Berdan avoided field service in a new campaign.[178]

Into Maryland

After the catastrophe near Manassas, what direction would the Sharpshooters' war take? Robert E. Lee quickly answered the question. His seemingly invincible Confederate army moved north soon after the confused battle of Chantilly, east of Centreville, a fight in which the USSS regiments did not participate. Although not moving forward at the same time, both Sharpshooter regiments became part of the field army George McClellan was charged with organizing to confront Lee. The campaign would culminate in the war's bloodiest day, with Antietam standing as a defining aspect of the life of the 2nd Sharpshooters especially. The record number of USSS dead in one battle, Second Bull Run, would stand for less than three weeks.

McClellan's most fervent critics had to respect the general's penchant for organizing and inspiring armies. President Lincoln wished he possessed a better choice for army leadership, but McClellan again received the job. The Union general even used his clout to request several changes to the army's senior officers. McClellan was also able to delay the court-martial of Fitz John Porter as the national emergency prevailed. The 1st USSS remained under Porter for the campaign, although many Fifth Corps troops rested in Washington's defenses well into the second week of September.[179]

With General Hatch taking over the division of Rufus King, the 2nd USSS, diminished greatly in numbers, still served under Henry Post. Walter Phelps Jr., slightly younger than Post, assumed brigade command. With their campaign of many unknows ahead of them, the 2nd Sharpshooters rejoined the 1st Brigade, 1st Division of the reborn First Corps. Joseph Hooker, whose fighting reputation as a Third Corps division leader marked him for higher responsibilities, took over the First Corps from the disgraced McDowell.

In their march north from Washington, Hooker's men moved along with the Ninth Corps as Maj. Gen. Ambrose Burnside oversaw the two-corps wing. Assigned to the army's right, Burnside's command protected against a rumored yet unlikely Confederate drive on Baltimore. At a loss regarding the size and location of Lee's Confederates, the Army of the Potomac did not march at a torrid pace after the first day's trek, which took the Sharpshooters from northern Virginia to Leesborough, Maryland, a total of about twenty miles. The men had started out on the evening of September 6, with their first camp reached by late morning the next day.[180]

The horrible summer impacted each company of the 2nd USSS in both numbers of soldiers and a dearth of officers. Again, an irresistible drive to save their country made the Sharpshooters see the importance of perseverance. Many Sharpshooters had become very accurate shots at a young age, after undoubtedly much solitary time outdoors free from parental or governmental constraints. Such gritty individualism defining the Sharpshooter archetype served the eight companies quite well on the march in Maryland, with so many doubts about the future and some difficulty when supply trains fell behind. Company H lacked a commissioned officer in the early part of the campaign. In total, both Vermont companies had fewer than forty men in the ranks while in Maryland.[181]

Tough conditions for unwell men withered the ranks even more. Amos Abbott completed the last march of his military career early in the campaign. Feeling sick for some time, Abbott did not depart with his company on September 6. Catching up with the 2nd USSS two days later, Abbott quickly went back to Washington on doctor's orders. He spent two months in a hospital before receiving a sixty-day furlough. Home to Concord, New Hampshire, on Thanksgiving Day, Abbott would receive a medical discharge in February 1863.[182]

The three Warner brothers of Company C who enlisted in 1861 moved forward in the campaign down one member. Robert, an officer although the youngest of the trio, had resigned his commission in late July, leaving Hiram and Horace in Maryland. Horace, born in 1826, was seven years older than Hiram. Efforts for the small company to expand its numbers through recruiting continued, with limited success.[183] In contrast to smaller states to the north, Pennsylvania failed to successfully recruit a full Sharpshooter company. The reasons that might explain the problem seem lost to history due to the relative lack of primary source information about the Keystone State marksmen.

Positives and negatives of the march grew obvious to James Matthews and his Maine comrades in Company D. The tough trek to Leesborough wore down the men as humidity and dust grew especially enervating during the morning of September 7. As a means to keep his men moving along, Colonel Post, the disciplinarian who managed to retain his soldiers' respect, fined those who could not keep up. Five minutes late to stack arms, Matthews would be docked $1 during a marching break. Later in the northern advance, Matthews at least could write of abundant apples, a great treat for marching troops when ripe enough. The men reached Lisbon, Maryland on the evening of September 11.[184]

The small town marked an important point on the National Road between Baltimore and Frederick. Lee's army began marching away from Frederick on the 10th in an effort to seize supplies and bountiful Union prisoners at Harpers Ferry, Virginia. Unknown to McClellan, Lee's force divided into five separate parts, with three of them using different roads in the quest to take Harpers Ferry, an endeavor under the command of Stonewall Jackson. Stuck with a languid advance due to McClellan's deliberate nature and cloudy strategic vision, Burnside's wing became destined for a dramatic leading role in the next several days.[185]

Walter Wallace Smith, Company G, 2nd USSS, wrote letters on consecutive days from Lisbon and New Market. He wished family to know "I am still alive," although, "Where we are going I can't tell." Feeling the difficult summer weeks in the immediate past, Smith added, "The Rebels seem to have the advantage in everything now a days but I hope their race is about done but I fear not." With cannonading to the west, Smith could not avoid destiny pulling his regiment toward the enemy.[186]

The men appreciated treats and kindness from Maryland's pro-Union population, most notably after their western turn toward Frederick. As Curtis Abbott wrote, marching "through the farms and villages of Maryland to Frederick, was enjoyed by the men on account of the show of friendliness among many of the citizens, especially in Frederick." The reception awaiting Burnside's wing of the army made indelible impressions on the First and Ninth Corps. With the Ninth camped west of Frederick and Hooker's men east of the city, McClellan crafted a plan for the wing to move forward against a Confederate rear guard holding passes in the South Mountain range.[187]

ON SOUTH MOUNTAIN

An intelligence coup rivaling nearly any in American military history somewhat ended the fog of war McClellan suffered early in the campaign. Twelfth Corps troops discovered a copy of Lee's plan for the Harpers Ferry attack and other movements. Known as Special Orders 191 or "The Lost Order," the misplaced Confederate plans informed McClellan of the highly divided nature of Lee's army. McClellan, without rushing his entire army forward, at least pictured a way to defeat the Confederates on Union soil.[188]

Even if they did not know all the details of McClellan's lucky break, Sharpshooters felt the compelling nature of the moment. As Curtis Abbott suggested, "Our men were in high glee.... Fortune beckoned and the night spread its dark mantle as a screen."[189]

Would September 14 live up to the grand hopes men held the previous night? Starting early in the morning, Burnside's troops advanced west, nearing two crucial gaps in the South Mountain range. Elements of the Ninth Corps engaged Lee's rear guard at Fox's Gap in the morning. Hooker's men, with much farther to march, targeted Turner's Gap on the opposite side of the National Road.

Although Hooker's corps was not the closest support for Burnside, the 2nd USSS and their comrades in the three divisions were ordered to reach South Mountain in the afternoon of the 14th. Orders the previous day demanded the divisions of Hatch and Ricketts follow close behind Brig. Gen. George G. Meade's Pennsylvanian Reserves. "It is expected that the march will be resumed with the utmost promptitude," First Corps headquarters noted.[190]

Ground around Fox's Gap had plenty of natural obstacles to assist Confederate defenders. The hills that the 2nd USSS climbed proved far more difficult. An experienced hiker not under fire and moving in perfect weather conditions might wither when facing the steep topography north of the National Road. The Pennsylvania Reserves charged on the far right of the advance, with Hatch's division closer to the road. With some gaps forming between the two divisions, the 2nd Sharpshooters had a chance to perform the crucial task of linking Meade and Hatch.[191]

Success of Hooker's charge could seize Turner's Gap and link up with the Ninth Corps to seriously threaten the portion of Lee's army not part of the Harpers Ferry operation. Stout Confederate resistance made the work difficult, but the Reserves, who had sustained more loss than any Union division on the Peninsula, proved up to the tough afternoon. At nightfall, the Confederates fell back along the front from Fox's Gap to Turner's Gap.

No Sharpshooters lost their lives on South Mountain. They did not engage the enemy as much as the Reserves or some other troops in Hatch's division. Tough as the climb had been, Curtis Abbott recorded an interesting insight that lessened the day's stressful toll.

> *This skirmish was especially interesting to the Vermonters from the nature of the ground. The advance was up the heights from rock to rock and amidst the trees. The very difficulties of the ascent brought back memories of their native hills and lent an inspiration to their efforts.*[192]

Night quickly fell for the Sharpshooters on the eastern slope of Turner's Gap. Minnesotan Joseph Dickey, in a letter two days after the battle, remembered hearing shooting continue until 10 p.m. An exhausting day, including the long trek from Frederick and the work on the mountain against a resolute enemy possessing excellent ground, helped some Sharpshooters get some sleep, even with some firing well after dark. Eerie feelings during the occupation of the first victorious ground of their military service likely gave way to a realization that the USSS could contribute to battlefield success.

As light increased the following morning, the marksmen and their First Corps comrades had an opportunity to examine the bloody ground in their possession. Moving up the hill with Adjutant Lewis Parmelee and some comrades, Joseph Dickey saw "no one there that was able to get away," a reference to the large number of fallen Confederates from the previous day.

Further images of war's horrors could be found. Company D's James Matthews noticed one Confederate officer riddled with bullets. The unfortunate human had been turned into "a perfect sieve," likely thanks to some Sharps Rifle rounds. Lines of Confederate dead could be seen along other areas the Sharpshooters occupied.[193]

With most of the First Brigade to the left of the Sharpshooters, Colonel Phelps witnessed similar effects of the fighting. He wrote of Confederate dead in heaps, evidence of how hard the enemy fought to keep the Union army east of the mountains. Phelps and soldiers in the three other brigades of the First Division lost General Hatch to a wicked thigh wound, although his inspiring leadership kept the division fighting hard. Never to return to his division, Hatch would receive a Medal of Honor for his heroics.[194]

Time to move out would quickly arrive. The Northerners would pursue Lee's men, and perhaps inflict an even greater blow before the Harpers Ferry attack force could reunite with their Confederate comrades somewhere west of South Mountain.

To the Antietam

Under the command of George Morell, the Fifth Corps division including the 1st USSS had not been idle for the previous few days. President Lincoln, fixated again on the safety of Washington, had offered more troops for the field army, although he refused the full extent of McClellan's request. On September 11, Porter was "ordered to-night to join you as quickly as possible," the president wrote McClellan, "I am sending you all that can be spared."

With about six thousand troops including the 1st Sharpshooters, Porter and Morell departed on the morning of the 12th after intense rain the evening before. Captain John Isler and the 1st USSS—411 enlisted men and 14 officers—moved out from Fort Corcoran, Virginia, barely two miles west of President Lincoln's White House desk. Across the three mornings needed to reach McClellan, multiple Sharpshooters used the phrase "forced marches" to describe the trek from Washington to the west of Frederick. High heat zapped the strength of many, some falling out for good. Fortunately, while heading farther into Maryland, dozens of recruits joined Isler's band.[195]

A long march to Brookeville dominated the first day's itinerary. Porter moved ahead of his infantry to greet McClellan on September 14, the same day of the fights for South Mountain. The division of U.S. Army regulars and McClellan's reserve artillery were then placed under Porter. This force remained unengaged to the east of the mountain gaps bellowing with artillery and musket fire.[196]

Although Morell's Division and the 1st USSS trailed the rest of the army, both the First and Fifth Corps took a role in the pursuit of the fleeing Confederates. With a Second Corps division moving ahead of Hooker as he rested his men on the morning of September 15, early reports suggested the enemy lost no time in escaping the trap of South Mountain. As the morning advanced, Porter's division of Regulars faced delays traversing Fox's Gap because General Burnside neglected to ensure his troops, exhausted from fighting the day before, did not block the road.[197]

Well ahead of Isler's ten companies, Post's 2nd USSS pressed ahead. Charged with finding stragglers from Lee's army and keeping even just a modicum of pressure on Lee's retreating force, the 2nd Regiment had a great opportunity to use their skirmishing skills on September 15. Danger lurked, as the Sharpshooters expected. Charles Kay, a twenty-four-year-old New Hampshire marksman, sustained a wound near Boonsboro, leading to a disability discharge ten weeks later. He lived until 1900.[198]

As at previous times when facing a major threat from McClellan, General Lee seemed unafraid, even with his haggard and battered army. The Confederates made a stand west of Antietam Creek, near the town of Sharpsburg. Still on the opposite side of South Mountain, Morell's regiments moved to join their army comrades.[199]

After a westward turn in Boonsboro, Northerners nearest Lee's men headed toward Antietam Creek. Hooker's corps and other troops created a jumble of men and supplies on the road, a setup not conducive to a rapid, organized attack against Lee's small force on the other side of the Antietam. Nonetheless, Hooker sent McClellan an afternoon message suggesting the Confederate line was not formidable. McClellan's lackadaisical arrival later in the afternoon presented evidence to some historians of the army commander's disinterest in further battle. Lee would seem to court disaster with a stand at Sharpsburg because one ford on the Potomac River to the rear was the Confederate army's only route of escape.[200]

While finally surveying the scene, McClellan envisioned an attack from the north of Sharpsburg that could sweep away Lee's army. Fog shrouded the lines on both sides of the creek until about 9 a.m. on September 16. With his cautious way of war, McClellan held off on ordering a move until about 2 p.m., even though he promised General Halleck forceful action in an early morning message. True to his preference for bold commanders leading important movements, McClellan sent Hooker and the entire First Corps west of the Antietam. Hooker's men did not instantly move; time was needed to get organized for the creek crossing. The 2nd USSS and the First Division used a ford about a half mile below a bridge the other two divisions traversed.[201]

In a report written four weeks after the battle, McClellan suggested the defensive ground Lee's army held granted tremendous possibilities to repel an attack. "Desperate fighting alone could drive them from the field," he opined, "and all felt that a great and terrible battle was at hand." These accurate observations called for the commanding general to concentrate overwhelming force at key points to defeat the enemy. However, McClellan failed to do so.[202]

Initially moving across the creek with only his First Corps, Hooker expressed concern to McClellan about a lack of supporting firepower. Meeting his commander after McClellan went west to observe his moving troops, Hooker said the enemy had the potential to push back his three divisions. This prompted McClellan's assignment of the Twelfth Corps to augment Hooker's numbers. Unfortunately, neither McClellan nor Hooker developed a concrete plan on how the additional troops, the smallest corps in the Army of the Potomac, would assist.[203]

Shooting began soon after the 2nd USSS crossed the Antietam in the afternoon of the 16th. Evidence does not place the regiment at the head of the division as skirmishers during the advance. Rather, Brig. Gen. Marsena Patrick's four New York infantry regiments led the way, halting west of the creek as Doubleday's other three brigades spanned the Antietam. Confederates soon noticed the movement, opening fire on the assembling troops. This barrage seemed to draw the Sharpshooters forward. The marksmen then played a role in decreasing fire from scouting Confederate cavalry. The early resistance, with the division still not fully across the creek, boded ill for making Hooker's advance meaningful. With parts of George Meade's division fighting to the north, darkness would soon inhibit the movement of troops. The First Corps had not been granted the time to reconnoiter the ground before a major attack the next morning.[204]

The first death in the battle of Antietam for Post's regiment—the tenth of the war—happened as Doubleday attempted to move his division beyond the creek. The sun was quickly sinking to the west. Wellington Tucker, given the first name of Arthur in state records, received a mortal injury while part of the force tangling with Confederates who were making a short stand. Tucker died later that evening as his twin brother Washington continued to fight for life after his wound received more than three weeks before along the Rappahannock. After the second twin's death a month later, the brothers were buried at a cemetery in Cherryfield, Maine.[205]

Confusion gripped First Corps units as they attempted to make the most of their ordered march on unknown ground. Hooker's divisions went north on the Williamsport Road before cutting across the country. Lines grew tangled as some soldiers crossed the path of friendly troops in the rapidly decreasing daylight. With all of the miscommunication, brigades of the same division lost contact with each other, some not arriving at their camp until hours after dark. Final arrival of Sharpshooters at their evening campsite must have caused plentiful relief. "Darkness came so soon," Curtis Abbott wrote, "that their advance of that night amounted to little more than a reconnaissance," one of limited utility. Finding their camp in the darkness, Post's marksmen and the rest of Phelps's small brigade took a position in the divisional reserve.[206]

The Sharpshooters did not have much to show for their disjointed march on September 16, but Doubleday's soldiers at least assembled along the Hagerstown Pike north of Sharpsburg. Symbolic of the confusion gripping Hooker's advance from the start, Doubleday's disheveled lines generally faced west, even though their enemy stood mainly to the south. Sleeping on their arms like their Northern foes, Confederates heard occasional firing during the overnight period. Tension filled the air for the large number of American warriors sensing a great battle looming.[207]

Hooker's confused battleline was poorly situated for the attack ordered for early on September 17. Weather conditions added to the unfortunate circumstances. "The night became dark and drizzly," the corps commander reported. Yet, living up to his reputation as "Fighting Joe," Hooker concluded, "the battle would be renewed at the earliest dawn."[208]

Watershed for the 2nd USSS

The tactical situation offered the 2nd USSS a great opportunity to act as skirmishers for Hooker's attack. Lamentably, perfect circumstances rarely occur in war. Instead of a prominent place at the apex of the First Corps spear, the 2nd USSS did not even move at the front of their own division. The marksmen charged at Antietam like many of their infantry comrades. A generally concentrated line of expert shots standing in the middle of a massive bloodbath failed to take advantage of USSS training as isolated troops using cover to pick off enemy artillerists or officers. The undesirable arrangement for the Sharpshooters created a perfect storm, resulting in their second bloodiest single day of the war.[209] The frightful toll would forever change the 2nd Regiment, leaving emotional wounds and an absence of known leaders the eight companies felt for the rest of their service.

Earliest daylight brought Confederate cannon fire in Doubleday's direction, creating chaos among the division's soldiers. With balls hitting the ground or flying overhead, William Humphrey, Company E, remembered the "lively work" the Sharpshooters began just to form a line. Granite Stater Edwin Chadwick summed up his feelings about the randomness of early morning cannon fire. "Shot and shell flew around us in a way that is not very agreeable when you cannot tell but that the next one may burst at your feet and send you into eternity," he proclaimed.

In the aftermath of their awakening by Confederate shells, the companies moved back to a point near the army's only New Hampshire artillery battery. This respite failed to last, as the marksmen were told to prepare for the assault.[210]

A problem plaguing McClellan's entire army at Antietam, lack of overwhelming power at the point of attack, gripped the First Corps early on. One brigade entered the eastern end of a cornfield D. R. Miller owned, forever known as "The Cornfield." Chopped up themselves, this brigade inflicted intense casualties on a Confederate brigade. Other Union units on the western side of the First Corps line went forward lacking coordination as Doubleday's men started feeling the stout resistance expected from the tested troops of Stonewall Jackson.[211]

Confederates admired the fine-looking lines of blue and green uniforms Hooker ordered forward. A staff officer facing the brunt of Doubleday's attack wrote, "The spectacle now presented was one of splendor and magnificence." The Confederate remembered, "as the enemy advanced we beheld one of the most brilliant displays of troops we had ever seen." Adding to the encomiums, the Southern officer declared, "their well-polished guns and bayonets gave a glamour and a show at once fearful and entrancing." More than seventy years after his terrible morning at Sharpsburg, a Louisianan showed respect for the men of the First Corps, including the 2nd USSS, by writing, "there were no slouches at the game of fighting" in the Union ranks.[212]

Leading his marksmen as part of Walter Phelps's small brigade, Col. Henry Post might have become a bit flustered with the lack of concentrated firepower. With Gibbon's brigade leading Doubleday's effort, Phelps was held back for a short time as the 2nd USSS stood in an awkward reserve position, a purgatory that did not last very long even after the brigade was ordered to lie down. At this early point in the battle, as William Humphrey, remembered, "the shot, shell, and bullets were flying."

Phelps sent Post forward with the goal of stabilizing the western flank of Gibbon's beleaguered Midwesterners. The green-clad men then faced a whirlwind

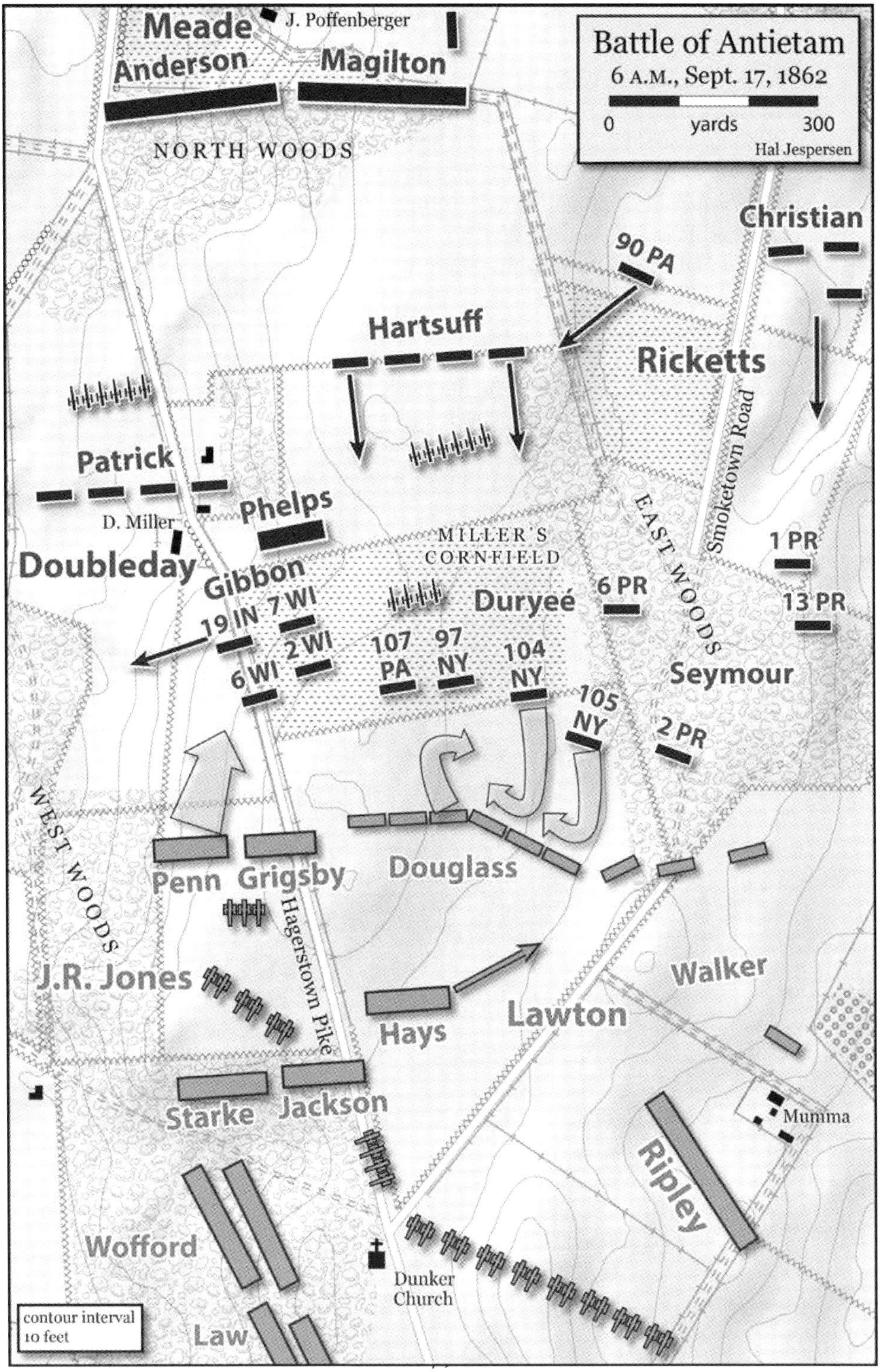
Battle of Antietam
6 A.M., Sept. 17, 1862
0
yards
300
Hal Jespersen
Meade
Anderson
Magilton
J. Poffenberger
NORTH WOODS
Christian
90 PA
Hartsuff
Ricketts
Smoketown Road
Patrick
Phelps
D. Miller
Doubleday
Gibbon
MILLER'S
CORNFIELD
EAST WOODS
1 PR
6 PR
13 PR
Duryeé
19 IN
7 WI
2 WI
6 WI
107
PA
97
NY
104
NY
105
NY
Seymour
2 PR
WEST WOODS
Penn
Grigsby
Douglass
Hagerstown Pike
J.R. Jones
Walker
Lawton
Hays
Starke
Jackson
Mumma
Ripley
Wofford
Dunker
Church
Law
contour interval
10 feet

as Phelps's small New York regiments also advanced. As Phelps reported, "The loss of the Second U.S. Sharpshooters at this point was severe."[213]

Finding much to shoot at on the other side of the Hagerstown Pike, the Sharpshooters received a special charge from Colonel Post. "Shoot down the color," he yelled after seeing Confederate flags. The Sharpshooters soon lost their commander. Post fell with a serious arm wound, a nonfatal injury. Although he made an effort to return to the Sharpshooters, Post never again led men in battle.[214]

Sharpshooters fell at an alarming rate. Table 1.2 lists those members of the 2nd Regiment who died from wounds sustained on September 17. The beloved adjutant was the unit's highest-ranking fatality. With the inspirational leadership that marked him as a great young officer, Adjutant Lewis Parmelee took the lead after Post's wound. As Lt. William Humphrey recalled, the adjutant "jumped up, ran down," then "picked up the flag." Humphrey added, "the staff

Only twenty-three years old, Adjutant Lewis Parmelee, 2nd USSS, lost his life near the Hagerstown Pike at Antietam on the morning of September 17, 1862. LIBRARY OF CONGRESS

was broken off near the colors," prompting Parmelee to stick "his sword into the broken staff," before raising the flag high and returning to the Union line. Unfortunately, Parmelee proceeded "but a few steps when he falls pierced by 7 bullets."

William Kerr, Company A, grabbed the fallen Confederate emblem, and then dashed away successfully. Nearby, Robert Twombly sustained his fatal head wound, as history records him losing his life while taking down an enemy flag. A fellow Granite Stater, 2nd Lt. John Thompson, Company G, also lost his life while credited with the effort to seize Confederate colors.[215]

Another officer to die, Michigan man John Whitman, was wounded while exhorting his men to the excellence expected of them for more than a year. Taking multiple hits, the seemingly doomed Silas Howard found the strength to remove the breech block from his rifle, tossing the important component to ensure a crafty Confederate could not use the excellent weapon.[216]

Table 1.2. Members of the 2nd USSS Killed or Mortally Wounded on September 17, 1862

Company	Killed or Mortally Wounded
Staff	Lt. Lewis Parmelee
A	Alex Livingston Edmund Sampare
B	Lt. John Whitman
C	James Law Leatus Pease Hiram Warner
D	Lemuel Clark Hilliard Coffin William Conant George Roberts
E	Byron McClallan
F	Joseph Everest Frank Wetherbeee
G	John Thompson Robert Twombly Joseph Winn
H	William Benson

Doubleday's men made some progress south of the Cornfield. The initial two brigades resisting Hooker's onslaught suffered severely. Confederates in support likewise felt the terrible fire that included Sharps Rifle rounds. "We took quite a beating," a Virginian in Stonewall Jackson's original brigade, remembered. Yet, as one of Gibbon's men wrote, the Confederates "made a grand stand," able to resist, give way, but still retain enough of a line to avoid a rout. The Badger infantryman added, "The Rebs fight like mad men. They will not leave the field until they are badly whipped."[217]

Sharpshooters lost to the fratricide included William Benson, Company H. The Vermonter proved "one of the strong, capable men" his comrades liked much. When such excellent soldiers fall, the reverberating pain can last for a lifetime for those left behind. Only twenty-two years old, Benson's wound still allowed the dedicated warrior to return home. He was born, died, and buried in the town of Landgrove, Vermont. He had been a corporal since February.[218]

The loss of Pennsylvanian Hiram Warner brought great pain to many. Home on recruiting duty for part of 1862, Warner returned to the 2nd USSS over the summer. Although he took part in organizing Company C, Warner

Three of the dozens of Confederates who died in the vicinity of the 2nd USSS at Antietam. LIBRARY OF CONGRESS

enlisted as a private. Nearly thirty years old at Antietam, Hiram's death led his sister to remember her great sibling. "He was one of the kindest and best sons and brothers," she averred. A brother-in-law added, "I don't believe that a better soldier has gone to the war."[219]

A bitter stalemate prevailed as the opposing troops hoped for succor. The Confederates provided aid first as a counterattack began to the south. James Kent illustrated how soldiers often become so focused on their immediate task that they do not notice dramatic changes happening that severely alter their situation. Kent wrote of loading and firing with great regularity thanks to the cartridge box he had on the ground. His actions illustrated the intense focus important to turning an excellent rifle shot into a dedicated soldier. However, charging Confederates under John Bell Hood forced back the advanced line of First Corps. Kent wrote that the desperate plea from a USSS officer was the first hint he had of Hood's bold dash against the Unionists south of the Cornfield.[220]

Hood's men withered under the concentrated fire of First Corps infantry and artillery, with two of Meade's Pennsylvania brigades inflicting much bloodshed. Sharpshooters Edwin Chadwick, William Humphrey, and James Kent recalled seeing General Gibbon himself directing the fire of cannons from the battery he commanded in the Regular Army before the war. The lethal lead severely tore apart the left of Hood's charging horde. Limbs, bodies, and fence rails rose high in the air from the canister Gibbon's artillerists unleashed. Humphrey remembered, "I saw an arm go 30 feet into the air and fall back again. It looked as though it had been torn off close up to the shoulder. It was just awful." A Texan agreed, suggesting the battlefield had become "littered with dead and the wounded."[221]

Reflections on Adjutant Parmelee

In an era of slow personal communication, worried family members often wondered about the fate of a loved one when hearing of a major battle. Noting newspaper reports about the regiment, Lewis Parmelee's sister Mary tried to cling to hope about her brother after first seeing him listed as wounded. Receiving more news nearly a week after the battle, Mary wrote on September 23, "I think we have no reason to think him alive." For all the 2nd Regiment suffered, Mary had the solace to note enemy troops had experienced great loss, as well. The Sharpshooters proved able to turn "the ground gray with rebel blood."[222]

With dedicated service over the past months, the late Parmelee earned much respect and admiration from his comrades in the 2nd USSS. "Tall and gallant," as a Vermont historian recorded, Parmelee left a mark on the regiment no one likely ever forgot. Charles Stevens denoted many of the adjutant's admirable qualities with a short encomium in the history of the Sharpshooters published in the nineteenth century. Parmelee proved "a great favorite in the regiment, a young man of excellent address and education, having passed through a course of studies at Edinburg." Gaining militia experience, Parmelee served in "New York city's crack regiment, the Seventh—or National Guard. He could quote all the great poets and prominent authors." Curtis Abbott deemed Parmelee "the beau ideal of a soldier," who very much looked the part. In addition, the young officer possessed "charming manners" making him "beloved" across the regiment.[223]

Benjamin Calef, who had considered Parmelee a dear friend and excellent team member at regimental headquarters long before Antietam, wrote a beautiful letter to Parmelee's father. Discussing the great courage Parmelee showed under intense fire on September 17, Calef noted what some might consider "seeming mockery" in the offering of "poor condolences in this your hour of affliction." However, "our deepest sympathies are yours & we morn the loss of a true friend, good soldier, & brave man, who has fallen in nobly defending a nation's honor."

Other letters the family received offered further solace. "I cannot suffer Lewis' death to pass without some notice in my pulpit," a pastor friend of the family wrote. Parmelee's friends and the nation's cause deserved such a tribute, he added. This comforting letter concluded, "I am, in much sorrow, & yet sorrowing not as those without hope." Another writer who spoke with other Sharpshooters after the battle noted the great respect Parmelee enjoyed. "One of Lewis' fellow officers remarked to me yesterday that he had never seen him so brilliant" as on the day of his death, leading the marksmen forward after Colonel Post suffered his harrowing wound.

Originally buried on the field along with many of his marksmen friends, the lieutenant's body was retrieved by his father, who had promptly journeyed to Sharpsburg after the battle. Parmelee's final resting place became Evergreen Cemetery, New Haven, Connecticut. Both of his parents had several years left to mourn their fallen hero.[224]

Immediate Aftermath

Dealing with the heavy toll of the morning battle, members of the 2nd USSS received a respite from fighting later in the day. The engagement proved the costliest in terms of casualties across the whole war, with more than twenty-three thousand men killed, wounded, or missing. Lee's troops did not immediately vacate Sharpsburg after scares in the middle and southern parts of the battlefield. The bold Confederate commander even refused to retreat that night after his army's nearly 30 percent loss. One Southern warrior surveyed the damage after his Louisiana regiment had only four men left standing, thanks in large part to USSS bullets.[225]

A Virginia infantryman who faced the 2nd USSS summed up the teetering fate of the two armies on September 17. The words indicated the nature of the fight in the immediate area of Miller's Cornfield, as well as the battle as a whole. In certain places "we repulsed the Yankees," the Southerner wrote, "whilst in others they repulsed us." Although the Union held the field, the weary Confederate opined, with a fair measure of truth when considering the losses, "neither party can claim much of a victory." A Badger infantryman who fought near the 2nd USSS suggested Antietam stood as "the most terrible fight that ever was fought on this continent."[226]

Ghastly sights awaited the 2nd USSS because, just like at South Mountain, the marksmen occupied the field, with the Confederates finally retreating in the overnight period beginning late on September 18. Part of a burial detail that found Lieutenant Parmelee and several fallen Sharpshooters, Edwin Chadwick witnessed the horrors across the landscape, including dozens of dead Confederates along the fence opposite the 2nd USSS position. He then hoped the horrendous bloodletting meant something, perhaps a rededication to making the war a conflict of short duration.

> *It is the testing of those who have been in nearly all the battles of the war that they never saw such desperate and bloody fighting. . . . If it is only the beginning of the end, the country may be satisfied with the dearly bought victory, but if the advantage is not followed up as it should be, as I am a little fearful it was not, it may well complain that so much blood is spilled for nothing.*[227]

Time spent on the distressing field perhaps justified the cost of September 17 for men in the 2nd USSS. Granite Stater James Kent, a member of Company G, counted eighty dead Confederates along the fence line where Sharpshooter bullets had flown in earnest during the battle. He added, "We piled a perfect windrow under the fences, where they lay, but it cost us dear." Talking to a Southern prisoner, Kent learned that the Sharps Rifle inflicted a grizzly toll on the enemy along the Hagerstown Pike. Knowing the unforgettable losses the 2nd Regiment sustained at Antietam, Kent added, "We are good for twice our number yet."

Walter Smith, Company H, wrote in early October with a less sanguine attitude. "I have seen about all the fighting I care about for the present," Smith bemoaned, "To see men picked up the way they were on the last Battlefield ought to be enough to satisfy almost anyone." Even a fervent abolitionist, the

Vermonter added, "would be satisfied to let the Generals close up the war" if witnessing Antietam's toll.[228]

Phelps's Brigade had only three hundred men in the ranks soon after the fight, something weighing heavily on the young brigade commander. The day after the battle, Phelps informed his wife of his promise to stand by his troops until the end. With more than sixty killed or wounded in Post's USSS regiment alone—approaching half of the green-clad soldiers engaged—the end might not have seemed far off.[229]

George McClellan presided over the army suffering so much. He was not a man who preferred to see wounded and dead soldiers, writing earlier in the year how a victory with five thousand casualties brought him no charms. The Union army possessed the field after losing more than twice that many in a day around Sharpsburg. McClellan's natural penchant for caution would play out over the next several weeks, but the battle at hand did not yet seem over. Desultory firing prevailed and some casualties were suffered on September 18. Potential for a fight lingered, with the 1st USSS destined to lose more men.[230]

Sharp Fight below Shepherdstown

Unengaged at the battle of Antietam, the 1st USSS constituted part of a Fifth Corps reserve division near the Middle Bridge, a span carrying the road from Boonsboro into Sharpsburg. With orders to move out on September 19, cavalry commander Alfred Pleasonton stalked Lee's retreating troops. Using the Fifth Corps to assist with the chase made sense; Fitz John Porter's two present divisions had not suffered much over the previous days. A third division under Porter, making a tough march from Washington, neared the undulating fields around Sharpsburg.

Escaping down the road leading to the only nearby ford across the Potomac, Lee's men dropped trees in an effort to slow down the Union pursuit. Orders from army headquarters required Porter "to push forward your pickets; ascertain if the enemy appears to be retiring, and if so, to mass your troops in readiness to move in any direction." Both of Porter's divisions on hand prepared to move into Sharpsburg.[231]

Fifth Corps men occupied the town early on September 19. Not used as skirmishers early on, the 1st USSS received verbal instructions from division commander Morell, who moved the marksmen to the front during the march through Sharpsburg. The Sharpshooters, Captain Isler reported, were to make their way to the Potomac, "and wait for further orders from General Porter." When the corps commander chimed in, a written directive commanded Isler to

Smoketown
Mercersville
Hagerstown Pike
Antietam Creek
Potomac River
Hitt (Upper) Br.
Keedysville
N. Woods
Miller's Cornfield
E. Woods
Pry's Ford
2 USSS Sept. 17
W. Woods
Pry
Dunker Ch.
Sunken Lane
Porterstown
Middle Br.
Sharpsburg
Shepherdstown–Boonsboro Pike
Rohrback (Burnside's) Br.
MARYLAND
Harpers Ferry Road
1 USSS Sept. 19–20
Boteler's Ford
Shepherdstown
WEST VIRGINIA
Antietam Iron Works
Antietam and Shepherdstown
0 miles 2
Hal Jespersen

keep the regiment "well concealed, and not to begin firing until he opened with the heavy batteries to our right unless the enemy should limber up."[232]

The 1st USSS moved out with some assistance. A Massachusetts company of sharpshooters, as well as two companies of the 4th Michigan Infantry, helped screen Porter's line. Difficult topography slowed the effort, but experienced troops quickly formed along the bank of the river, near the crossing with many names, including Shepherdstown, Boteler, or Pack Horse Ford. Flowing along the Potomac's course on the Maryland side of the river, the dry bed of the Chesapeake and Ohio Canal offered intriguing possibilities for the USSS as an elevated place to fire on the enemy.[233]

For the relatively low number of soldiers involved, the two sides commenced a cacophony of some intensity by late afternoon from opposite sides of the Potomac. Thundering cannons dominated the raucous scene. Original USSS historian Charles Stevens deemed the engagement "a brisk little action." The circumstances offered Sharpshooters a dream situation, the targeting and picking off of enemy cannoneers, a much safer situation than charging Stonewall Jackson like Post's eight companies did two days before.[234]

By late afternoon, even Porter, an officer steeped in caution, hoped for more than a minor clash against a paltry number of enemy troops. With Confederate cannons in plain view, the enticing idea of seizing the big guns led the 1st USSS to take part in a bold stroke. Even with the river flowing up to the waists of many, the charge was on to capture some enemy artillery. The suddenness of the valiant bolt, with the 4th Michigan moving out with the Sharpshooters, surprised several Southerners who had been ordered to remain at their post shelling the Northerners until the last possible moment.[235]

The crossing commenced as darkness quickly started to rule the area. Declining sunlight proved a bane to the 2nd Regiment three nights before when crossing the Antietam, but 1st USSS used the time of day to their advantage. The unexpected assault as twilight approached surprised the Confederates. Of the Southerners, a Michigan infantryman suggested, "They had not thought of an attack of that kind after dark." A Confederate eyewitness agreed, suggesting the small number of blue and green warriors appeared as a million soldiers crossing the Potomac. "The river was full of men over half way across, cheering and firing," the Confederate remembered.[236]

"One could hardly see the length of the line," suggested 1st USSS adjutant John Smith Brown. Thus, the Sharpshooter officer "hated to go" across the Potomac, which he deemed more than three feet deep at the ford. Yet, the risks of the attack brought reward and fame to the bold Union troops. Intrepid work in the small assault force earned a Medal of Honor for Corp. Cassius Peck, Company

F. The citation for the Vermonter's award declared Peck, "took command of such soldiers as he could get and attacked and captured a Confederate battery of four guns. Also, while on a reconnaissance, overtook and captured a Confederate soldier." Another Sharpshooter nabbed one of General Hood's couriers, allowing for additional glory for the 1st USSS during the bold venture.[237]

Peck's reputation for dedicated soldiering seems to have already been strong as he joined his comrades in the charge across the river. Many were pleased when the excellent soldier's bravery led to the nation's highest military award, officially handed down thirty years after the incident. In a recommendation letter for the medal, a comrade praised Peck's "fidelity and honor." The brave Green Mountain man "was always present with his colors for duty, and was noted for being one of the most unerring shots in the command."

Medal of Honor winner William Ripley lauded Peck as "gallant and faithful" in his duties when they served together on the Peninsula. When hearing of the award for Peck, Vermont's adjutant general wrote to the army in Washington. The state "thanks you for honoring one of her bravest and best."[238]

Captain Isler reported his pleasure at the conduct of the 1st Regiment during their work across the river. He gave special plaudits to Lt. William Winthrop, a thirty-one-year-old native of Connecticut, who led Company H. Isler wrote of Winthrop exhibiting notable skills "leading the line" to the Potomac and beyond, with the company commander "the first to set foot on Virginia soil" during the charge. Winthrop's acting status as company commander changed on September 22, when he officially earned the rank of captain.[239]

The astonishing action on the evening of September 19 cost the 1st USSS two lives: Henry Logas, Company A, and Wolverine Marvin Raymond, the first Company I man to die of wounds. Raymond had joined up in March 1862 at the age of twenty-four.[240] As a result of the battle at Shepherdstown Ford, 1st Regiment combat deaths for the entire war totaled thirty-six.

Orders returned the 1st USSS to the Maryland side of the river later in the evening. On September 20, several Union artillery batteries, firing over the river from high ground closer to Sharpsburg, thundered vociferously. Without losing more lives, the Sharpshooters took part in a confrontation much larger than the previous day. Staying on the Maryland side of the Potomac, Isler's marksmen took a position in the dry canal bed, assisting Fifth Corps troops across the river. A wicked battle ensued, proving especially costly to the new 118th Pennsylvania Infantry. A Wisconsin Sharpshooter witnessed much of the carnage. He hoped shooting from his fellow marksmen decreased the cost to their comrades. Multiple infantrymen did write that the USSS fire saved Union lives. Even in a limited role, "Our regiment fought bully," a Badger proudly wrote, helping to keep the ford in Union hands as the Confederates withdrew for good.[241]

Quiet Autumn

The Antietam campaign ended after Confederates fell back from Shepherdstown Ford. The moment began more than seven months without infliction of a fatal battle wound on a USSS member, their longest streak across nearly three years of active service. Myriad duties, including moves to new, more salubrious quarters, defined camp life for the green-clad soldiers. They would not leave the Sharpsburg vicinity until the closing days of October.

McClellan's evening visit on September 20 satisfied members of the 1st USSS, camped near the ford they fought for during the two previous days. Finding McClellan "looking pleased" about the army's position, a Badger marksman observed, "he does not look so fat and healthy as he did last spring. He works too much for his health." Then penning sentiments common in the army, the Sharpshooter deemed McClellan, "the man to command the army," meaning "the people should give him their confidence. The soldiers do, and it is not misplaced."[242]

Membership in the USSS had dwindled significantly since the companies started coalescing one year before. In addition to the horrendous losses from disease, wounds, and accidents, more than sixty marksmen had been killed or mortally wounded in action since Yorktown, with eighteen of those falling in about one hour along the Hagerstown Pike on September 17. Thus, mourning the loss of comrades constituted a common activity. The difficult emotional toll of the war often went unrecorded, but the surviving comrades would never be the same after losing so many friends.

Curtis Abbott undoubtedly spoke for many in the USSS. Recovering from a wound at Second Manassas, the Vermonter described the difficult days after Antietam, even as the men enjoyed a major respite from marching and fighting. "One sad result of a battle is to deprive the survivors of their tent-mates," the Vermonter lamented, "These autumn days were among the saddest ever experienced by the survivors of this army."[243]

Poor supply governed Sharpshooter lives during their autumn rest. Food of low quality caused grumbling, and the quantity of edibles left much to be desired. Army commander McClellan blamed Washington for the problems, with some modern historians suggesting Secretary of War Stanton intentionally kept victuals and new clothing away from the Army of the Potomac to make McClellan look incompetent. Whoever deserved the blame, William Ripley captured the flustered state of the 1st USSS in his history of Vermont's company, while also noting soldiers' efforts to improve their lot. Clothing, which might have been captured on the Peninsula or thrown away by enervated Sharpshooters on summer marches, was much needed by October. Moldy and wormy hard bread added to the woe, "and this at a place and time when it seemed to the soldiers that there could be no good reason why such a state of things should exist at all." Even with prevailing complaints, Ripley suggested, "time cures all ills, even in the army."[244]

On one of his trips to Washington as quartermaster, Benjamin Calef wrote home on September 28. Connected to both regiments even while the two USSS outfits remained in different corps, Calef said he had a chance to accompany the wounded Colonel Post to New York. He turned down the opportunity, but Post updated Calef soon after arriving to start what was thought as a short period of convalescence. "His wound is doing well and he is in good spirits," Calef wrote. He also had news of Hiram Berdan's condition. He noted the colonel had been improving lately after his supposed wound at Second Bull Run.[245]

More than 30 percent of those in the 1st Sharpshooters were listed as absent from roll call on October 2, as illustrated in Table 1.3. Sickness or wounds would not account for all of those absent, because some may have been on detached duty or home recruiting. However, the bulk of the 242 marksmen not in the ranks that morning likely were in hospitals or at home on extended leave due to illness or battle wounds. No historian can fully demonstrate the intense toll military life took on the volunteer soldiers of the Civil War, but these numbers from just one regiment paint a stark picture.

Table 1.3. Number Present and Absent 1st USSS, October 2, 1862

Company	Total	Present	Absent
A	59	34	25
B	94	88	6
C	99	75	24
D	33	20	13
E	69	47	22
F	108	82	26
G	95	63	32
H	72	47	25
I	93	51	42
K	75	48	27
Total	**797**	**555**	**242**

Source: First USSS Order Book, National Archives

Orders for men to go on picket duty on a regular basis kept marksmen somewhat in the practice of soldiering along Antietam Creek or the surrounding area. Thomas Connington recalled the restful time in October, "Went on picket occasionally where I might have written if I had not had so much company writing to do and being pretty well tired out."[246]

President Lincoln's visit to the inert army created memories for many Sharpshooters. Charles Stevens suggested Lincoln's inspection of Porter's command "would have been more gratifying" if the soldiers had "not been roasted for three hours by the hot sun" during the festivities. A Badger penned lines in an October 4 letter describing the president.

> *The President looked very plain, he dressed in plain black, even to a tall stove pipe hat, and he rode a black horse. I did not get a very good look at him, for he was on the move all the while, but from what I did see, I thought he had a very careworn look, and looked thinner than he did a year ago. He was loudly cheered by all the troops, except the Regulars, who I believe don't never cheer. He acknowledged the compliment by one of his smiles and uncovered head as he rode down the line.*[247]

Soon after returning to Washington, Lincoln ordered McClellan to advance his army. Lee's Confederates were making good use of their respite from Union advances to rebuild the South's principal army. McClellan did not move out for three weeks, time spent bickering with Washington. Concerns about the army's preparation for a new campaign had some merit, but McClellan—deemed an expert in logistics and organization—seemed to be using the issues as a pretext for caution. He appeared to lack the motivation to create solutions that would serve the army and country. Many across the army still held faith in McClellan, but even some of his allies began to wonder if the Army of the Potomac's commander had the will to win the war.[248]

Sharpshooter recruiting had borne fruit over the months that immediately passed. Dozens of future soldiers were still drawn to the purported perks of the USSS in the year after the original formation of the eighteen companies, perhaps because infantry life ostensibly had fewer charms. With so many on the rolls unable to perform duty due to injuries and sickness, the large number of new Sharpshooters bolstered the two regiments after the unforgettably rough summer. The two Vermont companies in the 2nd USSS added forty-eight men in October alone. Fifty-nine new members of the 1st USSS joined up in the first ten days of the month, with even more than that expected soon after.[249]

Veteran soldiers often questioned the utility and devotion of recruits, essentially suggesting the new soldiers lacked certain qualities, or even true patriotism. After seeing rookie comrades fight at Shepherdstown, however, an experienced Badger marksmen felt positive about those who had joined up earlier in 1862. Writing home in September, he opined, "The new recruits fight first rate, and were not very excited" while firing from the canal at Shepherdstown. Of course, having skilled comrades with many fights under their belt likely had something to do with the rookies' good performance. "I tell you the presence of old troops does a good deal to cheer on new men in a fight," the Wisconsin Sharpshooter added, "for they take it as a matter of course, and do not get scared so easy."[250]

A new member of Company F, 1st USSS, John Monahan, had enlisted in August. He departed Rutland, Vermont, at noon on September 30, with his train arriving in New York City at 10 p.m. The long trek to his marksmen comrades took Monahan through Philadelphia. Eight days later he arrived at Harpers Ferry, Virginia, reaching camp in time for four hours of drill on October 13. Five days later, he found guard duty "rather tiresome work."[251]

An army at rest and away from enemy fire still faced dangers. Unsurprisingly, sickness culled the ranks of the Sharpshooters during their rest. Companies across the two regiments lost men to disability as autumn advanced. More than a dozen permanently left the 1st USSS for medical reasons just from the four New York companies after Antietam through early November. Some of these men had been sick for many months, unable to perform duties as they bided their time in military hospitals.[252]

An excellent October 4 letter from a Wisconsin warrior in green mentioned several key elements of Sharpshooter life. The Badger unit

> *is generally very healthy, I think more so than any other company according to size in the regiment, which is in a very bad condition, for we have not got a field officer here . . . we have but three Captains in the regiment for duty at present; all the rest are either sick, resigned or suspended from command. As near as I can see Capt. [Frank] Marble gives good satisfaction to this company, as commanding officer. He just suits me for he seems determined to make every man do his duty, and he tries to do his. . . . Lieut. Stevens is still in Wisconsin recruiting for this company and with good success too, I should judge, by the way they come in. . . . Bob Casey who was shot through the throat is getting along finely.*[253]

The two New Hampshire companies in the 2nd Regiment only lost two to medical discharges in the period between Antietam through the first third

Captain Alfred Willett illustrates a central aspect of the history of the USSS, frequent changes in company leadership. The initial commander of Company I, 1st Regiment, Willett resigned in November 1862. U.S. ARMY HERITAGE AND EDUCATION CENTER

of November. This demonstrated some evidence that the problem of sick men departing the army had stabilized in certain companies. Nonetheless, several Granite Staters would receive discharges for Antietam wounds weeks, and sometimes months, after the battle. Able to take the field by mid-October, Darius Starr camped with Company F in the Sharpsburg area. "We have always been in the advance," Starr quipped later in the month. He wished other troops to gain glory on the front line as the Sharpshooters rested.[254]

Disciplinary measures proved once again that Sharpshooters sometimes lost their way. One bizarre incident impacted Joseph Carpenter, Company I, 1st USSS. The older soldier, expected to always exhibit "good moral influence" on his younger comrades, found himself sentenced to carry a log for two days while also being "publicly reprimanded in presence of the Regt." His infraction included exposing himself "in an obscene and indecent manner," which was "deserving the contempt of clean-minded men," according to regimental records. Major George Hastings was leading the 1st USSS when the October 19 sentence was recorded.

The month saw two members of the 1st Regiment docked $5 for straggling during the previous summer. Major Hastings also issued an order commanding "no rubbish must be thrown or left lying around within the limits of the camp." The major allowed officers to arrest anyone failing to meet the order's sensible demand. Detailed regulations about guard duty further displayed for the men how military authority still governed their lives, even when far from the enemy.[255]

Thomas H. Brown, a new recruit in Company E, 1st USSS, wrote several letters home during his service. He thought much about his family, with an October 23 letter frequently offering suggestions on managing the home front while he served in the army. Brown missed the opportunity for regular religious worship services, but treasured the testament he had received while passing through New York on the way to the army.[256]

"If the Union army had all the comforts of life it would be demoralized," marksman and philosopher John Monahan wrote in late October. His comment alludes to the expectation a soldier maintains about a harsh existence. At least the men mustered for pay on the first day of November, with Monahan denoting his "very tired" state as the month started.[257]

Due to wounds and sickness, some Sharpshooters with longer service than Monahan never saw their comrades in the field again. Maine's Silas Ward illustrated the frustration and difficulties sick soldiers faced, partially because of slow bureaucracy. Far from his comrades, Ward informed the state adjutant general of his six weeks at a New York military hospital. He asked for some time at home to get better. Able to walk, Ward did not request a discharge, just an opportunity to leave the confines of the hospital. State records show Ward received a disability discharge in October.[258]

Orders to build log houses offered soldiers the hope of an even longer break; more permanent structures pointed to winter quarters. The plans for wooden homes to keep out some cold fell by the wayside, as the two regiments prepared to depart the area around Sharpsburg.[259]

The End of McClellan

Life was about to get much more active for the Sharpshooters and the army as a whole. When the time finally came to march again, the Sharpshooters seemed ready to go, even with reduced numbers that likely appalled all those who mustered into companies of one hundred or more men a year before. The November

1 morning report for Maine's Company D, 2nd USSS, showed only twenty-six marksmen present for duty, with that same number of men sick. Sergeant Albion Morey had deserted the company on October 12, leading to further drain of experienced men in the battered outfit.[260]

Fine early November weather made the marching rather pleasant. Trekking through northern Virginia with the glorious Blue Ridge Mountains to the west, natural beauty attracted the eyes of those in the two Sharpshooter regiments. On their way south, elements of the 1st USSS protected part of the army's right near Snicker's Gap, a key crossing point in the Blue Ridge. Ordered to climb the impressive peak, with the danger of slipping and possibly even rolling down the mountain, the 1st Regiment could enjoy a fine view albeit for a short time. On the morning of November 3, the men marched back downhill to reach Warrenton, which served as a campsite for the bulk of the army.[261]

As Joseph Campbell wrote from Warrenton on November 4, "It has been a nice time to move." The warrior had been posted as part of the cattle guard, a key element of an army in the field. Soon, with portents of more mud and cold, snow blanketed the ground. With the Sharpshooters retaining their corps assignments of the previous months, Maj. Homer Stoughton's 2nd Regiment marched with the First Corps, now under the command of John Reynolds. Porter held on to Fifth Corps command, thus retaining oversight of the 1st USSS. The two regiments camped near each other around Warrenton.

Dramatic change beckoned. Even though he moved with some energy after finally advancing from Maryland, McClellan's time had run out. Lincoln ordered the change in army commanders the day after elections in several states. Ambrose Burnside took command. McClellan, who violated General Halleck's order to depart immediately, stayed around for a few days. Burnside, not keen to control the whole army, was now charged with quickly developing a plan to confront Lee's Confederates.[262]

Many soldiers viewed McClellan with great respect. George Marden felt sadness with the alteration in army leadership. Witnessing part of McClellan's review of the army as the general departed on November 10, Marden wrote, "He was received with the usual cheers," with the army "sorry to have him go." Still, his inability to forcefully confront the Confederates led some to believe McClellan's generalship included too many limitations. Artemas Cross, a Vermonter in the 1st USSS, noted that many in his regiment simultaneously held what appeared to be contradictory views on the displaced army leader. "I have not found a member of an old regt that believed we ever would take Richmond or subdue the south & they all adore McClellan," he observed. Cross concluded, "I leave you to judge if these two things have any relation to each other."[263]

McClellan's departure led the War Department to recall Fitz John Porter to face charges stemming from Second Bull Run. The Fifth Corps became Dan Butterfield's command. In another change of importance, Burnside organized the army into three grand divisions, each with two infantry corps. The 1st USSS marched with the Center Grand Division (the Third and Fifth Corps), led by Joe Hooker, who had just returned from convalescence following a bullet wound to the foot at Antietam. Stoughton's 2nd USSS joined the Left Grand Division, under William Franklin, who had the Sixth Corps as part of his large command.[264]

Prior to the army's departure from Warrenton, Col. Henry Post returned to the 2nd Regiment for a short time. "The men gathered to welcome him with cheers," Curtis Abbott remembered, "but the colonel seemed embarrassed." Field service proved too difficult, so Post went to Washington in an effort to find more marksmen recruits. Later in the month, he penned a heartfelt letter to his men announcing his resignation. Post hoped if anyone held hard feelings because of his focus on discipline, he would help them understand the need for oversight from superiors in a military organization. Nothing would please him more later in life, the colonel added, than to see his old soldiers again.

Post held the esteem of many, even if they preferred less structure in their soldierly life. Holding out hope for Post's completed healing process, Benjamin Calef wrote of his strong support for the colonel, "I wish he would return with what he deserves, a star on his shoulders." Summing up the thoughts of many, Curtis Abbott penned a short sentence to honor Post, "The respect which he won is immortal."[265]

Mud, something Civil War troops experienced with much consternation, became part of the Sharpshooters' existence on the way to Fredericksburg. While only about seven miles from the city on November 23, Joseph Campbell started a letter about the problems gooey ground created. Regarding nourishment, Campbell found crackers about the best food available, although he enjoyed a squash with some salt for supper. On the lookout for better grub, Campbell spied the gourd while marching the previous day.[266]

Sharpshooters found some positives on the southeasterly trek to Falmouth, across the Rappahannock from Fredericksburg. Michigan marksman Thomas Connington wrote of the items taken from the Virginia countryside. In addition to dry fence posts for fires, various farm animals and other sources of nourishment fortified the troops. The tenuous nature of army supplies necessitated the pilfering, Connington suggested.[267]

Bridge building equipment requested from Washington had yet to arrive when Burnside's army started arriving at Falmouth in the third week of November.

The delay proved fatal to Burnside's hope for a quick dash south to Richmond, the Confederate capital. The Union army was stuck for days while the bureaucracy tried to catch up to the army's pace and Burnside's vision. Rarely losing a chance to take advantage of an error from his opponents, General Lee used the time to occupy and fortify impressive heights beyond the town.[268]

With Hiram Berdan still on leave following Second Bull Run, Lt. Col. Caspar Trepp commanded the 1st USSS. In late November, Berdan felt well enough to draft an extensive correspondence, including some letters to President Lincoln, outlining his ideas for an expanded command, what he termed a Corps of Sharpshooters. He wished for time to recruit and find the officers to lead components of the new larger organization. As part of the idea, Berdan requested promotion to brigadier general.[269]

"California Joe No. 2"

During the Sharpshooters' autumn, a determined patriot began a long trip leading him to the ranks of the expert marksmen. Andrew Westervelt departed California in late October, first making his way to New York. On November 29, he penned a letter that would travel west, destined for publication in a California paper on January 3, 1863. Westervelt's optimism rings loudly in his letter.

> *I am now in Berdan's 1st Regiment, Co. A, as a "sharpshooter." I have enlisted for the war, with the determination of doing my duty in any capacity in which I may be placed. You may rest assured that I will not disgrace my name or any of my old Shasta or California friends. I have met with friends who have confidence in me from my reputation, you know, I have as a California mountaineer.*
>
> *I met Col. Berdan in the streets, and he welcomed me as a man he could place confidence in, and I stand in his opinion as California Joe No. 2 . . . give my regards to all my Churntown friends. Tell them I will do my duty, and keep them posted as to the war.*[270]

Westervelt kept his promise to stay in touch via letter with California during his service. Records demonstrate his enlistment in the Sharpshooters, although he appears to have served in multiple companies of the 1st Regiment.

December Despair

Members of the 1st Regiment started December with a level of optimism thanks to their camp at Stoneman's Switch, near the railroad bringing supplies from Aquia Creek. Plentiful wood allowed for regular fires and lumber for structures to keep out the cold. However, some of the same old problems prevailed: lack of food consistent in quality, quantity, or variety; slowness in receiving new clothes and shoes; and pay that never seemed timely. Even the return of knapsacks lost during the summer came with a major blow. Sharpshooters found their old contents, including journals and items from home, were missing.[271]

Small positives could be found in Berdan's companies. Vermonter Artemas Cross enjoyed the little things, albeit in cramped quarters. As he wrote early in the new month, Cross and three comrades shared

> *a tent about 5 feet square & 6 feet high, each of us carries a piece of tent. Our rations are hard tack, a kind of hard dry flat tasting crackers, & sometimes beef, beans, rice & a little sugar. The other day I bought 2 quarts of Indian meal off an old Negro woman with a silver quarter that I had & us 4 had 2 nice meals of hash pudding & sugar & it tasted better than any rice pudding that you ever eat.*[272]

In the 2nd USSS camp, inventive Vermonter Walter Smith wrote on December 1 about the process used to cook an excellent batch of beans. First, Smith dug a hole in the ground slightly larger than the pot, then he would

> *build a fire in it so by the time the beans are boiled enough the hole in the ground has a good bed of coals in it. Then put a piece of Pork on the beans & set in the pot of beans. Cover it with a plate or something then fill around & over the pot with coals & ashes & let them sweat till morning. When we get up we have as good a pot of beans as anybody.*[273]

Tragedy grew more likely each day the army stood around Falmouth. Lee contented himself by keeping an eye on Burnside's stalled force while the Confederates fortified beyond Fredericksburg. The way to Richmond blocked, Burnside continued to plan as he awaited the bridging infrastructure. Finally, on December 10, progress seemed likely, although Burnside struggled for a toehold on the far bank of the river. Street fighting, a rarity in the Civil War, grew in intensity as more troops crossed on the freshly completed bridges or on boats.[274]

South of the city, the 2nd USSS fanned out near the Bowling Green Road after crossing the river. Lively skirmish duty for Stoughton's companies proved the most difficult experience for the two Sharpshooter regiments at the disastrous battle of Fredericksburg. On December 13, more than three thousand killed and wounded were included in the casualty list for the First Corps after Left Grand Division commander Franklin incompetently managed the fight. In reserve to the north, the 1st Sharpshooters saw but did not participate in the carnage, where the Second Corps and divisions from other commands suffered horribly. The battle cost Burnside more than twelve thousand men, about the same toll as Antietam, but while inflicting perhaps six thousand fewer casualties on the Confederates than the dreadful day back in September.[275]

Caspar Trepp's warriors spent the battle on the east side of the river, but the 1st USSS crossed the Rappahannock on the morning of December 14. Trained men with Sharps Rifles could assist with scouting the hill Lee's men still held as Burnside prepared to evacuate back to Falmouth. The following day, four companies of the 1st Regiment served farther to the left, linking up with some of Franklin's skirmishers. As part of the force covering the withdrawal, two companies under Trepp manned the army's right until the morning of December 16. As some of the last organized troops across the river, Trepp's remaining marksmen helped bring back stragglers from the fighting over the previous sad days. Captain Frank Marble, Company G, led the last group of USSS members back to camp.[276]

A more dramatic denouement awaited the 2nd USSS about two miles to the south. The retrograde of the First and Sixth Corps led to the destruction of pontoon bridges in the waning moments of the Union presence on the Fredericksburg side of the river. Men from assorted companies across Franklin's command had to hustle to cross the bridges. Some Sharpshooters did not arrive in time. Four Minnesotans became Confederate prisoners for the want of a span to reunite with their comrades. Based on the postwar roster, of the four men captured that Stevens mentioned in his nineteenth-century history, three eventually returned to the regiment. One of those would die of a battle wound in 1864.[277]

The inability to save some Sharpshooters from capture epitomized the failed effort at Fredericksburg. Although much sorrow and fecklessness accompanied life in the Army of the Potomac in general and the Sharpshooters in particular, an abiding optimism prevailed, even after the lopsided rout at Fredericksburg. William Ripley may have grasped the idea as well as any other member of the army. In his history of the Vermont company of the 1st USSS, he discussed the positive demeanor part of the Union officer's mindset. "The men who composed the Army of the Potomac were in the field for a certain well defined purpose," Ripley opined, "and until that purpose was fully accomplished they intended to remain." Whatever the cost, "their ardor" abided, and no amount of Confederate resistance could "dampen their splendid courage."[278]

Even with the latent hopes to save the Union, sickness, poor food, and the biting winds of winter dominated life for the Sharpshooters as December closed. John Monahan felt "dreadful tired" on December 16 after being on picket the whole night. He sensed the "disappointed and demoralized" nature of the army after the Fredericksburg debacle. By Christmas Eve, the new Sharpshooter cooked up some applesauce while "thinking of home." Two days later, Monahan could at least write of "a very pleasant day."[279]

Members of the 2nd USSS had hard work to improve their campsite in the last half of December. Mainer James Matthews noted the necessity of gathering large quantities of wood near the regiment's temporary home, although water seemed plentiful. Soldiers felt the need to find a new location, then went to work. Christmas Day brought a period of intense activity. Unfortunately, brigade commander Walter Phelps had several complaints about the layout of the site, prompting an array of ordered changes.[280]

Strife between Colonel Berdan and Lt. Col. Caspar Trepp flared up before December's end. Berdan had returned to the field during the month, then expressed disdain for some of Trepp's choices. The dispute centered around Trepp's ideas about drill requirements for regimental officers. Bitterness in the relationship between the regiment's two senior leaders resulted in Trepp's submission of his resignation, an act he had attempted after prior problems with Berdan. The colonel ignored Trepp's request, undoubtedly because he knew of the lieutenant colonel's experience and the respect soldiers held for him.[281]

Dozens left the USSS as the year's final weeks went by. An examination of roster data shows the continued attrition of soldiers in the two regiments, even with no battlefield deaths sustained on December 13. Across the period from Burnside's army leaving Warrenton through the end of 1862, nearly seven weeks, the six companies from New Hampshire and Vermont had forty-six Sharpshooters depart through discharge or death from disease. Several of these soldiers had spent months in hospitals. Company F, 1st USSS, was hit the hardest during this period, losing twelve members. If recruiting successes had not occurred earlier in the year, military efficiency might have justified consolidation of the USSS into a small number of companies by the close of 1862. As John Monahan suggested in his diary on December 28, "People at home know nothing about the hard shape of their friends in the army."[282]

"A Distinct Arm of the Service"

Reunification of the USSS regiments began as dreary 1862 wound down. The process started when the 2nd USSS departed Phelps's Brigade for a new posting. "The whole brigade turned out to bid us goodbye," Ben Calef wrote of the assembly Colonel Phelps ordered. The colonel drew Calef's respect with "a very appropriate address," detailing what the men had been through together. After the order to stack arms, Calef added, "we were all mixed up shaking hands and taking our farewell."[283]

The 1st USSS would join their Sharpshooter comrades after returning from a foray to the Rappahannock. Finding no Confederates, Rudolf Aschmann, Company A, recorded the starkest memory of the jaunt: wading through ice-cold water at Richard's Ford, about fifteen miles west of camp. As William Ripley wrote, members of the 1st USSS became "agreeably surprised" after returning from the reconnaissance. Stoneman's Switch had also become home for the 2nd Sharpshooters.

Leaving 1862 behind, some Sharpshooters had fun on New Year's Day. A variety of games brightened the winter's routine, creating a merry setting for the reunited USSS regiments. Food ranged from oyster stew to donuts. George Marden used humor to sum up the fun. "We are eating and drinking and sleeping and taking little thought for the morrow," he averred. "If I were a squad of rebel cavalry, I think I could take the whole army."[284]

The Sharpshooters would not be expanded to match the request Colonel Berdan made to President Lincoln—and Berdan would not yet become a brigadier general. However, the Sharpshooters would spend nearly the rest of their service attached to the same brigade or division. An order from Burnside on January 14 formalized the reorganization that had brought the two USSS regiments back together. The order, which also noted the detachment of companies to different grand divisions, established, "The regiments and companies of sharpshooters in this army will form a distinct arm of the service, and will be under the command of Colonel Berdan, as chief of sharpshooters, who will report directly to these headquarters."[285]

The opening two weeks of January included time for typical camp duties. James Baker, Company C, 1st USSS, classified the period after Fredericksburg as a "dreamy state of inactivity." Smiles undoubtedly abounded when a round of new uniforms refreshed the men. "The boys all look green," John Monahan penned, "I am living finely." The outfits helped the USSS stick out on January 8, when General Burnside reviewed the troops, likely another opportunity for soldiers' morale to improve. Typical of the emotional roller coaster many Civil War soldiers endured, Monahan recorded maudlin thoughts soon after. "The country is bleeding to death," he sadly wrote on the day after Burnside's review, "Men must understand each other, or they will always war."[286]

Similar morose tidings with a tinge of optimism filled George Marden's thoughts in January 1863. The month found the New Hampshire soldier as acting assistant adjutant general in Berdan's command. "The fires of patriotism have grown dim," Marden opined, "and the knees of many have begun to tremble."

Trying to find some light from the faint winter sun, he continued, "the blood of these martyrs, who have fallen in this cause, is the seed of national liberty."[287]

Many knees likely trembled when orders arrived for a new effort against the Confederates. The lack of confidence many officers had in General Burnside proved to be less damaging to the movement than Virginia's mud. Starting off well enough on January 19, Burnside's effort bogged down after a deluge of rain turned roads into glue. Men, animals, and supply wagons mired in the unforgiving conditions.

Some USSS companies did not take part in what history calls The Mud March. Not attached to the advance, USSS companies assigned to the army's right flank fared well enough. Part of the doomed endeavor, John Monahan coined a highly memorable sentence on January 21 to define the army's experience. "We will all die if we have to stay here," the flustered Green Mountain man wrote. The next day he described his company's appearance with five words: "Clothes and guns all mud."[288]

Confederates happy to see their enemy struggling so mightily used humor to taunt Burnside's men. As Wolverine officer Thomas Connington wrote later in January, "to add insult upon injury," the Confederates created "a sign painted in big letters—*Burnside stuck in the mud*—it might be fun for them but it was death to us."[289]

Virginia's wintry goo doomed Burnside. Outraged at real and perceived lack of support from his officers, the army commander went to Washington, giving President Lincoln the choice of sacking several generals, including Joe Hooker, or accepting Burnside's resignation. After some thought, Lincoln picked the latter. Fighting Joe then became the new army commander. Burnside at least was out of the horrendous role of trying to make something of the winter after the debacles of the previous six weeks.[290]

"The Soldiers Could Not Be Too Perfect"

Across the winter, Thomas Brown, Company F, 1st USSS, wrote several letters that demonstrated his interest in news from home. He asked for updates about the health of his parents, while also providing advice for those managing another Vermont winter. He seemed content with his own circumstances, including a weight of 145 pounds on February 20, which prompted him to write, "I am gitin fat." With continued weight gain through the season, Brown would add seven more pounds. "I am thankful for my health," the prospering soldier concluded.[291]

Thoughts of home came to James Baker, as well, unfortunately for a tragic reason. Another officer in the company lost his mother to smallpox back in Michigan. The times meant a constant threat to health from an array of maladies, whether a person enlisted in the army or prayed for the safety of their soldier boys in the army. Writing about the sad loss of his comrade's parent, Baker hoped people would be grateful for any positives in their lives. "How very thankful we ought to be though we have been prostrated with diseases," Baker concluded.[292]

The lieutenant knew of the tragic loss inflicted on the USSS. For the first four months of 1863, the four Sharpshooter companies from Michigan lost thirty-four soldiers to discharges. Jeremiah J. Brown, a Wolverine in the 2nd Regiment, wounded at South Mountain back in September, received his medical discharge from a Baltimore hospital six months later. Moving to California later in life, Brown died in San Jose in 1910, seventy-one years old. Two of Brown's Company B comrades, teenager Jedediah Howe and forty-three-year-old John A. Huff, left the army early in the winter with disability discharges. Huff's January departure, for "functional disease of the heart & dropsy of abdomen contracted in the service" did not keep him from the army for the rest of the war.[293]

Capt. John Dewey, leading Pennsylvania's USSS company, departed in February. He endured myriad health complaints during his service, which included time under arrest after being absent without leave. Chronic diarrhea would plague the Keystone Stater for decades. In a sworn affidavit more than a decade after departing the army, Dewey deemed himself a "constant sufferer" since the beginning of his Sharpshooter experience. The wayward soldier lived until the last day of 1902.[294]

One of those who died of disease during the winter was Eugene W. Smith, who joined the USSS as part of the summer 1862 recruiting surge. Twenty-three years old, the Company I warrior lost his life in Falmouth on February 3. He rests at Fredericksburg National Cemetery.[295]

The sad culling of companies could not go unnoticed among those with field service from the beginning of the war. Again writing the discharged Charles Shepard back in New Hampshire, Joseph Rolfe noted the fine winter camp near Falmouth. The USSS did not "need quite so much ground" as the year before, Rolfe wrote, because "the old Co. is almost 'played out.'" He continued with news about promotions and men still with Company E, 1st USSS. "I guess the boys don't like Hooker any better than Burnside," Rolfe added, "but he can try I suppose."[296]

The USSS regiments found a home in the Third Corps, which Brig. Gen. Dan Sickles commanded. Berdan still had a semi-autonomous status while being attached to Amiel Whipple's Third Division. "Comparative comfort" existed for the Sharpshooters on duty as winter droned on. Joe Hooker exhibited skill in supplying the army and strengthening morale. The quality of food improved, with fresh bread common. Vegetables, unheard of during Burnside's tenure, bolstered moods across army camps. A new furlough system allowed soldiers some time back home during the winter, a major boost to their spirits. Furloughs also decreased desertion, another major problem Hooker dramatically lessened. The new commander also did away with Burnside's grand divisions, a cumbersome concept that added a layer above a corps commander without accomplishing much.[297]

Expectations that the USSS would never lose a high level of competence in military maneuvers required regular practice, regardless of the season. Drill and parades offered more than a way for the men to not completely idle away the cold months. The value of practiced repetition of important concepts and motions cannot be denied for any group of soldiers. Weather interfered with duties sometimes, but the Sharpshooters understood the necessity of going back to the basics during a period of limited activity. As Charles Stevens wrote in his USSS history, "Company and battalion movements it was very essential must not be forgotten—the soldiers could not be too perfect."[298]

Being on picket while facing the elements kept men miserable. In a February 21 letter, Lt. Thomas Connington complained mightily about the compulsory work. He called a four-day picket tour "the miserablest I ever spent in my life." Rain or snow fell for nearly the entire time at a pace surpassing other recent storms, the Wolverine added. Not wishing to appear too glum, Connington continued, "There is no use whining. I can stand as much of it as anyone but don't like it." The receipt of a wonderful letter from home propped Connington's spirits.[299]

Winter proved quite damaging to the relationship between Colonel Berdan and Lt. Col. Caspar Trepp. A great deal of paper would be consumed to draft the formal charges and countercharges the two men filed against each other, centering on the supposed cowardice of the other officer. None of this bureaucratic brawling led to guilty verdicts, but Trepp and some other officers were arrested and confined for parts of the winter. The malaise of the cold season could only be made worse for the Sharpshooters as their senior leaders pummeled each other through the court-martial process.[300]

Berdan's determined effort to keep Trepp away from his responsibilities did not seem to divide the Sharpshooters, who had measured up the two men long ago. At the start of a March 4, 1863 letter, Capt. George Hastings could speak for most in the USSS when he discussed the resolution of the case, which exonerated Trepp. Berdan had seemed determined to use the matter as a means to take firmer control over his men, but the effort backfired horribly.[301]

Sharpshooters on duty faced problems with the weather well into March. John Monahan wrote on March 6 what many marksmen likely experienced in a month that can bring harsh conditions, "On picket and am having a hard time.

I am very sick." Monahan might have envisioned better moments from the previous weeks when he could write of "a good fire and lots of reading matter" in his pleasant tent. Responsibility continued to call, however. After a short break, Monahan went back to the picket line on March 8.[302]

Weather occupied frequent space in the diary of Henry Bedell, Company K, 1st USSS. An artistic soldier who doodled eagles and other creatures into the pages of his diary, Bedell was shivering across the cloudy March 3. Conditions led to cancellation of the day's scheduled drill. Three days later while on picket, Bedell recorded another dreary day with wind. On the last day of March, he mentioned a major snow storm, while sketching a woman on the page.[303] Soldiers found interesting ways to pass the time as winter retained its grip over the feuding American armies.

Benjamin Calef expressed much in a March 7 missive. Overjoyed with two recent letters from his "Dear Lizzie," Calef noted the highly changeable weather, with sunny dryness soon followed by cold, rainy gales. He also expressed happiness about progress healing from an ankle injury, while also trying to support his correspondent; she seemed worried about him, a natural feeling a loved one had for their soldier hero. The letter displayed the variety of concerns any given Sharpshooter might have: weather, their personal health, and the well-being of family.

Whipple's Division assembled for review on March 14, an event Calef missed as he dealt with the chores of overseeing the USSS quartermaster's department. Calef wrote of the 14th being "a real raw March day," so he felt no disappointment at not being at the review. Later in the month, Calef expressed the languid state of his temperament as spring officially began. "I wish I could take hold with the same zest as last year," he averred, "but I cannot."[304]

Sharpshooters could not be faulted for trying to improve their position in the army. Dour days led some men to seek new commands. Captain Jacob McClure, still in charge of Maine's Company D, 2nd USSS, wrote the state's governor about an idea to raise new companies of Pine Tree State marksmen. McClure began the March letter, "I have the honor to ask for authority to raise a Battalion of Sharpshooters in the State of Maine." He noted some interest in the War Department for a group of four or five companies, under the command of a major, to bolster the number of expert marksmen in the army. McClure suggested the extra manpower pool available from the national draft offered the chance to recruit the best shots from those compelled into military service. The officer requested Company D should be allowed to go with him into the new battalion, something the U.S. Army likely would not have consented to. Even though McClure secured the endorsement of a brigadier general and Col.

Adelbert Ames, leading the 20th Maine Infantry, the state's battalion of sharpshooters took many months to organize.[305]

Junior officers in Maine's company bolstered McClure. In a letter later in March to Gov. Abner Coburn, McClure received praise for his hard work and skill in motivating men. The missive suggested,

> *Capt. McClure has distinguished himself in his Regiment & Brigade as an officer possessing superior qualifications. He has always been prompt, energetic & faithful in the discharge of his duties. He has been in mostly all the skirmishes & battles in which his Regt has been engaged, and on every occasion has exhibited the utmost coolness & courage. As a man, he is honest, earnest, intelligent and strictly temperate. He possesses an excellent judgement & sterling common sense. His conduct among both officers and men has been uniformly gentlemanly & courteous.*[306]

"As Long as There Remains a Traitor"

Company commanders, usually at the rank of captain, had a vital role to play in a Civil War unit. They were responsible for the lives of their men, even as roll calls counted far fewer than the one hundred soldiers a company included at full strength. With much to keep them busy, captains usually lacked the free time for letter writing, the best the men in the field could do to stay in touch with friends and loved ones. Captain Albert Buxton, leading Vermont's Company H under Homer Stoughton, had much on his mind when he took up pen and paper on March 13. The letter details the political views of one man; he could not speak for all of his soldiers. One could logically conclude, however, that the words Buxton used had strong support from his Green Mountain warriors. The captain felt great umbrage about some in the North he considered insufficiently supportive of the war. Buxton's thoughts on the Emancipation Proclamation, Lincoln's edict issued six months before declaring free all slaves in rebellious areas, offered a fascinating perspective.

> *At the time I enlisted in my country's cause, I was almost a democrat, but not the kind of democrats that they have at the present time. Now I am an abolitionist of the deepest dye and I am not ashamed to own it either. I am in favor of the President's Proclamation. I believe it to be a blow directed to the very vitals of this cursed rebellion; and in my opinion it is the only thing that will bring permanent peace to our land. There is a cowardly set at the North that are opposed to this Proclamation. They are opposed to the administration and to everything that is loyal and just. They are harping on what this war*

is costing the Government. They tell how demoralized the army is becoming, and they are trying in every possible way to discourage the true patriot. Now if these very men were in the rebel ranks with a gun in their hands (although they are too cowardly to fight), they would do less injury than they now do.

My motto is to fight as long as there remains a traitor that dares to raise his puny hand against that flag which shall yet wave triumphantly over every inch of southern soil. Yes, I say fight that treacherous host until they are subdued, if it costs half the blood and treasure of the North. The time has come when the people of the North should take hold of this matter as one man. It is a determined foe that we are contending with, and it needs our united efforts to crush the rebellion that has already brought sorrow and sadness to almost every home at the North.[307]

Seeing the President

Weather dictated much for the Sharpshooters in any season, especially in early spring. Darius Starr recorded an excellent day for gathering white oak firewood on March 27. The following day, however, brought rain, with "heavy thunder." Worse yet, a snowstorm soon arrived. John Monahan wrote of stiff winds bringing down some tents. The next morning, the Sharpshooters awoke to eight inches of snow. Making the most of the storm, Monahan noted how several of his comrades engaged in "a great snow balling match" that evening. Conditions turned bright on the morning of April 1, with George Marden thankful to see the sun.[308]

Although battle did not seem imminent, soldiers still had mortality on their minds. Pondering their own possible death led some Sharpshooters to caution family about contingencies. With so many people dying young in the nineteenth century, soldiers naturally might contemplate the death of loved ones, as well as comrades or themselves. In a haunting letter home on April 4, Thomas Brown declared, "there is meny of a family left fatherless by this war, and you may be to but I hope I shall be spaired to get home and I hope you all will be spaired till I get home again."[309]

A formal parade before President Lincoln occurred on April 8. With some of his family and friends along, the president inspected Hooker's army as more than one hundred thousand marched by. Lincoln had the opportunity to talk with officers and learn more about the army's condition. Sharpshooters took notice of the immense burden evident in the president's countenance. "He looks very much worn," John Monahan wrote on seeing Lincoln, a sentiment Wyman White echoed.[310]

Preparations for a special celebration had occupied the opening of spring in the USSS camp. The men determined that games and fun should mark the anniversary of the 1st Regiment's participation in the Yorktown siege. Officers from both regiments organized the jolly day, including the preparation of a program. Festivities began on the day after the presidential visit.

Sharpshooters could not conduct such a memorable carnival without shooting competitions. Only the finest marksmen in a given company had the chance to demonstrate their accuracy at what was special enough to be given capital letters. Charles Stevens noted the "Grand Shooting Match" began with a speech from Colonel Berdan. Samuel Ingling, Company I, 1st USSS, won the gold medal as the best shot in the brigade. His mettle served the Sharpshooters well for the rest of the war. Some officers, including Wisconsin's Frank Marble, also performed quite well with a rifle.[311]

After months away due to illness and hospital duty, Wyman White greatly enjoyed the celebration. He did not lose an expert's touch with a rifle during his absence. White finished second during the process of determining who would represent the 2nd Regiment's Company F in the finals of the shooting contest. White wrote of sack and foot races, cock fights, climbing a greased pole (something no Sharpshooter accomplished), and attempts to capture a greased pig as part of the Yorktown anniversary.[312]

As the days warmed, soldiers felt the pull of a new campaign. Four days after Lincoln's review, Hooker sent the president a letter outlining his plan. "I will have more chance of inflicting a heavier blow upon the enemy by turning his position to my right," with the bulk of his infantry advance, Hooker suggested. He hoped a large Union cavalry force could make mischief south of Lee's main defensive line, still along the strong bluff on the other side of Fredericksburg.[313] The basics of the plan mirrored Burnside's idea for what turned into the Mud March, but snow and mud would not hamper the spring offensive.

Their exact role yet undetermined, the Sharpshooters engaged in basic and important activities preparatory to marching orders. A large group of marksmen took part in a four-day picket detail, which started on April 12. On the return to camp, a Badger mentioned the presence of an old enemy. "A heavy rain soaked them as they marched back," he lamented, "again making mud plenty."

Additional preparations included intensified use of the USSS target range, with practice for individual soldiers or groups firing by volley. Men such as Ben Calef and George Marden kept busy working at Berdan's headquarters as the "general training" of the companies continued. Orders for issuance of eight days rations and sixty rounds of ammunition instilled the sense of inevitable battle across the Sharpshooter companies. "We are on the eve of great events," Darius Starr proclaimed on April 20. The hunt for Confederates would soon begin.[314]

In late April, the bulk of four corps marched up the Rappahannock to the west of Falmouth, then crossed south. With an alacrity true to his reputation, Hooker successfully placed half his army above Lee's Confederates, centered at a humble crossroads known as Chancellorsville. The Third Corps started the campaign at the other end of the line below Fredericksburg, along with the First and Sixth Corps. Hooker visualized a pincer movement, trying to keep General Lee guessing where the main blow would fall. Would the troops north of Fredericksburg crush the trapped Confederates while John Sedgwick, leading the three corps to the south, attacked the Confederate defenses from the opposite direction? Hooker bragged of Lee's "certain destruction," but the fates of war often refuse to tolerate a human being with such elevated visions of himself.[315]

Part Two

"The full measure of the penalty," May 1863–April 1864

Six infantry regiments across two other brigades joined Colonel Berdan's Sharpshooters in General Whipple's division at the start of the Chancellorsville campaign. With his two other divisions, Dan Sickles led more than 17,500 present and equipped men at the end of April. The strike force Hooker sent north of Fredericksburg, initially the Fifth, Eleventh, and Twelfth Corps, placed a strong collection of troops well north of Lee's left. These men soon received an excellent supplement, two divisions from Darius Couch's Second Corps.

The Third Corps held a reserve position early in the campaign, beginning with a march to the left along with the First and Sixth Corps. Parts of those two other commands faced enemy fire while crossing the Rappahannock south of Fredericksburg on April 29. With separate and powerful wings north and south of Fredericksburg, army commander Joseph Hooker hoped to fool the Confederates as to where the main blow would fall. No Union general had so baffled Robert E. Lee in the previous twelve months. Hooker's secretive march held the potential to bring a resounding victory, especially because the Army of the Potomac counted nearly two soldiers for each Confederate under Lee. If Hooker could damage the Southern supply line with cavalry, Lee would have had no choice but to retreat closer to Richmond to protect his army and national capital.[1]

Unfortunately for the Union cause and Hooker's historical reputation, a sudden tentativeness pervaded the Northern general's leadership. Instead of continuing his march south to crush Lee, Hooker held his northern flanking force back, forming defensive lines in the heavily forested area around Chancellorsville. Communication snafus with his corps south of Fredericksburg, along with cautious generalship there, precluded Hooker from coordinating the pincer movement he planned. Lee decided to risk much by becoming aggressive. Rather

Major General Daniel Sickles commanded the Third Corps at Chancellorsville and Gettysburg. LIBRARY OF CONGRESS

than retreat south, Lee would nearly empty the Fredericksburg line, then march to fight Hooker's force on the Union right.[2]

The USSS and their comrades under Dan Sickles had yet to play a role in the drama. Then, an active destiny called. Adding more troops to his force north of Fredericksburg offered Hooker a means to improve his chances against the always bold Confederate Army of Northern Virginia. In the early afternoon of April 30, the Third Corps was ordered to proceed "without delay, by the shortest road, concealed from view of the enemy to the United States Ford," eight miles due west of Falmouth. Sickles's march required "the greatest promptness," the order continued, with all three divisions expected to cross the ford by 7 a.m. on May 1.[3]

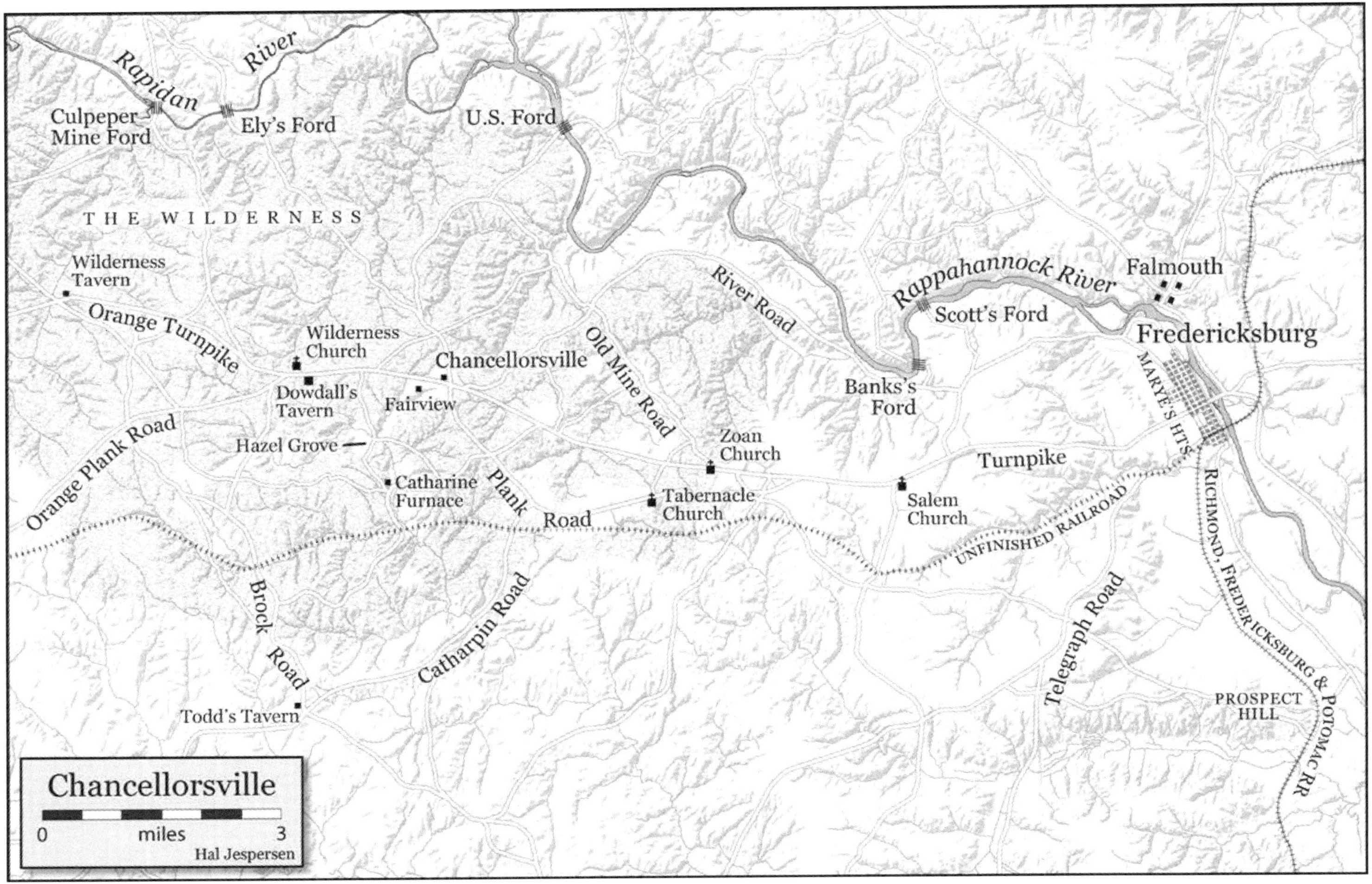
Chancellorsville
0
miles
3
Hal Jespersen
Rapidan River
Culpeper Mine Ford
Ely's Ford
U.S. Ford
THE WILDERNESS
Wilderness Tavern
Orange Turnpike
Wilderness Church
Dowdall's Tavern
Chancellorsville
Fairview
Hazel Grove
Catharine Furnace
Orange Plank Road
Plank Road
Old Mine Road
River Road
Zoan Church
Tabernacle Church
Salem Church
Turnpike
Banks's Ford
Scott's Ford
Rappahannock River
Falmouth
Fredericksburg
MARYE'S HTS
UNFINISHED RAILROAD
Brock Road
Todd's Tavern
Catharpin Road
Telegraph Road
PROSPECT HILL
RICHMOND, FREDERICKSBURG & POTOMAC RR

Division commander Whipple's instructions for the march, released from Third Corps headquarters at 1:15 p.m., ordered an immediate move to the ford. Slightly more than twenty miles had to be covered for the USSS and the rest of the Third Corps to meet their deadline. Soldiers were compelled to carry eight days of rations.[4]

The need for speed wore down the troops. John Monahan noted, "The boys throwed almost everything away," with "all very tired" after not stopping much for rest until 2 a.m. on May 1. Captain James Baker, Company C, 1st USSS, figured the day's march amounted to fifteen miles. Hartwood Church, six marching miles from U.S. Ford, served as the night's camp. By about 9 a.m., Berdan's men crossed the Rappahannock. Following their late arrival at the ford, marksmen still had about two miles to cover before reaching their prescribed position near Hooker's main force.[5]

Hours too late on the morning of May 1, Hooker ordered an advance with several brigades outside Sickles's divisions, while also ordering two Fifth Corps divisions to Banks Ford, closer to Fredericksburg. With Lee attacking other portions of Hooker's force, the effort to control Banks Ford had to be abandoned. Hooker instead selected to withdraw, a very controversial decision that withered the potential of his incredibly bold and well-managed flank march. This surrender of the initiative would prove devastating. No Union general confronting Lee did well after such an error, as illustrated by McClellan's catastrophe on the Peninsula and Pope's nightmare that culminated at Second Bull Run.[6]

The order calling for the day's advance required the Third Corps to halt a mile north of Chancellorsville, a logical position for a designated reserve force. Later on May 1, USSS companies stood near Hooker's headquarters in advance of Whipple's Division. By midnight, Berdan reported his men returning the short distance north to the division's camp.[7]

Sickles's men would not be in the rear for long. On May 2, they moved from north of the campaign's eponymous crossroads to a more open and prominent position more than a mile south of Chancellorsville. Sickles detached the USSS from Whipple, placing the marksmen under First Division commander David Birney, who, like Sickles, lacked military experience but would perform fine service during the inevitable battle. Berdan's companies reported to Birney at about noon on May 2.

Switching to the defensive seemed to energize Hooker. Lee, conversely, became flustered with his apparent inability to harm the Union army, which had spent many hours fortifying the forbidding confines of the forest around Chancellorsville. Never content with a static line of unknown offensive potential, Lee conversed with Stonewall Jackson about the possibility of striking Hooker farther to the west, after reports placed an isolated Union corps, Oliver Howard's Eleventh, two miles beyond Chancellorsville. Never afraid to dare, Lee divided his army again, with Jackson sent west. Lee held the southern and eastern portion of the line with only two divisions against Hooker's much larger horde.[8]

"A Smart Fight"

Witnessing Jackson's force heading west to attack Hooker's flank, Union troops south of Chancellorsville grew restive during the morning. Sickles's fighting temperament led him to grant Birney's request to send troops forward to disrupt what some considered to be Lee's retreat. Birney rightly deemed Berdan's men a great unit to assist with discerning Confederate intentions. The Sharpshooters went forward after crossing a new bridge over Scott's Run. Infantrymen in the 20th Indiana linked up with USSS elements as part of the advance. One Sharpshooter felt good after learning his Hoosier friends would help out that day. "We always thought when we had the 20th Ind. for support when we were skirmishing, we were all right," Nathaniel Sessions, Company I, 1st USSS, wrote.[9]

The 23rd Georgia, Southern troops left behind to guard the trains moving west with Jackson's flanking force, stood in the way. The afternoon quickly turned sour for the Peach Tree warriors, pressed by the Hoosier infantry and the USSS, with Union troops forcing the Georgians back. Attempts to rally around a foundry building proved futile as Berdan kept up the pressure on the enemy skirmishers, leading to the capture of dozens. "We speedily routed the skirmish line," a Vermonter in the 2nd USSS remembered.[10]

With additional efforts to flank the Confederates' main line, the ultimate gift awaited, the surrender of most of the 23rd Georgia. The impressive victory still took some work. "We soon came on the rest of the regiment," the Wolverine Sessions, remembered, leading to "a warm time with them." Wisconsin marksman George Cottrell suffered multiple injuries during the fight. With determination fondly remembered by a comrade, Cottrell kept firing. The first bullet struck near the hip, but equipment protected Cottrell's body. A bloody throat wound followed. The Sharpshooter writer remembered his brave friend, "appeared to care very little about being hit, but blazed away when occasion offered, apparently with a will." The determined Cottrell, a very young soldier born in 1845, would survive the war, dying in 1872.[11]

As the day appeared to be going against them, some Georgians attempted to escape from a railroad cut, but many returned to their line due to the hazards involved in running away from the intensity of Sharps Rifles. Eventually, close to two hundred Georgians became prisoners near the site known as Catherine's Furnace. The commanding officer of the 23rd Georgia lost his command through court-martial as a result of the tragic day. The USSS remained in the area until evening to monitor the ground south of the main Union position nearer Chancellorsville.[12]

John Monahan called the valiant effort against the Georgians "a smart fight." James Baker's strong leadership certainly helped. The Wolverine's work to keep his marksmen firing led one of his comrades to term Baker "one of bravest officers in the regiment." A Detroit newspaper echoed such sentiments about Baker. The lieutenant's "courage and bravery cannot be excelled," the story noted in reporting of the May 2 engagement.[13]

A company commander became the highest-ranking fatality for the USSS at Chancellorsville. Captain Dudley Chase led his men forward toward the Furnace on May 2, taking a round in his left arm. The subsequent amputation led to worsened conditions for the Minnesotan, who had risen to command of Company A after Francis Peteler's promotion in early 1862. Chase died on May 7, with burial at Groveland Cemetery, Minnetonka, Minnesota.[14]

Chase earned Berdan's mention in his initial report on Chancellorsville. Greater tributes came from a St. Paul newspaper, which deemed Chase "a brave and gallant officer" who was "universally loved." The fallen hero, a native of Maine, rose in the Minnesota city's esteem while making a productive life in his new state. "Here at home," the paper added, "where so many knew him as a good and worthy citizen, the news of his death will be deeply mourned."[15]

Three Wolverines were also listed as receiving fatal wounds on May 2: Alvin Smith, Marvin Wetmore, and Walter Christie. The trio of marksmen enlisted in 1862, with Smith and Wetmore killed in action, while Christie died ten days later at a Washington hospital.[16]

A Badger Sharpshooter called the terrain of their May 2 brawl "a brushy timbered hill." The relatively small battle became known as the "Fight at the Cedars," due to the large number of cedar shrubs in the area. General Birney announced "The Cedars" as an engagement that could be placed on regimental battle flags.[17]

"Our Loss Here Was Considerable"

The triumph against one Confederate regiment did nothing to stop the determination of Stonewall Jackson. By late afternoon, the Southern corps commander sent nearly thirty thousand men against the unprepared Eleventh Corps. The rout forced Oliver Howard's men back and essentially out of the rest of the battle. Accidentally shot by his own men after darkness descended, Stonewall paid with his life for the day's victory.[18]

The lateness of the hour and Jackson's fall halted the Confederate advance short of U.S. Ford or Chancellorsville. Nonetheless, the overnight period raised questions about the viability of the rest of Hooker's line. In special trouble, the Third Corps had two divisions well south of Chancellorsville on a spot known as Hazel Grove. Sickles formulated a plan for a night attack to solidify his command's hold in the area. The attempt led to multiple incidents of friendly fire without improving the tactical situation. Sharpshooters and their comrades fell back during the night. Confederate big guns lit up the sky, providing some memorable fireworks for the retreating marksmen moving north before dawn.[19]

The USSS then manned a new position west of Chancellorsville and north of the Plank Road. As Hooker's troops worked overnight on entrenchments to protect the salient around the crossroads, Confederate cavalry leader J. E. B. Stuart took charge of Jackson's infantry corps. Regardless of the shock delivered to the Union army the day before, reuniting the Confederate force stood imperative in Lee's mind on May 3. He ordered Stuart to advance quickly to join his wing with the rest of the Confederate army.[20]

Berdan held the 2nd USSS in reserve for the opening of what would be another brutal day. Elements of the 1st Regiment had a very active and important role as skirmishers facing Stuart's bloody opening attack. Boldness from Trepp's Company C, which included an early counter charge, demonstrated the intense grit within the hearts of the Sharpshooters. The Wolverines paid a hefty cost for their valor, with seven men lost to combat death on the day. One of them was Harmon Wise, known to the men as "Rough." Deemed "a good natured, ready soldier," Wise distinguished himself on his last day of life. The six additional members of the company who lost their lives on May 3 were Leonard Bissell, Byron Brewer, John Evans, Henry Hood, William Parker, and John Price.

The seven fallen Wolverines accounted for half of USSS members dying from Chancellorsville wounds. By the war's end, this terrible toll for Company C would stand as tied for the most marksmen's lives lost in a single company on one battle day. Of his soldiers' fate north of the Plank Road during the early morning, Berdan reported, "Our loss here was considerable."[21]

North Carolinians filled two of the brigades attacking Sharpshooters as the day opened. One Tar Heel in the 7th Regiment found the defenders' riflery and cannon rounds "withering," even with the generally wooded area across much of the advance. Leading another brigade north of the Plank Road, Dorsey Pender informed his wife about the stout resistance. These Confederate observations likely included witnessing Sharps Rifle fire from the USSS. Together, the two Tar Heel brigades sustained more than 1,600 casualties while helping to push Hooker's force back.[22]

A New York marksman penned short but descriptive thoughts of the unforgettable fight. Experiencing his hottest day of battle yet, he wrote, "Our men fought well, but nothing could resist the dreadful fire of the enemy."[23]

Hiram Berry, Third Corps division commander, lost his life leading his men during the morning. While both armies suffered immensely, Stuart's charging lines made steady progress. However, the Confederates proved unable to cripple Hooker's army. Disorganized by the morning's success, the Southerners "seemed to come in crowds rather than in any lines of battle," one of Sickles's Third Division staff officers reported after Berry's battered line retreated.

The army patched together a new defensive front north of the Chancellorsville crossroads, with the Third Corps manning the southern part of a large curve that protected the line of retreat to U.S. Ford. Other corps to the east and west of Sickles assumed strong positions with either the Rapidan or Rappahannock covering Hooker's flanks.[24]

Lieutenant Brewer's Determination

First Lt. Byron Brewer was the second USSS officer to die from Chancellorsville wounds. His mortal injury came while rallying men against the Confederate surge on May 3. Brewer had enlisted as a corporal in August 1861 at the age of twenty-three. With obvious soldierly qualities, he became a sergeant that autumn. Brewer continued to earn higher positions, as well as the respect of comrades. Edwin Wilson, a marksman in the same company, considered Brewer "a brave and accomplished officer, who was always ready and active in all emergencies." Falling to enemy fire on May 3 seemed like an appropriate end for a warrior hero like Brewer. According to Wilson, the lieutenant had envisioned his own death shortly before.

The fatal injury at Chancellorsville was not Brewer's first combat wound. With the true spirit of a Wolverine, Brewer had missed six months of active duty while healing from the brutal impact of a bullet at Second Bull Run. Earlier in the war, he suggested the Confederates could not craft a round to hit him. Facing a lengthy healing process, Brewer proved resolute in an effort to rebound. As Wilson remembered, "They shot him in the left breast" near Manassas, "and the ball went clear through him, cutting away a part of the left lung, causing a wound that would have killed nine men out of 10."

Receiving a March commission as a lieutenant, Brewer returned to duty, although, "In appearance, he did not look like the same person," Wilson wrote. Brewer spent the time back with his comrades while looking "pale and sickly." The young officer "would roam around and through the camp listless and dejected, and would frequently make the remark that the next battle would be his last." Wilson noted how members of the company attempted to remove such negativity from Brewer's mind, but the lieutenant's vision became reality. Wilson witnessed Brewer's "active part" the day before his death while on the hunt for the 23rd Georgia. During the May 2 advance, the officer "seemed to recover some of his old-time spirits."[25] The USSS would benefit from the revitalized Brewer for only one more day.

"A Cold, Particularly Disagreeable Rain"

The Army of the Potomac possessed a strong line as May 3 ended. Curtis Abbott noted noon as the time when the army formed up closer to the Rapidan and Rappahannock. The marksmen passed a generally quiet afternoon while resting a bit behind the lines. On the 4th, the USSS formed not far west of the Bullock House, less than a mile north of the Chancellorsville crossroads. Skirmish duty, no doubt a predictable fate for the Sharpshooters, led the men even closer to their unyielding Confederate foes.[26]

The work of the day proved dangerous to all, deadly to some. Sharpshooters losing their lives to May 4 wounds included another Company C Wolverine, Sgt. Porter Barker, as well as Granite Stater Daniel Morse. Along the Third Division line, the men lost their commander, Amiel Whipple, a career soldier who had graduated in the top 10 percent of the 1837 class at West Point. The spinal wound inflicted by a Confederate sharpshooter led to Whipple's death on May 7. Thus, Sickles lost two of three division commanders during the battle.[27]

A Wisconsin marksman noted that Whipple had earned the approbation of the USSS in the short time of their connection. The Badger suggested, "He was much respected by our boys for the manly and fearless manner in which he entered into the contest, and great sorrow has been expressed at his fall."[28]

USSS members beyond the main line attempted to decrease the chance of a bold Confederate finding more targets. Berdan himself took a detail of ten volunteers from his command with the special mission of targeting Southern sharpshooters. Although too late to save Whipple, who fell at about 10 a.m., Berdan reported his select band doing a fine job forcing some hidden Confederates back. The USSS "held the ground gained" from the enterprise, Berdan added, "so that no more casualties occurred from the enemy's fire."[29]

Destined to live nearly fifty more years, John Monahan saw his career as a Sharpshooter end on May 4. His short time in military hospitals allowed him to write descriptions of his last few days as a soldier. "The boys are very sore," he wrote of his fellow patients on May 7. Two days later, Monahan recorded he "slept all day," with May 11 a time of being "sick and sleepy." Soon he would be on his way home to Vermont.[30]

Taking a reserve position later on May 4, the USSS received some ammunition and rations, both items vital for the tired men. Higher officers busied themselves with a discussion about next steps. Hooker supported a withdrawal of the army via U.S. Ford, something some of his corps commanders resisted. A campaign begun with so much potential ended in what George Marden called "a cold, particularly disagreeable rain" that for a time seemed able to wash away bridges designed to facilitate a safe retreat. The soggy march back to Stoneman's Switch became the Sharpshooters' last service of the ineffectual Chancellorsville endeavor.[31]

Impressions of the Dismal Campaign

"We made some history, but accomplished nothing," Wyman White penned regarding early May 1863. The disaster and retreat stunned many in the army. Starting with his unmatched trek around Lee's left, Hooker's plan had the makings of a brilliant drive capable of winning the war. Depths of despair did not seem to linger, however. For the Sharpshooters, after a return to Stoneman's Switch, the campaign epitomized what a group of expert marksmen could achieve, the capture of the 23rd Georgia. The dangerous labors of the previous week and the army's failure, however, ensured the USSS returned to camp "worn out with fatigue, and considerably downcast."[32]

Hooker attempted to instill deep pride among his men after the failed effort. In general orders issued on May 6, the commander "tenders to this army his congratulations on its achievements of the last seven days." His army "will give or decline battle whenever its interest or honor may demand." Even without victory, Hooker concluded, "We have no other regret than that caused by the loss of our brave companions," who fell "in the holiest cause ever submitted to the arbitrament of battle."[33]

A Badger Sharpshooter, reviewing the campaign in a letter to his mother, did not retain the fighting spirit Hooker hoped to stoke with his order. Frank Smith listed an array of bad news, including the death of General Whipple. He wished to "speedily" be back home because the May disaster made him wish "never to mix up again in the turmoil of Battle."[34]

George Marden had a role in the action, something quite enlightening as he was generally assigned to quartermaster work and communicating orders to the two Sharpshooter regiments. In a May 8 letter, Marden discussed key aspects of the Chancellorsville fight, including his assignment from Berdan to work the battle line. "The bullets began to whistle uncomfortably close," Marden opined, "but in a few minutes I got so excited I did not think of them." He considered the capture of the 23rd Georgia "a most splendid affair." Overall, Marden concluded, Chancellorsville proved "our skill in skirmishing and our ability to shoot so accurately and rapidly." Even when facing the truculent Confederates trying to overwhelm Hooker on May 3, Marden suggested, "I was never so impressed with the superiority of sharpshooters over infantry."[35]

Even as the failed campaign rankled, Sharpshooters often retained a fighting attitude. Andrew Westervelt suggested the Confederates should be thankful for Hooker's retreat. "We could have whipped the rebel army there if we had not given them up and re-crossed the Rappahannock," California Joe Number Two declared.[36]

Thoughts of missed opportunities did not translate into the Sharpshooters' complete loss of confidence in Hooker. "We are somewhat disappointed, but not discouraged," Albert Buxton informed a Vermont paper. The army's "confidence in him remains unshaken. We believe he will yet lead us on to victory," he added. The letter also noted how Loring Wyman, a member of the company, lost all fingers of his left hand to a Chancellorsville wound. Wyman spent many months of service in the Veteran Reserve Corps before leaving the army in early 1865.[37]

In writing a letter home to Michigan on May 8, William Denny, 2nd USSS, noted the difficulties of the campaign, as well as the wounding of Corp. Llewellyn Blanchard, a respected teenage member of Company B. Denny retained plenty of motivation to discuss positives, as well as his confidence in Hooker. Regardless of the army's losses, he suggested, victory will occur.

> *We are all in excellent spirits. We know that we have not been defeated, and we further know that we gave the rebs a terrible thrashing. I never saw the men more jubilant. The army of the Potomac is now perfectly united, and more determined than ever to destroy Lee's army. We all have the greatest confidence in "Fighting old Joe," and we of the 3d corps feel proud of our commander, Gen. Sickles. . . . In the thickest of the fight the Sharp Shooters particularly distinguished themselves.*[38]

The mien of the marksmen provided a necessary level of buoyancy after Chancellorsville. Later in May, Dan Cummings, a Maine lieutenant, updated his father about the status of Company D. "We are rapidly recovering from our late reverse," the missive began, "and under the glorious Hooker we shall soon be in condition to meet them again." Of their army commander, Cummings declared, "The Army both love and fear him." Of his immediate superior, the lieutenant added, "your friend Capt. McClure of our Co. is well and ready and anxious" to battle the Confederates again."[39]

Trepp versus Berdan Again

The latent hostility between Hiram Berdan and Caspar Trepp grew into another series of allegations after Chancellorsville. Roy Marcot, Berdan's modern biographer, suggests Trepp held the high ground in the argument. However, Berdan should receive the benefit of the doubt in this instance. Vain and ineffective as a leader of the Sharpshooters overall, Berdan was not always wrong while serving with his men in the field.[40]

Trepp expressed great angst about his superior officer in a letter soon after Chancellorsville. Ben Calef delivered the message in person to the judge advocate-general's office in Washington, prompting a May 11 reply from a military justice official. In response to the bureaucracy's request, Trepp crafted another document, detailing his concerns about Berdan's lack of time along the firing line of the 1st USSS in early May. Secretary Stanton received the letter, which Marcot logically considers a development that denied a general's star to Berdan, a promotion he had sought for many months.

Writing to the assistant adjutant general of the Third Corps, Trepp repeated concerns about Berdan's lack of field presence. He suggested the brigade commander was not on the line of the 1st Sharpshooters as they moved toward Catherine's Furnace on May 2. Then, Berdan failed to man the line of Trepp's companies on the following day, when they suffered a great deal from Confederate fire.

Trepp's letter to Secretary Stanton further detailed Berdan's actions, or lack thereof, at Chancellorsville. Trepp suggested a court-martial should be convened, followed by Berdan's dismissal from military service. While these maneuvers took place, Berdan himself was writing President Lincoln, requesting creation of additional Sharpshooter units. Recruiting was sorely needed, Berdan added, because of the "decimated" condition of the two USSS regiments already in the field. To fulfill the vision and mission of the Sharpshooter line of service, Berdan opined, simply filling up the existing organization would not suffice.

George Hastings, wounded at Chancellorsville, worked with Trepp in the effort to undercut Berdan. On his way to the rear with a shot to the knee on May 3, Hastings wrote of having talked to Berdan, who had posted himself out of contact with the enemy. The wounded officer allowed Trepp to use his name, as Hastings hoped, in the effort to deny a promotion for Berdan. The disgruntled officers held the additional hope of keeping Berdan from controlling more Sharpshooters that he might end up recruiting.

Although a strong regimental commander and quite knowledgeable about the use of Sharpshooters, Trepp's charges against Berdan suffer from a notable fallacy. As a brigade commander, Berdan could not be expected to always stand with skirmishers or even the regiment in closest contact with the enemy. Perhaps some level of cowardice explains why Trepp and Hastings did not see Berdan in the front with the Sharpshooters at Chancellorsville. However, a brigade commander could not be court-martialed for failing to advance with a line of skirmishers all the way to Catherine's Furnace. Likewise, a good reason may have existed for Berdan to remain in back of the line during the main Confederate attack north of Plank Road on May 3. He was leading a two-regiment brigade, not the 1st USSS alone. Trepp's charges do not stand as a case of failed leadership by a brigade commander.

As part of Berdan's effort to expand the Sharpshooters in the late spring of 1863, he received a May 29 endorsement from General Hooker for promotion to brigadier general. In a letter to one of Lincoln's assistants, one of the arguments Berdan made in favor of his own promotion was a concern about his family's inability to receive a pension if he fell in battle without an official commission. Lincoln echoed that concern, but this was not necessarily supportive of a promotion for the Sharpshooter chief. The president's words suggest Berdan's commission as colonel may not have been official.

After so much ink, Berdan was denied a promotion. Trepp's post-Chancellorsville writings likely impacted the determination to withhold a star from Berdan, as well as the possibility that Berdan lacked a political sponsor in the U.S. Senate. The military bureaucracy already knew of some instances of Berdan's questionable choices as a leader, especially his two years of disputes with subordinates and his periodic disappearance from his men under fire.

Berdan's focus on recruitment in the late spring of 1863 certainly had merit. Other members of the USSS witnessing the thin ranks in their companies could naturally wonder if the Sharpshooters were going to wither away. The lack of consistent recruitment success from early in the war haunted the dream of a "distinct" Sharpshooter line of service, again demonstrating that the army failed to craft a workable vision for the betterment of the USSS. Would the eighteen companies simply dissolve due to sickness, wounds, and death?

"Irksome" Time before Another March

In army returns dated May 10, the Third Corps had slightly less than thirteen thousand men and officers present and equipped. Brig. Gen. Charles Graham, who led a brigade of Pennsylvania infantry at Chancellorsville, rose to command of the Third Division after the death of General Whipple. For the Sharpshooters, the general dullness of a defeated army in repose prevailed. William Ripley recorded the weeks after Chancellorsville as a time when "nothing of moment took place to essentially vary the monotony." Drills, parades, and reviews abounded. On a few occasions, a special plea for USSS marksmanship came into camp. However, the men who rushed to some portion of the picket line never faced prolonged problems from Confederates along the Rappahannock.[41]

Matters negatively impacting lives raised USSS stress levels in other ways. Concerns remained about outside officers gaining leadership of companies. Ira Northup had been acting as captain of the Pennsylvanian Sharpshooters since the departure of John Dewey in February. Northup enlisted the help of several comrades, including the respected "Fighting Parson" Lorenzo Barber, to argue for promotion to captain and continued leadership of Company C. State records include multiple letters on the contentious matter, which would have placed a New Yorker from Company B, 1st USSS over the Keystone Staters if Maj. Homer Stoughton's preference prevailed. The regimental commander's effort failed, much to the delight of the Pennsylvanians, who would see Northup gain the two bars of a captain.[42]

After returning to Stoneman's Switch, staff member Ben Calef had to share accommodations due to problems finding or replacing tents. Having spacious arrangements earlier in the war, Calef found the new reality "anything but agreeable," until an additional tent went up on May 15. His letter of the following day noted a work trip to Washington in which much had to be done. The time away permitted reunions with old friends, giving the harried brigade quartermaster some relaxation in the capital.[43]

One of the administrative improvements Hooker made across the army was the proliferation of brigade or regimental bakeries. The increase in fresh bread fueled soldiers for months, leading to an obvious morale uptick. Using the motivation from superiors to become a creative cook, James Matthews, a Maine Sharpshooter, happily built an oven in May, a process taking up two days. He then baked a custard to mark the happy moment.[44]

While life droned on for the Sharpshooters and army, Confederate commander Robert E. Lee planned and discussed merits of a new campaign. Like the year before, he had sights on an invasion of the North. From the Third Corps picket line south of Fredericksburg, Colonel Berdan reported a June 2 movement of Confederate troops toward the city. Additional evidence painted a picture of an enemy force ready to vacate Fredericksburg.[45]

The opening Confederate move out of Fredericksburg led to Union cannon fire from across the Rappahannock. With orders to prepare for a departure from camp, George Marden called the transition from quiet routine to a new campaign "quite sudden and unexpected." At the same time, events did not instantly change. Ten days passed between the USSS picket line reports of Confederate movements to the breaking of camp at Stoneman's Switch. Nonetheless, the growing anticipation made marksmen realize another campaign imminently awaited. Marden could only guess about the two regiments' fate. He expected another move across the river, but "I do not propose to waste any ink on speculations or forebodings."[46] With whatever the future, he and his USSS comrades would soon become very busy.

Hooker correctly figured Lee began a move out of Fredericksburg to head north. He suggested the time seemed logical to attack the small contingent of the enemy still around Fredericksburg, then move south toward the Confederate capital. This violated the Lincoln administration's clear directive to always ensure the safety of Washington. With dozens of miles separating elements of the Confederate force, the president responded to Hooker with a suggestion to chase Lee, then strike his army on the march. "If you had Richmond invested to-day," Lincoln averred on June 10, "you would not be able to take it in twenty days." Instead, the commander-in-chief declared, "I think Lee's army, and not Richmond, is your sure objective point." With the message garnered from the president's veiled order, Hooker readied his army for a long march followed by a showdown with the confident Confederate warriors.[47]

Soldiers began to feel ready for the challenge. Dull routine would no longer suffice as the warmer weather made a new march feel necessary to purge the sour taste of Chancellorsville. As 2nd USSS Vermonter Curtis Abbott declared, "Their camp on the hillside so pleasant in the previous winter, was now irksome. No member of Co. H was sorry at the initial movement." The new endeavor would take the men two states to the north and the most famous battlefield of the war.[48]

Heat Dominates June

Shortly before breaking camp, Hooker shuffled troops in the Third Corps. With battle losses, the Third Division disappeared, if only for a few weeks. The two USSS regiments transferred to David Birney's First Division. Although the marksmen retained a semi-official detached status, with Berdan reporting directly to Birney, organization charts placed the USSS in the Second Brigade under Brig. Gen. John Henry Hobart Ward. The Sharpshooters' brigade comrades included the 20th Indiana, 3rd and 4th Maine, 86th and 124th New York, and 99th Pennsylvania.[49]

Lee's vanguard had been moving for more than a week before the bulk of the Army of the Potomac gave chase. June 11, the same day of the Third Corps' reorganization, marked the first notable movements for the Sharpshooters. The USSS covered almost fifteen miles to open what history would call the Gettysburg campaign. Berdan's marksmen and the rest of the Third Corps stood as the troops northwesternmost in the entire army. The move had been ordered after cavalry leader Alfred Pleasonton requested infantry support. Used as pickets along the river, the 2nd USSS temporarily served with the Second Division, under Andrew Humphreys. During a rest period, members of Company H visited the grave of their comrade Warren Stevens at Rappahannock Station, the site of the regiment's first notable combat the summer before. After a short break, the Sharpshooters headed to Bealeton, farther to the northwest. With orders to limit wagons and strictly enforce rules against straggling, the Third Corps was expected to make excellent time.[50]

Banal weeks after Chancellorsville may have seemed endless, but Union soldiers likely pined for a quiet camp soon after the new campaign began. Harsh conditions quickly replaced the feckless days following the May defeat. Regardless of the orders against straggling, some men across the army simply could not keep up due to the humid conditions and dusty air. By the close of June 15, several infantry corps concentrated within a few miles of the Bull Run battlefields. The Sharpshooters camped in old Confederate entrenchments. In the first four days of the march, which included a break of more than a day, the Sharpshooters covered nearly sixty miles.[51]

The march to reach Bull Run seemed especially severe to a Vermont Sharpshooter.

> *The men were already tired and foot-sore, the day was a hot one, with what little air there was stirring in our back, and the dust was very annoying. They say the order was to go to Centreville before camping, but that the medical officers said that it would not do to try to reach there; and we went into quarters for the night about two miles beyond Manassas Junction, only fourteen or fifteen miles from where we started in the morning. I have heard of quite a number who fell dead on the way, while many more were sun-struck, the road being lined with stragglers nearly all the way. I had to fall out myself, but was able to come into camp about dark. If the marching had been done early in the morning and in the evening, devoting the hottest part of the day to rest, the men could have gone twice as far with less fatigue and loss of life; but the leaders do not have to go on foot with fifty pounds weight on their backs.*

Able to call on the optimism abiding in so many frazzled Sharpshooters, the Vermonter extolled the fortitude of his comrades by suggesting, "The boys are in the best of spirits."[52]

After some rest, the men moved to Centreville on June 18. Simple pleasures offered some relief, but disappointment dogged many Sharpshooters. James

Matthews found some satisfaction with a bath in Bull Run. His attempt to supplement army rations failed, however. He found the clams he caught too tough to eat after cooking.[53]

A prolonged break from longer marches occurred after the army approached its namesake river. The time was used to allow stragglers and the sick to catch up as much as possible. Slight camp alterations and picket duty constituted life for the Sharpshooters across the next six days.[54]

Vermonter Thomas H. Brown despaired in Centreville on June 18. He referred to the march as "a hard hot time," with a dearth of water the primary problem. The emotional toll of lost comrades dogged Brown, as well. His letter noted the death of his friend John Meader, who died from the effects of an accidental axe wound to his knee before the men left Falmouth. Meader's widow, a native of Ireland, outlived her husband by half a century.

Four days later, Brown updated his son Horace from a Gum Springs, Virginia camp, using a few sentences to sum up his current status. He recorded the predicted expensive sutler supplies, such as fifty cents for a pound of butter, with that much cheese fifteen cents cheaper. Beloved tobacco cost $1.50 a pound. At such costs, Brown noted he had not tasted butter or cheese since the previous winter. Rains during the march caused a great deal of misery for the men, Brown added. Sharpshooters sometimes walked into fields to stay off muddy roads. Deeply lamenting the loss of his friend Meader, Brown still found the motivation to endure.[55]

On June 24, James Matthews had enough to eat, but the variety of the grub seemed appalling. The Maine man had "plenty of mutton" for breakfast, followed by a lunch of "pig and mutton." Supper amounted to "pig" only.[56]

Ben Calef wrote home on the same day to express his exhaustion. Still not out of Virginia while elements of the Confederate army marched into Pennsylvania, Calef deemed the June ennui "the meanest campaign we have ever had." He very much preferred battle to such horrendous marching.[57]

George Marden also updated the home front on Sharpshooter life during the new campaign. He very much enjoyed the break from marching. He admired the beautiful opening in an oak grove where he sat, because, "There is no dust to wear out the eyes or cause the teeth to grit." With a band playing and plentiful flags flying, "We are on a regular picnic." Marden suggested that the breakfast he enjoyed before starting duty consisted of many wonderful foods, including veal cutlets and fresh milk. As a soldier in the field, however, Marden knew reality could overtake the army. "It is not impossible that a great battle may commence any moment," he bemoaned.[58]

Closing in on Gettysburg

Most of June 25 passed with the men marching to pontoon bridges at Edward's Ferry. Many soldiers did not stop their trek into Maryland until the next overnight period. The day's effort—"perhaps the hardest march of the Sharpshooters' service," Curtis Abbott suggested—likely exceeded thirty miles. Confused orders added to the woe of the Sharpshooters' long day as their guide struggled to find the USSS campground.[59]

Clouds and some drizzly moments dominated central Maryland when the march resumed after only a few hours of rest. At least soldiers enjoyed cooler temperatures. Michigan diarist Henry Bedell jotted notes of rainy moments, as well as long stretches on the road. The grand Maryland landscape received its due when the young corporal wrote, "passed through a fine country," including the mouth of the Monocacy River.[60] Natural beauty could take the minds of some off their enfeebling plight.

USSS staff officer Ben Calef witnessed the difficulties of the march north into Pennsylvania in the summer of 1863. U.S. ARMY HERITAGE AND EDUCATION CENTER

With a diary covering much of 1863, Henry Bedell, Company K, 1st USSS, penned many impressions about his army life. U.S. ARMY HERITAGE AND EDUCATION CENTER

As with their experience the summer before, soldiers in the Army of the Potomac remembered the very positive response from residents of the Old Line State. Again, Frederick's happy citizens filled the streets to express appreciation for their protectors. Seeing cheering people along the roads and receiving water and edibles bolstered the marching warriors, readying them for further trials and the confrontation with their Confederate foes.[61]

A Badger Sharpshooter wished the home folks to know about the kindness of Marylanders. Troops seeing comrades fall dead from heatstroke while on the march felt emboldened thanks to citizens' liberality. "The boys were well treated by the inhabitants," the soldier wrote, "getting most anything they called for from the farmers, who in very many instances refused to take pay for what they so liberally furnished." Near Taneytown, only a few miles from Pennsylvania, Rudolf Aschmann, officer in Company A, 1st USSS, remembered one kind farmer who had parked his wagon along the line of march. The Marylander had bread, cakes, bacon, honey (an especially loved treat for Civil War soldiers), and other wonderful victuals.[62]

The Confederates scattered across the south-central part of the state, including a force preparing to invest the state capital of Harrisburg. General Hooker continued to press on, but then a bombshell landed, a dispute with Washington about control of the Harpers Ferry garrison. Bitterness between the army commander and general-in-chief Halleck led Hooker to offer his resignation, which President Lincoln promptly accepted. George Meade, junior in seniority as a major general to several other corps commanders, became the army's leader.[63] Meade was the fourth commander of the army in eight months.

Cavalry and infantry continued advancing as Meade attempted to balance competing demands in his orders from Halleck. The Army of the Potomac was required to turn back Lee while also protecting Baltimore and Washington. Major General John Reynolds, one general senior to the new commander who respected Meade as his chief, oversaw the westernmost Union force, including three corps of infantry.

The Sharpshooters and all of their comrades under Reynolds marched into Pennsylvania from camps in Emmitsburg, Maryland. Early on July 1, Union cavalry and infantry confronted the Confederate advance west of Gettysburg. A valiant stand by two cavalry brigades, as well as the First and Eleventh Corps, proved vital to the army's ability to hold the town as a spot to rally the entire army.[64]

Third Corps men moved up across the afternoon and evening of the opening day of July. Too late to take part in the engagement, which led to a Union retreat without the Confederates gaining the high ground east and south of town, the Sharpshooters strained once again under the demands of a military march. William Ripley estimated the afternoon trek to the fields immediately south of Gettysburg amounted to ten miles, with a faster pace especially difficult. The Sharpshooters left Emmitsburg at 4 p.m., arriving on the battlefield shortly before dark.[65]

Curtis Abbott recalled the fading daylight casting long shadows across the fields south of Gettysburg. Gazing east of the road, the Vermonter remembered being able to discern two hills that would be prominent in American military lore: Big Round Top and Little Round Top. After a short rest, the Sharpshooters moved closer to town, nearing Cemetery Hill, the spot where retreating Union forces coalesced earlier in the afternoon.[66]

Berdan's USSS regiments included nearly five hundred men when arriving at Gettysburg. The 1st Sharpshooters counted almost three hundred, with Homer Stoughton's eight companies fielding less than two hundred. At the start of the new month, Company A, 2nd USSS faced the possibility of a major battle with forty-two men in the ranks, two more than the June 1 total. This surprisingly good net addition—the highest total to open a month the Minnesotans would have in the rest of their history—honors the men who endured such a grueling march. Hundreds across the army fell behind on any given day, with some Sharpshooters—including a Wisconsin officer—left in Frederick hospitals due to the torrid pace.[67]

While Sharpshooters marched to their Pennsylvania destiny, others fought for their lives in hospitals, with some losing their final battle. Suffering from respiratory problems and away from the 2nd USSS for months, Sgt. William Graham, Company B, had been admitted to a Baltimore hospital on June 19. As both lungs filled with fluid, pneumonia caused his demise. Graham died in Baltimore on June 30, with burial in Philadelphia.[68]

Those in the ranks and able to handle the journey from Stoneman's Switch proved themselves the stoutest of American warriors. The men in green trying to gain a good night's rest at Gettysburg steeled themselves for their participation in what remains the largest battle to ever occur in the Western Hemisphere.

Berdan's Reconnaissance

Robert E. Lee expended a great deal of thought in the overnight period and into the morning of July 2 before deciding on a plan for the second day of battle at Gettysburg. Lee wished to roll up Meade's left flank, an area including Birney's Division. Lee's orders sent two divisions of the Confederate First Corps under James Longstreet to the southern terminus of the army. The vision focused on moving up the Emmitsburg Road to push aside any Union units. Longstreet would then occupy the ground between the parallel heights known as Seminary Ridge and Cemetery Ridge.[69]

Meade, seeing the advantages of remaining on the defensive east and south of Gettysburg, only needed to hold what he already possessed. Understanding enemy plans required scouting and keen eyes to the west. Cavalry often performed such a role, but discussions during the morning led senior officers in the Third Corps to plan a reconnaissance with a small number of foot soldiers. Colonel Berdan would lead the effort, which brought on a small but highly memorable clash as morning turned to afternoon.

The Union scouting party included four companies of the 1st USSS (D, E, F, and I), a total of one hundred marksmen. Brigade comrades in the 3rd Maine joined the effort. The entire force likely did not number more than three hundred men. Heading out at about 11:30 a.m. based on orders from Major General Birney, Berdan would report, "I moved down the Emmitsburg road some distance beyond our extreme left and deployed the sharpshooters in a line running nearly east and west, and moved forward in a northerly direction parallel with" the road.[70]

Hours before Longstreet's assault force filled in farther to the south, Cadmus Wilcox commanded a brigade of Alabamians on Lee's right flank. The Southerners moved south, setting the stage for a bloody fight with Berdan. The 11th Alabama, marching in open ground, moved ahead of the regiment on its right, the 10th Alabama. As a result, the 11th Regiment walked into an ambush. Sharpshooters waited to unleash their shots until the Alabamians exposed their flank. As Wilcox reported, the 11th "received a heavy volley of musketry on its right flank and rear from the enemy, concealed behind ledges of rock and trees."[71] The closing phrase of Wilcox's report complimented the trained USSS, who preferred to allow terrain to determine firing positions. The Sharpshooters certainly benefited from the insufficient work of the 11th Alabama's skirmish company.

The initial rounds of fire likely came exclusively from the Sharpshooters, as the 3rd Maine Infantry trailed the marksmen. Exuberant with success in the opening moments, the Sharpshooters moved forward, dropping a mounted Confederate officer and several enemy soldiers. Of the Southern warriors in the front of Wilcox's force, a Vermonter would recall, "I did not see a man of this skirmish line escape."[72] This was, unfortunately, the best moment of the reconnaissance for the Sharpshooters.

Berdan likely wished the infantry support had moved up in the same line as the USSS, because the 10th Alabama quickly responded to assist the surprised troops in the 11th Regiment. A brisk engagement between the opposing units took place on either side of noon. The Maine infantry "supported us handsomely," Charles Buchanan, a New York Sharpshooter, recalled in an 1889 speech dedicating the USSS monument on the field. The Northerners needed to support each other, as Buchanan added, because "our skirmish firing was met by volleys of rebel infantry."[73]

With their position in the front of the advance, USSS members used trees and rocks to bolster their defensive position. Spread out in a skirmish line like the Sharpshooters, the Maine men suffered due to the more open ground they held. The topography created the difficult tactical situation of the two Union regiments seemingly merging into one another. As 3rd Maine commander Col. Moses Lakeman lamented in his report, his troops "filled the intervals" between the Sharpshooters. The "decided disadvantage" of the 3rd Maine's position became more obvious as the Alabamians showed no interest in leaving their ground.[74]

Perhaps after less than twenty minutes of fighting, Berdan ordered a necessary retreat. Some suggest the suspected cowardice of the Chief of Sharpshooters might have played into the decision to abandon the advance, but Berdan acted with reasonable motives. His soldiers were not going to dominate the moment against an entire Confederate brigade. Moving back to the east, Berdan reported the presence of the enemy, leading to a cascade of decisions that altered the course of the entire battle.[75]

Allegations and Lies about the Reconnaissance

Years after the war, a Maine newspaper labeled Berdan's reconnaissance "a most audacious performance." The words seem true, and the Sharpshooters, with their Maine comrades, did prove that a large number of Confederates stood west of the Emmitsburg Road by noon. The teamwork the two regiments performed to confront Wilcox's Brigade bolstered the honor of both the 1st USSS and 3rd Maine.[76] Unfortunately, harsh words and downright lies clouded the historical record for decades after the fateful work against the Alabamians.

Colonel Lakeman and some in the 3rd Maine questioned Berdan's leadership during the encounter west of the Emmitsburg Road. Lakeman grew so perturbed he suggested Berdan did not command the reconnaissance. The Maine officer may have felt as if he had control over the expedition. Disturbed by Lakeman's words, Berdan wrote the colonel soon after learning of their difference of opinion. Lakeman refused to retract his contention of being in charge of the July 2 foray.[77]

Whether motivated by Lakeman's canard, or simply trying to buttress his own large ego, Berdan found an opportunity to falsely elevate the importance of the July 2 reconnaissance. In an 1888 speech, Berdan made ridiculous statements about the midday clash with Wilcox. Many people, including Confederate General Longstreet, echoed Berdan's sentiments, creating a poorly reasoned and historically inaccurate history of the small engagement on the battle's second day.

Admitting his men fought Wilcox's troops, who were not even assigned to Longstreet, Berdan's speech stressed the view that the reconnaissance engaged the large Confederate flanking force. Berdan also suggested great prescience in fighting at the key moment to ensure the Confederates would not capture the Round Tops, central to holding the Union left. In another address, Berdan suggested he faced "the most critical moment of my life" during the reconnaissance. Buttressed by an "all-inspiring feeling of loyalty to the Union," Berdan would stay and fight. He stood ready to sacrifice all the men under him west of the Emmitsburg Road to buy time for more Union troops to bolster the threatened flank.[78]

These statements made no logical sense. Berdan did not stay long west of the road. He showed no penchant for sacrificing three hundred men at the time due to the quick retreat he ordered. Also, his reports at the time showed no effort to inflate the reconnaissance by suggesting his men halted an entire enemy corps. Berdan's speeches and writings to that effect decades later amounted to the visions of an older man looking to glorify his own leadership. Berdan was not the savior of Little Round Top. Many other brave men who did not live through the day, or who died of wounds soon after, deserve such fame as their final shroud.[79]

Unfortunately, others agreed with Berdan at the expense of historical truth. Charles Stevens's history of the USSS turns the small band under Berdan into the seminal soldiers of the entire war.

> *The heroic deeds of Leonidas and his 300 Spartans, betrayed and slaughtered by the Persian hosts, has for ages been recounted in verse and story. But no greater display of heroism, no more self-sacrificing spirit of patriotism can be cited in the annals of war, than was this courageous attack of Berdan's 300 on the marching columns of 30,000 foes. And surely, it may be fairly said to be a turning point in the Rebellion.*[80]

The boldness and fortitude of the USSS cannot be doubted, but Stevens's grandiose wording constitutes the most idiotic statement related to the Sharpshooters ever printed. Like Berdan, Stevens admitted Wilcox's men were attached to A. P. Hill's Corps. At the time of the brawl between Berdan and Wilcox, Longstreet's men were miles away. That fact alone should have led a regimental historian to doubt the veracity of any claim that the USSS and two hundred men from Maine delayed Longstreet.

Other Sharpshooters perpetuated an incorrect view of the midday fight. Interestingly, one marksman's praise of Berdan as the one who saved the day at Gettysburg noted the lack of faith across the USSS in their leader before the reconnaissance. At the time the four companies moved out, Lewis Allen remembered, the one hundred Sharpshooters doubted Berdan's motives. "He was ambitious to exchange the eagle he wore for a star," Allen opined. After the midday battle, "the few of us who came out alive believed that our slaughtered comrades had been offered as a sacrifice" to Berdan's covetous dream of becoming a general. The version of history Berdan hawked led Allen to change his mind, the letter continued.[81]

Contemptuous of Berdan—and unafraid of any repercussions—Caspar Trepp wrote harsh words about the decisions made as the reconnaissance advanced. Because the band of three hundred marched down the Emmitsburg Road, Trepp reported how the Confederates could easily see the blue and green soldiers moving into position west of the road. As Trepp explained, "All this time we were marching or halting in plain view of the enemy. For this violation of rules of secret expeditions, we paid dearly."[82] One need not agree with Trepp to understand the plight of the Union reconnaissance. The small group was heavily outnumbered, unable to accomplish much besides discerning the presence of the enemy well south of the Union's Third Corps line.

Some may suggest Trepp's definitiveness on the matter reflected his lack of respect for Berdan, because the colonel's failure to keep his band concealed did not change much. The 11th Alabama did not expect to be hit by the Sharpshooters at the moment of first contact. Moreover, exactly how the marksmen and Maine soldiers could have moved to and beyond the road without being at all detected can be questioned.

Nonetheless, Trepp accurately noted the cost of the endeavor. Whatever Berdan's attempts to elevate the reconnaissance, battle losses cannot be sugarcoated. Overall, the fight with Wilcox inflicted more than sixty Union casualties, including nineteen Sharpshooters hit, five of whom sustained mortal injuries.[83]

Capt. Charles McLean, the highest-ranking fatality, led Company D on Berdan's jaunt. Only twenty-five years old, McLean had a leg amputated after being taken prisoner, then lost his life on July 4. The young officer earned many friends and much respect during his time with the USSS. Having received a promotion to lieutenant in November, John Hetherington rose to the vacant captaincy in the New York company.

Smith Haight was another member of the company to die in action during the reconnaissance. One seriously wounded New Yorker, Sgt. Edwin Nelson, rebounded to return to his comrades for the rest of their service.[84]

Second Lt. George Sheldon, Company I, died on the field, with original burial near where he fell, by a large live oak tree. Later, Sheldon's body was taken to Gettysburg's new national cemetery. Sheldon originally enrolled in Company C, transferring to his new command in February 1863 after his promotion. In describing Sheldon, Ed Wilson remembered, "a more manly young fellow never wore shoulder-straps." The deceased had been "a most promising young officer."[85]

A New Hampshire Sharpshooter nearly thirty-nine years old, Charles Thatcher lost his life to a wound sustained on July 2. Dying nearly three weeks later in Gettysburg, he rests at the national cemetery in town President Lincoln would dedicate the following autumn. Although a native of the Granite State, Abraham Cooper fell as part of the Vermont company. His remains returned to New England, where he rests at Pine Grove Cemetery, Hillsdale, New Hampshire.[86]

Once again, a fight for the USSS led to some men struggling for many months in hospitals before returning home with a discharge. Company F's George Wooley, who had enlisted in September 1861, lost an arm at Gettysburg. Facing tough times in a hospital, Wooley's discharge would not occur until January 1864.[87]

Both Sides Move to Battle

The four marksmen companies on Berdan's foray seemed to have retreated toward the Union center, essentially unengaged for the rest of the momentous day. After Berdan's reconnaissance, however, much bloodshed remained across a wide front on July 2. Hard work for fourteen other companies and most of Meade's army beckoned.

As they faced attacking divisions from all three of Lee's large corps, George Meade's soldiers stood tall. Topography created an incredibly strong defensive position for the Army of the Potomac at Gettysburg. Unfortunately, the marksmen should not have been where they were when Confederate attacks began. As originally ordered, Third Corps commander Dan Sickles manned a line on Cemetery Ridge from Little Round Top to the north, eventually reaching the left of the Second Corps. In perhaps the most controversial decision of the battle, Sickles pushed his men to the west, clearly not meeting the intent of Meade's order. Despite a faulty understanding of Longstreet's location, Sickles's advance rested partially on a concern that Berdan's reconnaissance had highlighted the danger of looming Confederates to the south.

The new Third Corps position did have the merit of occupying higher ground around a peach orchard along the Emmitsburg Road. Yet, the corps stood isolated after the western move, with both flanks unprotected. In a grand debate over the decision for decades after the war, Sickles and others showed a penchant for exaggerating and lying just like Berdan. Rightfully so, historians generally support Meade rather than Sickles.[88]

Did Meade leave too much discretion for Sickles, trusting a subordinate in whom he did not have much confidence? With his mind fully occupied as leader of the army, perhaps the commanding general cannot be blamed for failing to ensure Sickles complied with the directives of headquarters about the Third Corps line on July 2. A modern article does a good job of clearing Meade of negligence on the matter.[89] Nonetheless, a better outcome was possible. Meade did not deserve the odium Sickles heaped on him after the war, but the army commander could have done more to perfect the disposition of Union forces on the left before Longstreet's attack.

Like all other times in their history, the Sharpshooters lacked control over the decisions of generals. Ideally, the marksmen would have stood united with their Third Corps comrades across a mile of Cemetery Ridge, with firmly protected flanks and plenty of nearby support. Instead, USSS warriors again had to make the best of their circumstances. By the time John Bell Hood's Confederate division moved ahead with a major attack at 4 p.m., the 2nd Sharpshooters held the far left of the entire army, posted away from supporting infantry. The marksmen stood west of the Round Tops in an effort to delay any enemy infantry looking to take control of the Union army's southern flank.[90]

With an array of difficulties confronting Lee as he planned the attack, the most problematic was the absence of some troops under Longstreet. George Pickett's Virginians would not reach the field in time to participate in the bloodletting. Evander Law's regiments, however, would be central to the attack. Those tough soldiers started July 2 about twenty-five miles away from where they would hit the line of the 2nd Sharpshooters. A rapid march brought the brigade to Longstreet's main encampment west of town by about noon. From there, several miles of a wayward march finally brought Hood's entire division, with Law's men in the vanguard, to a position along the Emmitsburg Road. The Round Tops stood tall to the east.[91]

Whatever reasonable doubts existed about Sickles's move to the road, the surprise the Third Corps' advance inflicted on Confederate leaders charged with opening the attack served the Union cause well. General Hood and his officers did not expect to see Union infantry to their immediate north along the grove known to history as *the* Peach Orchard. The astonishment Confederate leaders experienced on seeing a large number of Union troops in an unexpected area temporarily masked the error Sickles made in choosing a position supported only by fruit trees.

Although the highest ground in the vicinity stood behind Homer Stoughton and his eight companies, the 2nd Sharpshooters manned good positions west of Big Round Top. Still, the area the Sharpshooters and Birney's Division had to defend stretched far too long for the number of men available. As General Longstreet wrote, Birney formed "a broken line" from the Peach Orchard well to the southeast in the valley bordering the Round Tops, including the area of Plum Run. In his statement on Birney's position, Longstreet used words to detail one advantage the 2nd Sharpshooters would possess in the struggle. Hood's men would attack across difficult ground "obstructed by boulders."[92] Such natural features offered trained marksmen good places to shoot while disrupting an orderly Confederate advance.

As a Third Corps division commander, David Birney witnessed much bravery from the USSS at Chancellorsville and Gettysburg. LIBRARY OF CONGRESS

Withered Southern optimism translated to strong initial advantages for Stoughton's men and other defenders near the Round Tops and on undulations such as Houck's Ridge, the spot General Ward selected for much of his brigade. Evander Law remembered the undesirable situation in an article after the war. "The position occupied by the Federal left wing in front of us," Law suggested, "was now fully disclosed to view, and it was certainly one of the most formidable it had ever been the fortune of any troops to confront." He considered Big Round Top "a huge sentinel guarding the Federal left flank." Law also mentioned the copious woodlots, which invariably diminished an attacking column's ability to see a sufficient distance.[93] Due to the trees and ground, Law did not know that some of the best marksmen mustered into Union service stood between the Confederate lines and the heights farther east.

To comply with Lee's literal orders, Longstreet, Hood, Law, and other senior Confederates should have ignored the Round Tops. The attack was to advance up the Emmitsburg Road, but so much had changed since Lee received the morning reports used to generate the July 2 plan. The looming Confederate divisions could overwhelm the Peach Orchard, but besting Sickles would disrupt Lee's timing, a vital element of the attack because multiple corps had to be coordinated in the effort to strike the Union line. Besides, leaving an unknown number of Northerners to the right and rear risked a counterattack as Longstreet's brigades moved north. With so much time of the day already gone, the necessity of an attack overwhelmed all other considerations, regardless of how confused Confederate regimental commanders and others had become about their true goal.[94]

The impulse drawing Confederate brigades east, away from Lee's intended path, plunged thousands of some of the greatest troops any Southern army fielded during the war toward Homer Stoughton and his 170 marksmen in the 2nd USSS.

Confusion about the Initial 2nd USSS Position

Pinpointing the location of the 2nd USSS at the start of Hood's attack requires some historical sleuthing due to the lack of agreement across both contemporary and modern sources. Several maps place the line in multiple places hundreds of yards apart. Eyewitnesses created confusion by not offering enough clarity on the matter. Historians can lament but not condemn the Sharpshooters for failure to provide solid answers to future generations. They had far too many more pressing items to consider that afternoon.[95]

Pursuant to Major Stoughton's report, his men moved multiple times in the hours before Hood's line appeared to the west. As the far left of the army, the eight companies held the important goal of covering Plum Run Valley, the ground immediately north and west of the Round Tops. After their morning placements, the 2nd USSS received orders from General Ward to advance at around 2 p.m. In the Green Mountain officer's report produced less than a month later, Stoughton

> *moved forward to a brook some 200 yards beyond a second cross-road running perpendicular to the Emmitsburg pike, and intersecting with it in front of Sugar Loaf hill [Big Round Top]. I sent forward scouts to reconnoiter the ground. I then rode out perhaps the distance of half a mile, and discovered the enemy's skirmishers advancing on my right, which, being unsupported by any connection with skirmishers on my right, I was compelled to withdraw to protect my flank. In this position we had but little time to wait. The enemy's skirmishers advanced to the top of the hill in our front, and immediately after they placed a battery directly in our front, and being too far for our range, I*

sent forward a few men under cover of woods on the left, and silenced one piece nearest us.[96]

How close did the marksmen stand from Hood's two brigades when the attack opened? Were Stoughton's eight companies together in a single line? Definitive answers to these questions cannot be provided, but an analysis of sources offers some clarity. The modern 2nd USSS history places a line of skirmishers from north to south at the Bushman Farm, with the right flank near the spot of Company D's monument. This is the closest to the brigades of Law and Robertson that the USSS could have stood at the opening of the attack, perhaps 275 yards. Conversely, an excellent account of Law's Brigade at Gettysburg puts the eight USSS companies along Plum Run nearly at the base of Big Round Top. Stoughton's men so far east would have stood well over half a mile away from Hood's front line. That seems too far from the opening attack.

One reason for some authors preferring the Bushman line could have been Stoughton's scouting mission earlier in the day that ventured to the Emmitsburg Road. The Maine monument's placement argues for this line, as well, but logic points to a line farther east, for multiple reasons. First, Stoughton noted the Confederate battery was too far for the Sharpshooters to target. Second, the Sharpshooters lacked superior lines of sight so close to Law and Robertson due to the woods that partially concealed the Southerners. Third, why would Stoughton want his small band so far to the west when his men could hit targets twice as distant in a line much closer to the Round Tops?

Most persuasively, the relatively low number of casualties to the Confederate artillery Stoughton mentioned suggests the cannoneers were not pressed hard by elite shots trained to damage those manning the big guns. A modern and very detailed review of unit strength and loss at Gettysburg places 260 cannoneers in a pair of batteries on either side of Hood's front two brigades. These units offered great targets for the USSS, but the batteries combined for only nine casualties at Gettysburg, with Union counterbattery fire likely accounting for some of the wounds. If the USSS originally stood relatively close to the cannons, far more artillerists should have fallen, even when fire from Stoughton's companies led Confederates to abandon the big guns for a time.[97]

Modern articles present the best option for the spot of the opening stand of the 2nd USSS. At this location, the Sharpshooters stood on the rocky and uneven ground not far west of the Slyder House, with some marksmen positioned to the north of the family's home. Using rocks for cover, the Sharpshooters on such a line had better lines of sight while the distance from Law and Robertson diminished risk from infantry fire early in the Confederate attack. A

Minnesota historian listed six hundred yards between the antagonists at the 4 p.m. opening of Hood's charge, which would have placed the USSS companies on the broken earth connecting the Bushman and Slyder properties. Moreover, the observant Curtis Abbott, Company H, remembered a line not far west of the Slyder structure. In addition to the rugged ground, a short rock wall topped with rails, bordering the north-south lane below the house, offered the men some good protection.[98]

Sharpshooters against the Tide

Wherever the 2nd USSS took positions on the afternoon of July 2, no doubt can exist about the utility of their bold effort to slow Hood's opening attack. As Law moved out, his fellow brigade commander to the immediate north grew quite confused. Jerome Robertson, leading Hood's old Texas Brigade, had orders to keep his left on the Emmitsburg Road as his right connected to Law's line. With Law fixated on the Round Tops, his Alabamians bolted east from the road, heading straight for Stoughton's marksmen. This naturally created a gap between the two leading Confederate brigades, prohibiting a more coordinated attack. In his battle report and in multiple letters after the war, Robertson expressed his befuddlement. The mutually exclusive orders "caused some separation of my regiments," the flustered general reported, "which was remedied as promptly as the numerous stone and rail fences that intersected the field through which we were advancing would allow."

Facing enough problems due to the contradictory orders and tough ground, Robertson remembered a ferocious Union response to the opening of Hood's assault. A proficient skirmish line covered the entire front of Robertson's soldiers. Frequent bursts from each Sharps Rifle brought death and confusion to Law and Robertson's early advance.[99]

Still, Southern warriors "firing and yelling like demons" seemed very determined on this day. With the valley lower than the road, Confederates moved downhill slightly as they faced the opening fire from Stoughton's line. Artillery rounds, mainly from a battery on Houck's Ridge, formed another indelible memory of the Union's resistance. Great thirst plagued many Confederates in Hood's line due to the especially long day for Law's men, as well as the lack of full canteens. Although adding to their fatigue, several officers dismounted to seem less visible to the Sharpshooters.[100]

More than thirty-five years after the harrowing moments, an Alabamian delivered a speech about how he and his comrades faced the Sharps Rifle fire of the 2nd USSS.

The men sprang forward as if at a game of ball. The air was full of sound. A long line of Federal skirmishers, protected by a stone wall, immediately opened fire. Grape and canister from the Federal battery hurtled over us as we descended the hill into the valley. We rushed through our own battery while it was firing and receiving the fire from the enemy's guns. Men were falling, stricken to death. . . . The younger officers made themselves conspicuous by rushing to the front, commanding and urging the men to come on, while Adjutant General Terrell was doing what he could to restrain the impetuosity of the Fourth Alabama, calling on the men to observe the Fifth Texas. . . . Immediately to the right, Taylor Darwin, Orderly Sergeant of Company I, suddenly stopped, quivered, and sank to the earth dead, a ball having passed through his brain. There was Rube Franks, of the same company, just returned from his home in Alabama, his new uniform bright with color. . . . He shortly afterwards met the fatal shot.[101]

While inflicting pain and death against their enemy, a small number of even the best marksmen could not stand for long. Dyer Pettijohn, a Minnesotan serving on skirmish line duty as the attack opened, wrote that a group of Confederates moved stealthily on the right of Stoughton's men. The enemy escaped detection until the Southerners captured multiple Sharpshooters, including Pettijohn, who was doomed to the status of prisoner for the rest of the war.[102]

The bulk of Stoughton's men were able to get away. The marksmen soon scattered as hundreds of Confederates appeared able to flank the 2nd Regiment from the north. William Oates, leading his 15th Alabama from the center of Law's early front, remembered, "When crossing the little run, we received the first fire from the Federal infantry, posted behind a stone fence near the foot of Round Top mountain." The fire Robertson found rather problematic did not faze Oates horribly. He continued, "Our line did not halt, but pressing forward drove our enemy from the fence and up the side of the mountain." Law's writings seconded the relative ease with which Confederates dislodged the Sharpshooters.[103]

Some Sharpshooters stood at their initial position longer than others. Curtis Abbott wrote of the brave and respected Captain Buxton, on the right of the Company H line, calling for a retreat. Men on both sides of Buxton started to fall back, destined for a climb up Big Round Top. Abbott also saw some green-clad soldiers, who he deemed "the bull-dogs of the line" staying to send one last round at the looming foe. These more stubborn Sharpshooters then were "crowded in before the bayonets of the on-coming host."[104]

Stoughton's men, originally in a line likely more than a half-mile long, resisted well at the early stage of the fight, but the varying impact of their fire, as

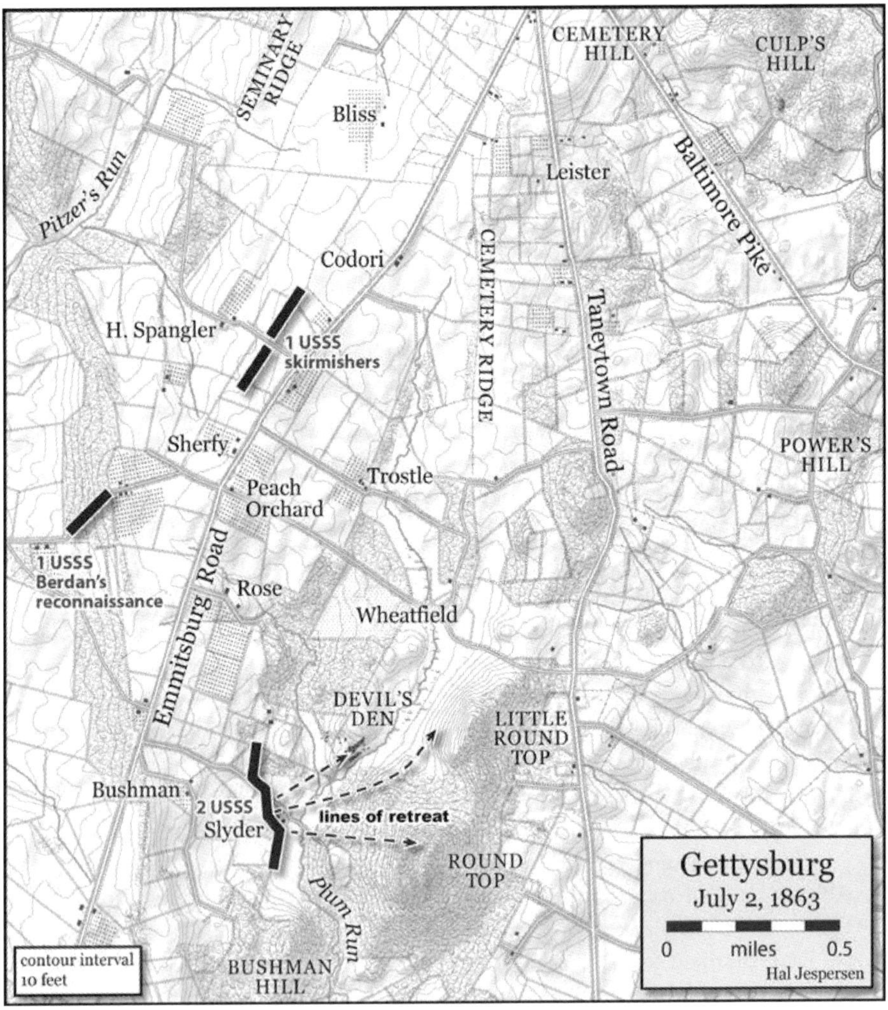

CEMETERY HILL
CULP'S HILL
SEMINARY RIDGE
Bliss
Leister
Baltimore Pike
Pitzer's Run
Codori
CEMETERY RIDGE
Taneytown Road
H. Spangler
1 USSS skirmishers
Sherfy
Trostle
POWER'S HILL
Peach Orchard
1 USSS Berdan's reconnaissance
Emmitsburg Road
Rose
Wheatfield
DEVIL'S DEN
LITTLE ROUND TOP
Bushman
2 USSS Slyder
lines of retreat
ROUND TOP
Plum Run
BUSHMAN HILL
contour interval 10 feet
Gettysburg
July 2, 1863
0 miles 0.5
Hal Jespersen

Confederates recalled, should not be a surprise. The leading two Confederate brigades included about 3,700 men. Accepting the short period of initial resistance as the Confederates overlapped the flanks of his line, Stoughton reported, "The Second Regiment did splendid execution." Wyman White wrote of the extensive and effective fire from his comrades in green coats. Each Confederate to fall meant one less to press those defending ground closer to or on the Round Tops.[105]

Texan John West remembered a very brutal few hours near the middle of Robertson's line. Artillery fire and the Sharpshooters had presented the most telling resistance to the advance. Shells tore through the Confederates even before the infantry moved east. In updating his son on the hail of cannon fire and Sharps Rifle rounds, he lamented, "I felt all the time as if I would never see you and little sister again." Tough work continued for the troops in Hood's front brigades as they progressed east. Dealing with the streams, fences, and terrain proved quite enervating, especially later because "Yankee sharpshooters were on the higher mountains, so as to have fairer shots at our officers."[106]

West pointed to the most important service any USSS companies provided at Gettysburg. Although Stoughton's small band could not stop the enemy's resolute regiments, their true effectiveness came soon after the 2nd USSS scattered in front of Hood's bold advance. Heading in different directions, some companies moved to Houck's Ridge, offering support to elements of Ward's line. Others knew Big Round Top offered a great defensive position. Using rocks, trees, and the hill, additional fire created a great deal of confusion for Confederate officers.

A vital decision William Oates made dramatically diminished Law's striking power when the brigade needed every possible rifle to continue eastward. With the USSS appearing in multiple positions, the Alabamians then received fire on their right flank. Oates obviously worried about the problems that could befall his men if he pressed east without confronting elements of the 2nd USSS to the south. After a second volley from Sharpshooters hit Oates's lieutenant colonel Isaac Feagin, costing him a leg, Oates changed course, giving chase to those Sharpshooters on the high hill. This violated Oates's order from Law to head to Little Round Top.[107] Writing a very friendly letter to Stoughton a quarter century later, Oates expressed much respect for the USSS. Heading to his right, Oates remembered,

> *The Forty-seventh Alabama swung with me. My advance dislodged you, but as you fell back up the south front of [Big] Round Top, you kept up a lively fire on my advancing line, which returned it but without much effectiveness, as your men, being trained sharpshooters and skirmishers, kept well under*

After fighting in the valley to the west, several members of the 2nd USSS found their way to either Little Round Top (left) or Big Round Top on the battlefield at Gettysburg. LIBRARY OF CONGRESS

> *cover, taking advantage of the boulders which line the mountain side. When over half-way up your fire ceased, and henceforth to the top I did not see one of your men.*[108]

Knowing they had drawn two Confederate regiments away from the main attack, the marksmen on the big hill had no reason to confront a Confederate force of vastly superior numbers. The exact destinations of each Sharpshooter who went up Big Round Top cannot be known, but some may have fled south, away from the action. Those USSS members going in the right direction had more service to offer pressed comrades.

Further Resistance from the 2nd USSS

Hobart Ward's main line, in a good spot along Houck's Ridge, struggled against Hood's front line and the supporting brigade of Georgians under Henry Benning. Meanwhile, a Fifth Corps brigade under Col. Strong Vincent began manning the southern slope of Little Round Top as a means to fortify the Union left. Some Sharpshooters found their way to assist Ward or Vincent.

In a post-battle report, a lieutenant from the 4th Maine Infantry wrote, "Some of the Second U.S. Sharpshooters fell back through our line, and reported the enemy advancing a column on the hill to flank us, at the same time a few shots of the enemy were fired on our flank." The exact number of Sharpshooters assisting Ward on Houck's Ridge remains unknown, but they undoubtedly contributed some shots against the Confederates under Law, Robertson, and Benning. Using the rocks of Devil's Den as protection likely became a priority for the USSS.[109]

Sharpshooters proved able to concentrate their fire, sometimes reaching counterproductive levels of redundancy in their shooting. With a hot day and facing a tough fight, many Confederates paused at Plum Run to have some water. A Texan officer tied his cool and wet bandana around his head before continuing east. The unfortunate Lone Star lieutenant likely did not have time to think about the danger of making a colorful target for some of the North's best shots. When the officer's body was later recovered, Confederates counted eleven bullet holes in the blood-soaked bandana.[110]

Swarming Confederates pushed Ward's men back after a spirited brawl for the possession of Houck's Ridge. A key Southern target became a New York battery under Capt. James Smith, which placed four guns forward, with two to the left of the infantry line. A struggle of epic and tragic proportions erupted. Through the maelstrom, a Texan remembered, "On we went, yelling and whooping." Colonel Elijah Walker, 4th Maine, fell with a wound during the desperate minutes. With USSS assistance, the Mainers repelled an attack on the brigade's left shortly before Confederate frontal assaults finally pushed through to capture part of Smith's battery.[111]

The costly conquest of the ridge and control over some cannon proved a mixed blessing for certain Southerners. Sharpshooters still on Big Round Top ensured not all of the enemy lived long to celebrate the capture of the Union guns so damaging to Hood's advance across Plum Run Valley. As Curtis Abbott remembered of the Confederates at the captured cannons, "Many who came to admire them remained to sprinkle them with their blood, for the Sharpshooters on the slope of Round Top, falling back to avoid capture, within easy range dealt the full measure of the penalty." The distance separating the USSS members on Big Round Top and Confederates falling at the captured cannons likely exceeded a half-mile.[112]

A small group of green-clad soldiers assisted farther east as the 20th Maine famously fought to keep Confederates from overwhelming the left flank of Vincent's Brigade. Captain Walter Morrill, Company B of the 20th Maine, reported how about fifteen Sharpshooters, very likely Company B, 2nd USSS, made their way to Little Round Top. Morrill used these determined marksmen as part of his command. Detached from the rest of the 20th Maine, these men protected ground farther east than the main line of Vincent's infantry. The small band's position included a stone wall, contributing to the element of surprise.[113]

After their sojourn on Big Round Top, Williams Oates and his two regiments pushed to attack the 20th Maine as more Confederates pressed Vincent's three other regiments. Morrill's group would blast the unsuspecting right flank of the Alabamians moving to attack Vincent's men. Plenty of rocks covered ground between the antagonists. Thick bushes and other biomass inhibited vision for the defenders. Captain Morrill admitted to an infantryman comrade the difficulty of seeing the enemy from the location of his company and the attached USSS members. Nonetheless, several attempts to take the hill met firm resistance. After the brigade commander fell to Confederate fire, a determined charge from the left of Vincent's line would include Morrill and the USSS contingent posted at a great spot to strike the right and rear of the Alabamians.[114]

The impetuousness of the rush against Oates proved decisive. Able to blow through Stoughton's first line of defense and take Houck's Ridge, Hood's Division could not breach Little Round Top. At key locations during the attack, members of the 2nd USSS stood tall alone or with infantrymen to unleash withering volleys into the enemy. The Confederates "were too much worn out and exhausted" to prevail, a Lone Star warrior opined. Besides, Union fire flew "as thick as hail, and we were compelled to get behind the rocks and trees to save ourselves."[115]

The Cost and Benefits of Stoughton's Stand

Although the bulk of Stoughton's forty-three casualties at Gettysburg fell on July 2, somehow only two members of the 2nd Sharpshooters—Minnesotan John O. Dolson and Company F's Henry Richards—died from the effects of wounds. The lives sacrificed across Ward's entire brigade translated to time for other Union troops to man defensive positions on Little Round Top and other targets of Confederate firepower that afternoon. With Lee's army extended across a disjointed line for miles, coordinating Longstreet's effort with attacks to the north proved far too difficult, even for a commander of Lee's talents.

John Dolson's story includes a major spelling error leading to transportation of his body to North Carolina after he died at a Union hospital two months after Gettysburg. He had the misfortune of being listed as the same age as a Tar Heel soldier from the state's 2nd Regiment named John O. Dobson. A team of dedicated historians in the twenty-first century discovered the error after reviewing a range of records, including many very difficult to read. Dolson was given a new marker and stone at his gravesite in Raleigh, North Carolina.[116]

Henry Richards, who died on an amputating table, had earned respect from his comrades with a kind heart and reserved manner. Before leaving for war, Richards, thirty-nine, had planted trees along the road leading to the cemetery in which he would be buried in Portsmouth, New Hampshire. The street was renamed Richards Avenue to honor the lost patriot.[117]

Richards had demonstrated great promise before the war, exhibiting traits that led to an offer of an officer's commission. Instead, the quiet and devoted New Hampshire warrior mustered in as a private in his company. He suggested the fate of an enlisted man suited him better, especially because of the fine rifle he would undoubtedly get to wield as a member of the USSS.[118]

All of the sacrifice at Gettysburg came with a feeling of great accomplishment in USSS ranks. A wounded Vermonter suggested the men in green did much to dictate the outcome on July 2, and therefore the final success of Union arms. Without the 2nd Sharpshooters, as Manilus Holbrook proudly wrote, "history might have recorded a different ending of that the greatest of all battles."[119]

Confederates could share Holbrook's sentiment after a protracted fight with elements of the USSS. If compliments from the enemy offer the most respectful honor to fallen soldiers, the Sharpshooters lost defending Plum Run Valley rest quite satisfied. In his letter to Homer Stoughton, Williams Oates lavished great praise on the Sharpshooters for their stout defense. Oates outlined how the USSS inflicted a large number of casualties in the two Alabama regiments he oversaw.

> *The great service which you and your command did was, first, in changing my direction, and in drawing my regiment and the Forty-seventh Alabama away from the point of attack. You drew off and delayed this force . . . from falling on Vincent and the Union left at the same time of the attack of Law's other three regiments, the Texas and two Georgia brigades in front, and but for this service on your part I am confident we would have swept away the Union line and have captured Little Round Top, which would have won the battle for us. Again, when Vincent had fallen and I was within 150 yards of the top of Little Round Top, you forced me to retire by appearing in my rear and opening fire on me.*[120]

In his memoirs, Oates wrote of hoping to remain on Big Round Top, then turning the hill into a Confederate bastion.[121] This unrealistic vision for a better Confederate outcome at Gettysburg does not detract from the colonel's correct belief that the Sharpshooters' delay of two regiments had a major impact on the battle that unfolded.

Although Berdan's reconnaissance earlier in the day needed lies to achieve mythical status in the war's history, the stand of the 2nd Sharpshooters required no exaggeration to become immortal. Words from a speech about the reconnaissance seem more appropriate for Stoughton's glorious afternoon. Charles Buchanan's oratory dedicating the New York companies' monument west of the Emmitsburg Road used an intriguing phrase to characterize the midday fight against Wilcox. He proclaimed the four USSS companies acted "like a thunderbolt to the rebels, from a clear sky." In addition to providing a pithy book title, Buchanan's words ring more accurately for Stoughton's eight companies at Gettysburg, the finest and most impactful combat performance in the history of either Sharpshooter regiment. Regardless of his penchant to twist truth for his own purposes, Hiram Berdan precisely summed up the elan and grit of his men when opening the last paragraph of his battle report by proclaiming, "I trust that the sharpshooters lost none of their reputation at Gettysburg."[122]

"Peace to Their Remains"

Fighting for the day did not wrap up when Sharpshooters helped save the Union left on and below the Round Tops. In the morning, the six 1st USSS companies not on Berdan's reconnaissance started forming a skirmish line west of the Emmitsburg Road and north of the army's left flank. The marksmen had orders to not fire unless fired on, perhaps to minimize Confederate aggressiveness while Sickles pondered ways to improve his position. Nonetheless, much Sharps Rifle ammunition was expended for hours as the Southerners unsurprisingly seemed ready to fight. One Alabamian wrote of the "brisk fire" the two competing skirmish lines kept up for hours before the forceful attack of more Confederate brigades later in the day.[123]

The six companies did not appear to form a solid line at the very beginning of their service west of the road. The sharp eye and strong leadership of Capt. Frank Marble oversaw the three companies on the right of the regiment's line. Infantry from the 1st Massachusetts on the right and 5th New Jersey to the south added some muscle to the line during the day. Some skirmish companies stood on open ground, while others had the benefit of shelter from areas of thick forest. The Union line stood perhaps six hundred feet west of the Emmitsburg Road.[124]

USSS members engaged the Southern skirmishers with a good deal of success prior to the Confederate attack meant to complement Hood's effort to the south. One Wisconsin marksman wrote of the fate of an unfortunate target. The Badgers

> *became engaged with the enemy in front, and one line of skirmishers of about 125 men having approached in plain view within about 300 yards, were*

scattered like chaff, most of them going down. One poor fellow "treed," and succeeded in dodging balls until he had put in three shots, when he fell like a log. The tree was "barked" all around, the size of a man.[125]

As Hood's assault unfolded, growing evidence of additional major attacks from Lee's men to the north quickly materialized. The Union skirmishers west of the Peach Orchard soon found more work than they could handle, apparently falling back a considerable distance while staying west of the road. Based on the orientation of Confederate units later in the day, Cadmus Wilcox and his Alabamians had a chance to best some additional companies of the 1st USSS.[126]

Wilcox reported his line starting their attack 750 feet from the Emmitsburg Road. He noticed the USSS and other skirmishers using a fence for protection, then wrote of the push of his superior numbers scattering the advanced Northerners. Holding great faith in Wilcox, the brigade moved ahead feeling the day would bring a resounding victory. As a member of the 9th Alabama, on the left of Wilcox's advance, suggested, "our line moved onward, straight onward" as Union bullets, "thick as hail-storms in winter, were falling on every side."[127]

Against the bold Confederate attack, Union skirmishers across multiple regiments, including the 1st USSS, did not remain for long. Once again this day, a portion of the USSS gave way to Confederate legions. The fight brought another day of anguish to the Badgers of Company G. With four Wisconsin men lost—Eli Fitch and William Woodruff killed outright, joined by the mortally wounded Henry Lye and Eli Vincent—the company sustained another severe toll.[128] Comradery, the glue of an army, created indelible memories, prompting a surviving Sharpshooter to remember the quartet of fallen marksmen. At Chancellorsville, Woodruff

had a narrow escape by a ball grazing his forehead, and knocking him over, inflicting, however, no greater injury than a headache. He was noted for his kind and good-natured disposition to those around him. Fitch had been with us but a short time, but evinced a determined spirit, and fired away with a will. . . . He was hit while falling back. Sergt. Lye enlisted in the original company. . . . He was born in England [and] one of our liveliest and most humorous members. . . . He died a hero in every sense of the word. Eli Vincent was a fearless and determined soldier, and one of the best marksmen in the two regiments of Sharp shooters. When he went into battle he meant "business." . . . All of these men will be greatly missed by those of their comrades who have survived them. They sacrificed their lives for their country's good. Peace to their remains.[129]

On the left of Company G, Wolverine Simon Roosa sustained a fatal wound while confronting the Confederate surge. A New York native born in 1829, Roosa would die in a Philadelphia hospital on July 18. He rests in the city's Mount Moriah Cemetery.[130]

After pushing Union skirmishers back, the Confederates stormed the main Third Corps position around the Peach Orchard, with both sides losing men at a rapid pace. The overwhelmed Sharpshooter companies retreated toward Second Corps lines farther north on Cemetery Hill, with a patchwork of Meade's units working to stem the disaster. What seemed like an unbearable Confederate assault ended thanks to further Union resistance, the disorganization and exhaustion of the attackers, and the waning light of day. The wicked afternoon ended with the Army of the Potomac bent, but far from broken. Thanks to a strong reinforcement during the afternoon with the arrival of the Sixth Corps after a forced march that began the evening before, Meade was not going anywhere.[131]

Gettysburg Denouement

Not content with two days of near success, Robert E. Lee stayed focused on finding a way to crack his entrenched enemy. Historians cannot overstate the audacity of Lee's decision to stay on the field and attack one more day with his weary and damaged army. Like at Antietam after bloody fighting against his stout foe, Lee accepted great risk in the search for unknown rewards. Great confidence in his Southern army compelled Lee onward in search of an overwhelming victory. His tool for the day west of town would be a large division of Virginians under George Pickett, the last of Longstreet's command to become engaged. Portions of two divisions under A. P. Hill would go in on Pickett's left in the desperate exercise against the Union center on Cemetery Ridge, the heart of Winfield Scott Hancock's Second Corps. In an effort to soften Hancock's line, Lee ordered a massive bombardment by artillery prior to what would be immortalized as Pickett's Charge.[132]

The Virginians under Pickett faced enough problems trying to punch through Hancock's brigades. They also received intense musketry fire from their right flank after curving northeast. The defenders, Vermonters from the First Corps close to mustering out, gained some support from other units, including a small number in the USSS. Although they arrived late in the attack, Sharps Rifle fire from the marksmen added to the hellish cacophony of the Pennsylvania afternoon.[133]

Capt. Abraham Wright, leading Minnesota's company, would sustain the second of what would become four wounds of the war while manning the left of the Union defense against Pickett. Many years later, he retained vivid memories of the dying moments of the war's most famous attack. Third Corps units did not have the luxury of time when sent to assist Hancock's pressed troops. Wright remembered the 2nd Regiment moving north "not on a double-quick, but a run" in a line of four men each. Nearing the left of Hancock's position, the regiment then moved into line of battle, greatly extending the Sharpshooters' front. Formed behind the troops originally defending the area, the marksmen "commenced firing over the heads of those in line, for they were on their knees or otherwise low."

Wright and the Sharpshooters fired only a few shots before seeing many of the charging Confederates raising their hands in surrender. In addition to taking some prisoners, Wright witnessed a large number of enemy soldiers retreating between the Union line and the Emmitsburg Road. "We could have picked off many of them," the captain opined, "but our bullets would have gone very close to the heads of our own men, and, somehow, we did not have much desire just to kill some one." Sharpshooters also took part in an effort to capture some Confederate artillery.[134]

Curtis Abbott also recalled the charge's waning moments. Some prisoners being taken to the rear obviously seemed like good news to the marksmen arriving late in the attack. Looking west like Captain Wright, Abbott noticed fleeing Confederates "disappearing behind the hostile ridge, like the fleeing clouds after a storm." Abbott added that both USSS regiments contributed to a skirmish detail later sent toward the road.[135]

The brief fighting on July 3 robbed the Sharpshooters of more lives. Wolverine Harrison Higby, who enlisted in August 1862, would die on July 18 from his wicked injury, a bullet to the lower left leg leading to amputation. Multiple hemorrhages led to the Wolverine's death. Shards from a Confederate cannon ball inflicted a fatal wound on George White, Company G, 2nd USSS. From the town of Antrim and in his early twenties, White had enlisted in the autumn of 1861. He was buried at Gettysburg National Cemetery. Minnesotan Benjamin Hamlet was another marksman added to the butcher's bill on July 3.[136]

The doomed charge ended Lee's effort to make something of his Pennsylvania invasion. William Ripley rightly believed the Army of the Potomac "had been signally successful" in its brilliant defensive stand at Gettysburg.[137] At several points on the field, from Berdan's overhyped reconnaissance through spirited groups of skirmishers later on July 2, to the closing moments of Pickett's Charge, the USSS served quite well.

Sergeant Richard Tyler added to the laurels he earned as a soldier. Away from Pickett's Charge, he assisted with the capture of about twenty Confederate prisoners in the area west of Little Round Top on July 3. The unfortunate captives had been trapped in the big rocks around Devil's Den due to the hellfire from both armies on the previous day. Quite hungry and dejected, the Confederates appreciated the kindness from Tyler, who assured them fair treatment as prisoners of the USSS.[138]

On July 4, the 2nd USSS almost lost their Fighting Parson. Lorenzo Barber took a trip to Emmitsburg after learning a collection of the regiment's mail could be picked up there. On his way back to Gettysburg, the chaplain ran into a Confederate patrol. They made a mistake in keeping just the mail; Barber—who the Southerners wrongly deemed a noncombatant—went back to his green-clad comrades. Curtis Abbott gleefully remembered how Barber, "one of the most belligerent of our fighting men," returned to his Sharpshooter comrades.[139]

Much of the Confederate force remained in the vicinity of Gettysburg on Independence Day. Several USSS companies again answered the call to man a skirmish line west of the Emmitsburg Road. As hundreds of dead and wounded littered parts of the field, one historian deemed the day's firing "the sharpest picket work ever done" by the USSS until the fight along the North Anna River nearly a year later. As a result, July 4 brought additional fatalities to USSS ranks. The killed were James Kent and William Beard, two New Hampshire warriors, and Sgt. Josiah Gray from Maine. Gray lost his life ten feet away from his comrade James Matthews. The round hit Gray from the right while the noncommissioned officer sat behind a tree. The trio of fallen became the last of the eighteen members of the two marksmen regiments to suffer a mortal wound at Gettysburg. Beard had sustained a serious injury at Antietam.[140]

Colonel Berdan reported his two regiments expended 14,400 rounds of ammunition across their three days at Gettysburg.[141] Exhausted from the summer's march and days of intense battle, the Sharpshooters awaited their next mission. Where would the fates of war take them next? Could Meade's men destroy Lee's army before they escaped to Virginia?

Coming to Grips with Gettysburg

Before the eighteen USSS companies could confront the unknown future, they had to endure the immediate aftermath of the most horrible battle of the war. The stench of death pervaded Gettysburg's fields and woods. By July 5, several Sharpshooters worked on burial parties, with Caspar Trepp overseeing the putrid chore. In total, Third Corps men buried nearly 1,500 on the battlefield, 300 more than Trepp mentioned in a conversation with Rudolf Aschmann.[142]

The Gettysburg campaign brought the greatest victory for the Army of the Potomac to date. However much the Sharpshooters wished to contribute to final peace for their tattered country, they had to heal from great fatigue, intense battle action, and the emotional difficulties of losing more friends. George Marden, serving as assistant adjutant general to Ward's Brigade, succinctly overviewed the state of the USSS and his own fragile condition in a July 5 letter to his mother. The Sharpshooters had "constantly been under fire" during the battle, he wrote, with the big fight leading to "favorable but not decisive" results. "I have not had my boots off for four nights," he continued, "and for forty-eight hours of the time had not a mouthful to eat."[143]

Vermonter Thomas Brown shared Marden's feeling that the battle did not seem to offer a conclusive outcome, perhaps because the two armies combined for more than forty-five thousand casualties. His July 6 letter home included hopes for the future while deeply sensing the immense human toll of what would become the war's costliest battle. "I can tell you it is hard to see so many men slain," Mrs. Brown read.[144]

The horrid aftermath of the battle likely contributed to one Sharpshooter's decision to desert on July 7. John W. E. Robinson, Company F, 2nd USSS, had enlisted in the autumn of 1861, but he never returned to his comrades after his unapproved absence near Gettysburg. More than a century later, a family member requested a change to Robinson's service record, suggesting he had a young family to take care of in New Hampshire. "Many like him," the descendant of Robinson pleaded, had no thoughts of being disloyal, but they could not ignore problems back home, sporadic pay from the army, or lingering sickness due to military service. The government denied the 1970 request to change Robinson's historical status as a deserter. The troubled Granite Stater later enlisted in a Massachusetts heavy artillery outfit.[145]

As the men dealt with their traumas, senior officers made fateful choices. Lee faced the dilemma of evacuating his army and thousands of wounded from enemy territory, forty-five miles from the safety of the Potomac River. With his forces still dispersed across miles of ground west and north of Gettysburg, a miracle seemed necessary. Lee skillfully managed the initial stage of the retreat, especially vital given the need to protect against Union cavalry raids. Sudden attacks targeting the extended Confederate wagon trains or Lee's wearied infantry could have brought devastating results.[146]

General Meade's initial thoughts focused on the status of his victorious army. With his own strained supply system and bone-tired legions, Meade could not simply rush after Lee's fleeing columns. At least from the perspective of his bosses, Meade failed to find the proper balance in General Orders 68, issued on the afternoon of July 4. The missive thanked the Army of the Potomac "for the glorious result of the recent operations." Meade wished his men to know their sacrifice "will be matters of history, to be ever remembered." Yet, the war went on. "Our task is not yet accomplished," Meade added. He then earned scorn from Lincoln with a McClellan-esque view that he planned "to drive from our soil every vestige of the invader." Meade's caution made an intense pursuit with overwhelming attacks on Lee's retreat highly unlikely. Lincoln suggested Meade did not seem interested in trying to crush the Confederates, just see him flee.[147]

With General Sickles losing a leg near the Peach Orchard, David Birney had temporary command of the Third Corps. William French was appointed permanent commander on July 7, the same day his soldiers left Gettysburg. The march south led the Sharpshooters to familiar places, such as Emmitsburg, Frederick, the Maryland passes of South Mountain, and then through the country toward the Potomac. Sharpshooters grew disgusted with the disrespect from some Pennsylvania farmers compared to the nicer residents in Maryland. Keystone Staters did not seem as devoted to providing treats and water as those one state to the south. As Sharpshooter historian Charles Stevens wrote, "This difference in disposition and feeling seemed very strange to the soldiers."[148]

New Yorker Harrison De Long wrote with great pride about what the army accomplished in Pennsylvania. "The soldiers are in good spirits," he informed a friend later in July, "and it is safe to say that the Army of the Potomac never stood up more manfully in any fight than at Gettysburg." De Long hoped the soldiers' intense grit and endurance in early July made the Northern home front proud. He at least figured the result of the war's worst battle worked to cast aside "the idea that the army must have some particular pet General to command it to accomplish anything."[149]

As the final act of the Gettysburg campaign, Lee's army stood near Williamsport, Maryland, attempting to cross the rain-swollen river. Cautious in his pursuit over the last several days, Meade pondered options while expressing worry about the impressive Confederate works built near the Potomac. One sharp fight along the river on the southern part of the opposing lines did not harm Lee notably, with the bulk of his army fleeing before Meade pounced. History does not criticize Meade much for failing to inflict more damage, although Curtis Abbott recorded concerns from his Vermont comrades. "There was much expression of dissatisfaction in the company," he recorded, "when it was found that the Confederate army had recrossed the Potomac without another battle." A Badger in the 1st USSS seemed less sanguine about a fight against Lee at Williamsport. He wrote of the enemy "very strongly entrenched among the hills."[150]

Moving Back to Virginia

Word of Lee's escape led to more doubts within the Lincoln administration regarding Meade's performance, triggering the general to offer his resignation. General Halleck smoothed over the tension to avoid another sudden change at the top of the army, which would have been the third in six months. Meade did not fear facing Lee, he simply thought the armies' positions in the Williamsport lines failed to offer much of a chance to overwhelm the enemy. The risk seemed too great. As George Marden opined, the Confederates had "dug like rabbits" in the previous days to create an "immensely strong position."

As the USSS marched south, they traversed Sharpsburg. Members of the 2nd Regiment passed the horrible area around the Cornfield where so many comrades lost their lives ten months before. The Third Corps—now back to three divisions thanks to a large number of new regiments—then joined other corps that spanned the Potomac at Harpers Ferry on July 17. Back in Virginia, Meade kept the army east of the Blue Ridge as Lee continued his retreat on the west of that beautiful mountain range.[151]

Reaching Upperville on July 18, twenty miles southwest of Leesburg, the Sharpshooters faced good marching conditions, as well as benefits from the summer harvest. A highly prized item in nature's bounty offered much pleasure. "The height of the blackberry season," William Ripley wrote, led USSS members onto properties "full of the most delicious specimens." Thanks to the fresh fruit, healthier and happier men continued the march.[152]

The Sharpshooters did not face the torrid pace they suffered the previous month. Battle beckoned, however. Meade stood "embarrassed at not ascertaining anything definite in regard to Lee's movements," but he found a chance to strike through Manassas Gap near Wapping Heights, a few miles east of Front Royal. Hoping to pull Confederate forces into a larger engagement, Meade sent General French and the Third Corps forward. Working in their traditional role as skirmishers, although entering the fight in different waves of Union troops, the USSS performed quite well while losing the life of another comrade, New Yorker Thomas Carey. Badger Sgt. William Babcock lost an eye in the fight, while Albert Sisson, not yet twenty years old, took a rather painful bullet to the leg. He never again served with his comrades.[153]

Some familiar regiments such as the 20th Indiana and 3rd Maine worked with the USSS at Wapping Heights, keeping the pressure on during the day without orders for a major attack. The 2nd USSS sustained no casualties, although members of the regiment captured some prisoners. General French, concerned about the perceived vulnerability of his flanks, remained cautious. Receiving afternoon orders to push with more rigor, the highlight of the battle came at about 5 p.m., way too late for French to make much use of the Union sacrifice during the tough day. A grand assault from the New York brigade Dan Sickles organized early in the war threatened much havoc, but Lee's forces slipped away to the south. Marden found the infantry's effort northwest of Wapping Heights "as handsome fighting as I have ever seen. . . . We had a splendid view of the charge." The staff officer had again found himself on the USSS line of battle, overseeing companies on the right of the earlier advance. "I had some narrow escapes," Marden wrote in a July 25 letter.[154]

Perspective from Walter Smith countered Marden's positive view of Wapping Heights. Smith suggested the army had a great chance to inflict damage on a part of the Confederate army. The day's battle "was not much of a fight & not very creditable to our Generals," Smith complained to his parents. The Union force "fooled away so much time at Manassas Gap," he added, that the day did not land a major blow, even as Lee's army "was plain to be seen moving past the Gap with their trains."[155]

Within a few days, the Sharpshooters would enjoy a prolonged rest. Unable to make anything more of the foray through Manassas Gap, Meade continued moving down the eastern side of the mountains toward old stomping grounds along the Rappahannock River. The Sharpshooters reached Warrenton and the area to the south near Sulphur Springs on the 26th. Like the summer before, potential small fights were a possibility along the Rappahannock, so the men kept up their guard. At least extended days of marching ended for weeks. With plentiful fresh water, USSS members immediately partook in a pleasing summer respite. As Curtis Abbott remembered, the men "lingered" near the river.[156]

Late July's weather did not bother the men much, with temperatures comfortable for the season. USSS members started the robotic life they expected, with picket duty, drills, inspections, and plenty of time in camp. On July 28, Company K's Henry Bedell received a new pair of shoes. As he went out on picket, he added new socks to his outfit, likely making for a happy Sharpshooter. On the first day of August, Bedell noted that he "remained in camp all day."[157]

Many men felt the loneliness of life across the relatively idle weeks. Vermonter Thomas Brown wrote his wife on July 28, "I long to get home again but it is hard to tell when the time will come." Like before, Thomas Connington displayed great sadness at times, as outlined to his sister on the 30th. "It has been a very lonesome and long time since the last letter from you," he bewailed. "I am almost used up with marching." The summer break arrived at a good time for the frazzled Sharpshooter.[158]

A former Sharpshooter suffering at home found nothing to enjoy in life. James Larrason, who had been home in New York City since a wound on the

Peninsula, was disconsolate to the point of suicide. With a bag full of stones, Larrason jumped off a ferry boat in late July. In the note he left for his wife, Larrason suggested poor treatment while hospitalized in the army left him in chronic pain down his entire right side. Feeling useless to anyone, Larrason suggested ending his life offered the best solution. He signed the tragic note, "Your unworthy husband."[159] The case of Larrason illustrates the tragedy the Civil War left in its wake, with invisible scars inflicting much pain.

August's typical heat began to impact the comfort of marksmen in the field. Inventive warriors found ways to help men forget loneliness and summer's discomforts. Curtis Abbott wrote of his industrious Vermont friend Henry Campbell, a man with experience driving cattle. On the other side of the river Campbell procured a big Virginia steer. The doomed animal ended up feeding many men. As Abbott wrote, "a glowing coal pit" cooked the turning meat, which was then "basted and seasoned after the fashion of our forefathers."[160] Such good times undoubtedly boosted morale.

Even with the necessity of picket duty, Harrison De Long enjoyed the area around Sulphur Springs. He referred to the spot as "a great resort for the Southern Chivalry in the summer time." The destruction of war severely damaged buildings at the site, however, making the grounds, "not much the appearance of fashionable watering place." Still, the New Yorker concluded, "It is a very healthy country," a fine spot for the army to rest for a while.[161]

Better food and a decrease in summer's heat later in August likely buttressed the health of most USSS companies. Roster information demonstrates far fewer Sharpshooters left the army due to disease or wounds in the last five months of 1863 compared to earlier periods. Across the twelve companies from Maine, Michigan, Minnesota, New Hampshire, and Vermont, only thirty-eight Sharpshooters received medical discharges or died of disease from August through the end of the year. This positive trend, especially good in the wake of the number of surviving wounded from Chancellorsville and Gettysburg, possibly reflects stronger immune systems and better conditioning compared to earlier in the war. Of course, the smaller companies partly explain the lower numbers of discharges.[162]

Some excellent leaders departed because of wounds or sickness in the closing months of 1863, including the Wolverine from Company C James Baker, a talented and revered officer hit at Wapping Heights. A New Hampshire Sharpshooter who exhibited strong leadership, Benjamin Brown, departed with a disability discharge in August. He had risen from corporal to second lieutenant in only a few months. Another Granite Stater, Daniel Buckingham, tried to recover from a wound at Gettysburg, but he died of disease in his native Ohio on November 26. His loss was not attributed to the wound sustained in July.[163]

Albert Isham, who suffered a major knee wound at Chancellorsville, departed the Badgers of Company G, 1st USSS in the autumn. One Sharpshooter in the company wrote, "Isham was a splendid soldier, and much sympathy is expressed for him." Only twenty-three at the time of his discharge and a native of New York, Isham lived for more than six decades, dying in California in 1928.[164]

Hannibel Tichout, Company H, 2nd USSS, became one of the highly unfortunate men lost during the last five months to disease. He checked in to a hospital on September 13, having suffered from typhoid fever for much of the summer. Reported with a wide range of bodily debilities, treatments for Tichout included lead and opium, a sign of the limited medical knowledge of the time. "He sank gradually, dying on the 26th," according to a government publication. Only twenty years old, Tichout had enlisted thirteen months before his death. The Vermont patriot rests at Alexandria National Cemetery, Virginia.[165]

Berdan Gone for Good

Hiram Berdan had been away from the USSS since late July, when once again senior army officials wished to know the reasons for the colonel's absence. Shortly before departing, Berdan had changed a list of USSS officers authorized to travel north on recruiting duty, prompting a written protest from Caspar Trepp. Trepp's July 28 letter included disgust about Berdan's effort to alter the list of officers with permission to depart the regiment for a time. After all, Trepp wrote, Berdan had earlier deemed himself in "off duty" status.[166]

While Trepp again fumed over Berdan's actions, senior officials wondered what Berdan was doing away from his command without permission. Weeks of telegrams and letters attempted to learn Berdan's whereabouts. Some in the army doubted his authority to be away from his regiment. By early September, documentation from a Regular Army officer noted Berdan's recruiting work in New York City. Nonetheless, on September 9, a member of the War Department in Washington wired a general in the city, "Please order Col. Berdan to rejoin his command forthwith."

On September 12, while the army wondered about Berdan's actions and location, the colonel received a twenty-day leave of absence from the Department of the East, headquartered in New York City. A medical officer had written a supplementary note, suggesting continued problems with the contusion from a shell, likely a reference to Berdan's putative wound at Second Bull Run. The medical officer deemed the founder of the USSS "unfit for duty" because the wound tended to hemorrhage at the colonel's slightest exertion. One wonders if Berdan simply left the army because he did not wish to spend the colder months in the field, using contacts in New York to justify in writing his departure from the Sharpshooters. Berdan likely did not wish to request a medical leave from a surgeon with the army because such a request could have been denied.

Later expansions of the leave, including fifty more days beyond October 20, filled in the rest of Berdan's military experience. Updates to his medical record appeared in December, with physicians noting Berdan's inability to travel without bleeding, rendering service in the field impossible. Berdan ended his career with an honorable discharge on the second day of 1864.

Berdan's modern biographer suggested an August 1863 denial of promotion to brigadier general probably ended the colonel's commitment to military service. This sensible conclusion, along with Berdan's wish to avoid the rigors of army life, likely had led to an unjustified absence from his men starting in late July. The colonel's sizable ego undoubtedly found satiation in 1868 when Berdan received brevet promotions to brigadier and major general for Chancellorsville and Gettysburg. He returned to the life of an inventor, becoming involved in a major patent infringement lawsuit against the U.S. government. The founding father of the USSS died in the national capital on March 31, 1893, at the age of sixty-eight.[167]

An Active Two Months

Vermonter George Clay faced the summer realizing the importance of good health for a soldier. Writing home on August 25 from his camp near the Rappahannock, Clay first announced his happiness about enlisting, rather than being drafted. He saw some vacant places in the regiment, including marksmen still missing in action from Gettysburg. "Soldiering is hard business for me," Clay added, "but I can stand it very well, if I am not sick." He suggested hospitalized soldiers are "half taken care of," with unnecessary deaths occurring regularly.[168]

Mail often created the happiest moments for a Sharpshooter. Thomas Connington replied to his sister's kind missive on August 27. His letter outlined the army's efforts to keep idle soldiers focused on their fate. Drills, picket duty, and inspections proved quite tiresome, Connington complained. With death frequently on the minds of both correspondents, Connington passed along his condolences to a family at home who recently lost a son and daughter. With fickle fate dictating lives on earth, Connington did not expend much time talking about the possible outcome of the war. He humorously said the progress since Gettysburg might close out the conflict over the next few weeks, "but we have thought so ever since we have been in the field."[169]

Charles Stevens penned a September 1 letter from Sulphur Springs. The Wisconsinite exhibited a writing prowess while in the ranks indicative of the future USSS historian. Reviewing Company G's service in the war thus far, Stevens listed eighteen engagements from skirmishing near Big Bethel in late March 1862 through Wapping Heights sixteen months later. Stevens deemed the company's record great enough to "certainly satisfy our friends at home that we have endeavored to do our duty to our country in its efforts to crush this wicked rebellion." Determination to win still burned bright among his Badger comrades, Stevens concluded, with the soldiers prepared for "a vigorous prosecution of the war until the entire Union is restored to its former prestige and glory."[170]

Sulphur Springs served as camp for about six weeks. Andrew Westervelt witnessed signs of the Confederacy's weakness, even as he hoped for better health for himself. Lameness in a foot had been bothering the Californian in the 1st USSS. "I hope to see the end of this war within a few months," the marksman averred on September 9. "By all accounts the rebels must be seeing hard times." The major defeats at Gettysburg and Vicksburg, Mississippi earlier in the summer pointed toward an eventual Union triumph. Hoping such an idea would soon be reality, Westervelt added, "There are many deserters from the rebel army, and they most all say the Confederacy is about played out."[171]

Down time allowed Vermonter Thomas Brown a chance to clean his prized Sharps Rifle. He detailed the effort to one of his children in a September 15 letter. With a weapon looking very shiny and beautiful, Brown informed his son that the rifle recently ended the lives of feral hogs roaming the Virginia woods, destined, no doubt, for Sharpshooters' cooking fires. Brown also repeated concerns about death, with hopes of being home again soon. Like many of his comrades, Brown asked for a return letter.[172]

Wolverine Gardner Clark informed his wife of the army's partial move south, with cavalry and infantry engaged in some skirmishing on the way. The Sharpshooters followed soon after, reaching Culpeper on the evening of the 16th. Historian Charles Stevens noted how some men fell out on the march, and then spent time foraging. As usual, many stragglers caught up to their USSS comrades the following day. A large number of doomed turkeys could be seen mulling around the Culpeper camp, with privates doing their best to hide the largess from officers.[173]

Some Sharpshooters had little time to set up a new campsite before picket duty called. Henry Bedell went out on September 18, staying posted all night through 11 a.m. the following morning. With regular duties prevailing, the army made efforts to keep the men happy. Several Sharpshooters received new green uniforms on September 21. At their camp between the Rappahannock and Rapidan, the men found much rest when not on picket, with no imminent signs of a new campaign.[174]

Near the start of autumn, from Walter Smith's perspective at least, Meade's force had overwhelming numbers that likely could be put to better use. "I don't know how large our Army here is now," the Vermonter admitted, "but I think it is large enough to thrash what few Johnnies there are in front of us."[175]

Harrison De Long shared Smith's wonder why the army did not make use of the good weather. "Everything is favorable for an advance," the New York marksman opined in a September 29 letter. "The roads are good, and the army in fine condition, the weather being cool enough for all military purposes." De Long suggested an effort against General Lee now would be preferable to an advance pestered by "cold storms and muddy roads."[176]

Rudolf Aschmann recorded three generally idle weeks through early October. In constant flux, the organization of the Army of the Potomac underwent further change as summer turned to autumn. The two Sharpshooter regiments no longer shared a brigade, although the marksmen remained under division commander David Birney. The 2nd USSS, led by Lt. Col. Homer Stoughton

As a brigade commander in the Army of the Potomac, French aristocrat Regis de Trobriand would become quite familiar to USSS members.
LIBRARY OF CONGRESS

remained in Ward's Brigade. Trepp and his 1st Regiment joined another Third Corps outfit, the excellent troops under Brig. Gen. Regis de Trobriand. The wealthy Frenchman would earn a solid reputation throughout the war. Working in law and as an author after immigrating to the United States in 1841, de Trobriand had begun the Civil War as colonel of the 55th New York Infantry.[177]

Changes to Birney's camp, dictated by the relocation of other divisions, likely made soldiers think new marching orders beckoned. Lee's army, which had just lost Longstreet's First Corps, sent west to assist beleaguered Confederates in Tennessee and Georgia, still worried General Meade. Unsurprisingly, Lee moved around the Army of the Potomac, then headed north. Meade ended up blocking Lee's effort to threaten Washington. The Confederates then sustained heavy casualties in a reckless charge against well-posted Northerners along the Orange and Alexandria Railroad.[178]

In a campaign not amounting to much, USSS members earned some encomiums from General Birney. With a concern that Lee's penchant for flank attacks could cause trouble early in the march north, the USSS guarded the division's left, sending some pesky Confederates flying westward. The men spent tense days and nights looking for the enemy. While on the move during the day, one Wisconsin Sharpshooter wrote, "The roads were good and the weather cool." Even while lugging "packed knapsacks and haversacks with 60 rounds of ammunition," he continued, "the men made good time."[179]

Elements of the Third Corps confronted Confederates in battle on October 13 near Auburn, east of Warrenton. As part of a battle line, then moving ahead on a charge, the 1st USSS gained additional laurels from Birney. Along with the 3rd Michigan Infantry and a Massachusetts battery, Trepp's men received credit "for their gallantry in repulsing the enemy's attack on the head of the column." De Trobriand witnessed a spirited effort on the day, thanks to his bold troops. "The enemy had not time to give us a volley," the general reported. A Company G man wrote, "Three rebel dead lying in the woods near where we entered, proved to us that we had been having a bout with dismounted rebel cavalrymen."[180] In a campaign lacking the drama of larger fights, the Sharpshooters could at least rest knowing their reputation still stood high with superior officers.

Charles Stevens suggested the Sharpshooters' charge at Auburn, although a relatively minor affair, demonstrated the superiority of breech-loading rifles, "our men continually firing as they ran after" the skedaddling Confederates. Company K's Jonathan Breed sustained a potentially fatal wound to his right leg during the bold advance, but the quick action of comrade Joel Race saved the marksman's life. With Race tying a handkerchief around the leg, then twisting the fabric tight with a bayonet, Breed survived.[181]

In the afternoon of the following day, the Sharpshooters trekked to Centreville, not far from Washington. With the two warring armies temporarily stymied southwest of the Union capital city, Dan Sickles returned to see some of his Third Corps troops. Angling to regain corps leadership, Sickles became flustered when Meade spurned the maimed general. In his short visit with the army, however, Sickles felt the appreciation of his men. Members of the USSS and others across the three divisions had raised money to purchase a carriage and horses for Sickles. Ovations for the wounded general resounded along Third Corps lines. Sharpshooter Gardner Clark deemed the civilian soldier Sickles one of the best leaders in the army.[182]

Euphoric over the short return of Sickles, the mood among Sharpshooters turned to somber necessity on the following day. The army made an example out of a Michigan infantryman who had deserted. Regiments across Birney's Division turned out on October 16 to see military justice implemented. Formed in two lines, as a Badger Sharpshooter wrote, Birney's troops saw the condemned soldier,

> *marched solemnly behind his own coffin, the band in front playing the dead march. He appeared resigned to his fate, and walked firmly along to his last resting place. After a short prayer in his behalf by the minister attending him, his eyes were bandaged by the Division Provost Marshal and he took his seat on the edge of his coffin which was by the side of his grave. Soon after twelve muskets poured forth their contents at a distance of six paces, and Henry C. Beardsley of the 5th Michigan regiment fell dead in his coffin pierced by eleven bullets, one gun containing a blank cartridge.*[183]

Deciding he could not work his maneuver to any advantage, General Lee turned back south, heading once again to the land between the Rappahannock and Rapidan. His greatest accomplishment during the October effort, the destruction of about twenty miles of train track and some bridges, forced a delay in the Union's pursuit. As Meade waited for a repaired supply line, the Sharpshooters rested near Bristoe Station, then moved west to Warrenton. Farther south by early November, Meade looked for some advantage with his enemy once again protected on ground along the Rappahannock.[184]

From Bristoe on October 23, Thomas Connington penned another letter. He blamed a frigid river crossing for the large number of colds among his USSS comrades. He found time to provide advice to his sister, who had complained about going to school. The captain expressed a view of the importance of education.[185] As the shadow of national conflict continued to dominate lives, this one Sharpshooter focused attention on his family, however far away they lived from the war zone.

Near Catlett's Station the following day, a Vermonter wrote an update to an "Absent Friend." George Clay recalled the difficult marching across the previous two weeks, while noting the celebration of his twenty-third birthday the day before. "I hope before I see another Birthday I shall be at home with my friends," the optimistic marksman added. Turning to the weather, Clay found the rain of the night before quite cold, although he did not expect the less-than-ideal conditions to cause problems for the army.

Clay's tone partly sprang from the recent receipt of a letter from home. The marksman's reply outlined several aspects of his life, allowing his correspondent to better picture a soldier's existence. Clay detailed the difficulty of marching many days in a row while carrying a great deal of weight, from food to blankets and ammunition. The Vermonter detailed the items to illustrate the "pretty hard day's work" put in for a marching soldier.

Two major items Clay predicted in this letter would be reality for him in the short and long term. He proved correct on General Meade's ability to get the army moving again after the delays due to repair of the supply line. On a personal level, although Clay would not be home in one more year to celebrate his birthday with friends, he had many more left.[186]

"Hell on the Rappahannock"

After moving his troops closer to Lee, Meade envisioned an advance on November 2, but the specific plan received a veto from President Lincoln and General Halleck. Flustered with the disapproval of what he deemed a good idea, Meade remained eager for further action. Four days later, he outlined a course for his entire army. The troops would advance against separate fords of the Rappahannock, potentially dealing a severe blow to opposite wings of Lee's force. French's Third Corps "will move at early daylight to Kelly's Ford," Meade ordered, with the cautious corps commander given a key role. Wyman White recorded that a march of eleven miles was required before reaching the river.[187]

Pennsylvanian Ira Northup wrote proudly of the 2nd USSS leading three infantry corps to the day's battle; Birney had placed the 2nd USSS in front and the 1st Regiment along his flanks during the march to Kelly's Ford. Deploying his troops near the ford, including two batteries, Birney found very strong enemy fortifications.[188]

Unsurprisingly, the Sharpshooters began vital operations on the army's left. Before crossing the river, some marksmen used their expertise with a rifle and training as soldiers to complete deadly work. A Wisconsin Sharpshooter used some technical terms to describe the moment later in the month,

> *Corporal Jno. W. Johnson (of Co. G) from near Madison, plumped one man through the middle of the back at 700 yards raise of sight. . . . The wind was blowing hard at the time, and although Johnson considered the chances poor for hitting his man at that distance, under the circumstances, yet upon being urged, exclaimed "By great! I'll try him," and did so, allowing two feet for windage.*[189]

By early afternoon, the marksmen moved across the ford in water about three feet deep, pushing Confederate skirmishers back to the opposite bank. USSS members then engaged their entrenched enemy. With the more distant firing not having the best effect, a more active phase unfolded.[190]

With de Trobriand's Brigade reinforced by the 2nd USSS and 20th Indiana, the French baron took the lead role in the day's drama. "The enemy, who did not expect us there so soon, offered little resistance," he averred. In a charge more consequential than Auburn the previous month, Rudolf Aschmann soon planted the 1st USSS regimental flag on the Confederate works. The brigade commander wrote of surprise being key to the moment's success. Men across de Trobriand's command seized dozens of prisoners.[191]

Charles Mead, Company F, 1st USSS, declared, "we skedaddled most of them" after the quick move to the other side of the Rappahannock. However, the Confederates had enough time to unleash some strong fire into the charging Northerners, costing the lives of seven Sharpshooters. Thomas Brown saw a friend, Patrick Murray, fall with a shot to the head. Fortunately, Brown wrote home, the brave and excellent soldier never knew what hit him.[192]

Trepp's additional battle dead included William Fitzgerald (Company B), Henry Townsend (Company C), James H. Reed (Company D), New Hampshire's Samuel Munroe, and Elbridge Jewell, a Wolverine in Company I. The sole combat fatality from the 2nd USSS was William McFarland from Maine, who would die on December 1 after losing both legs to shellfire. A wife and three children grieved back home in Ellsworth.[193]

Fitzgerald, only nineteen years old, succumbed to his horrible wounds on November 29. He struggled through difficult days after the shot fractured an elbow joint. After excision on the following day, an amputation of his arm occurred on the 12th. Additional procedures on the stump could not alter the doomed Sharpshooter's fate.[194]

Typical of combat operations during the war, some wounded men suffered severely for months. Edward Southworth, Company C, 1st USSS, lost a leg as a result of the fight at Kelly's Ford, his second wound of the year. He spent seven months in military hospitals before the inevitable medical discharge, followed by a return home to Michigan. The devoted and maimed Sharpshooter lived until 1910.[195]

Isolated groups of Sharpshooters contributed to the capture of prisoners as the Kelly's Ford action wrapped up. Thomas Connington received credit as he and a comrade nabbed several Confederates. In writing home a few days later, Connington reported more prisoners fell into Sharpshooter hands than Trepp had in his whole regiment. Receiving great praise for their work, the success further buttressed General Birney's reputation. He managed the attack quite well, with one historian suggesting the general "elicited the admiration of all."[196]

Much glory awaited the northern wing of the army, as well. The Sixth Corps took the prominent part at Rappahannock Station, a site the USSS would have found familiar. The day's work cost Meade more than six hundred casualties, most of those on the right with the Sixth Corps. Although USSS members mourned more lost friends and tentmates, the marksmen could relish the major accomplishment on November 7, their most meaningful success since Gettysburg. Meanwhile, the Confederates, who lost two thousand men along the Rappahannock on the day, fell back several miles to positions below the Rapidan.[197]

Meade's excellent plan, strongly implemented across his whole front, walloped Lee's army. One Badger Sharpshooter, suggesting the attack delivered "Hell on the Rappahannock," hoped "The Devil's to pay on the Rapidan" sooner than later.[198] The men would get their wish after more rest in November, but paying the devil one river south would bring fewer positive results than Kelly's Ford at a greater cost than the USSS desired.

Moving to Mine Run

Rainy days kicked in later in November. Badger Frank Smith found time to write home with an update on November 12. He felt quite positive about recent developments, including reoccupation of Fredericksburg by a portion of the army. After the trek and battle netting hundreds of prisoners five days before, the Sharpshooters grew quite happy near Brandy Station. Smith continued, "The rebs built nice log huts and were calculating to stay here all winter." The largess included the capture of a good deal of Confederate mail.

Vermonter Charles Mead also approvingly gazed at the rows of Confederate log huts around Brandy Station. The extensive construction provided evidence of Lee's plan to remain between the rivers for the whole winter. Meade foiled that goal with the attacks of November 7. He used the Confederate huts to shelter his own army, making Brandy Station a base for the next several months. Some Sharpshooters wrote of construction work in mid-November because Meade had more men than could be housed in the seized log homes.[199]

While Meade pondered the Army of the Potomac's next move, always inventive and industrious soldiers used the land's bounty to improve rations. Sharpshooters panned out in various directions trying to see what food could be found. As Curtis Abbott remembered, "The men of Co. H enjoyed the nuts and persimmons with which their camp at Brandy Station could be provided from the abundance in the surrounding countryside."[200]

When not building, on picket duty, or performing typical chores, Sharpshooters lounged on the property of John Minor Botts, a prominent Virginian who had opposed his state's secession. After Confederate cavalry horses feasted on Botts's 2,200-acre farm earlier in the autumn, Botts gleefully wrote of the Confederate retrograde after the fighting of November 7. Still, William Ripley considered Botts a "so-called loyalist," due to his constant demands for the Union army to repair his fences after troops used the rails for firewood. Across more than two weeks, fixing fences took up much time for Sharpshooters ordered to placate Botts, the fastidious host of Meade's army.[201]

George Marden echoed William Ripley's view of Botts. "I have rather a diminished idea of his martyrdom," the USSS staff member noted on November 13. Even with the orders to repair damaged fences, Marden suggested the Sharpshooters enjoyed much about camp, including "a fine oak grove." He added, "The weather has been remarkably favorable to us." The marksmen could rest some knowing of the additional laurels the Kelly's Ford operation brought. "The Sharpshooters did well and got a great deal of praise," Marden opined. "As skirmishers they have no equals in the Army."[202]

Lt. Col. Homer Stoughton spent time at camp in Brandy Station on the issue of recruitment, a matter close to the hearts of company commanders across the 2nd USSS. In a November 22 letter to Maine's governor, Jacob McClure informed his chief executive of Stoughton's particular interest in more Pine Tree State marksmen. McClure illustrated the problem by mentioning Vermont's work to increase Sharpshooters in the state's "three decimated companies." The Maine captain added that those capable of signing up as a member of the USSS "would not enlist in any other branch of the service." McClure concluded with optimism about a future when more Sharpshooters gladly mustered in to add to "the honorable name that those remaining few have so justly won."[203]

Regardless of the thin ranks throughout his command, General Meade did not wish to stay immobile for the whole winter. A drive for continued victory turned his gaze south of the Rapidan. General Lee maneuvered into a fine defensive position along Mine Run, twenty miles west of Falmouth, with the Confederates stretched for several miles close to the Rapidan. Meade saw an opportunity, with the hope of placing the Army of the Potomac on Lee's right, closer to Fredericksburg than the Southerners. Mother Nature forced a delay due to continued cool autumn rains. Meade's latest foray then began on November 26.[204]

Leaders Lost, Leaders Gained

"I have a right to be hopeful," Meade wrote his wife the day before his army began moving toward Mine Run. With bothersome weather improving, he had crafted a plan more complex than the successful moves against the Rappahannock earlier in the month. Coordination of his force became paramount if anything could be gained from the Mine Run endeavor. With his army taking multiple routes, Meade's troops targeted a rendezvous point near Robertson's Tavern, along the Plank Road. The tavern stood nearly ten miles west of Chancellorsville.[205]

General French had clear instructions to "close up on the Second Corps" at Robertson's Tavern. Mixed-up instructions and confused senior officers across French's three divisions destroyed Meade's vision for a swift and coordinated strike south of the Rapidan. After crossing the river on Thanksgiving Day, a Green Mountain Sharpshooter in the 1st Regiment wrote of "frequent and long halts," with skirmishing heard to the south and west. George Marden described the ground across which the men moved as "a swampy woods." With the Sharpshooters and Birney's brigades in the rear of French's command, the lead division, under an inexperienced general, took the wrong road. Instead of being part of the reunited army farther south, the Third Corps encountered Confederates at Payne's Farm, slightly more than two miles north of Robertson's Tavern.[206]

In an area rightly called the Wilderness, men, beasts, and cannons bogged down. Large bodies of troops moved, as William Ripley suggested, "while blindly groping about in the mazes" of underbrush and woods. The limited vision in an area of known enemy occupation led to orders from French for Birney and other division leaders to, "Look out well for your right flank. . . . Throw your flankers well out, and make them strong." The order seemed especially justified; an hour after the missive to Birney, French was informed of the Second Corps engaging the enemy farther to the south, near Robertson's Tavern.[207]

Contrary to Meade's plan, the Third Corps became engaged without forming a link with other parts of the army. As a result of the topography and the order of march, the fight at Payne's Farm began for two of French's divisions well before Birney could arrive with his excellent veteran brigades. With the chaos in front, Birney reported that his orders from General French called on the First Division "to form a second line in rear of the center of the first line," meaning the division would support their Third Corps comrades already engaged. Well into the afternoon and therefore considerably behind schedule, French committed to battle at Payne's Farm.[208]

Still in different brigades under Birney, the two USSS regiments joined opposite wings of the division's line. Passing the battle primarily in battery support, the 2nd USSS suffered no fatalities on the confusing day. An incident potentially fatal to some Vermonters in Company H led to four injuries after a great shot from a Confederate cannon blasted part of a tree into members of the 2nd Regiment. Some of the stunned soldiers went to the rear for treatment after the incident.[209]

Not far away, Trepp and his ten companies confronted a more dangerous situation. Moving up to support other heavily pressed troops who had been under fire for about two hours, the 1st USSS worked to improve a rail fence, located on the edge of a line of timber. The marksmen then blazed away against hundreds of experienced and tough Virginians. The enemy sent "a galling fire" from the other side of a clearing, perhaps six hundred feet from the Sharpshooters. As Birney reported, "The musketry fire was incessant, and the enemy made constant efforts to break through my line."[210]

The two opposing sets of American warriors shot each other down until darkness quickly descended. Of their role in a line of infantry regiments, "not a man flinched," a Green Mountain marksman remembered, although their fate acting again as infantry in a line of battle led to "some grumbling." The historian of the 17th Maine, to the right of the 1st USSS, suggested the woods assisted the brigade by protecting men from the worst of the Confederate fire, even as the enemy drew closer. Yet, the Confederates seemed intent on knocking the entire Third Corps back.[211]

New Yorker Rudolf Aschmann estimated that about thirty of the forty-one casualties in the 1st USSS fell in under thirty minutes. With their active work on November 27, the unit had eight more men added to the list of those killed or mortally wounded.

The highest-ranking death was the gloomy but dutiful Thomas Connington, whose early doubts about service in the USSS did not keep the officer from a stern dedication to duty. A comrade penned a letter to Connington's family to express his sadness over the loss of a fine officer. On the following day after examining the ground where Connington fell, some marksmen found that Confederates had already buried the Michigan lieutenant. The family read of their deceased kin as "a faithful and true man" on which a regiment could depend. "I was always proud to call him friend," the letter continued, "and since his noble death more than ever before." In the missive's concluding praise, the writer noted, "None braver or better have gone forth to battle for our country."[212]

Fascinating stories define other Sharpshooters lost at Payne's Farm. John Wilson Irwin Chidsey, a New Yorker in Company B, had only lived twenty years, but he left quite an impact on his family and fellow marksmen. A friend in the company, Harrison De Long, wrote Chidsey's father about the tremendous respect the departed Empire Stater had earned. Chidsey set an impeccable example, the grieving father read, because his son was the best soldier in the company.[213]

Additional lost lives were New Yorker William Hafen, Travis Doty from Company C, Elbridge Hosmer from Vermont, Badgers John W. Johnson and Frank Smith, and two from Michigan, Leander Ballard, and William E. Showers. Struck above the left eye, Hosmer held on to life for a short time. Charles Mead recalled the maudlin scene when Hosmer was buried in early December. Many felt intense sadness for their lost friend, who had a wife and two children back home. Showing great commitment to his country's honor, Hosmer exuded heroism and the sheer determination of an American patriot.[214]

Pvt. Sherrod Brown, a Vermonter in the 1st USSS, would receive a medical discharge six months after his wound at Payne's Farm in November 1863.
LIBRARY OF CONGRESS

Even while losing more members and a respected officer like Connington, other Sharpshooters exhibited great bravery at Payne's Farm, therefore inspiring their comrades. Charles Baker suffered a mouth wound, with the Confederate round dangerously close to the throat. The original USSS historian wrote that Baker "spit the ball out" in response, setting an example of gallantry for his comrades. Also, three days after his twenty-fourth birthday, Ohio native Eliakim Blakeslee, Company C, the regiment's color sergeant, feared not as he performed his vital duty. The resolute Wolverine had already earned a strong reputation for tremendous courage. He added to those laurels on November 27. By spring 1864, Blakeslee would rise to lieutenant, then regimental adjutant.[215]

The sacrifice of the battle yielded little but broken hearts and distressed marksmen. Confidence in General French became another casualty of the day. With the inability of French's command to reach their ordered destination, as Curtis Abbott lamented, "the 3rd corps was now losing its prestige."[216]

"One Whose Loss Will Be Severely Felt"

The tenacious Confederate division holding off the Third Corps north of Robertson's Tavern withdrew to safer ground in the overnight period. The USSS marched south in rainy and muddy conditions on November 28, with much of the next day spent studying the Confederate position. Meade, who lobbed a great deal of consternation at General French for failures since departing Brandy Station, still looked for advantage. By the time the army regrouped near Mine Run, reshuffled lines placed John Sedgwick's Sixth Corps in advance of French. Robert E. Lee, a skillful military engineer, knew he possessed excellent ground along Mine Run. Staff officers under Meade began to accept a harsh reality: Extensive loss of life could be expected if the Union army attacked.[217]

Unsurprisingly, Mine Run found many Sharpshooters on a picket line beyond the small stream. Captain Albert Buxton of the 2nd USSS took a group of men to investigate an area with heavy concentrations of underbrush and trees. The band found Confederates posted behind impressive entrenchments. Those on duty in the overnight period experienced more drenching precipitation and general misery from a lack of rest.

The Mine Run campaign provided eerie previews of Sharpshooter life that would begin in the spring of 1864. Days brought use of the marksmen as infantry, bothersome rains, and unpredictable and seemingly endless hours manning picket lines with the enemy behind breastworks. The "swampy morass" at Mine Run at least included a house between the lines stocked with hens, turkeys, and other edibles, which benefited some Sharpshooters.[218]

On the closing day of November, Meade inflicted a level of justice against General French by parceling out all three divisions, leaving the uninspired corps commander without troops. Birney's men held positions generally in support of artillery, but both USSS regiments, as could be expected, remained part of the division's strong skirmish front. Two other excellent units, the 3rd Michigan and 124th New York, joined the Sharpshooters in a "provisional brigade" on November 30. These men held the expectation of leading a major attack against Lee's forbidding entrenchments. Sharpshooters crossed Mine Run over temporary bridges without drawing much Confederate fire.[219]

A few nonfatal injuries across the companies occurred in the early hours near Mine Run. On the left of the 1st USSS, Company B had multiple casualties as they warily approached the enemy's fortifications. Sergeant Alexander Dupont, one to fall with a wound, his second of the war, had enlisted in August 1862 when thirty years old. Although a later enlistee, Dupont clearly performed duties well while serving with his New York comrades.[220]

Lorenzo Barber took his place of danger with his comrades, like usual. Although the cold weather delayed the loading and firing process, plentiful shooting occurred, with the "Fighting Parson" joining the list of the USSS wounded. After targeting some Virginia hogs between the lines, Barber took a bullet to the leg. Taken north to an Alexandria hospital, Barber's leg and life endured. The beloved friend and chaplain to the Sharpshooters would spend seven months in hospitals, a highly regrettable absence to his comrades in green.[221]

Overall, the Michigan infantry officer leading the provisional brigade reported a total of thirty-six casualties across his four regiments on November 30, several being captured infantry on the right of the line. The biggest loss was Caspar Trepp, who died early the following morning after a shot to the head. Lt. Rudolf Aschmann, nearly hit by the fatal round, witnessed the wound to his "dear, fatherly friend." The round entered near the left temple and exited above Trepp's right ear. Placing the doomed officer on a stretcher, six soldiers moved their fearless commander to the rear. Later, the skirmish line of the USSS also moved back.[222]

"I regret to say that the command has experienced a serious loss in the death of Lieutenant-Colonel Trepp," David Birney reported. "Well liked by the men," as one Green Mountain Sharpshooter wrote of Trepp, his death meant the entire USSS said goodbye to "one whose loss will be severely felt." After an initial burial, General Birney ordered Trepp disinterred, because he did not wish such an excellent officer to rest in enemy soil. Final burial awaited at Green-Wood Cemetery, Brooklyn, New York.[223]

The regiment, now under the command of Badger Frank Marble, took the news of Trepp's death quite hard. Still in Washington recuperating from his Chancellorsville wound, George Hastings felt saddened on hearing of Trepp's death. Not far from a medical discharge, Hastings lauded Trepp as "a true and gallant soldier." As Hastings wrote, he had been informed by a fellow officer, "the men all feel as if they had lost a father." Regarding the possible replacement of Trepp, Hastings bemoaned, "We have no one who can fill his place as he filled it." Although focused on the rigid command structure in military organizations, Trepp retained tremendous respect from his men, deservedly so.[224]

William Ripley, the regiment's original lieutenant colonel, noted how Trepp's focus on military protocol did not damage his reputation. "He was a severe disciplinarian, even harsh; but was endeared to the men by long association in the field, and was sincerely lamented." Fellow officer Charles Stevens added of Trepp, "In his death the Sharpshooter service lost a careful and skillful officer, one who had become well known through the corps for his promptness and efficiency in executing movements intrusted to him." Stevens added Trepp acted with especial valor at Mine Run. He suggested Trepp's manner displayed a nervous sense, perhaps because the leader envisioned the horrible cost the USSS would sustain if they were called on to charge.[225]

Compounding the tragedy of their leader's demise, Trepp's wife would die of typhoid fever less than two months later, leaving three minor children, Christine, Harriet, and Robert. The youngsters ranged in age from six to two years old when their father died. A devoted group worked to ensure the children received some benefits from the government, with the usual bureaucratic process undoubtedly taking a good deal of time. The guardian for the orphans wrote in May 1864 to enlist the State of New York's help in the process to bolster the support for Trepp's progeny.[226]

"Uncle Sam's Sassy Sogers"

On the day of Trepp's deadly wound, Meade intended to launch an attack. Giving Second Corps commander, cantankerous Gouverneur Warren, nearly half the army to strike Lee's right, Meade also ordered John Sedgwick to assail the enemy's left. Confident the previous day, Warren demurred after further study of the Confederate line. The army leader then called off his November 30 plan, refusing to mourn the lost opportunity. In early December he wrote how he would give up command before ordering thousands to needless slaughter.[227]

George Marden wrote of the bitter cold descending in the new month. The troops pulled out, with pickets and many members of the USSS the last to leave on the morning of December 2. Some men essentially sleepwalked back to camp, with a Sharpshooter sometimes having to firmly shake a comrade to remain alert enough to continue the trek. Some green-clad warriors did not finish the retreat until December 3. Returning to camps around Brandy Station one week after the campaign began, the USSS settled in for winter.[228]

The Mine Run campaign stood as the largest engagement for the USSS between Gettysburg and the Wilderness, a period of ten months. In addition to the loss of the beloved Trepp, nearly fifty Sharpshooters sustained wounds, causing expected absences from the field for many, some of whom endured long hospital stays.

As deaths from disease and wounds continued, the military retained capital punishment for some cases of desertion. With all their devotion to country and the drive to risk life for the cause, certain Sharpshooters felt sympathy for doomed soldiers who fled their responsibilities. Marksmen wrote of a Maine infantryman who was executed on December 4. Four men carried the hopeless deserter's coffin behind him as a band played the dead march. At the fatal moment, George Marden averred, "The prisoner fell dead into his coffin" after the firing squad performed their duty. Opining as a soldier and philosopher, Wyman White considered officers to blame for the wayward warrior who had been subjected to the firing squad. White concluded the condemned man should not have been executed.[229]

With nothing gained along Mine Run, members of the public far from war wondered about the possibility of ever gaining victory worth the cost. Doubts of a daughter about the army's fortitude led to a pointed response from Minnesota Lt. Owen Evans. In a December letter, he corrected his daughter's analysis of Mine Run. "We have the flower of the rebel army to fight," the experienced father conveyed. Evans added, "Meade acted very wisely in returning with the full strength of his army." Evans also dissented from what he described as his daughter's implication that Meade "likes rest better than fighting." Evans suggested the army wants "the rebellion crushed so effectively that it can never again raise its hydra head." Even with his effort to correct his daughter's impressions of the Mine Run fiasco, he implored her to put forward ideas about the war.[230]

Doldrums of the cold season in the USSS camp dominated life for weeks. Construction of new homes—or improvements to existing structures—warmed the Sharpshooters and kept men more limber and happier than lazier soldiers. Thomas Brown—with tentmates John Page, James Guthrie, and Alvin Babcock—worked hard across the first third of December to upgrade their housing. A vital fireplace became part of the cramped hut, but the necessity of taking up space for heating could not be denied. The motivated quartet hoped to stay in their "perfect" house for the whole winter, which they did for most days.

Before the next summer ended, two of the four Green Mountain men sharing the hut would be dead.[231]

Gathering firewood became a necessity for Sharpshooters not on picket duty. A Badger suggested the lack of timber seemed the only drawback to camp on the Botts farm. Once again complaining about the abuse of his property, Botts gained a guard over a respectable hardwood grove. Thus, soldiers had to spend more time bringing biomass to camp. In some cases, wagons would cross more than a mile filled with the necessary heating resource.[232]

Like those bringing in firewood, some picket details had to walk several miles to reach their area of responsibility, adding to the amount of cold those Sharpshooters faced. Labor meant warmth due to activity, but Sharpshooters on duty shivered from the elements. Men likely preferred sitting near a fireplace, some made of stone, while in their uninsulated huts. A penchant for idleness prompted one Badger to change the acronym of their organization. USSS members became known as Uncle Sam's Sassy Sogers over the winter, the last word a reference to those turned into lazy or unmotivated people.[233]

In a December 20 letter home, Gardner Clark, a private at the start of the war who rose to captain of Company C, 1st USSS in late 1863, wondered about the fate of his country.

> *Today I was thinking what slaves we all are. Slaves to stronger minds than ours. Slaves for good or ill as fate may decide. We give up our own individuality to an organization and then follow its footsteps like beaten hounds. By what right have a few who hold the reins of the U.S. Government precipitated a long and cruel war upon thirty-million of their fellow beings. They say to preserve Human Liberty as our forefathers left it. Is it not just possible they are thrusting a worse bondage upon us than relieving us from tyranny?*[234]

Such an attitude does not seem like the naïve ramblings of a young soldier upset with his fate. By this point, Clark was a devoted and experienced warrior of the nation's fratricide. Regardless of any individual's views of the Lincoln administration or any particular political mindset, questioning the intentions of government during such a challenging time seems natural. Clark neither abandoned nor worked against his cause. Rather, he was simply worn down by the war. The nature of continuous operations in a seemingly perpetual conflict could easily be seen as contrary to the American ideal of freedom as a birthright. Feeling like a slave in the army might be expected from an apprehensive American soldier during any war. After all, Clark's nation had been founded by those concerned about the possibility of a military dictator destroying liberty.

A counterpoint to Clark's worst-case scenario found expression in William Ripley's history of Company F, 1st USSS. After his discussion of the Payne's Farm fiasco of November 27, the Medal of Honor winner suggested a higher cause made the war necessary.

> *To the misjudging, war doth appear to be a worse calamity than slavery; because its miseries are collected together within a short space and time as may be easily, at one view, taken in and perceived. But the misfortunes of nations cursed by slavery, being distributed over many centuries and many places, are of greater weight and number.*[235]

With the government campaigning for experienced soldiers to sign on for additional service, the issue of reenlistment occupied the minds of many across the eighteen companies. Bonus payments, furloughs home, and patriotic ardor led many to sign up again. Two days before Christmas, Capt. Jacob McClure wrote Maine's adjutant general, "I have honor to inform you that my company has enlisted to serve three years from the 21st day of December." The stalwart officer added his belief that the Maine men soon expected to head home for a short time away from the army.[236]

One hundred percent of the twenty-one present members of Company H, 2nd USSS, reenlisted in December. These motivated Vermonters went home as a group for their furlough starting on January 7, 1864. They returned, Curtis Abbott proudly recorded, in late February, ready for the rest of winter and eager to see the horrible and bloody war conclude in victory.[237]

Extended time on picket may have decreased the desire for a longer term of service for those teams of Sharpshooters on duty in the period around Christmas Day. Manning the picket line meant a trek to the Rapidan, about six miles from camp. Henry Bedell's detail stood in December's weather for seventy-two hours, with two days of rations delivered to the group of eagle-eyed marksmen. The long time away from a more comfortable hut ended nicely on the 27th, as Bedell and his band received a ration of whiskey.[238]

Wyman White originally intended to not reenlist. As of the day before Christmas, White stood as one of only four marksmen in his company to not sign up for more than three years of service. Perhaps the inducements for another tour of duty, including a large cash payment, did the trick. Maybe the speech Lieutenant Colonel Stoughton delivered in favor of reenlistment worked some magic. For his own reasons, White changed his mind on Christmas Day, obligating him for more time in the military, while granting him a wintry sojourn home. The Granite Stater's furlough would start early in the new year, with his return to the regiment occurring on March 18.[239]

Because of their firm intent to see the war through, Sharpshooters reenlisting before 1863 ended did not need the inducement from division commander Birney when he requested men elect to sign up for more service. Birney's January 2 statement summed up the pride he felt across his brigades, including the brave marksmen he knew well. Birney wrote of his men perceiving "that he has never called on the division without a hearty and cheering response." Birney expressed confidence that a large number would reenlist. He must have grown quite pleased when he heard of the status of the 2nd Sharpshooters. Army data from January 5 noted 189 men in the regiment had agreed to become "Veteran Volunteers," the phrase to describe soldiers deciding to stay in the army.[240]

Opening Weeks of Fateful 1864

When he picked up a blank diary on New Year's Day, Charles Ford, Company I, 1st USSS, did not know if he would live through the entire year. The young marksman also may have been too modest to accept he would fill each day with a plethora of tidbits about service in the USSS, leaving history one of the greatest primary sources on Sharpshooter life. His first entries included remarks about the bane of a Civil War soldier's winter. Rain falling on the last day of 1863 continued as the calendar flipped to January. New Year's Day opened with a goopy mess around camp as gloomy skies still dropped precipitation. At least on the following day, a hard freeze made the ground solid for Ford and his comrades.[241]

As the harshest part of winter began, family members wished to improve the lives of their Sharpshooter heroes in Virginia. The unmotivated William Greene, Company G, 2nd USSS, was one who received treats from home. Greene's January 4 letter to his mother detailed the items she had mailed to Brandy Station. Although many such packages arrived with spoiled items, the cold weather allowed Greene to enjoy and share a supper of pork spare ribs with two tentmates. Greene also found much use for other edibles—such as pies and doughnuts—as well as the needle and yarn. One comrade especially liked the tobacco Mrs. Greene provided. Plans for making hoe cakes and flap jacks would be supported, Greene wrote, by the yeast his diligent mother put in the package.[242]

Kindness from the home front included gifts from strangers. On January 10, Sharpshooters and some infantry comrades moved to a camp two miles closer to Culpeper with vital new hand protection. A Badger Sharpshooter wrote of being situated at Camp Bullock, named to honor "a Philadelphia gentleman" who paid for mittens for each member of Birney's Division, about seven thousand pairs. For more vigorous marksmen, boxing gloves received extensive use across winter weeks.[243]

Weather did not turn horribly cold as January advanced. Thaws brought problems in the form of the unforgettable Virginia mud, but seasonable nights made picket duty somewhat bearable. Dress parades and inspections could be performed if Old Man Winter did not act too unmercifully, but days of hard rains were recorded throughout January. With pleasant temperatures occurring later in the month, routine duty defined life for the marksmen.[244]

From the 1st USSS camp on January 27, George Marden began a letter home, "Incidents of which to compose a letter are as scarce as hen's teeth." Soldiers learned to make small changes to their lives as a means of improving their daily conditions, Marden continued, giving proper credit to experience as a great teacher. "The weather is of course as unfailing for a topic as it was in the days of Noah," the comedian warrior continued, with very nice warmth seen for a few days after the downpours. One problem, Marden suggested, was the dearth of snow that would make an evening sleigh ride to view the moon quite memorable. Marden then detailed an unfortunate lifestyle choice many soldiers made.

> *Tonight there will be a great drunk as the sutler has just come from Washington. Drunkenness seems to be an epidemic. They take turns. First one officer and then another. The men follow suit as they have opportunity. . . . The Third Corps had a great ball at 3rd Division Head Qtrs. Monday night. I did not go though I had an invitation. It turned out as I expected, a great drunk.*[245]

The party Marden mentioned received coverage in the New York press. Looking more on the bright side than Marden, a reporter deemed the grand event the "first army ball of the season." The large house hosting the festivities, which a Third Corps division commander used as his headquarters, stood a mile south of Brandy Station. General Meade's chief of staff Andrew Humphreys joined the gala, although the invited President Lincoln missed out.[246]

Furloughs resulting from reenlistments contributed to the relatively quiet state of the USSS camp through several weeks of early 1864. Less experienced Sharpshooters, or those choosing to not extend their time in the military, had concerns about staying warm, not getting mail, and finding enough to eat each day. Sickness nagged Charles Mead through early February. He then found sundry amusements to occupy time when not on duty, including card games and chess. Mead recorded sounds of fighting on February 6, when part of the army and some Sharpshooters forayed to Morton's Ford on the Rapidan. Soaked and muddy soldiers trekked back to camp the following day to no advantage. A similar theme played out at the end of February in a jaunt to James City. Without fulfilling a major military purpose, the Sharpshooters logged some exercise and time away from camp's routine. Summing up the James City trek, Caspar Kent wrote home, "all nearly tired out, I assure you." Expressing Sharpshooter optimism, he closed, "The weather is warm and pleasant again and after we get rested we shall be good as new again."[247]

Those heading home on furlough sometimes had a longer time away than expected. Maine's James Matthews had gone north on January 7, bound first for the national capital. By the 11th, he enjoyed breakfast in Boston, with arrival home in Rockland, Maine, during the evening of January 13. Able to add time away from Virginia due to the recruiting duty to which he was assigned, Matthews did not rejoin the army for several weeks. After the southbound trip, he reached Washington again on February 27.[248]

Even the long-absent William Greene received a furlough after he elected to reenlist. The soldier who absconded more than a year did not garner the government's scorn to the point of losing his right to go home for a time. Only back with the Sharpshooters since December 1863, Greene traveled to New Hampshire shortly before Matthews went north. Like the Company D man, Greene found extra duty in New Hampshire, including work at a hospital in Concord. He would depart home in late March, rejoining Company G, 2nd USSS on April 1. Three weeks later, he wrote his mother, with the implication of using the private care he was receiving from a doctor to act lame in hopes of avoiding more difficult duty.[249]

Mud and monotony had ruled the weeks of February and March for Sharpshooters in Virginia. Joseph Barton, only two months away from a mortal wound, found simple pleasures in the food available in early March. "The government gives us soft bread and hard tack," the Vermonter in Company H, 2nd USSS wrote with delight. He also devoured "beef and pork, coffee, & shuger, beans & dried apples. We live first rate and cook our own meels, steep our own coffee. I own a coffee pot."[250]

Transition to Spring

The biggest change for the army as winter turned to spring in 1864 resulted from the decision of President Lincoln to reward Ulysses S. Grant for his achievements in the Western Theater. The most successful Union field commander of the war, Grant rose to lieutenant general, the highest-ranking individual in the army. Meade retained command of the Army of the Potomac—and deserved credit for positive changes to the army's administration in recent months. Yet, greater boldness seemed necessary to improve outcomes for the Union's effort in Virginia, even considering the poor supply situation and number of desertions in Lee's army. To avoid political entanglements, Grant would bypass Washington through service in the field alongside Meade. Grant's elevation meant fighting in earnest would prevail when warmer weather returned.[251]

Andrew Westervelt—California Joe No. 2—wrote home to Shasta County after Grant's initial visit to the army. The fresh injection of Grant's leadership buoyed Westervelt, who knew the purpose of the sacrifice he had witnessed since joining the 1st Sharpshooters. In an April letter, which departed Virginia, and then traveled 3,500 miles for publication back home, Westervelt declared,

> *I think, when the true history of this war is written, that the Army of the Potomac will then show how many brave men have fallen while we were defending the emblem of freedom. Many has been the Generals who have led us, but I think we now have as able a man as can be found, . . . I wish I could tell you some of the stories which we get from rebels who desert and come to us. It is said that four hundred came in to day in a body, and I have no doubt of it, as we see the account of their arrival in Washington every day, . . . It is hard to think how many men have been used up in the regiment, as we are almost the first in a fight . . . there never was another body of men in any regiment who possessed any more courage than the men in this regiment.*[252]

Another major change occurred as Meade received authorization to consolidate the number of corps in his army. After their great losses in leadership and personnel since Chancellorsville, neither the First nor Third Corps truly recovered. The two corps disappeared, with the USSS joining the Second Corps under Winfield Scott Hancock, finally returned from a serious wound at Gettysburg. Like the months before the change, the Sharpshooters stood in different brigades under David Birney, leading Hancock's Third Division. Old comrades from the Third Corps brigaded with the USSS. Homer Stoughton's 2nd Regiment served with Hobart Ward in the First Brigade, while Alexander Hays led the Second Brigade, including the 1st USSS and eight infantry regiments. Major Charles P. Mattocks, from the 17th Maine Infantry, commanded Berdan's old outfit.[253]

In early April, General Hays referred to his brigade as "the finest command in the army," and he may have been right. The experienced leader still hoped for promotion to major general, something he craved in letters. Sharpshooter Perrin Judkins worked on Hays's staff, along with marksman Cpt. Frank Marble, who would hold a brigade position for the rest of his excellent service. Hays wrote of his happiness with those who served him, deeming his staff "exceedingly pleasant boys."[254]

Harrison De Long, Company B, 1st USSS, especially liked one result of the Third Corps' demise, the departure of "veteran whisky sucker" Maj. Gen. William H. French. Losing his command, French was assigned to Philadelphia. De Long lacked an understanding of why French's orders took him to the city, but "I presume he can get gin cheaper" away from the army.[255]

As Grant's elevation and corps reorganization played out, target practice and instruction prevailed. On March 18, a shooting schedule went into effect for members of the 1st USSS. From 11 a.m. to noon six days a week, companies would alternate at the shooting range. More training occurred in a school for noncommissioned officers, created on April 6. The classes aimed to instill the wide variety of rules and practices expected of those important members of a regiment. Any sergeant not on duty was compelled to attend.[256]

Initially doubtful about the army's decision to create Sharpshooter companies, General Hays found much to commend when seeing the marksmen train. In an April 17 letter, the brigade commander praised the USSS as a group of soldiers who "will strike a man invariably at five hundred yards and a horse at eight hundred." In reference to earlier qualms about the Sharpshooters, Hays continued, "They are improving very fast."[257]

As part of the army's very active early spring, new USSS members made their way to Brandy Station. A group of inexperienced soldiers departed Lansing, Michigan soon after mustering in back home in late February. With a stop in Washington, the men soon made their way to camp. After joining their comrades in Company B, 2nd USSS, one unidentified Sharpshooter penned an update to a Michigan newspaper.

> *We are in sight of the Blue Ridge mountains. They appear to be about four miles off, but are really fifteen. We have a very nice camp ground on top of a hill. The 1st U. S. S. S. are just above us. . . . When we first arrived, we were set at work on our log shanties, or tents, which is quite an undertaking. They are eight by eleven feet, and about four feet high; then there is the cloth or shelter tents that go on the top of these, which makes very comfortable quarters. We should have had ours finished, if we could have had an axe, but they being very scarce, we have to wait our turn. Four of us occupy one tent.*

Although the rookies had not yet received rifles, they seamlessly transitioned from civilian to soldier. The Wolverine's letter included an overview of a Sharpshooter's daily schedule, starting with the 6 a.m. bugle call to get out of bed. After breakfast, the men performed drill or other ordered work until noon. Necessary activities revved up again after lunch, with lights out at 8 p.m.[258]

Other states' recruiting efforts across the months after Gettysburg bore fruit, with the Pennsylvania company adding six new members in April. Additional soldiers returned to several companies from long periods in hospitals, or as paroled prisoners. Minnesotan Albert Corwin had come back to Company A in the autumn after being captured at Chancellorsville. Later, the unfortunate Midwesterner left again due to nagging medical problems. Because of the continued drain of manpower from sickness, the Minnesotans only had thirty-four members at the start of May.[259]

Recruits and the relatively healthy returning to camp could not always keep up with the drain from sickness each month. Fortunately, USSS companies with historically high numbers of disability discharges saw reduced instances of such problems through the first four months of 1864. Neither the New Hampshire nor Vermont companies in the 1st USSS lost any members to discharges during the opening third of the year. Still, many men left the ranks, including nine from Company E, 2nd USSS. The Vermonters lost members to death, disability discharges, or transfers to the Veteran Reserve Corps. Losses included the short time as a soldier for Andrew Berry, Company G, 2nd Regiment. He had enlisted in February, only to die two months later of typhoid fever at Brandy Station. Berry shared qualities with Robert Twombly, of the same company, who lost his life at Antietam. Both men lived in Tamworth, New Hampshire, with death before their twentieth birthday, followed by burial at Riverside Cemetery.[260]

Weather and the quantity of supplies improved as April advanced. As he prepared for his birthday early in the month, Company F's Charles Mead dodged a good deal of rain, a frequent irritant across many days since Mine Run. With many in the 1st USSS deciding to not reenlist, some men began counting down the days until muster out, as early as August for some of the regiment's members. Rudolf Aschmann tallied only twenty-six present in Company A as the men prepared for Grant's opening salvos against the Confederates. Although hit hard by illness across previous months, the 1st Regiment's Vermonters had more than forty in the ranks as April wound down, an indicator of productive recruiting.[261]

Warmer days brought signs of the next campaign, with a decrease in mud very much appreciated. Reviews before generals or other dignitaries gave the army a chance to display the power Grant would wield. Gardner Clark's April 13 letter noted his attendance at a review, followed by an evening brigade dress parade. The soldiers might loathe such festive occasions due to the marching required just to arrive at the event's location. At least Clark happily noted both Meade and Hancock's attendance.[262]

Soldiers feeling ready and confident had to perform much work to earn the esteem of their commanding officers. As a Vermonter in the 1st USSS informed a newspaper in an April 24 letter, "we have done a *heap* of *getting ready*" for the looming campaign. In addition to preparing all equipment, a move in the camp of the 1st USSS brought further labor, including the need for intense work gathering more firewood. The letter expounded on the preparations of the troops for the unknown action ahead, "Our time has been nearly all occupied lately, by reviews, and inspections, till it seems to me that our *appearance* must suit the most difficult taste . . . even the white gloves have not been forgotten." Perhaps General Grant grew impressed when reviewing the Second Corps two days before. Although finery in a marksman's dress and the honed bearing of well-trained troops cannot automatically win battles, a confidence comes from competence and good showings in front of senior officers. Hoping to fight as well as they looked, the Vermonter humorously wondered, "How can the rebellion stand before white gloves, and well-polished brasses and—boots?"[263]

Festus Spencer, a Michigan Sharpshooter also composing a letter on April 24, devoted much of his comments to family matters. He expressed thanks for his mother's recent package, including a newspaper and chocolate. The Sharpshooter then acknowledged he had not reciprocated sufficiently to her kindness. Spencer held strong positive feelings for family, including his "Dear Sister." He hoped all would accept "tons of affections." Cognizant of what the warming weather would mean, the Sharpshooter expected an end to the army's generally inactive winter weeks.[264]

Table 2.1 illustrates the placement of the two USSS regiments in David Birney's Division on April 30, 1864, five weeks after the dissolution of the Third Corps. As part of the highly respected Second Corps under Winfield Scott Hancock, the Sharpshooters knew their fighting destiny called. They joined nearly thirty thousand men present for duty across Hancock's four infantry divisions.[265]

Even with dozens of new recruits, the Sharpshooters had unfortunately lost some excellent members in the closing weeks of their idle time near Brandy Station. Jacob McClure, who had worked hard to implement the Sharpshooter concept as early as the summer of 1861, received a disability discharge on April 12. He wrote home about "not being able to perform the duties of a line officer, and march through an active campaign." With the loss of Daniel Cummings, another officer gone a few weeks before, the Maine contingent in the 2nd USSS would go forward under the command of Stephen Barker, who McClure had recommended for the vacant captaincy.[266]

Table 2.1. The Sharpshooters and Birney's Division April 30, 1864

Third Division, Second Corps, Army of the Potomac
Maj. Gen. David Birney
First Brigade
Brig. Gen. John Henry Hobart Ward
2nd United States Sharpshooters
20th Indiana
3rd Maine
40th New York
86th New York
124th New York
99th Pennsylvania
110th Pennsylvania
141st Pennsylvania
Second Brigade
Brig. Gen. Alexander Hays
1st United States Sharpshooters
4th Maine
17th Maine
3rd Michigan
5th Michigan
93rd New York
57th Pennsylvania
63rd Pennsylvania
105th Pennsylvania

Source: Official Records, vol. 33, 1038.

Weather across April did not always cooperate with the army's need to drill and prepare for another bloody spring campaign. Charles Ford's 1864 diary listed snow on April 2, followed by the invariable mud, which must have flustered Sharpshooters on work details, such as those once again bringing wood to camp. "Very dull times" prevailed on April 10, with the following day dominated by "nothing going on" due to the mud. Police detail, postings on the picket line, brigade dress parade, and the reviews before senior leaders meant some of

Ford's days had more meaning. Water and mud could still conquer for a time. Undoubtedly frustrated, Ford wrote on April 16, "Woke up laying in the water, raining hard."[267]

Rain could not disrupt the grand strategy of attacking and weakening Confederate armies. Overseeing all U.S. Army operations across the entire nation, General Grant originally envisioned a swift move of Meade's Army of the Potomac, assisted by Ambrose Burnside's unattached Ninth Corps. Such a maneuver toward Richmond would allow Meade to link up with Benjamin Butler's Army of the James, advancing west along their namesake river. Uniting Meade and Butler's forces served as Grant's primary aim, as he wrote his Washington-based chief of staff Henry Halleck on April 29.[268]

Of course, Robert E. Lee's undersized yet highly motivated Confederates had a say in how the Union's spring offensive would unfold. General Grant's plans ensured USSS members a role in the inevitable combat. Having seen tremendous sacrifice at some of the largest battles of the war thus far, even the most prescient member of the Sharpshooters likely could not envision how much May's hellfire would cost. The deadliest month of combat for the marksmen was about to begin.

Part Three

"The many brave boys we have lost," May 1864–February 1865

Through the centuries, soldiers have learned the fickleness of life. Change for Civil War troops seemed a constant, as described in the diary of Michigan Sharpshooter Charles Ford for the first two days of May. After closing April on police duty and firewood detail, Ford jotted down "clear and pleasant" to describe weather at the opening of the new month. By the evening of May 2, a major wind and rain storm displaced the great conditions, souring moods, and leading men to scramble to batten down loose objects and tents.[1]

Inclement conditions failed to dent the pull of war. Orders issued on the 2nd outlined a grand vision for the advance of Meade's army. General Hancock and the Second Corps would cross the Rapidan at Ely's Ford, four and half miles northwest of Chancellorsville. With the Fifth and Sixth Corps spanning the river at Germanna Ford, the Sharpshooters advanced with Hancock as the easternmost infantry under Meade. Guided by cavalry and with the assistance of engineers, bridges would facilitate the army's crossing of the river, with alacrity expected. Each man was ordered to lug six days of rations and fifty rounds of ammunition on their person, increasing the weight each rested warrior already carried.[2]

A flurry of activity occurred in the USSS camp as the men prepared for the new campaign. Packing began in earnest on the morning of May 3. The Sharpshooters departed from a relatively new camp; a sanitation improvement had required the short move. Leaving the site seemed bittersweet to some, as the pleasant spot melded with warmer weather to refresh men from the relatively dormant colder months.[3]

With many generals planning and issuing orders, philosophical missives home were written earlier in the evening. Penning the final sentence his wife would ever see from her husband, General Hays noted, "All our boys are well" and hopeful for the campaign.[4]

Caspar Kent, one of the many Sharpshooters who would not survive the spring offensives, updated a Vermont newspaper with an extensive letter later in May. He recalled the sense of readiness the USSS and the whole army felt while still north of the Rapidan. Although midnight on May 4 was the ordered time to start the move south, Kent timed the brigade's departure from camp near Brandy Station at 10:30 p.m., ninety minutes ahead of schedule. "We left camp very quietly, not a bugle or drum was sounded," Kent recalled. Sharpshooters departed for the bloodiest month in their history rather calmly, "as though we were going out on drill to be back in an hour or so."[5]

Shortly before dawn on May 4, the Sharpshooters rested north of the Rapidan. Birney and his brigades moved across the river later in the morning, with the day's camp established around Chancellorsville by early afternoon. Evidence of the previous spring's battle abounded in the woods. Charles Mead picked up a skull he considered Confederate, without certainty as to the cause for which that particular solider died. Shells, bullets, and other detritus of Hooker's flubbed fight could be seen. As historian William Ripley wrote, USSS members "found also the graves of some of their lost comrades, buried where they fell, while in many places human bones shone white and ghastly in the moonlight."[6]

Looking around the temporary camp on the old battlefield, Caspar Kent recorded scenes of the past, while enjoying two rare but highly desirable commodities: quiet and safety. Despite finding bones "bleaching the ground," Kent wrote of pleasant images seen from the concluding part of the march on May 4, when the USSS bivouac would be established near remnants of the Chancellor House.

> *We passed over the same ground where if you recollect I wrote you by moonlight one year ago, but how different now from then! Now it is still as death, and but for the rude marks left by shot and shell and the breastworks, one would think that Virginia never heard the barking of the iron dogs of war. One year ago, too, we had to speak at the top of our voices to be heard, for shot and shell were crashing on every side.*[7]

Regardless of the maudlin memories a camp at Chancellorsville could bring, Meade's overnight start to the army's march across the Rapidan had taken advantage of darkness. Yet, Confederate signalmen on hills near Mine Run only needed daylight to detect the moving Union horde. Fortunately for the Army of the Potomac, the river crossings happened without much incident and in a timely manner.[8] Little else would go right over the next few days.

Confusion Begins in the Wilderness

For the second consecutive May, Union military fortunes encountered enormous problems in the Wilderness. Planned for weeks and formulated into sensible orders, the movement of the Army of the Potomac became as intractable as the tangled undergrowth giving the name to the region south of the Rapidan. Like Hooker's mess at Chancellorsville the year before, a battle in the cramped confines of seemingly limitless forest had not been part of Grant's original vision. A position due south of Mine Run was the goal, facilitated partly by the USSS and the rest of the Second Corps making a rapid march to Todd's Tavern and beyond.

Meade erroneously expected the Confederates would remain protected in their Mine Run entrenchments. Due to the boldness of Robert E. Lee, however, Union troops first engaged the Confederates about two miles west of Wilderness Tavern, well east of Mine Run. A rookie Union cavalry general utterly failed to detect the bold advance of Lee's heavily outnumbered infantry, bringing a halt in the march of the entire Fifth Corps. Instead of controlling events as Grant and Meade envisioned, four divisions of one corps would form a north-south line against Lee's move toward the east. The disastrous fighting in and mainly south of Saunders Field on the Orange Turnpike, with the Second Corps miles away, created a large gap between the wings of Meade's army. For the next two days, the army's senior leaders would be unable to satisfy a basic aspect of their orders, "Corps commander will keep in communication and connect with each other, and co-operate whenever necessary."[9]

Before the latest fiasco unfolded, Sharpshooters arose early on May 5 after about fifteen hours of rest around Chancellorsville. Thirty years later, William Kent remembered waking up that fateful day still feeling his dusty throat and sunburned face from the marching that had opened the campaign. Taking the advance, Birney's two brigades needed until 9:30 a.m. to reach Todd's Tavern. USSS companies marched on the flanks of the division to scout for the enemy as much as the consuming woods allowed. Pursuant to the plan from headquarters, Hancock would have marched west for several more miles to reach the assigned position. Confused about Confederate intentions, headquarters ordered Hancock to halt when his men reached Todd's Tavern. After a short break, late morning orders altered the destiny of the USSS. Instead of continuing west, Birney's men turned north on the Brock Road, to a crucial intersection with the Orange Plank Road. The USSS needed to cover nearly five miles to reach the crossroads. John "Captain Jack" Wilson, 1st Regiment, would report Birney's brigades "proceeded with all haste." They arrived in a timely manner to help begin two days of some of the worst and most concentrated bloodletting in the history of American warriors.[10]

Birney's brigades reached the division of George Getty, part of the Sixth Corps sent south to halt a bold advance of men under Confederate Gen. A. P. Hill. Meade very much wanted a rapid lunge from Hancock's entire command. Such a western thrust was necessary to link the Second and Fifth Corps. Unknown to Meade, Hancock and the four divisions nearby would need much more time to concentrate along the Brock Road. To satisfy his orders, Getty wished to strike Hill. Hancock would send Birney's men forward to assist after Getty became engaged, with the USSS playing a part in the confused brawl to the west. With the trackless and forbidding forest, Caspar Kent labeled the area of battle, "the most lonely place I ever saw."[11]

Sharpshooters from northern New England may have especially enjoyed serving near a brigade of Sixth Corps infantry. Five Vermont regiments, who would lose more men to battle death than any brigade in all Union armies, had a crucial role to play on May 5. Getty's command included two other excellent brigades. With Hancock's growing assemblage of battle-tested divisions, a great opportunity existed to rout the pugnacious Hill and his bold Confederates. Alas, the gods of war dictated another outcome across the late afternoon and evening of May 5.[12]

Major General Winfield Scott Hancock led the Second Corps and the two USSS regiments into the hellfire of the Wilderness and Spotsylvania Court House. LIBRARY OF CONGRESS

Captain John Wilson, Company B, 1st USSS. BRIAN T. WHITE COLLECTION

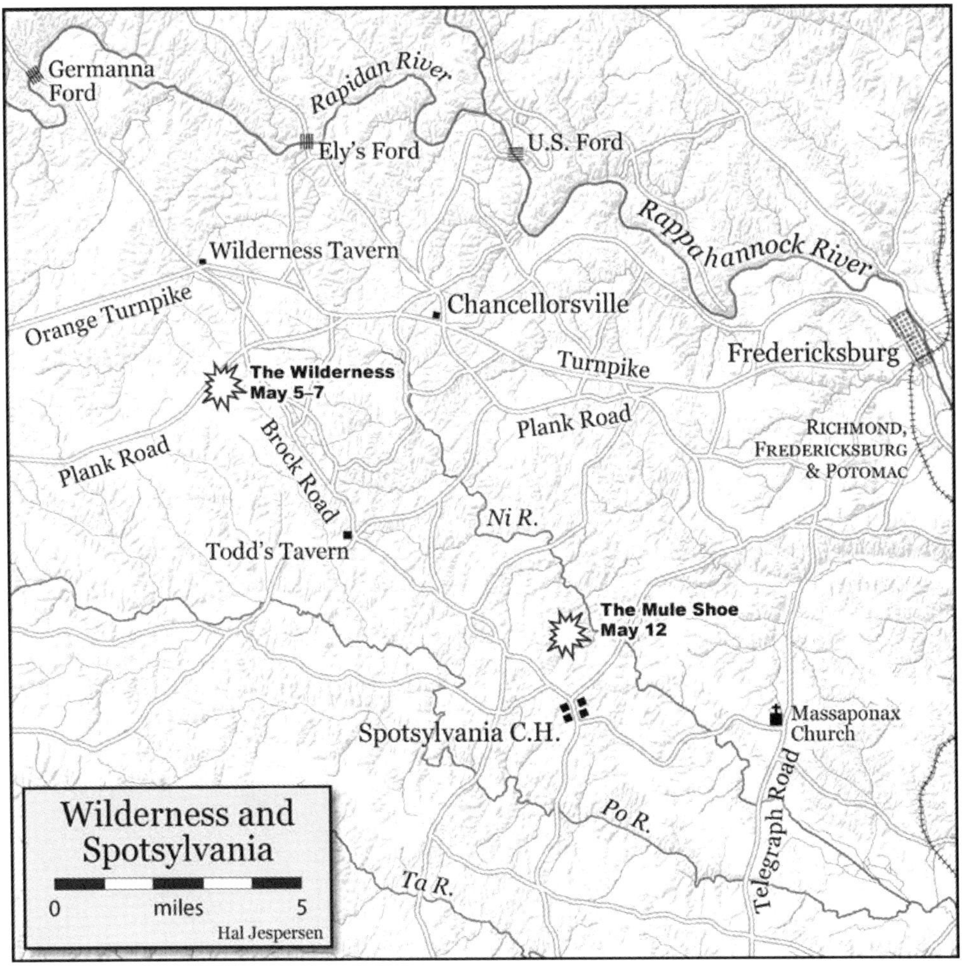
Germanna Ford
Rapidan River
Ely's Ford
U.S. Ford
Rappahannock River
Wilderness Tavern
Orange Turnpike
Chancellorsville
Fredericksburg
Turnpike
The Wilderness May 5–7
Plank Road
Brock Road
Plank Road
Richmond, Fredericksburg & Potomac
Ni R.
Todd's Tavern
The Mule Shoe May 12
Spotsylvania C.H.
Massaponax Church
Telegraph Road
Po R.
Ta R.
Wilderness and Spotsylvania
0 miles 5
Hal Jespersen

The ground of the advance, what Hancock deemed "a perfect thicket," dictated the type of fight that developed. Charge and counter-charge with poor vision and disrupted formations defined the hours for the warring divisions. Of the undergrowth, a Maine infantry officer remembered, "The low foliage was so dense you could not see beyond pistol range." Because of the thick, unmanaged forest and weeds, troops could often not hear other units engaged even with the intense firing across a wide front. For much of the forward move west of Brock Road, Vermonter William Kent rarely saw anything beyond the Sharpshooter comrades on his immediate right and left.[13]

The Confederates held good ground in their defense against Getty and Birney, "repelling assault after assault," as a Tar Heel remembered. Gaining confidence in their ability to dominate their foes, some North Carolinians believed pressure could force the enemy back. They quickly ran into deep trouble along Brock Road, which Hancock's men had been turning into an impressive line of entrenchments. Still, some Sharpshooters found themselves in tough circumstances. Charles Mead wrote of his inability to see an advancing enemy line until the Southerners marched close to his position. Comrades nearby had already fallen back.[14]

David French was one of the first USSS members to suffer a fatal battle wound in the horribly deadly month of May 1864.
BRIAN T. WHITE COLLECTION

What Capt. John Wilson deemed "quite a skirmish" greatly impacted one company of the USSS. Starting in the late afternoon, five Vermonters in the 1st Regiment sustained fatal wounds. In addition, Badger Michael Costello fell with a wound costing a leg and then his life. As the only USSS members to die from injuries that day, the marksmen might be considered lucky. Regiments in Birney's command suffered far more than the Sharpshooters in many instances as the waning daylight added to difficulties across the lines south of the Plank Road.[15]

The five lost Company F marksmen were: Artemas Cross, William Domag, David French, Edward Trask, and William Wilson. Buried at Fredericksburg National Cem-

Only twenty-three years old, Maj. Charles Mattocks, commanding the 1st USSS, became a prisoner of war at the battle of the Wilderness.
MAINE STATE ARCHIVES

etery, Cross, an 1862 enlistee, had yet to reach his nineteenth birthday. Finding his resting place near Burlington, Domag's parents had several years to lament their lost warrior. French fell six years after his wife's death, while Trask lost his life not far from where he suffered a shoulder wound one year and a day before. In all, nearly 25 percent of the company's men suffered wounds on May 5, a devastating loss to a command familiar with bloody experiences.[16]

Brigadier General Alexander Hays died from a shot to the head on May 5, costing the 1st USSS their brigade commander. With the capture of Maj. Charles Mattocks, the 1st Sharpshooters also lost their regimental commander. Hays, a West Point classmate of Ulysses Grant, received a wonderful encomium from the army's highest-ranking officer. Vermonter William Kent remembered feeling a "shudder" when seeing the dead Hays shortly before moving out for the day's battle. Although doubtful of the Sharpshooters at first, Hays learned to respect the green-clad warriors in his brigade, and the feelings were mutual.[17]

Casualties in the 2nd Sharpshooters were relatively light on May 5. The men manned a reserve position in Ward's Brigade after serving as skirmishers in the unremitting forest. Providing fine service later, members of the 2nd USSS helped haul off an abandoned cannon between the lines.[18] The deaths of men from only two of eighteen USSS companies suggest some elements of the 1st USSS also had positions behind the main lines for much of the fighting.

William Kent could thank his knapsack for preventing a possibly fatal injury. Hit in the back, the surprised Green Mountain marksman inspected his personal items in the evening. A Confederate bullet went through blankets, paper, tobacco, and other items without breaking his skin. The notable welt between his shoulder blades constituted the worst aspect of the difficult moment for Kent, who settled down on the battlefield with a group of four other Sharpshooters for the very dark and eerie overnight period.[19]

The Union's brave warriors had inflicted much misery on their opponents. One Confederate brigade at the apex of the slaughter lost more than a thousand men on May 5. Accurately summing up the Southern experience across the frightful hours south of the Plank Road, a Tar Heel officer remembered, "We had to contend against large odds till near sundown." Another cogent Carolinian could not believe what he had witnessed that day, when men in blue and green fought incredibly hard to push back the brave Confederate division willing to fall to the last man. He recorded thoughts of the day's "slugging match" as the opposing soldiers fired at each other a few yards apart, then ceased after reaching the utmost brink of human endurance. As Granite State Sharpshooter Wyman White recalled, the stubborn nature of the fighting dictated the excessively violent outcome, even as the lines of the contending forces changed very little.[20]

DEADLIEST DAY

A grim stalemate in the area around the intersection did not leave all men inactive from the exhausting fight as the evening's darkness settled in. Some soldiers went forward in an effort to bring in wounded comrades. As Charles Stevens remembered, the stretcher bearers worked feverishly "in that black, grim, dismal wood." The compassionate Vermonter Caspar Kent assisted some wounded marksmen to a hospital, where the fatigued soldier worked for two days.[21]

The death Kent may have avoided through his hospital work would call him far sooner than he wished. On May 6, however, he escaped the costliest day in the history of the USSS. For the contending armies in general and the Sharpshooters in particular, the new dawn brought hours of exponential devastation. More than thirty Sharpshooters would either die or succumb to wounds sustained on the second day of fighting in the Wilderness.

Hancock could not have felt surprise near the end of May 5 when he received the next day's orders from Meade. The curt wording exemplified the army commander's gruff personality and the obvious stress he had suffered across the previous twenty-four hours. "You are required to renew the attack at 4.30 o'clock to-morrow morning, keeping a sharp lookout on your left. Your right will be relieved by an attack made at the same time by General Wadsworth's division and by two divisions of General Burnside's corps." The promise of supporting troops likely bolstered Hancock, who would oversee Union operations on that part of the field.[22]

Like the day before, headquarters could easily envision all parts of the Union force melding into one unit. Keeping the linkage proved impossible, as did coordination of an attack when Meade could not order Burnside to do anything. The Ninth Corps had two divisions heading southwest behind schedule, with another division sent south on the Brock Road to bolster Hancock's entrenchments. All parts of Burnside's command would assist the Second Corps in some way during the day, but far later than uninformed headquarters personnel could imagine.[23]

With permission to delay the attack by thirty minutes, Hancock rolled out his force at 5 a.m. The tide swiftly started pushing back the scattered Confederate units south of the Plank Road, with the USSS taking a leading role. Parts of the 1st Regiment seemed to have had a traditional flanker role, working on the sides of Hancock's advance, although sources suggest part of the regiment also joined the charge of the main line. Along with the 2nd USSS, those Sharpshooters near the front of the charge found themselves in an undesirable spot for marksmen. Like the 2nd Regiment at Antietam, much of the USSS served as infantry on May 6. Their rapid-fire near the front of Hancock's lines undoubtedly assisted with the charge, but the eight companies under Homer Stoughton became desired targets of Confederate muskets and big guns.

With several other brigades assisting, the Sharpshooters—starting out north of the Plank Road—took part in an assault "made with great vigor and impetuosity," as William Ripley suggested. Curtis Abbott recalled the cramped formation creating difficulties. "The Sharpshooters were wedged between the other regiments, without room to deploy in line of battle" early in the charge, he wrote. Much "huddling and confusion" existed, which made the advance far less perfect than lines smoothly drawn on battlefield maps.[24]

Overwhelming numbers compensated somewhat for any alignment problems soldiers encountered. The deafening musketry of the daylight surge drove the enemy a respectable distance west, thanks to what a Maine infantryman called Hancock's "grand wave of battle." Charles Mead estimated "about a mile" as the length of the Confederate retrograde. Whether on the sides or on the front of the attack, the Sharpshooters had to step over many dead from the first day's brawl.[25]

Chaos swarmed over the Confederate defenders, especially after Fifth Corps troops chipped in from the north, further denting the Southern ability to resist Hancock. "The attack and the defense were alike of the most desperate nature," a Second Corps historian remembered. A Confederate, formed with his brigade of South Carolinians in a reserve position the previous evening, wrote of Hancock's charge, "The pressure was irresistible."[26]

Sharpshooters along the Plank Road had infantry and artillery targets to choose from later in the morning attack. Intense heat and choking smoke proved quite bothersome, playing a part in the waning Union progress. A far bigger challenge soon materialized. The arrival of James Longstreet's Confederate divisions, rumor of which led to Meade's warning to Hancock about the army's left flank, had saved the day for Lee.[27]

Charles Ford informed his diary of the wicked backlash Longstreet delivered. The Wolverine marksman concisely recorded, "The rebs broke us and drove us back." A North Carolina infantry officer fondly recalled Longstreet's powerful advance, where one line halted and repelled Hancock's minions, "leaving the ground strewn with Federal dead." In addition to more lost comrades, Sharpshooters could long remember the Rebel Yell emanating from Longstreet's tough soldiers, what Charles Stevens deemed, "the most hideous music imaginable."[28]

Hancock's troops found their way east, but not all units ended up back in the Brock Road entrenchments. An unsecured left flank, which had occupied the thoughts of senior officers since the Second Corps had marched north from Todd's Tavern, became a notable problem for men west of the Brock Road by late morning. Four Confederate brigades, guided east and north by an unfinished railroad grade, appeared out of the wooden abyss, with Sharpshooters and more of Birney's troops caught again in the vortex. Like Hancock earlier in the morning, the Confederates found their impetus faltering as more Union troops began to rally, bringing a relative lull to the smoky hell south of the Plank Road.[29]

Another round of fighting, which started at about 4 p.m., rocked the Sharpshooters and their comrades, this time acting on the defense with good breastworks and fine artillery support. Wyman White remembered enemy fire that hit Hancock's line quite hard. The Granite Stater sustained two hits to his knapsack, one of which went all the way through. Nonetheless, Confederate dreams of forcing back all the divisions under Hancock withered quickly, quashed like saplings in the Wilderness cut down by bullets and shells. By creating a good deal of smoke, fires in the woods and across the Union entrenchments worked in the Confederates' favor for a time, but the solid position Hancock created stood as a roadblock against Union disaster.[30]

Courage from USSS color bearers along the Brock Road entrenchments added to the laurels marksmen earned on May 6. Eliakim Blakeslee, Company C, once again demonstrated a determination to do or die as the protector of the 1st Regiment's colors. In the other USSS outfit, James Madison Tarbell, only twenty-one years old, had been promoted to color sergeant after his reenlistment over the winter. At the Wilderness, he held the standard aloft, continuing to cling to the staff even after being wounded in the right arm. The brave James, who served in the company alongside two brothers, Thomas and Abner, would receive a discharge on the last day of 1864 after his tough, unforgettable service in the Wilderness.[31]

James, known to the family as Madison or "Maddie," experienced much subsequent trouble from his wounded arm. The damaged limb would be amputated in 1903, several years after he had moved to Kansas. The determined and respected Sharpshooter died in 1917, remembered as "a fine gentleman, kind and jovial to all."[32]

"Throwing a Pearl Away"

Darius Starr, less than a week away from becoming a prisoner of war, referred to May 6 as "the hardest infantry fight I ever saw." Staggering numbers support Starr's conclusion. As shown in Table 3.1, thirty-two USSS members suffered death or mortal wounds on May 6, 1864, the most lethal day the Sharpshooters would ever know. All but six of those fallen soldiers stood in Stoughton's 2nd Regiment. Once again, the expert shots had been ordered to charge in a conventional battle line, becoming easy targets for Confederates manning excellent defensive positions. If the veterans in the eight companies thought nothing could be worse than Antietam, the undergrowth, smoke, and hellfire of the Wilderness changed the minds of every marksman.[33]

The bloodbath claimed lives across fourteen USSS companies. Seven lost on the day in both Companies E and H, 2nd Regiment stands as tied with Company C's toll at Chancellorsville for the most marksmen dying from battle wounds inflicted on a single company in one day.

Albert Buxton, the highest-ranking Sharpshooter fatality on May 6, died from shock on an amputating table not long after his leg wound. Deemed "a brave and valuable officer," Captain Buxton would be the second of three brothers lost in the Civil War. Two of Buxton's siblings died from disease in the nation's fratricide. Of the fallen commander he knew well, Curtis Abbott remembered, "The company mourned his loss, as a family of brothers would the loss of their eldest."[34]

Thomas Jefferson Tarbell, another officer lost in a Vermont company, received his mortal wound the day after his twenty-ninth birthday. He would die in October. Eight years senior to his brother James, the two Tarbell brothers had enlisted on the same day, October 16, 1861. Thomas, an original sergeant in Company E, rose to second lieutenant in early 1864. Like thousands of other soldiers, the eldest Tarbell Sharpshooter suffered in the years before the war, losing his wife and a young child in 1860. The fallen officer rests at Sugar Hill Cemetery, Wallingford, Vermont. Four lines inscribed on his tombstone lament,

Table 3.1. Sharpshooters Killed or Mortally Wounded on May 6, 1864

Company	Name
1st USSS	
A	George Blake
B	Joseph Marr
C	Lewis Bebee
D	Christian Schneckenberger
F	Jacob Lacoy
K	Jasper McBain
2nd USSS	
A	Alfred Hamlet
B	Elias Haggerty
	Thomas Hawkins
C	Samuel Howard
	James Rude
D	William Lee
	James Pendleton
	Franklin Stanwood
	David Ward
	John Wilson
E	Daniel Davis
	William Davis
	James Leach
	Samuel Maxham
	Wallace Robinson
	Thomas Tarbell
	Alvin Walker
F	Leone Bamford
G	Joseph Floyd
H	Samuel Bigelow
	Albert Buxton
	George Currier
	George Jones
	James Maynard
	Lewis Pike
	Myron Sheldon

Bravely he fought and nobly he fell,
Neath the starry flag he loved so well.
Tearfully we've laid him low in the grave,
Peacefully rests here our Soldier brave.[35]

Sergeant Jasper McBain, Company K, received six wounds. He died a prisoner two days after his horrible injuries. A Wolverine in the 2nd Regiment, Thomas Hawkins would be buried in the new Arlington National Cemetery after his July 1 death. Pennsylvanians Samuel Howard and James Rude fell from head and heart wounds respectively. Franklin Stanwood, only three months after enlisting and not yet nineteen years old, lost his young life in the infernal woods far from his Maine home. The teenage marksman rests at Maquoit Cemetery, Brunswick.[36]

An even younger marksman fell on May 6. Samuel Bigelow had enlisted the previous December before turning seventeen years old. He would die at a New York hospital in mid-June. Bigelow appears to be the youngest USSS member to die in battle, having been born in April 1847.[37]

Due to the confused surroundings, dense smoke, and battle lines quickly changing, several other marksmen would spend time as prisoners because of

The three Tarbell brothers, Company E, 2nd USSS, appear in this photograph. Thomas, seated on the right, was mortally wounded at the Wilderness on May 6, 1864. James, seated on the left, suffered a wound that day, which led to his discharge. Abner, standing behind his brothers, joined the regiment in early 1864. JADE SCHMITT WANGER COLLECTION the May 6 brawl. Later in the year, captivity took the lives of additional Sharpshooters, including two from Company H, 2nd Regiment.

When looking back on his battered company and the USSS in general as a result of May 6, Curtis Abbott expressed great sadness and even anger. "The army was throwing a pearl away in such use of these men," the Vermonter lamented, "who as skirmishers in this wood on the flanks of the attacking columns would have done far more execution with only a fraction of the loss." A Green Mountain historian seconded such a notion by writing, "the men could have done better service with less loss as skirmishers and sharpshooters."[38] Alas, dozens of soldiers who signed up for a "distinct" service of high honor would end their military careers, or even their lives, charging like infantry against strong Confederate lines in a dark and dangerous Virginia forest.

Fourteen More Lost

After the horrible ordeal, the Sharpshooters and every other American warrior in the area likely felt immense fatigue and emotional turmoil from long marching and intense fighting. For the terrible loss, more than seventeen thousand casualties in Grant's four corps, little immediate advantage materialized from two lurid days of fighting. As Grant wrote Halleck, "We can claim no victory over the enemy, neither have they gained a single advantage." Yet, the general-in-chief did not view retreat as a tenable option. He could not abandon his hope of uniting with Butler's army near Richmond. After a day of planning and probing the enemy, Grant began designing a night march for Meade's three corps and Burnside's divisions. They would move south with confidence, rather than retreat across the Rapidan. Grant expected a quick march to Spotsylvania Court House, which would ideally place the Union army between Lee's Confederates and their national capital.[39]

Before the grand move to Todd's Tavern and beyond, some Sharpshooters stood close to the advanced lines near Confederate positions. Firing there likely accounted for the death of Joseph Call, from Maine, the only 2nd Regiment member to die of a May 7 wound. Sources do not confirm with certainty Call met his demise earlier in the morning. However, Hancock reported at 9:15 a.m. of the death of a Sharpshooter along the Plank Road, about a mile west of the main line of the Second Corps. The lack of any other 2nd USSS deaths on the day suggests Call might have been the victim mentioned in Hancock's dispatch. Details about Call's life are scarce, except that he had enlisted earlier in 1864 at the age of eighteen, another very young Sharpshooter to die at the Wilderness.[40]

Later in the morning, the army attempted multiple reconnaissance operations aimed at uncovering if Lee made changes to his lines in the overnight period. On a day expected to not offer a great deal of bloodshed, the 1st USSS would lose thirteen more lives. Death's keen grip on the marksmen simply did not wish to let up. The regiment's reconnaissance mission moved west along the Plank Road before 11 a.m. Colonel John Crocker, original leader of the 93rd New York, took charge of the expedition. He had earned brigade command on May 5 after the death of Alexander Hays. The force included a good deal of infantry in addition to the contingent of marksmen. The intrepid band's goal was "to ascertain if the enemy were there." Crocker needed a strong force, even as Hancock remained concerned about Confederate designs against his southern flank.[41]

Crocker's men did not enjoy a pleasant stroll through the Virginia woods. Random Confederate shots hit in the vicinity of the reconnaissance party from early in the march. Moreover, May 7 offered many ghastly sights and tense moments as both armies wondered what their enemy had in mind. Sharpshooters moving out saw bodies and much burned-over forest on their foray, which had Crocker's New York infantry in front. The hundreds of soldiers likely went west of the Brock Road for about a mile, the spot of Hancock's scouts the evening before. Brisk firing began near the Confederate entrenchments, placed on a rise of ground that undoubtedly offered relatively good views of the Union advance.[42]

"The enemy had us in a bad spot," Charles Stevens suggested of the fight erupting with notable fury. The Sharpshooters lacked good firing positions against the protected Confederate line. Charles Ford felt as if the enemy had drawn the blue and green troops nearer than necessary to expand killing opportunities. "We got close to them before they opened," the Wolverine jotted in his diary. "Finding the enemy entrenched in force," a Maine infantryman remembered the impenetrable Confederate line as seemingly endless as the Virginia woods.[43]

Crocker's force did not stay long in the treacherous spot. By 11:25 a.m., Hancock could report, "General Birney has slowly retired without being followed." Using similar language, Sharpshooter Curtis Abbott explained, "Their errand being accomplished, they retired." In the horrid albeit short fight, more than fifty in the Northern group fell, with an especially terrible toll taken in the ranks of the 1st Sharpshooters. Thirteen in the regiment died as a result of the day's work, with the lost men representing eight companies. Rudolf Aschmann noted his regret at leaving the body of John Ulrich due to the necessity of retreat. Two other New Yorkers were added to the butcher's bill, including Lt. Michael McGeough of Company H.[44] All lost members of the regiment on May 7 are shown in Table 3.2.

An 1861 enlistee in Company G, 1st USSS received a serious wound to the arm during the confused and short May 7 fight. Sergeant William Sweet,

Table 3.2. Members of 1st USSS Killed or Mortally Wounded on May 7, 1864

Company	Name
A	John Ulrich
D	John Phinney
E	Bernice Scales
F	Edwin Giddings
	Edward Lyman
	Joseph Hagan
G	John Denniston
	Israel Ingalsbe
H	Michael McGeough
I	Albert Finch
	George Merrell
K	Darius Hall
	Orville Parker

nearing his twentieth birthday, would be sent home for a time before returning to his comrades after the healing process.[45]

Due to the large number of recruits from earlier in the year, Curtis Abbott suggested the inexperience of several soldiers made the short engagement of May 7 an important time of leadership for veterans of the USSS.

> *Fresh troops are said to be giants in their first encounter, dwarves in their second, and veterans after. One of Co. H's veterans in his journal of May 7th, evidently written just after the advance, says, "They have scared our boys so it is hard to make them stand. They look to the old men for an example. I hope I shall set a good one. May God help me to."*[46]

Unable to retrieve their dead and wounded from the scouting mission, the Sharpshooters experienced a "dreadful quiet" in the charred and bloody Wilderness, "while the stench was suffocating." Grant's ordered move south began with other elements of the army while the Sharpshooters kept an eye on the terrain west of the Brock Road. The Second Corps would remain near the Plank Road for a short time, but the men would soon travel to new fields filled with American corpses.[47]

Between the Wilderness and Spotsylvania

As with the plan to move quickly through the Wilderness a few days before, the Union army bogged down, ruling out a swift shift to Spotsylvania Court House. A southerly night march for multiple infantry corps down the Brock Road turned into a quagmire. Hancock's original orders put the Second Corps immediately behind the Fifth in the marching column, but cavalry and wagons impeded progress. While waiting for his regiment's turn to march, Charles Ford found the body of a Vermont infantryman he knew, then ensured a burial on the field.[48]

After some brisk engagements for other parts of the army, Second Corps men found themselves only as far south as Todd's Tavern as another haunting evening closed in. Elements of the USSS remained north of the army at first, still holding positions from the previous days. Called south on the morning of May 8, the marksmen manned portions of a new firing line that day. Along this position, two Sharpshooters would lose their lives while working in a detached capacity. Brigade staff member Lt. Perrin Judkins, from Wisconsin, was killed while inspecting a firing position. The 2nd Regiment's fatality, Anson Jillson, Company F, lost his life while serving with the army's sole New Hampshire artillery battery.

Originally buried near the site of his fall, Judkins's final internment would be at Fredericksburg National Cemetery. Showing excellent leadership after a quarter century of life, Judkins had moved forward to direct soldiers in firing positions along Laurel Hill, south of Todd's Tavern. "While gallantly galloping to the front," Charles Stevens wrote, Judkins was "unhorsed by a rebel shell." An eyewitness called Judkins "most heroic" at the moment of his fatal injury.[49]

Company A, 1st Regiment, took part in a bold maneuver on the 9th, with Rudolf Aschmann one of the officers leading the effort. The isolated group of Sharpshooters captured some Confederates south of their main line. The regiment did not lose a man on the day, a fortunate—and likely unexpected—outcome.[50]

May 9 began a three-day period about which 1st USSS commander, Capt. John Wilson reported, "nothing of especial interest" transpired. "The boys are in very good spirits, but very tired," Caspar Kent wrote to summarize the status of the USSS on the 9th. Six miles southeast of the fighting in the Wilderness, Kent witnessed continued desolation in Virginia's woods, as if the fate of the Sharpshooters would be perpetual agony in charred fields and obliterated undergrowth. "The weather is very warm, and the woods are all on fire and it looks like the city of destruction," Kent added. While manning firing positions, the Sharpshooters lost one life on May 9, Russel Perkins, Company C, 2nd Regiment. Like hundreds who served in the USSS, and the Pennsylvania company in particular, little can be documented about Perkins. His death marked the fifty-fifth Sharpshooter to suffer a fatal combat wound across the five days south of the Rapidan.[51]

Also on the 9th, much of the Second Corps crossed the Po River, minor progress in the attempt to overwhelm Lee's lines. More slaughter seemed inevitable. Winning another race against the Army of the Potomac, the truculent and stubborn Confederates held a long line north and west of Spotsylvania Court House. Robert E. Lee looked for some advantage from his good position. Lee had a special interest in the possibility of attacking isolated Second Corps divisions south of the river. Battered and as weary as any Sharpshooter, the Southern warriors acted as if no Union army could push Lee back against the ramparts of Richmond, about forty miles away.[52]

After withdrawing to the other side of the Po on May 10, soldiers in Birney's Division generally found themselves in reserve positions on a day when several Sixth Corps regiments to the east charged Lee's works. Limited success illustrated the resolute nature of the Confederates and the excellent defenses made from existing terrain and hard entrenching in a short period. On the following morning, Caspar Kent summed up the day, "The cannonading and musketry were terrible."[53]

Near the Fifth Corps, Sharpshooters had a supporting role during the major assault on the evening of the 10th. Lieutenant Colonel Stoughton took a shell hit that broke two ribs, a mishap that would take him away from the 2nd USSS for a short time. Brigade commander Ward also sustained a wound. His days with a field command soon ended. General Birney brought charges against Ward the following day for drunkenness.[54]

With Stoughton away, Maj. Edward Rowell took command of the 2nd Regiment. Born in Concord, New Hampshire, in 1835, Rowell displayed excellent leadership skills, becoming an original second lieutenant in September 1861. He assumed command of Company F in June 1862, then became a major at the start of July 1863. Although not officially mustered in as a lieutenant colonel, Rowell had been appointed to the rank in February 1864.[55]

During the frustrating day for troops across Grant's line, Joseph Quick, another Pennsylvania marksman, died from a wound on May 10. Philip Sands, an exceedingly tough member of Company B, 1st Regiment, took a serious wound to a leg, which led to amputation. Suffering in hospitals after his fourth battle injury of the war, Sands would die on November 4 at Carver Hospital in Washington. The thirty-one-year-old New Yorker rests at Woodlawn Cemetery, Bronx, New York. Charles Stevens remembered Sands as "well-liked by all," and "one of Company B's best men."[56]

Charles Mead enjoyed some turkey for breakfast on May 11, thanks to an officer's work capturing the unfortunate fowl. Veteran Sharpshooters likely had visions of Yorktown across the arduous and stressful day. Focused on entrenched Confederates while trying to keep low behind their own protective structures and ground, USSS members faced a bitter stalemate after the previous day's major attacks. Loose, sandy soil assisted with the rapid creation of makeshift trenches as firing continued across the lines. Then, rain brought misery, especially when downpours began. Adding to the bleak day, artillery firing could fill the air with deafening noise as well as deadly missiles.[57]

Even with the stormy conditions and danger from the enemy, scouts from Birney's Division, likely including some Sharpshooters, were able to advance into woods close to Confederate positions. Long-range USSS shooting brought down some Confederates. Three 2nd USSS men ran out of luck on the firing line or in isolated places in the Second Corps front. May 11 included the loss of teenage New Hampshire marksman John F. Kennedy, a native of Scotland. He would die in a Washington hospital five days later, with burial at Arlington National Cemetery. Company B's two lost Sharpshooters, Richard Warfle, another 1864 enlistee, and Sgt. George Woodman, added to the butcher's bill.[58]

Death across miles of front with no discernable tactical advancements did not change General Grant's strategic thinking. He had been pondering a major shift in the army's lines early in the day. A 7:30 a.m. circular required corps commanders to "ascertain what force is sufficient for holding securely their positions and what number of troops will then remain free for use in offensive movement or in extending the front of the army." Headquarters was asking senior officers "to reduce the number of men holding" defensive lines "to the lowest number possible." A new grand maneuver, destined as one of the most famous attacks of the war, called the Sharpshooters again.[59]

"The Memorable 12th of May"

Grant's idea for a shuffle of Meade's lines followed by a vigorous attack at a single point sent the nineteen thousand men of the Second Corps nearly five miles to the east. The soldiers then formed into lines nearly a mile due north of a key Confederate position. Known as the Mule Shoe for the curved shape protruding north, the salient seemingly beckoned an attack. Not only could the spot be hit on three sides, but General Lee had made a fateful error on May 11, deciding to remove cannons from the extensive area protected by trenches and strong log breastworks. Could the intense labor of the previous several days to strengthen the Mule Shoe save the position from a Union attack Lee failed to envision?[60]

The fateful order arrived at Birney's Division in the late afternoon of May 11. The men would move soon after dark. Rainy and cool weather during the night march made soldiers across Hancock's divisions quite miserable. With efforts to ensure a quiet march in the dark, Charles Stevens remembered, "The very stillness of the entire movement presaged a big fight." Men arriving at the launch point for the attack had hours to wait in the dark rain, adding to the unpleasant nature of the move. Francis Barlow, commanding the division on Birney's left in Hancock's assault formation, suggested the overnight period amounted to a "mass of darkness, mud, and rain."[61]

USSS members who participated in the attacking force did not write much about the Mule Shoe position. A Second Corps staff member accurately described the area in a letter written more than a quarter century later. "It was on high ground, was well intrenched, and in every way an ugly-looking place to assault."[62]

One Massachusetts infantryman remembered, "Just as dawn appeared it was so foggy we could see but a few feet ahead." Any dour feelings among the USSS did not prevent the marksmen from once again lining up as infantry for the grand charge. Originally on the flanks and in a skirmish position, the Sharpshooters surged forward with the whole Second Corps. They faced very little opposition from a thin Confederate skirmish line. Birney's men had more strenuous work during their advance compared to Barlow's Division on the left, which marched over less difficult ground. Nonetheless, brigades from across Hancock's command hammered the Mule Shoe at nearly the same moment.[63] The carnival of death quickly began.

Brutality unmatched on nearly all other fields of the war could catch the eye of any American soldier in either army at the Mule Shoe. In a letter to his wife published in a newspaper, Caspar Kent described some of the battle's horrors and the aftermath he saw in the following days. His words demonstrate the two key aspects of the day: a highly successful opening surge of Union troops and targeted Confederate counterattacks. Carnage abounded.

> *I could tell you of things that would make your blood run cold—where our brave boys charged and took the rebel works, and the rebels charged nine successive times to retake them, but failed at last. It was in a thick woods and the small trees and underbrush were all cleared away by the rain of lead and iron that we sent into the rebel column. Our loss was not very heavy, but the rebel dead, dying and wounded lay three to seven deep; our stretcher bearers pulled out wounded that had five dead piled on top of them; it was a sad sight, but*

the roar of musketry and the booming of artillery drowned every other noise save the command of the officers in the immediate vicinity.[64]

Sergeant Grove Scribner, Company H, 2nd USSS, took time away from other duties to move one skulker forward. The timid Sharpshooter, acting in a manner his comrades expected from an unmotivated soldier, had lingered behind the advance. Scribner, twenty-three years old, demanded the laggard join company comrades closer to the Mule Shoe. Curtis Abbott suggested Scribner informed the coward that "he could stop a bullet just as well" as the braver USSS members, which prompted the scared marksman to move forward. This approach to discipline, Abbott averred, saved Scribner—who had suffered a wound a week earlier—from having to call men to guard an arrested marksman.[65]

A Maine infantryman in the same brigade as the 1st USSS described the initial wave of Union troops going into the salient in a "pell mell, helter skelter" fashion. Nonetheless, thirty minutes after the opening rush of his corps, Hancock reported the seizure of the outer line of works, soon followed by the control of a second Confederate line deeper into the Mule Shoe. Several Sharpshooters fired into the enemy from the flank of Birney's advance after moving forward from the right of the line. With great verve, the Second Corps "broke the very keystone of our arch," one South Carolinian admitted of the initial Confederate catastrophe.[66]

The overwhelming force of the charge bogged down in the confined space of the Mule Shoe, an area of barely half a square mile. As Sharpshooter and historian William Ripley suggested, "The Union troops were now a confused mass of rushing men," with brigade, regimental, and even company formations quite disheveled. Blasts of Union fire still could tell on Confederate formations. The large number of prisoners to rush to the rear added to Hancock's disorganization. The time seemed right for Lee to counterattack. The USSS and the rest of their corps would thus have much to endure on what Capt. John Wilson, still leading the 1st Sharpshooters, labeled "the morning of the memorable 12th of May."[67]

Waves of Confederate reinforcements ensured the day's battle would be protracted and horribly bloody. A Second Corps staff member described his foe, "Furious at the disaster that had come upon them, they fought like tigers." Knowing they might have been fighting to salvage their army, not just the Mule Shoe, Southerners lived up to their reputation as warriors. One suggested divine intervention might have played a part for the Confederates, as fog later in the morning confused the Northerners and diminished their ability to take advantage of the seized ground.

As the Mule Shoe action continued, other parts of the Union line tried to break Lee's will, especially the Ninth Corps to the south. Confederate resistance proved formidable. Birney's men suffered from inconsistent protection on their right flank, a concerning fact that did not lead to disaster, just stressful moments for generals and men on the firing line as hellfire raged for hours.[68]

By a quirk of fate, New Hampshire Sharpshooter Jonathan Chase suffered three separate Confederate shots to his right foot on May 12. Originally part of the 2nd Vermont Infantry, Chase became a Sharpshooter while home in late 1863. With bones destroyed, details about Chase's Mule Shoe injuries were found printed in a national multivolume study of Civil War medicine.

> *One ball entered between the lower extremity of the tibia . . . passed outward and downward, and made its exit near the sole of the foot. . . . Another ball passed through the foot, severely injuring the three outer metatarsal bones and the tendons. . . . The third ball entered on the inner side just about the union of the great toe with the metatarsal bone.*[69]

"This Didn't Look Like Advancing"

Rain came on later to make life even worse for the Mule Shoe combatants, with heavy firing accompanying the unwanted precipitation. "Darkness brought with it an abatement, but not a cessation of the struggle," William Ripley noted. He estimated 3 a.m. on May 13 as the end of most firing while the Confederates evacuated the Mule Shoe. Since the morning before, Lee had worked to build a new line less than a mile below the northern tip of the Mule Shoe. His strong new position stood against Grant's battered but still numerous minions.[70]

New Yorker Harrison De Long found much to praise in how both armies fought at the Mule Shoe. He deemed the Second Corps' opening charge near dawn as "the most brilliant operation of the war." Better support would have created "a total rout of the rebel army," he averred. Yet, "I never saw men fight so well as the rebels," De Long continued.[71]

The four Union corps sustained about nine thousand killed, wounded, captured, and missing on May 12. Across the eight days starting on May 5, the Union suffered thirty-three thousand casualties, almost one-quarter of Grant's infantry. Several limitations in the Army of the Potomac's leadership had become evident since the opening of the campaign, with a lack of trust brewing between Grant and Meade. For all the sacrifice, the army had at least inflicted much damage on the Confederates. Yet, the Union line at the Mule Shoe was only eleven miles southeast of Ely's Ford, where the USSS and their Second Corps comrades crossed the Rapidan to open the campaign.[72]

The wicked fighting on May 12 took the lives of nine USSS members, as shown in Table 3.3. With fatal casualties now totaling sixty-nine since May 5, the vicious Mule Shoe cost the USSS the second set of twins to fall in combat. George Denniston lost his life on the 12th, five days after his brother John was fatally wounded in the Wilderness. John's body remained unclaimed, but George found his final rest in Arlington National Cemetery. The Badger marksmen were only twenty-two years old.[73]

Charles Stevens deemed Lewis Crowell's demise "a particularly sorrowful death." After falling back with the 1st Regiment to replenish ammunition, the Granite Stater sustained a bullet under the left shoulder while resting with some comrades. Gilman Crowell, brother of the deceased, assisted with the burial on the field. Confederate fire, Stevens continued, came in "on all sides thick and deadly" wherever Sharpshooters seemed to be on May 12.[74]

Among the walking wounded, Sergeant Grove Scribner, the motivator of skulking soldiers, took an enemy bullet, costing him time away from his Vermonters. Although seemingly perpetual, the hellish battle ended. "The rain has stopped and it is very warm," Caspar Kent wrote on May 13, with the new dawn bringing little firing. Sharpshooters helped the wounded and worked on burial or skirmish details during the day. Clearly, the marksmen also had a great deal of emotional trauma from the horrible attack of the day before. Processing such unspeakable violence would take far longer than one morning, especially while men remained in danger.[75]

Table 3.3. Sharpshooters Killed or Mortally Wounded on May 12, 1864

Company	Name
1st USSS	
A	Frederick Schuessler
C	Daniel Tillapau
E	Lewis Crowell
F	John Bowen
	Thomas Brown
G	George Denniston
2nd USSS	
B	Charles Cronkite
	Chauncey Slaght
	David Waggoner

For all the Union success tallied in the number of prisoners and the permanent break scored against the Mule Shoe, George Marden did not seem impressed with the progress. On May 13, he referred to the Mule Shoe as "about all the ground we have gained since the first of last week." Marden continued,

I heard that the rebels had left and our army was advancing. On the strength of this I thought I would go up and see the ground. The first thing I found after wallowing through six miles of mud up to the knees of my horse was the 5th Corps digging away at breastworks. . . . This didn't look like advancing. A little brisk musketry fire was going on, and I was told it was skirmishing. So much for the story of the rebels retreating. Hereafter I believe only what I see.[76]

The worst week of the war for the Sharpshooters led the philosophical Caspar Kent to hope for imminent peace. In the May 13 letter to his wife, he wished for a final push that would force Lee to surrender.

If we are successful, we think this is the last battle of the war, for it is reported that Lee says if he is defeated he shall surrender. Oh, I hope he may be and peace declared, and we be permitted to go to our loved ones at home, and know that our work was not in vain; that in all our sufferings and trials we have but done our duty, for we have restored peace to our nation, our homes and firesides are safe . . . when I think of the many brave boys we have lost I almost despise the whole rebel race.[77]

General Grant again attempted to discern Lee's plans by maneuvering to hit the Confederates at an opportune location. With many troops spending the night in the Mule Shoe, the Second Corps took part in the prowl for the enemy. Hancock sent a missive to headquarters at 5:30 a.m., "Our sharpshooters have advanced 800 yards into the enemy's works," with little discovered. After taking some time to mull over the morass of death created the day before, Wyman White hauled in a captured Confederate. The New Hampshire warrior nabbed his human prize near the center of the salient as comrades inspected the surrounding area.[78]

Danger awaited Sharpshooters as they moved south to investigate Lee's new position. The day brought death to the seventieth USSS member in the eight-day-old campaign. An enlistee from the summer of 1862, Henry Mattocks, Company F, 1st USSS, had been wounded at the Wilderness, then again on May 13. He died near the Mule Shoe, with Caspar Kent holding his dying comrade's head in the final moments. Mattocks rests at Fredericksburg National Cemetery.[79]

Death and Maneuver

Hope and prayers for victory at Spotsylvania undoubtedly helped Sharpshooters cling to whatever optimism they still possessed. The Confederates stood up to Grant's challenge with strong breastworks south of the Mule Shoe, as well as excellent lines to the west all the way to the Po River along Laurel Hill. Victory remained only a dream in the minds and letters of enervated marksmen and other Union patriots.

The Second Corps retained generally stagnant lines around the Mule Shoe on May 14. With the Fifth and Sixth Corps moving on muddy roads from the right flank of the army to south of Hancock's divisions, danger awaited Sharpshooters on skirmish patrols for the next two days. Once again approaching Confederate lines, the USSS encountered an enemy ready to keep the heat on Grant's soldiers. The 1st USSS suffered eight casualties on the 14th during a sharp little fight near the McCoull House on the southern part of the Mule Shoe salient. Charles Ford, firing about one hundred rounds on the day, recorded a turkey, rather than the enemy, as his only confirmed kill.[80]

Additional isolated engagements increased the death toll through May 15. At the end of the two days, four more Sharpshooters sustained fatal injuries: Frank Edgerton (Company C, 1st USSS), John Bohnet and Stephen Tyler (Company B, 2nd USSS), and John Brown (Company F, 2nd USSS). Brown, only eighteen years old, became another teenage Sharpshooter to die in action during the month. Wyman White remembered an annoying aspect of Brown's personality, a tendency to say "Go to hell" frequently. The youngster spent less than three months as a soldier before his demise near Spotsylvania Court House. The lost Wolverine Tyler fell at the age of forty-four. A New York native, Tyler, in common with thousands of Civil War veterans, reposes in Fredericksburg National Cemetery.[81]

What next for the stalemated armies? "We hear a hundred rumors today about the war," Caspar Kent noted on May 16. As firing continued, the Sharpshooters settled in for more deadlock across the Spotsylvania lines. Grant ordered probes of Lee's position, then started shifting his forces in a vain effort to create an advantageous area for an attack. USSS members moved west to occupy some abandoned Union entrenchments, facing a small amount of Confederate fire. Due to sickness and wounds, Sgt. William Smith served as acting captain, Company H, 2nd USSS. Two days later, the company's new leader, William Newell, took charge. He had originally enlisted as a sergeant in November 1861.[82]

The enemy retained possession of excellent defensive positions, complicating any effort for Grant to find an advantage from reshuffled Union lines. May 17 was the quietest day for the USSS in two weeks. "We laid around," Charles

Ford jotted down of the day, with William Ripley labeling the day as the first "of uninterrupted repose" since packing up near Brandy Station earlier in the month. The rather lazy day provided fine weather to offer a good deal of rest to the USSS, a blissful collection of hours that must have seemed like an oasis among the ravaged terrain and scent of death.[83]

The largest attack since May 12 occurred on the 18th, with the Sharpshooters and Birney's Division in reserve northeast of the Mule Shoe. Failure met the effort, which should have been an unsurprising result to anyone in either army. By late evening, Birney's men moved south a short distance, as the entire army began to feel for a better position south of the Mule Shoe, the early stages of a grand drive toward the North Anna River.[84]

After fruitless bloodletting on May 19—another day when Birney's men acted in support without being heavily engaged—the Second Corps led the Union attempt to reach the North Anna before the Confederates. Hancock's isolated divisions worried Grant to some extent, with Lee's resilient troops always a threat to a detached Northern force. Untouched by war, the lovely scenery impressed some USSS members. With the importance of Hancock's lonely drive south, little threatening occurred on the march until May 21, when Sharpshooters deployed near the village of Bowling Green, seventeen miles south of the Mule Shoe. Driving beyond the town thanks to the help of cavalry, the Second Corps remained detached from the rest of Grant's infantry through the 22nd.[85]

Death from battle came to the 2nd USSS on the 21st, inflicted on Company E, which suffered the highest number of fatal combat injuries across the regiment's service. Calvin Hinkson, another marksman generally lost to history, fell near Bowling Green five months after enlisting.[86]

On the following day, many Sharpshooters enjoyed fine supplements to army rations after taking part in a foray a short distance south of Hancock's main line. Pudding and other joyous delicacies pleased the palates of some marksmen after investigating a structure labeled County Poor House. "Lived high," Charles Mead penned of the experience. William Ripley wrote of Sharpshooters on the reconnaissance who

> *proceeded to gratify a soldier's natural curiosity to see what might be found on the premises to eke out their unsatisfactory rations, and, to their great delight, found chickens, mutton, milk and eggs in profusion, upon which they regaled themselves to their hearts' content. If these, thought the delighted men, are Virginia poor house rations, the poor of Virginia are greatly to be envied.*[87]

"Wild Dismay"

Able to move his army seemingly by sheer will, Lee won the race to the North Anna. Elements of Grant's army moved along different roads to the river on May 23. The USSS and Birney's men answered the call to assail a small fort Confederates had created a short distance north of the river. The 2nd Regiment opened skirmishing near the position, as companies B and G of the 1st USSS supported a battery to the left. Soon, a major assault developed to seize the fort, known to history as Henagan's Redoubt, after a Confederate brigade commander. His South Carolinians did not have much of a chance against a very experienced and well-led Union division, but they inflicted a stunning loss on the USSS before retreating across the North Anna.

A South Carolinian near the redoubt had a fine view of the advancing Northerners. One Palmetto State marksman reportedly hit a mounted officer from about a mile away with a Whitworth Rifle. Nonetheless, the Confederates could not resist the pressure from Birney's imposing lines of battle, especially after the 7th South Carolina's left flank collapsed.

One Southern officer bellowed that every man was for himself in the effort to escape the onslaught. Caspar Kent enjoyed witnessing how the attackers forced the Confederates to cross the river quickly. "The cheers of our boys could be heard above the din of battle," Kent wrote three days later, as Confederates "fled in wild dismay." Curtis Abbott also rapturously saw the grand flight of the enemy. He noted the capturing of prisoners and the primary benefit of the swift Confederate collapse: the salvation of Chesterfield Bridge. Control of this fine span allowed Grant and Meade to send forces south of the river. To the west, Fifth Corps units made a lodgment south of the bridge that evening, making May 23 a rather successful day.[88]

Begun in the late afternoon, the fight had extended into evening, lasting nearly two hours. One Second Corps officer wrote of Birney's advance making a grand spectacle across beautiful ground. He acknowledged "a thrill of admiration" while witnessing the attack. The delightful sense came over the soldier, "not only because of the success that resulted, but also because the occasion was a rare one," with the forming of troops, their advance, and the capture of the fort able to be seen.[89]

Six marksmen in the 2nd USSS would die in attainment of the victory. Twenty-six-year-old Stephen Barker, who succeeded Jacob McClure at the head of Company D, would suffer in hospitals for months after a hit from a shell that mangled a leg near the thigh joint. With a medical discharge on November 30, Barker's fatal injury did not cause his demise until soon after the war. Another excellent young leader, Barker rose up the ranks of his company, having originally enlisted in November 1861.

Maine company commander Stephen Barker sustained a fatal wound near the North Anna River.
BRIAN T. WHITE COLLECTION

Henry Bickford, another Maine man, joined the death toll. The four other members of the 2nd Regiment to die from May 23 wounds were Minnesotan George Palmer, Vermonters John Law (Company E) and Alexander Whipple (H), as well as Luther Crane, a New Hampshire warrior. Born in the town of Bethlehem in 1840, Crane enlisted in Company G in the autumn of 1861. He would die in a Washington, D.C., hospital on June 18, nearly four weeks after a bullet had entered one side of his body and exited the other. The Granite State marksman rests at Mount Washington Cemetery in his native town, not far from the tallest peak in New England.[90]

After forcing the Confederate brigade back, USSS members guarded the Chesterfield Bridge, near the conquered redoubt. Birney's great success north of the river did not change the strategic picture in the area. Forced yet again to gaze at the enemy without the ability to control events, Grant struggled to find the advantage. Erroneously thinking the Confederates had started to retreat, the general-in-chief called for more boldness on May 24. Instead of falling back closer to Richmond, however, Lee's men quickly erected some of the most impressive defensive works a field army would construct during the entire war. Lee the brilliant military engineer undoubtedly felt quite able to deflect Union attacks from his superb position.[91]

Later in the morning of May 24, the two USSS regiments became some of the first Second Corps troops to cross Chesterfield Bridge. No USSS members sustained fatal injuries in the crossing or during the short time south of the river. Lee had the numbers and position to attack Hancock's Second Corps and some supporting units across the day, but sickness limited the Confederate general's ability to oversee a major attack. Taking a cue from their foes, Sharpshooters assisted in the creation of breastworks while on the south side of the river. Rain hampered the effort of the soggy Sharpshooters.[92]

With the Southern army in between wings of his own force, Grant lacked a good chance of success against Lee's North Anna entrenchments. As Sharpshooters idled away time not far from the Confederate defensive works, a wonderful delivery uplifted the marksmen. George Marden arrived with regimental wagons, bringing many goods for the soldiers, including letters and treats from home. As William Ripley noted in his company history, "As it was the first sight the regiment had had of its baggage for twenty-two days, the arrival was the signal for great rejoicing." Unfortunately, not all USSS members received a letter or package.[93]

Detecting the limited chances to get at the Confederates behind their bastion of earth and wood, Union troops south of the river completed a complicated retrograde after winning nothing of note. The time for a new flanking effort had arrived, with a tough march ahead. Late in the evening on May 26, the grand move began, as Lee attempted to thwart Grant's latest attempt to head south.[94]

Sharpshooters stood as some of the last troops to leave Hancock's position south of the river. Leading the 1st Regiment in the dark toward an isolated position close to the Confederates, John Wilson nearly moved himself and some of his men into enemy lines. Able to correct the error, Wilson and his men spanned the river before helping to burn Chesterfield Bridge. Eli Cook, an 1862 enlistee who was a sergeant at age twenty, earned further laurels by directing a squad of the USSS to fire on Confederate cannons south of the river. The big guns had been making life difficult for the troops escaping the clutches of their poor North Anna position.[95]

Difficulties below the Pamunkey

Grant directed another lunge to the southeast of the Confederate army, with the plan to cross the Pamunkey River, a curving stream beginning eighteen miles north of Richmond. The confluence of the North and South Anna created the Pamunkey, which flows southeast on the Peninsula until emptying into the York at West Point Landing, a site familiar to veteran 1st USSS members. The marksmen would not march so far east in the new campaign. Meade's army instead spanned the Pamunkey near Hanovertown, about fifteen miles northwest of Grant's new supply depot at White House Landing, another location veteran Sharpshooters could recall from two years before.

A tough trek in what Charles Ford observed as "quite warm" weather filled the next two days. The journey later on May 27 became highly memorable. Although the soldiers were allowed some breaks between their start near the North Anna and their ending spot near the Pamunkey, enervation abounded. Charles Mead—appreciative of one short rest about 9 p.m. to get some water—

still wrote of being as tired as humanely possible when stopping for the night early in the new day.[96]

With the Pamunkey crossed at Nelson Bridge near midday on May 28, the pattern of the previous three weeks repeated itself. Grant had once again stolen a march on Robert E. Lee, but the Confederates quickly responded, with Lee finding another fine defensive position. The exhausted American armies would face each other south of the Pamunkey near Totopotomoy Creek, a marshy patch of land in which the main Confederate line stretched southeast. The southern end of Lee's line rested just north of Mechanicsville and Gaines Mill, which undoubtedly reminded some Sharpshooters of the Seven Days, the disaster not quite two years prior.[97]

The Sharpshooters and the rest of the Second Corps continued south, forming beyond Horatio Wright's Sixth Corps, which had been the first Union infantry south of the Pamunkey. Unsurprisingly, construction of breastworks began again. Grant and Meade's headquarters, established near the river, buzzed with activity as the Eighteenth Corps started marching north from Butler's army to augment the Totopotomoy line.[98]

The new day of May 29 brought relative rest as the armies hunkered down in lines on either side of the creek, with Meade's corps generally north of the stream. Hot sunshine made for discomfort for those laboring on entrenchments or merely laying around. Birney's Division and the USSS manned the right of the Second Corps, with Hancock's ranks near the historic Shelton House, a structure in existence more than one hundred years before the American Revolution. Soldiers along the creek faced Confederates recently added to Lee's army under the command of John C. Breckenridge, former vice president of the United States, who ran against Lincoln in the 1860 presidential election. Like other Southerners in recent weeks, intrepid Confederates had worked quite efficiently to create excellent breastworks as they stood against Hancock. One Virginian, who said the digging and construction work did not begin until the evening of May 30, dubbed the soldiers' creation "a very respectable earthwork."[99]

Intense levels of skirmishing, rather than a general battle, ruled the last two days of May for the Sharpshooters. Before daylight on the 30th, USSS members started finding some isolated positions for their firing either on their own skirmish details or farther back of Lee's main line. A duo of companies—C and G of the 2nd Regiment—went to the right together. Artillery fire added to the roar as two American armies dueled for control of the wretched terrain south of the Pamunkey.[100]

Smarting from a relatively minor wound to his chin, Capt. Rudolf Aschmann would spend part of the evening lamenting the loss of his goatee.

Other New Yorkers gave far more. Thaddeus Haddon, Company B, was killed in action on May 30, becoming the first USSS soldier to receive a fatal wound along the Totopotomoy. A second member from the company, Francis Snyder, born in Germany in 1839, would die on June 12 from a wound sustained in late May along the swampy creek bed. The brave man who died for his adoptive country rests at Alexandria National Cemetery, Virginia.[101]

In an 8 p.m. order, Second Corps headquarters expressed the need to protect Hancock's right, as well as the cannons posted near the Shelton house. Birney would be focused on the guns north of the structure, across the Atlee Station Road. In addition, "A strong skirmish line," including some USSS companies, "should be thrown out well to the front and around the flanks all night."[102]

Rest would continue to be an elusive commodity for the Army of the Potomac in general and the Sharpshooters in particular. On the morning of May 31, the 2nd USSS earned laurels for a bold move against a Confederate position. In front of the division as skirmishers, while the 1st Sharpshooters manned a position near Swift Run, Major Rowell and his regiment advanced with skill and determination. Exhibiting great courage, Sgt. Warren Fletcher, Company G, was seen leading a band of marksmen, helping to nab several prisoners. The entire regiment took dozens of Confederate captives. Curtis Abbott remembered Rowell's bold action during a charge while other 2nd Sharpshooters "made a close race with the major." The audacity and celerity of the move contributed to the number of prisoners seized, estimated at eighty in multiple eyewitness accounts. Hancock wrote headquarters to applaud the "extremely spirited" work, without naming the 2nd USSS specifically.[103]

Wisconsin Sharpshooter Warren Fletcher received praise for his bold action in late May 1864. LIBRARY OF CONGRESS

The dash at the Confederates cost the 2nd USSS three Vermont lives: George Brown and Horatio Bruce of Company E, as well as Joseph Barton of Company H. Bruce, who would die at Armory Square Hospital in Washington on June 20, rests at Woodbury Center Cemetery in Vermont. Barton, who enlisted in late 1863, also ended his life in a capital hospital, with burial at Arlington National Cemetery.

An additional Sharpshooter would be lost to wounds as May ended. John Snyder, another New Yorker but apparently not related to the fallen Francis, sustained a mortal wound on the 31st as part of Company H, 1st Regiment. [104]

"A Feeling of Intense Satisfaction"

The six Sharpshooter lives lost along the Totopotomoy meant eighty-seven members of the two regiments fell with fatal wounds in May 1864. One-third of all USSS combat deaths occurred between May 5 and 31, by far the most devastating month of the war for the marksmen.

Army commander George Meade's orders required each soldier to pack five days of rations on their person starting on the morning of May 31. As the calendar turned to June, headquarters rightly expected more intense fighting along the disjointed battlefront. In the overnight period bringing the new month, Charles Mead recorded getting two hours of sleep. Some soldiers in Birney's Division had worked on a new line of entrenchments after the commendable advances to the right front on the 31st. With the Sixth Corps vacating the entire northern flank, destined for an overnight march to the south, Birney's small detachment, the northernmost infantry in the army, was too exposed and threatened seriously in the event of a flank attack. The men withdrew toward their original lines, swiftly abandoning their new breastworks in the small piece of the Confederacy they conquered just hours earlier.[105]

Many Sharpshooters had a chance to take a reserve position in the woods to begin June, a change of scenery away from death, heat, and misery. Still, some companies heard the call of picket duty. Several of those unfortunate marksmen would not be withdrawn from their position in front of the division until early on June 2 as a new destiny called the USSS.[106]

Birney's men did not stay long on the army's right flank. Grant and Meade determined better chances for offensive operations existed south of the Totopotomoy, along lines closer to Richmond. Elements of the Sixth and Eighteenth Corps would launch a series of attacks in that area on June 1, with modest gains for the casualties incurred. To augment the chances of success as the army slid closer to the Confederate capital, the Second Corps would be the next troops to head south.[107]

"A forced march," as William Ripley wrote, awaited the men on the dark night. Few other impressions from USSS members document the difficult evening. Birney's biographer summed up the experience of the division by blandly describing the march south as a "movement which had become so familiar to it during the preceding thirty days." The men covered about ten miles. In an evening message to the Second Corps commander, Meade wrote a personal note to Hancock, "Every confidence is felt that your gallant corps of veterans will move with vigor and endure the necessary fatigue."[108]

Marching in unknown territory without the benefit of daylight—to say nothing of the soldiers' run-down condition—contributed to a delay in Hancock's arrival. At this stage of the campaign, one may also wonder about the impact of the emotional toll on the USSS and their infantry comrades. The Second Corps had endured terrible hardship in the previous four weeks. Birney's Division had suffered nearly six thousand casualties since crossing the Rapidan. In the shorter time from the North Anna onward—even without a major battle for Hancock's three divisions—the corps sustained nearly 1,700 casualties.[109]

Divisions under Francis Barlow and John Gibbon arrived on the army's left flank first, hours later than Grant hoped, with Birney's men destined for a reserve position after reaching Cold Harbor close to noon. Hancock's twenty-eight thousand soldiers stared down their Confederate opponents across the Cold Harbor mire, a location adding to the risk of sickness from fetid water and overall poor sanitary conditions. Both warring American armies had pushed their troops to the breaking point.[110]

Bullets and shells would deal out staggering amounts of death on June 3. With Birney's brigades generally inactive, the USSS did not take a notable part in the attacks across the entire front. Sustaining about six thousand casualties on June 3, the assault Grant ordered and Meade oversaw gained less than the efforts of two days before. During the wicked day, Confederates in front of Hancock stood on ground the USSS and Fifth Corps infantry defended at the battle of Gaines Mill.[111]

As thousands of their Second Corps comrades were mowed down in the opening part of June, the Sharpshooters' lack of participation in major Cold Harbor attacks did not keep them from bloodletting and death on picket or skirmish details. USSS companies spread out for the next several days, finding positions across Hancock's three-division front.[112] While working hard and facing danger fewer than ten miles from the office of Confederate President Jefferson Davis, seventeen marksmen suffered fatal wounds. Table 3.4 lists these Sharpshooters by regiment, company, and date of mortal wound.

Table 3.4. Sharpshooters Killed or Mortally Wounded at Cold Harbor

Date of Wound	Regiment	Company	Name
June 3	1st	A	Frederick Baumann Frederic Strenger
	1st	C	James Curtis
	1st	F	Alvin Babcock
June 4	1st	C	Johnson Robinson
		F	Joseph Bickford
		G	Conrad Murat
		I	Benjamin Shay
	2nd	E	Asa Sanborn
June 5	1st	C	William Thompson
June 6	2nd	F	David Jameson
June 9	2nd	D	Jason Kelly James Salley
June 10	2nd	A	James Millet
June 11	2nd	E	Alanson Packard
		H	Carmillus Warner
June 12	2nd	G	Warren Hackett

Losses in the 1st Regiment on June 3 likely stemmed from three companies' support of the Second Corps picket line, which stood in some places close to the impressive Confederate works. According to Charles Mead, a stray shot inflicted multiple wounds on Alvin Babcock, who held on to life until July 1.[113]

A native of Maine, Minnesota marksman James Millet, an original member of Company A, had reenlisted at Brandy Station in late 1863. Nearing thirty years old and more than six feet tall, Millet rose to corporal before losing his life on June 10, with burial at Cold Harbor National Cemetery.[114]

Combat deaths during early June do not include Russel Harding, a Maine Sharpshooter. James Mathews suggested Harding was lost to action at Cold Harbor. The noted diarist, who was not with the 2nd USSS at the time, reported an incorrect tidbit. In the annual report of Maine's adjutant-general, Harding—who had joined the USSS less than four months before—was noted as dying from disease on June 2. Born in 1846, he rests at Arlington National Cemetery.[115]

Warren Hackett, the last USSS member fatally injured at Cold Harbor, was another 1864 enlistee to die early in his service. Life ended for the New

Hampshire marksman, still just a teenager, three days after his June 12 wound. Bugler Almon Griffin, one of the wounded men that day to survive, appears in the historical record as a similar soldier to William Greene, the marksman who deserted only to return. Griffin was away from Company F, 1st USSS for more than a year, returning in time for his first wound, at Chancellorsville, then a second combat injury on June 12. He would live to be eighty-eight years old.[116]

Charles Ford gladly noted the reprieve from work thanks to a truce on June 6. With the chance to clean guns and relax during a time in the rear, USSS members still knew their duty when ordered to take multiple days of rations on picket and in the Second Corps front lines. In some cases, small groups of Sharpshooters patrolled the nearby area, perhaps even to the Chickahominy, not far from Birney's left flank.[117]

Building and improving fortifications occupied much time for Sharpshooters at Cold Harbor. Some fraternization with the enemy occurred while the Sharpshooters tried to endure the first half of June. Still, the obligations of their service remained. William Ripley wrote of the USSS mindset as they manned the Cold Harbor front, often in small groups seeking out one excellent opportunity.

> *Service of this independent nature had a peculiar fascination for these men. In fact, sharp shooting is the squirrel hunting of war. It is wonderful to see how self-forgetful the marksman grows—to see with what sportsmanlike eyes he seeks out the grander game, and with what coolness and accuracy he brings it down. At the moment he grows utterly indifferent to human life or human suffering, and seems intent only on cruelty and destruction; to make a good shot and hit his man, brings for the time being a feeling of intense satisfaction.*[118]

Another Flanking Move

Pride about their prowess with a rifle and service to their cause could not erase the stark reality of Cold Harbor. Like their infantry comrades in the opening weeks of the spring campaign, USSS members had experienced heartbreaking wounds, intense marches, limited fresh water, and the looming possibility of their own instant death. No one in the Cold Harbor trenches likely had endured more problems at any other part of their lives than the previous month, including service earlier in the war. An inability to receive regular mail from home hurt Union troops especially hard in June.[119] As many Sharpshooters noted during their military service, a letter from a loved one—above all things—had the ability to instill the hope needed to endure.

Once again faced with a resolute enemy behind strong fortifications, Generals Grant and Meade developed plans to continue their campaign of maneuver against Robert E. Lee. Marching away from the works so close to the enemy made secrecy incredibly difficult to achieve, but Grant had no desire to waste thousands of additional lives in the dank ground of Cold Harbor. With orders to depart on the evening of June 12, the first goal for Hancock and the USSS would be Long Bridge on the Chickahominy, about ten miles below their entrenchments. Ensuring Lee would not withdraw with celerity to hit Benjamin Butler's Union force to the south before the Army of the Potomac arrived became one of Grant's major goals of his latest maneuver.[120]

As Hancock's command departed the dreary Cold Harbor front, fifteen members stood in the ranks of Company F, 1st USSS. While crossing the Rapidan five weeks before, the company had forty-three able to perform duty.[121] The withered ranks of other USSS components still contained excellent and experienced soldiers. Even those who had mustered in earlier in 1864 had seen enough battle and privation to be worthy of standing among the heroic enlistees of three years before.

Circumstances required another overnight march for the USSS. The men in green reached the halfway point of the march immediately after crossing Long Bridge. Memories of the Peninsula campaign likely grew strong for veteran Sharpshooters, whose course took them slightly east of Glendale and Malvern Hill, storied locations in USSS lore. By late evening on June 13, the well-managed move of the army brought the Second Corps close to Wilcox's Landing at the James River—ten miles southeast of Malvern Hill. The soldiers camped just east of Harrison's Landing, the cramped and sickly end of McClellan's retreat after the Seven Days.

Curtis Abbott referred to the "forced" nature of the march. Likewise remembering the pace of the journey, Charles Mead suggested General Birney "struck his gait" after the spanning of Long Bridge. Another tough part of the night and following day, a lack of good water, undoubtedly brought much concern and frustration. However, USSS members seemed to take their fate in stride, with accounts of the journey to the James not stressing the difficulties. Perhaps the fine rest to be had after the march, plentiful corn, and the ability to bathe in the river led the men to quickly disregard the enervation they experienced.

As he did with vitality in describing other parts of USSS history, William Ripley painted a lively picture of Green Mountain men of the 1st Regiment having fun in the James.

Soon the water was alive with the dirty and tired men, their hands and faces of bronze contrasting strangely with the Saxon fairness of their sinewy bodies, as they laughingly dashed water at each other, playing even as they did when they were school boys in Vermont. It was a luxury which none but those who have been similarly situated can appreciate.[122]

Overall, Grant and Meade did a good job keeping the interests of the foot soldiers at the top of their priorities during the major shift in the army's position. Yet, fresh beef and other army victuals were inconsistently available at positions on either side of the James. Such supply delays were expected after such a rapid movement of the whole army. On June 14, the Second Corps began boarding steamers to cross the river. Fresh fruit soon became another reason to temporarily forget the negatives of the previous few days. Charles Ford and William Greene, men in different USSS regiments, both penned fond memories of the cherry trees in numerous quantities south of the river. A feast of the wonderful treat served to brighten moods while satiating palates.[123]

The bane of Grant's spring thus far, lack of coordination among his forces, became quite a problem on June 15. On an incredibly fateful day, a portion of the Eighteenth Corps, freshly returned to the Army of the James, attacked the northeastern fortifications of Petersburg, Virginia. The city had become an important transportation hub and supply depot for the Confederates. Not far away with orders to head toward the city, Hancock and the Second Corps would arrive in the evening. A grand historical debate surrounding the decision to not launch a larger attack capable of seizing Petersburg continues to this day. The USSS and the rest of Birney's Division were the first men from Hancock's command on the scene capable of assisting with a renewed attack that might have won a resounding victory. Darkness instilled caution in the high command close to the fighting, including the bold Hancock. Instead of a strong and harmonized effort between Meade and Butler's separate armies, only a slight advantage would be won on the mid-June night. Nine-and-a-half more months would be needed to finally take possession of Petersburg.[124]

Opening Blood of the New Campaign

Focused on their own personal exhaustion and hunger rather than the foibles of their generals, marksmen northeast of Petersburg had a limited ability to rest, eat, and prepare for the ferocity in their immediate future. Confederate artillery fired regularly during the morning of the opening day of the USSS presence at Petersburg. The unnerving shells made the Northern soldiers know the

Confederacy intended to fight on, even with a relatively small number of troops who had their backs to the wall.[125]

Intense fighting starting on June 16 would prove terribly costly for the soldiers in green and blue. General Meade grew confident the attacks could overwhelm Confederate defenses before Lee and his vaunted Southern warriors arrived to buttress Petersburg's thin lines. Input from engineers, limited due to the inability to identify the full extent of the forces defending the city, led Meade to order a general assault for 6 p.m. on the 16th. The army commander had been absent from the field until early afternoon. General Hancock commanded forces at the front up to that time.[126]

Skirmish duty began the short yet bloody epoch for the USSS. Curtis Abbott recorded daylight as the moment green-clad warriors moved forward. Both Sharpshooter regiments responded to the call. As Captain Wilson reported, his 1st USSS found "the most suitable place for sharpshooters." The men had an important role, based on a morning order General Grant sent to Hancock. "Push the reconnaissance in your front carefully to ascertain if an advance can be made, and at what points best," the highest-ranking officer in the U.S. Army wrote the Second Corps commander. The lines of a relatively small number of Sharpshooters covered more than their own brigade as the two resolute enemy armies pondered ways to damage each other. Second Corps division commander Francis Barlow observed the enemy moving troops to positions in front of Hancock's men, an undesirable omen casting a shadow over plans for the next few days.[127]

Near Confederate elements along Harrison's Creek, men in green manning advanced positions started to fall hours before Meade's planned attack. As Charles Ford recorded on the 16th, "Jim Heath was shot." The Wolverine, who had enlisted in the summer of 1862 at the age of thirty-one, would die two days later, with final burial at City Point National Cemetery. The sacrifice of the veteran Sharpshooter occurred early in the day as the USSS helped force Southern skirmishers back. This action cleared the area of advance for the day's main effort, the evening attack Meade ordered.[128]

Heath proved a rarity among the USSS during its field service. He wielded an advanced target rifle with a scope. As noted near this book's opening, a telescopic sight often proved cumbersome, adding substantially to the weight of a rifle. Nonetheless, Captain Wilson deemed the fallen Michigander's rifle an important tool for future work. He ordered a Wisconsin marksman to take the heavy yet lethal weapon to the rear for safe keeping.[129]

Wilson's small command of less than two hundred Sharpshooters lost two more to fatal wounds that day. New Yorker Sgt. Thomas Smith would die after a serious leg injury. Caspar Kent, one of the Vermonters in the 1st Regiment who regularly wrote home, also lost his life on June 16. Of those surviving wounds, Stephen C. James, another New Yorker, had celebrated his twenty-third birthday the week before. The devoted marksman's right arm injury did not rob him of his military career, as he quickly returned to his comrades. A Midwesterner later in life, James would die in Iowa in 1907.[130]

The 2nd Regiment suffered one battle death during the June 16 fighting. Ira Blake, born in Canada in 1835, had married in 1860. In addition to his widow, the marksman—who sustained a major hip wound at Petersburg—left a young son. A resident of Tamworth, New Hampshire, Blake had been promoted to corporal two months before his mortal injury. He held on in an Alexandria, Virginia, hospital until October 27, with burial at Ordination Rock Cemetery in Tamworth.[131]

Casualties in the USSS would have risen much higher on June 16 if the units had taken a leading role in the evening assault. Other elements of Thomas Egan's Brigade, including the good friends of the USSS in the 20th Indiana, played a prominent part in the carnage. From their numerous positions, Sharpshooters participated in firing on the Confederate line. The Union seized a small amount of ground near a Confederate battery by day's end, a minor consolation for the intensity of the brawl and more than two thousand casualties across Meade's line. General Egan took a hit from enemy fire during the attack, costing him more than two months away from his soldiers. Colonel Henry Madill, 141st Pennsylvania, assumed command of the brigade.[132]

In a note to Grant, General Meade exaggerated the gains from the June 16 fighting. He reported Birney's "considerable progress," perhaps making the general-in-chief overly sanguine about the work ahead. Meade informed Hancock of the imminent arrival of most of Lee's Army of Northern Virginia. Thus, even with limited information about existing Confederate defenses, Meade wrote to his most trusted subordinate, "Our only chance is now" early on June 17. With his Gettysburg wound causing much trouble, Hancock left the field for some rest. General Birney then took temporary command of the Second Corps.[133]

Staying in their advanced positions overnight, Sharpshooters found limited sleep, with daylight quickly arriving in the late spring. The day brought further bloodletting, most notably an overwhelming dawn advance from the Ninth Corps, south of the USSS. These men under Ambrose Burnside captured additional ground. The victory could not fully dislodge the Confederate defenders, especially after further Ninth Corps attacks failed horribly. As Union forces inched closer to Petersburg, both sides likely sensed a protracted battle would be necessary. Northern and Southern troops speedily created or improved defensive works along the opposing lines.[134]

In a dangerous and confined spot, men in Company F, 1st USSS, started to deplete ammunition stores. Showing the honed soldierly qualities he exhibited along Shepherdstown Ford nearly two years before, Cassius Peck made a dash for more rounds for his Green Mountain comrades. Successfully returning with the .52 caliber cartridges, Peck added laurels to his fantastic record.[135]

To the right of their 1st Regiment friends, Sharpshooters along the skirmish line of the 2nd USSS lost the services of commanding officer Maj. Edward Rowell, who received a Confederate bullet to the hip. Rowell—in charge of the regiment due to Lieutenant Colonel Stoughton's continued absence—would survive as the senior Sharpshooter casualty during the opening days east of Petersburg.

The second day of fighting for the city added seven Sharpshooters to the USSS death toll, as illustrated in Table 3.5. Many felt the loss of highly respected Sgt. Maj. Caleb Jacobs. The highest-ranking enlisted man in the 1st Sharpshooters hailed from Wisconsin. Taken from the front to medical care, Jacobs lived long enough to write a farewell note he wished comrades to pass along to his family. "Tell them I enlisted to save my country, and if need be, to die for my country," Jacobs's final missive declared. "Tell them I never regretted that I enlisted. I am glad I have served my country, and do not regret to die for it," the message concluded, as printed in Stevens's history of the USSS.

USSS historian Charles Stevens suggested Jacobs "was in all respects a true patriot and a splendid soldier." The unfortunate passing of the devoted marksman led to the promotion of Charles Buchanan. Very much respected, Buchanan would be a lieutenant before the end of August. Known as one who never missed

Table 3.5. Sharpshooters Killed or Mortally Wounded on June 17, 1864

Regiment, Company	Name
1st USSS	
B	James Seward
C	Robert Sheldon
F	Henry Barnum Charles Mead
G	Sgt. Maj. Caleb Jacobs
2nd USSS	
F	Sexton Williams
H	Leavitt Burroughs

Vermont diarist Charles B. Mead was killed in action in the early part of Union operations at Petersburg.
U.S. ARMY HERITAGE AND EDUCATION CENTER

duty while setting a strong example for others, Buchanan, affectionately called "Buck" by his comrades, was a veteran of nearly three years in the USSS while still only twenty years old.[136]

Excellent diarist Charles Mead's life ended about ninety minutes after a morning bullet wound. His brother Carlos (known by his middle name, Eugene) added additional words to Mead's diary after his death. The fatal ball entered the right side of the marksman's head above the ear after having passed through a six-inch pine log. Eugene would survive the war after being taken prisoner later in June. Charles Mead, only twenty-one years old, rests at Pleasant Street Cemetery, West Rutland, Vermont.[137]

Two More Costly Days

Fresh from a trip south that started in Vermont, new Sharpshooter Eugene Kelley updated his family in a July 18 letter. He had missed the recent fighting, but already knew the terrible cost of the war. "The 2nd Corps has suffered very, very much," he declared. Hunger affected Kelley early in his army experience, with limited food for a time as he was transported from Fort Monroe to the camp of the 1st USSS. "But we live like kings now," he added, with "better beef than you can find in Vt and plenty of it."[138]

A major attack, ordered for early on June 18, was not needed to take the Confederate defenses immediately in front of Meade's army. The Confederates withdrew to better ground even closer to Petersburg. Quickly moving up several hundred feet, Second Corps men reached the Hare House, which naturally became a prominent location for USSS activity.[139]

Sharpshooters promptly formed into small groups, a now familiar arrangement, before moving ahead. George Riley Tower, a cagey veteran in Company H, 2nd USSS, went forward after an order to inspect a small structure between the lines. Taking some comrades with him, Tower's brave band ended up attracting a good deal of enemy fire. Equally courageous, Confederates interested in nabbing some prisoners moved ahead, with Tower captured while others fled. He soon escaped from the Southern clutches, eventually mustering out in 1865. Only twenty years old, yet a veteran for more than three years, Riley lived until 1923.[140]

Charles Ford undoubtedly spoke accurately of the third day of combat east of the city as he noted, "heavy firing all day." The close nature of the shooting received a poignant description in William Ripley's history of the Vermonters in the 1st USSS. As he wrote, "The shooting here was at very short range, and correspondingly accurate." Several members of the regiment found fine shooting positions while sitting in chairs recently used by the Hare family. Not far away in the family's garden, Confederates attempted to hold their new position. The USSS appeared to have the advantage thanks to the good protection afforded within the damaged yet standing Hare House. Ripley then quoted a captured Alabamian, impressed with the accuracy and determination of the warriors in green: "It was only necessary to hold up your hand to get a furlough."[141]

Occupying the Hare structure and surrounding elevated terrain constituted the day's only easy Union victory. Robert McAllister, ordered to take men forward at midday, felt great forebodings about the fate of his excellent and experienced brigade. Because Confederates needed little time to make their new line incredibly formidable, a great leader like McAllister could comprehend the forlorn nature of the endeavor. Quickly forced back, several of his regiments suffered to no advantage. The afternoon attack led to the war's highest casualty total for a single outfit. The 1st Maine Heavy Artillery lost more than two hundred dead and four hundred wounded, with fallen Second Corps troops littering the rise up to the Southern breastworks and batteries.[142]

The poorly supported attacks of the 18th at least had covering fire from the Sharpshooters, who continued to pop away from the Hare House and nearby ground. Although avoiding a role as charging infantry, some Sharpshooters could not escape death on June 18. Eight marksmen would sustain life-ending wounds on their third day outside Petersburg, as illustrated in Table 3.6. The mortally wounded Silas Whitcomb made a journey to Philadelphia for treatment, where he died on July 7. Henry Eldred contracted tetanus after the amputation of his

Table 3.6. Sharpshooters Killed or Mortally Wounded on June 18, 1864

Regiment, Company	Name
1st USSS	
H	William Hicks
K	James Stevens
2nd USSS	
E	Harry Culver Henry Eldred Silas Whitcomb
G	Henry Colby
H	Amos Chase Edward Demary

left leg. He died at a Washington hospital on the same day as Whitcomb, with his internment at Arlington National Cemetery. Harry Culver experienced a far longer period of final suffering. His life did not end until early 1865.[143]

A father back in New Hampshire would lose his second son to the war as a result of Sgt. Henry Colby's wound on June 18. Doomed to a sad and protracted period of misery, Colby died in October at a Washington hospital. The previous year, Henry's brother, an infantryman in the 11th New Hampshire, died of disease in Kentucky. The two brothers rest near each other in Pleasant View Cemetery, Springfield, New Hampshire.[144]

Brave Capt. Charles Merriman, Company F, 1st USSS, took a gigantic risk in the overnight period into June 19. Inspired to help some wounded comrades, Merriman gathered several filled canteens, then proceeded from the relative safety of the main line to provide water to wounded soldiers in the area between the contending armies. Merriman apparently spent several hours in the darkness on his errand of mercy, returning unharmed to his company.[145]

Visions of the horrible carnage proved a notable memory for Sharpshooters. Harrison De Long vividly suggested, "A more dreadful sight cannot be imagined than where our charges were repulsed." The New Yorker added that killed and wounded men "had to lay between the lines, in open fields, for several days without being removed." De Long concluded, "The endurance of the soldiers was overtasked" in the previous days, making for a very costly opening to the army's effort before Petersburg.[146]

During his three years of service in Company F, 1st USSS, Charles Merriman steadily rose in rank while exhibiting administrative competence and battlefield bravery. LIBRARY OF CONGRESS

In a letter on the 19th, George Marden wrote, "Our division got a terrible repulse," when describing the attacks of the day before. "Rowell's wound is severe but apparently not dangerous," he correctly added. Limited in his capabilities after the injury, Rowell would muster out in November, then live another thirty-five years. Perhaps sensing an optimism about the fate of Rowell, Marden realistically predicted the army's future, "The general look of things is favorable still and must ultimately be more or less successful."[147]

Marden's letter described some positives, such as the ground gained during the attacks starting on June 16. Looking on the bright side when considering the future could not erase the mid-June tragedy inflicted on the USSS. Three marksmen—New Yorker Daniel Vandebogart, Edward French, Company E, 1st USSS, and George Tuttle, Company B, 2nd Regiment—received mortal injuries on the 19th near the Hare House, where the USSS remained until the evening of June 20. Twenty-two of the forty-two marksmen who would lose their lives to battle in the Petersburg campaign, the last nine months of USSS field service, fell in the four days beginning on June 16. As David Birney's biographer opined, "It was evident the enemy was strong and secure, and the work of the week had been unsatisfactory."[148]

A NEW EFFORT TO THE SOUTHWEST

As had been made clear to General Grant for weeks, attempting to overwhelm Confederate earthworks usually brought sorrowful levels of human loss without major advantages. During the evening of June 18, Grant suggested to Meade, "our men should have rest." The U.S. Army's senior officer retained his fighting spirit, however, also informing Meade, "we will try to gain advantages without assaulting fortifications." Accepting his reality, Grant pondered a new idea, a movement of forces, including both USSS regiments, to a new line below Petersburg.[149]

Moved back more than a mile from the main line after being relieved by elements of the Ninth Corps, the Sharpshooters received rations and a short period of rest and relative quiet. Due to Grant's pugnacious nature, the men did not remain idle for long. Birney's troops would support the Sixth Corps along the Jerusalem Plank Road on the southern flank of the army. The move to the south offered an opportunity for Meade to control ground near the Weldon Railroad, a vital supply link for the Confederates defending Petersburg. If the railroad could be destroyed, General Lee and his dwindling army would be required to retreat, which would leave Petersburg and possibly Richmond in Union hands.

USSS members bemoaned the new order to move out. As a New Hampshire marksman remembered, the order to a reserve position after three days on the front line had created "the expectation of rest." Such a preferred result of Grant's new effort to the south did not become reality. Coordinating the movement of troops proved quite perplexing. Perhaps the men had been worked beyond human endurance. As the green-clad Granite Stater added, "Had a hard march; many fell overcome with heat."[150] June 21 was about to get much worse.

The 2nd Regiment could at least celebrate the return of their leader, Homer Stoughton, who had been absent for more than a month. Advancing with his men as a screen for the Second Corps, Stoughton sensed trouble immediately ahead while reporting to officers in Barlow's Division. Pressed forward by an unfamiliar brigade commander who had his facts wrong, members of the 2nd USSS notified Stoughton of concerns about the possibility of Confederates flanking them through undergrowth reminiscent of the Wilderness. Stoughton ordered the pressed men back, which undoubtedly helped save some from capture. However, Stoughton himself and about twenty other members of the small regiment became prisoners.[151]

Not yet twenty-three years old, Capt. Samuel Murry, Company F, also found his way to Libby Prison, the second time in the war the young officer was captured. A member of the regiment described Murry's harrowing afternoon on June 21.

> *In the impetuosity of the first attack our Captain found himself unexpectedly in the presence of five rebels, who advanced from concealment and covered him with their rifles. . . . Five bullets whistled over his head and plowed up the dirt around, and by the aid of a good pair of legs the Captain reached his company. But he was fated to have a sight of Libby, and at the next*

advance his position brought him between two converging wings of the rebel skirmishers, and, together with some companions, he was delivered to the provost guard.[152]

A wound to William Newell, commanding Company H, led Sgt. Walter Wallace Smith to the command of the Vermonters. Newell never returned, gaining a medical discharge in October. Hurt by a piece of his own sword when a Confederate round shattered the metal, forcing part of the weapon into his hand, John Hetherington, Company D, 1st USSS would receive a September medical discharge.[153] The loss of so many to death or wounds served as an unfortunate opening moment of what would be a horrendous two days for the entire Second Corps.

Such a bitter pill for the Sharpshooters constituted only a small part of the general problem during the advance toward the Jerusalem Plank Road. The Second and Sixth Corps did not link up in the tangled ground, which led Barlow's Division to expose its southern flank to eager Confederates. Routing of the line on June 22 caused Second Corps troops to choose between a retrograde or a Southern prison camp. Skirmish fire from USSS members and brave infantrymen helped stem the disaster, as the Second Corps rallied in breastworks previously constructed. Still, Grant and Meade's grand vision stood in tatters.[154]

Gorham Plummer, one of the unfortunate marksmen grabbed by the Confederates, soon found himself at Andersonville Prison, Georgia. He had enlisted in Company D, 2nd USSS earlier in the year. Plummer never saw Maine again, dying at the fetid prison near the end of August.[155]

Bitter feelings among senior officers of the Second Corps threatened a rupture in the command's leadership. Attempting to honor his own troops led temporary division commander Gershom Mott to pillory Francis Barlow and John Gibbon, his fellow generals who manned either flank. Giving credit to his skirmishers, which included many USSS soldiers, Mott suggested blame must lie elsewhere. "The falling back and losing some prisoners by two brigades of this division," Mott wrote, "was occasioned by the giving way of the troops of the First and Second Divisions, respectively, on my left and right."[156]

Whatever the bickering between generals, mortal combat injuries to four more USSS members became the saddest tale for the marksmen on this difficult jaunt to the army's new left flank. The doomed foray below Petersburg killed Barney Leddy and Peter Laflin (both from Company F, 1st USSS), Julian Dodge (Company F, 2nd USSS), and Charles Howard (Company H, 2nd USSS). Howard had fallen during the confused retreat of the advanced line.[157]

Summer's Misery

With important work to do behind the lines, George Marden spent June 23 at City Point, procuring clothing and other necessary items for USSS members. He wrote of the dry summer creating extensive dust, the ultimate contrast to the damp, muddy conditions that could bother Sharpshooters in any given season. Marden witnessed the horrid sights in hospital wards, thinking deeply about the astronomical cost of the war. Yet, "Petersburg still stands," he wrote.[158]

Perhaps embarrassed by the command's worst battlefield performance of the war, Second Corps troops smarted over the cost of the failure near Jerusalem Plank Road. The number of USSS members present and fit for duty appeared frighteningly small. In addition to the fatalities from combat, the two regiments combined for slightly more than one hundred casualties in the second half of June, including thirty-three captured or missing. Of the forty-seven Sharpshooters in heavily battered Company F, 1st USSS who had crossed the Rapidan in early May, only ten remained in late June.

During the first two weeks near Petersburg, the Second Corps had more than 6,600 men killed, wounded, or missing. General Hancock, returning to command his battered men later in June, classified the scamper south of Petersburg as "a disaster" that "seriously tarnished" the fame of the Second Corps. In an order issued on the 27th, Hancock suggested, "The war is one of endurance." Upset at the disgrace of June 22, the Second Corps leader then informed his men that those soldiers running away "will be shot down" if they abandon their comrades while under fire.[159]

Warm weather and water of low quantity and quality hindered the Sharpshooters, who still had regular picket duty in their temporary camp south of Petersburg. As George Marden wrote on June 26, "I wish we might have some rain." With temperatures quite high for days, Marden continued, "Fresh meat spoils almost before the hide is off." A thunderstorm later in the night failed to bring much rain, even if the decrease in temperature seemed welcome for a short time. At least the men in green had consecutive days in reserve, able to find whatever rest their tired bodies allowed. The marksmen remained near the Jerusalem Plank Road.[160]

George Crandall, Company C, 2nd USSS, had much on his mind as he wrote home on June 26. "Mother you must know that I am quite lonely," he bemoaned, regretting the departure of his brother Simon from the Keystone State outfit. Concerned about his mom, Crandall continued, "I suppose you are making money this Summer. I hope you are but I am afraid you will work yourself to death and then it won't do yourself good." Facing mortal danger themselves, Sharpshooters could temporarily cast aside the stressors of the Petersburg

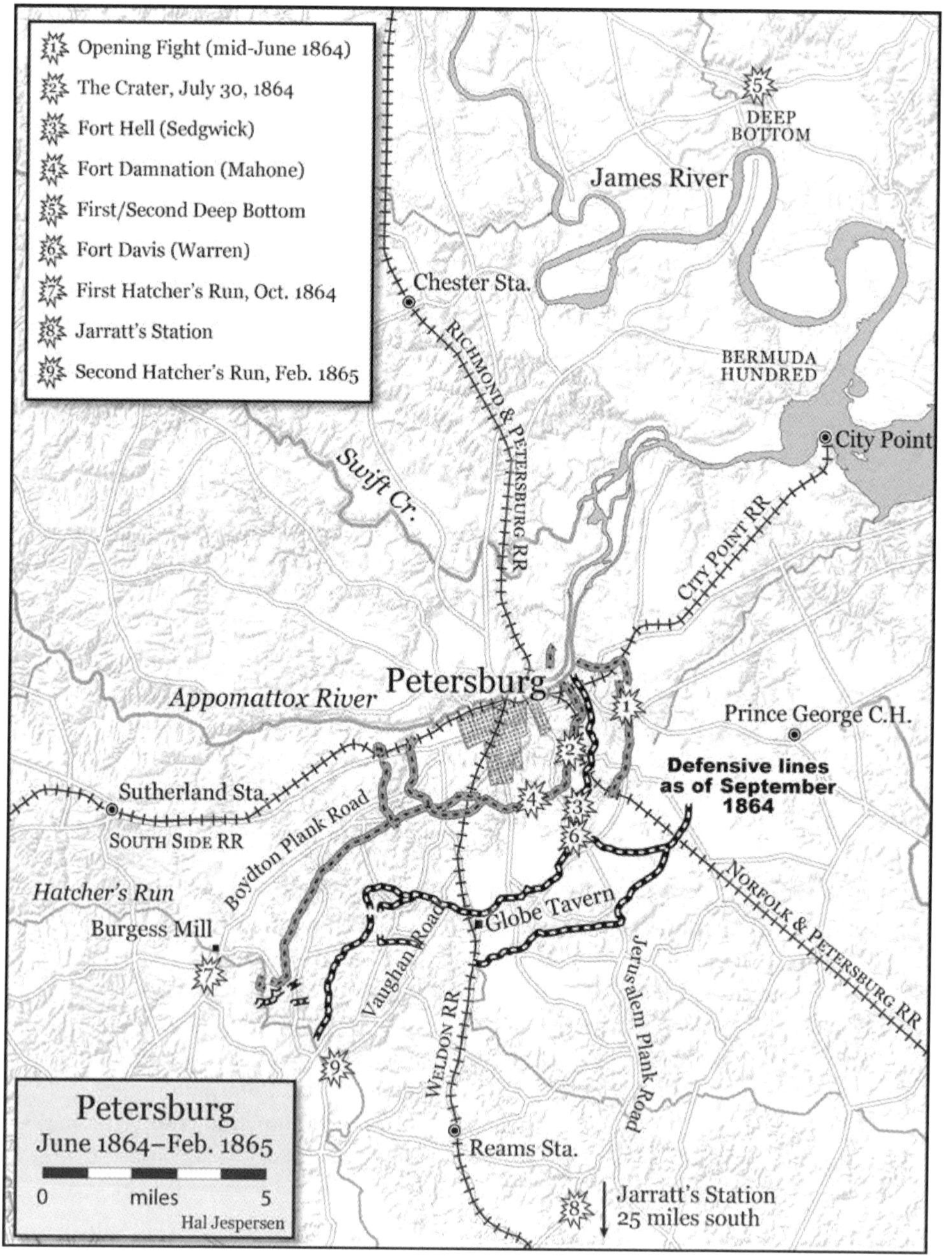
1 Opening Fight (mid-June 1864)
2 The Crater, July 30, 1864
3 Fort Hell (Sedgwick)
4 Fort Damnation (Mahone)
5 First/Second Deep Bottom
6 Fort Davis (Warren)
7 First Hatcher's Run, Oct. 1864
8 Jarratt's Station
9 Second Hatcher's Run, Feb. 1865
DEEP BOTTOM
James River
Chester Sta.
RICHMOND & PETERSBURG RR
BERMUDA HUNDRED
City Point
Swift Cr.
CITY POINT RR
Petersburg
Appomattox River
Prince George C.H.
Defensive lines as of September 1864
Sutherland Sta.
SOUTH SIDE RR
Boydton Plank Road
Hatcher's Run
Burgess Mill
Globe Tavern
NORFOLK & PETERSBURG RR
Jerusalem Plank Road
Vaughan Road
WELDON RR
Reams Sta.
Jarratt's Station 25 miles south
Petersburg
June 1864–Feb. 1865
0 miles 5
Hal Jespersen

front to worry about the health and safety of family members hundreds of miles away.[161]

While serving on picket in late June, Curtis Abbott noted the conversations opposing soldiers would have. As at other times during the war, the fraternization led to some trading between the two armies. Soldiers generally avoided shooting while in their isolated posts. Abbott seemed to relish light moments with his enemy. However, he felt the Southern soldiers got the better of any trading. As the Vermonter remembered, "Only our tobacco chewers ever claimed to realize fair profits."[162]

Humorous takes on fraternization with the enemy could not erase the stigma senior officers usually placed on trading or talking with Confederates. William Greene noted orders on June 26 for USSS members to head out on picket with the express goal of ending such interaction between members of the warring armies. The overnight work's efficacy went unrecorded, but more men from the brigade soon joined the Sharpshooters on their errand. Days across the rest of the month included a slight move to a new camp, as well as restful periods trying to dodge the heat.[163]

Table 3.7 displays the organization of the two brigades under David Birney that included the USSS at the end of June. Familiar infantry regiments from Third Corps days joined with some heavy artillerists with muskets as comrades of the Sharpshooters.

Days droned on as July started. USSS marksmen found a nicer camp in the woods on the 1st. Some back pay accrued to the Sharpshooters early in the month, with Charles Ford recording $62 received on July 3. He etched feelings of boredom in his diary during this time as picket beckoned regularly. "We are laying still in camp," he wrote of his resting site on the 6th. Entries devoid of any change from the quiet and hot status quo continued for days.[164]

Once again taking up a writing instrument, George Marden noted additional aspects of life in early July letters. He pitched his tent in an isolated area at the new USSS camp. He viewed the location away from comrades necessary because Marden felt unwell. Always trying to find positives, he noted, "It is doubtless as favorable a spot as can be found near the train, but bad enough at that," mainly due to the heat. Marden recorded temperatures in the shade topping one hundred degrees on July afternoons. "Luckily," he wrote, "there are not mosquitoes and under ordinary circumstances I can get along comfortably during the night."[165]

A Michigan infantryman summed up the state of war in mid-July, "This army still lies in front of Petersburg, looking at the johnnies, and fortifying." Basic duties for the Sharpshooters prevailed, along with a lack of notable

Table 3.7. The Sharpshooters and Birney's Division June 30, 1864

Third Division, Second Corps, Army of the Potomac
Maj. Gen. David Birney
First Brigade
Col. Henry Madill
2nd United States Sharpshooters
20th Indiana
17th Maine
40th New York
86th New York
124th New York
99th Pennsylvania
110th Pennsylvania
141st Pennsylvania
4th New York Heavy Artillery, 1st Battalion
Second Brigade
Brig. Gen. Byron Pierce
1st United States Sharpshooters
5th Michigan
93rd New York
57th Pennsylvania
63rd Pennsylvania
105th Pennsylvania
1st Massachusetts Heavy Artillery
4th New York Heavy Artillery, 2nd Battalion

Source: Official Records, vol. 40, I, 221–22

activity. Back in a familiar place on a work detail, Charles Ford noted Sharpshooters spent time leveling the remnants of the Hare House. Much of the toil occurred in the evening, with an all-night effort to improve lines of sight and protective features of the terrain. By July 16, Ford penned, "Very dry and dusty" to describe conditions that would prove bothersome for days. Confederate mortars and small arms fire persisted as annoyances. With a lack of action,

Sharpshooters continued to labor on projects, with one detail digging new roads in the rear of the Fifth Corps.[166]

Drying soil due to the intense sun made the Petersburg lines appear as a wasteland. Walter Smith commented on that ugly aspect of life by writing, "There is not a green spear of grass to be seen near here." Hopes for rain and temporarily cooler weather generally failed to offer relief to the USSS and their comrades.[167]

George Marden surveyed the army's fate in multiple letters later in the month. He summed up the USSS experience since early May with the phrase, "constant marching and fighting." With much to lament as a hot sun dominated life, Sharpshooters could still find some positives. "We are certainly better off than ever before," Marden opined. "Our Army is on a fine and convenient base of supplies, and I do not think Lee has it in his power to drive us away. Whether we advance or not, he will always find us here and ready for him if he shall think us too troublesome neighbors." Marden correctly noted that the manpower advantage of the North would limit Lee's chance of any lasting victory. "We can replenish our Army," the USSS staff member wrote, "but he cannot his."

Something rankled Marden, nonetheless, leading him to consider how the great sacrifice had yet to seem like a grand triumph.

> *We have had no decided victory and it will take calculation to figure out our gains. We thought we were making progress every step of the way from the Rapidan to Petersburg and as long as one flank movement after another kept the public in excitement it was satisfied and looked confidently for the end. . . . There is not a battlefield from the Wilderness to the James where we can claim a fair and square out and out victory. . . . The surface of affairs presents a very curious view and one not very flattering to us. But a closer examination looks better.*[168]

In an update to a Wisconsin newspaper, a Company G marksman recorded the notable drop in available men. Thirty-nine Badgers had crossed the Rapidan in early May; only twenty-four remained on July 22. As a veteran seeing the impact of wounds across the war, the writer cogently added, "A few of the wounded will probably never return, the nature of their wounds being such as to prevent it." An almost eerie "somewhat quiet" status quo in recent days left little time for rejoicing, the Sharpshooter continued. A lack of combat never seemed to last under Grant's leadership. A level of optimism remained as the soldier ended his short letter, "The boys generally are well, and hope well for future results."[169]

Vermonter George Clay penned short letters on July 25 and August 6 from camp near the Hare House ruins. Like so many of his comrades, Clay expressed heartfelt thanks to a relative for sending him a letter. He noted frequent thoughts of family while dealing with the difficulties of army life near Petersburg. Clay included an update about his brother and company comrade Smith, who had enlisted over the previous winter. Clay added short descriptions of the horrible fighting in recent weeks, especially recounting May 12 at the Mule Shoe, but he focused on other matters, with the weather being a natural topic. He hoped for rain "enough to lay the dust if nothing more." In the August letter, Clay expressed his fondest wish, to "never see so many dead again as I have this summer."[170]

Clay's letters served as bookends to a significant military maneuver that sent the Sharpshooters north of the James to a location known as Deep Bottom. The marksmen and a sizable force from the Second Corps and Union cavalry had orders to see if an attack from the north could compel General Lee to take troops from the Petersburg defenses. A threat to Richmond, the Deep Bottom expedition could also lead to a successful attack from Meade's army still around Petersburg. Heading out on the evening of July 26, the soldiers reached City Point, then crossed the Appomattox River near Bermuda Hundred. The fatiguing trek led the Sharpshooters to span the James River once again, with the total distance of the march nearly topping twenty miles. The 1st USSS served in their same brigade, commanded by the colonel of the 1st Maine Heavy Artillery due to the illness of Brig. Gen. Byron Pierce.[171]

Hancock's effort, including some fighting on ground close to the old Glendale battlefield, proved stillborn. The 2nd Sharpshooters, once again having Regis De Trobriand as brigade commander, had an expected posting in front of their division, in the vicinity of two farmhouses. They did not see much chance of making a go of Union leadership's goals. As a result, USSS men played a limited role in engagements across multiple days.[172]

What history calls First Deep Bottom quickly fizzled. General Grant decided the venture had no chance of notable success worth the cost. Ira Northup, still leading the lone Pennsylvania company in the USSS, wrote his dear wife on the last day of July to explain the unfortunate lack of progress at First Deep Bottom. The captain described the deafening noise Confederate mortars and cannons made. He estimated that 250 yards separated the opposing forces, an easy distance for Sharpshooters to do some damage. The penchant of both armies to quickly build protective fortifications limited killing possibilities for the marksmen.[173]

The 1st USSS, serving on a temporary detail with the Eighteenth Corps, remained north of the rivers after their brigade started the return trip south on the evening of July 28. The only combat fatality in the Sharpshooter companies at First Deep Bottom was German native Adam Friedmann, Company A, who fell on the 30th, the last day the Sharpshooters manned works on their short trip north. Dropped from the rolls early in the war as a deserter, Friedmann had remained away from his comrades from March 1862 until his apprehension twenty months later. Docked pay and forced to serve the cause, he became the twenty-seventh Sharpshooter to suffer a fatal injury in the Petersburg campaign. In his forties when he died, Friedmann, a very reluctant warrior, rests with many Civil War soldiers at Poplar Grove National Cemetery, Virginia.[174]

In his report covering the opening weeks of summer, well-liked John "Captain Jack" Wilson showed great respect for the soldiers in his ten companies. "Much credit is due the officers and men of this command for the promptness with which every movement has been executed," he proudly reported. Captain Jack concluded, "Those that have fallen we refer to with respect, love, and admiration."[175]

More Summer Blues

The most inventive effort Union forces attempted to seize Petersburg exploded before 5 a.m. on the morning of July 30, as First Deep Bottom wrapped up. A shaft brilliantly dug out by Pennsylvania coal miners in the Ninth Corps ignited with the force of four tons of dynamite. The ensuing battle, the bloodiest day in the history of Burnside's corps, rightly echoes through history as an utter catastrophe. With much new blood filtering through Virginia's soil, Grant, Meade, and the army bureaucracy sat at the drawing board to again ponder their options.[176]

Avoiding the pernicious waves of death resulting from the mine explosion and the battle of the Crater on July 30, the USSS companies returned to a familiar camp as the month ended. The provision of several days of rations on the 31st possibly removed some of the disappointment and lack of clarity marksmen felt after their deadly yet unproductive time around Deep Bottom.[177]

On the last day of the month, Eugene Kelley wrote of the massive amounts of shelling and musketry in Second Corps lines during the battle of the Crater. Such unpleasantries added to the woe facing the new soldier. He also requested that his friend try to keep a mutual acquaintance from enlisting in the army. Kelley concluded the missive with a plea for more letters. Sadly, in less than three weeks, the rookie marksman would die of disease.[178]

August started with bleak prospects for victory as the heat continued. Comparative quiet ruled USSS camps for two weeks. Writing on August 3, William Greene outlined several aspects of his life, in answer to questions from his diligent and wonderful mother. Instead of having her send more shirts, he described the process used to clean the only shirt among his accouterments. Because he used his blouse as a top covering when he washed the shirt, Greene requested no additional clothing from home. He did not wish to carry the extra weight.

Greene included an update about company comrade Augustus True. Although not listed in the New Hampshire state roster as suffering a battle wound, True apparently contracted some kind of major skin problem. Greene's letter informed his mother of True's recent operation in Washington. A pound of rotten flesh was removed from the New Hampshire kid's thigh.

Four days later in an evening letter, Greene updated his mom about the day's supper. He rejoiced in having tea, soft bread, and boiled cabbage to accompany his regular pork. He added words of pleasure about a Cuban cigar as a special treat for the night. With days often passing without much to do, Greene indulged in the bad habit of borrowing a good deal of money he had a limited ability to repay. Greene listed debts to the sutler, company officers, and a fellow Granite Stater in the 1st USSS.[179]

Greene's August 9 letter made passing mention of an unexpected movement of the Sharpshooters on the evening of the 5th. Called on to make a quick march without packing up, the marksmen advanced under a mile before the emergency abated. The action appeared to be a response to concerns that the Confederates were attempting to ignite a mine of their own. After the crisis passed, Sharpshooters marched back to camp without having added to their casualty lists. Curtis Abbott noted the special calls for Sharpshooter prowess at other times during their August lull. Requests for USSS acumen occurred "as often as a battle took place on any part of the long line."[180]

George Crandall wished he could be with his brother Simon, ten years George's senior, based on an August letter the Pennsylvanian wrote. The two had served in Company C together earlier in the war.

> *Glad to hear that you have been transferred to York, PA. I was surprised to hear that your wound has healed up so soon. Simon you say you are lonesome. Where you are, I suppose you are. I now have to appreciate you in your circumstances, but I will say this for your own good, to be contented wherever you are and stay away from your Co. as long as you can. Get transferred in the invalid Corps if you can for it would be far Better than the front.*[181]

The elite unit would not avoid casualties for the entire month of August. Once again, the Second Corps answered the call for a show of force north of the James. The latest attempt to break through to Richmond from the area near Glendale proved as futile as First Deep Bottom.

On August 12, Sharpshooters packed up and started moving north on another wretched trek. Dust and heat plagued the journey to City Point. Sunstroke dropped many in the Second Corps, including some in the USSS. The remainder of the move back to Deep Bottom included a steamer ride. The use of boats had a furtive intent; Grant hoped General Lee would assume the soldiers in ships were heading to the Shenandoah to bolster Union forces there against a detached Confederate force. A much larger engagement than First Deep Bottom, two corps engaged Confederates north of the James in August.[182]

On their return to Deep Bottom, the marksmen found themselves under the leadership of Maj. Gen. David Birney after being attached to the Tenth Corps, part of the Army of the James. Birney's promotion to corps command was certainly a deserved reward for the nonprofessional soldier.[183]

Delays in unloading troops frustrated Hancock's plan from the start. As he lamented, "Many of the boats were not adapted to the transportation of troops, and considerable delay was caused in landing." Soon after finally disembarking, soldiers in blue and green moved forward as skirmishers, fighting heavy thickets as well as Confederates. A dearth of progress hindered the Second Corps. Nonetheless, the Tenth Corps made the most of their chance after the Confederates weakened the defensive line in front of Birney to counter Hancock's position above Glendale. After neither side made much progress, skirmish firing defined the next few days for soldiers across the Union line.[184]

For the second consecutive month, heavy fighting would not define the Sharpshooter experience at Deep Bottom, with the green-clad warriors alternating between picket lines and a reserve position. Captain John Wilson added to the respect his men felt for him as he valiantly stood among them when under fire. As a Company G man fervently penned, Wilson prowled "everywhere along the line, on horseback, acting as he always does, in a brave and fearless manner." The fine officer would soon muster out, but his last fight as a warrior in green proved a microcosm of his distinguished career. In his final report, discussing Second Deep Bottom, Captain Jack noted his men captured six Confederates, including one officer.[185]

Whatever optimism the mid-August action placed in Sharpshooter hearts, fruits from the fighting north of the James proved elusive. After the vexing futility of Second Deep Bottom, company historian William Ripley wrote of soldiers learning how little control they have over their fate. "The men were beginning to understand that marches and battles were not always for immediate effect at the point of contact." Essentially, Union troops became the means for army leadership to experiment with the best way to crack the Confederate defenses around Petersburg.[186]

The two members of the USSS to die at Second Deep Bottom both fell on August 15, a day when the USSS served as skirmishers, advancing in front of their brigade all the way to the Charles City Road. Badger Levi Ingalsbe, whose sibling Israel fell at the Wilderness, died on August 16 at the age of twenty. A comrade remembered him as "a good and true soldier," who was "greatly missed by his few remaining comrades." Ingalsbe suffered a major wrist wound, as well as a mortal shot to the bowels. The only other USSS member to die at Second Deep Bottom, Franklin Dolton, had served in Company I, 1st USSS, since early 1862. He previously sustained a wound at Payne's Farm.[187]

Wolverines in Company K would lose the services of recently promoted 1st Lt. Richard Tyler after a wound cost the excellent soldier an arm. As his time before discharge wound down, Capt. Rudolf Aschmann, a young soldier of great merit, took a bullet about six inches above his right knee on the 15th. The Swiss native would lose the limb to amputation. "It seemed a hard fate," Wil-

During the Petersburg campaign, Union troops lived in quarters such as these in Fort Sedgwick, commonly known as Fort Hell. LIBRARY OF CONGRESS

liam Ripley wrote of Aschmann, who was only five days away from receiving his discharge for having served three years.[188]

Another difficult march brought the USSS back to a Petersburg camp on August 19. The Sharpshooters manned lines near the Jerusalem Plank Road around Fort Sedgwick, about a mile-and-a-quarter south of the Crater. Sharpshooters and others stationed in the area called the undesirable location "Fort Hell," mainly because of the intensity of Confederate fire in the area. A steady rain likely felt great to the marksmen returning from Deep Bottom, even to those tired men called out on picket duty soon after reaching camp. Darkening the mood, Confederate shells made an expected but unwelcome appearance in the summer evening. Ever appreciative of his mother's kindness, William Greene used some money received in the mail to buy cakes and some cheese, with the marksman deeming the treat highly rewarding.[189]

Companies Start to Muster Out

Due to their rapid organization in the summer of 1861, Sharpshooters in Company A, 1st USSS completed their third year of enlistment before any other of the marksmen units. Many of the muster-out notes for members of the company list August 19 as their day of departure. The bravery of the nonnative soldiers who served so well greatly honors the nation's historic commitment to immigration as a way to improve the United States. Company C men, excellent soldiers from Michigan, received their discharges on August 20.[190]

Some others in the 1st Sharpshooters counted down the days until their discharge. In an August letter, a Badger wrote, "On the 23d of September company G's time will be out, but there are but few of us to return," a reference to the hellish sacrifice across three years.[191]

Men in the dissolved components of the 1st Sharpshooters who still had time to serve, recruits from 1862 and later, generally transferred to another USSS company. For example, on September 9, New Hampshire's Company E, 1st USSS, had men with an ongoing service commitment move to either of the two companies from the state in the 2nd Sharpshooters. After original enlistees served out their terms, a company with few remaining members continued to exist, albeit for a short time. Transfer of those Vermonters remaining in the 1st USSS to 2nd Regiment companies occurred in December 1864. Those only serving three years in the company left the army in September.[192]

Emotions pulled individual Sharpshooters in different directions when they considered whether to reenlist. Each man had a strong desire to see the rebellion finally put down, but the marksmen could legitimately claim their honorable service of three years was enough. Demands of families, business, and other aspects of life need not tarnish those who wish to go home after a job well done. As the excellent soldier and Medal of Honor winner William Ripley believed, the 1st USSS had crafted "an honorable record, on which no stain rested, and second to that of no body of men in the army." In Ripley's great Company F, which suffered more battle dead than any other USSS outfit, only twenty-five of the original enlistees remained through the late summer of 1864. Only six of those twenty-five Vermonters chose to reenlist as the company's three years expired.[193]

Reenlistments proved far more numerous in the 2nd Regiment, sustaining the unit until the dissolution of the USSS. Perhaps the longer period of combat operations made members of the 1st Regiment wearier of military life. Or, maybe they felt greater disappointment in the army's failure to support the Sharpshooter companies. Regardless, as William Ripley suggested, no disgrace attached to those in the USSS who did not wish to continue their service after three harrowing years.

USSS companies remaining in the sweltering Petersburg malaise hoped to expand their numbers through productive recruiting. First Lieutenant Edgar Crockett, Company D, 2nd Regiment, wrote Maine's adjutant general on August 26. Only eighteen members of the company were present for duty, with seven on detached service, likely in a work party. At twenty-seven members, the company's number of absent, sick, or wounded men topped those on duty. Crockett hoped the state could do more to fill the ranks, suggesting he would accept new soldiers from those "drafted men suitable for this arm of the service."[194]

Another Second Corps disaster—which the Sharpshooters missed because their division remained near Fort Hell—likely made many USSS members hope their discharge date could arrive sooner. Hancock's two divisions in the action, once again along the Weldon Railroad, brought further infamy to the once proud Second Corps. The futility of the effort at Reams Station in late August illustrated the sheer exhaustion dominating Union men at Petersburg. Several inexperienced regiments contributed to another disappointing result for Hancock during the horrid engagement. The feckless effort once again fostered a schism in the leadership of the Second Corps, but Grant's troops at least had firmer control over the vital railroad thanks to the success of the Fifth Corps. Thinking of his next steps, Grant started planning for a greater victory by pressing his lines westward, which could place great strain on the smaller Confederate army's ability to hold rail lines and Petersburg itself.[195]

Now a battalion due to the reduction in companies, the 1st USSS temporarily gained a new leader, Henry C. Garrison, who had joined Company C in the summer of 1861. Moving into the officer ranks in the autumn of the following year, Garrison suffered a wound at Gettysburg, then mustered as captain the following October. Garrison was only twenty-five years old when he took the helm of the diminished band of Sharpshooters. In the 2nd Regiment, leadership went to Capt. Adolphus Guest, who had joined Company B as a first lieutenant in April 1862.[196]

With new commanders at the top of the two Sharpshooter outfits now totaling only fifteen companies, USSS members stood under familiar faces at higher levels of their military organization. Brigadier General Gershom Mott led the Third Division, Second Corps. The 2nd Sharpshooters surrounded themselves with familiar comrades in Regis de Trobriand's First Brigade, including their good friends in the 20th Indiana. The brigade included several other excellent regiments with Third Corps lineage, as well as the devastated yet still large 1st Maine Heavy Artillery. In Mott's Second Brigade, under Brig. Gen. Byron Pierce, the 1st USSS also served with reliable infantry comrades, such as the excellent 5th Michigan and 141st Pennsylvania.[197]

William Greene, a soldier of subpar motivation, often spent his war service breaking the rules. Even with the dangers from the enemy and their own officers who might be sticklers for military discipline, soldiers on opposing picket posts did not necessarily view each other as targets, as Greene's productive trading demonstrated. A friendly September 1 encounter with a Confederate placed William Greene in what first appeared as a tough spot after his return to camp. The New Hampshire warrior found himself under the eye of brigade commander de Trobriand. Greene expected detention from the provost guard. Instead, de Trobriand expressed an interest in a Richmond newspaper, which Greene quickly acquired from one of his Southern "friends."[198]

Myriad chores called the Sharpshooters across September's first week. Improving defensive works likely occupied some time for the marksmen. Their shooting prowess became more valued, as the trench lines snaked their way along not far from the enemy in many places. Police duty was assigned to Charles Ford in early September as fatigue pressed rather hard on the Michigander. "We do not get very good rations lately," the tired Ford bemoaned, with hardtack and pork on the regular menu. Weather at least helped, with cooler temperatures and some signs of rain.[199]

Great news for the Union cause soon arrived. After several months of battle and maneuver, Maj. Gen. William T. Sherman's force occupied the important Confederate city of Atlanta, Georgia. Union forces in Petersburg celebrated the achievement with a one-hundred-gun salute, which prompted the Confederates to start firing along the lines, including near Fort Hell. Charles Stevens reported seeing enemy mortar shells rise and fall in the night. The "bright, expansive explosions," the USSS historian recalled, "presented a scene never to be forgotten."[200]

Officers dutifully tracking an array of data for their companies demonstrated how war could damage equipment as well as men. In a September 6 inspection report, Capt. Charles Merriman, Company F, 1st Regiment, logged the destruction of twenty-eight haversacks, seven canteens, and five knapsacks. The items had become "unserviceable" after experiencing "6 months to a year" of wear and tear. Additionally, Merriman tallied a value of $42.54 for equipment one soldier had thrown out on the march, based on a list of charges for lost or damaged items in the third quarter of 1864. How the soldier paid for such waste remained undocumented. Merriman's papers illustrate regular and extensive equipment losses across the whole year in the heavily damaged company.[201]

The first combat death since June in the 2nd USSS occurred on September 9. Recruit John H. Thompson, who joined Company B in February, lost his life near Fort Hell. Little details are known about the Wolverine in green who died in his twenty-third year. He rests at Rose Cemetery, in his hometown of Bath, Michigan. Along with many others, Thompson's name found immortality in stone at the Clinton County Veterans Memorial in St. Johns. Thompson would be the last of thirteen members of his company to die in action.[202]

"To Carry the Point at a Rush"

Surrounded by fortifications, capable soldiers, and artillery—including mortars designed to lob ordnance in a high arc toward the enemy—Fort Hell likely could not be taken without major loss of Southern life. Yet, brigade commanders such as the stringent de Trobriand could not condone all fraternization, which could potentially decrease soldiers' zeal to harm the Confederates. Nonetheless, exchanging goods and sharing friendly conversations with Southern soldiers remained a part of the Petersburg experience for many soldiers, including Sharpshooters.

Curtis Abbott suggested that Union leadership's opposition to fraternization led to a plan for a midnight attack, what the Vermonter dubbed "a nocturnal surprise." Perhaps truth resides in Abbott's idea that senior officers called for an attack to deter conversations between members of the competing armies. However, the leader of the 20th Indiana had proposed a night attack as a means to decrease the threat to his men, who had taken several casualties in the vicinity of Fort Hell.[203]

A plan articulated late on September 9, Special Orders 77, set the stage for the assault. As written by de Trobriand's assistant adjutant general, the order included dramatic language.

Lieutenant-Colonel Meikel, commanding Twentieth Indiana Veteran Volunteers, will take his regiment and the Second U. S. Sharpshooters in front of that part of your line which extends on the left of the new redoubt built on the Jerusalem plank road. The movement will be executed at 12 o'clock to-night most quickly, and so as to remain unnoticed by the enemy's pickets. At 1 a.m. Colonel Meikel will carry the enemy's rifle-pits from a point marked by a single tree on the left of the Jerusalem road, including the point known as the Chimneys, where he will be supported by some companies of the Ninety-ninth Pennsylvania Volunteers, under Colonel Biles' command. From the point of attack marked by the little tree alluded to he will establish on the left a new straight line of rifle-pits, connecting with the present one at the next projecting point of woods. He will occupy and defend his new line, if attacked, until after sunrise, when the two regiments under his command will be relieved by the advance of the present line of the Third Brigade. It is deemed preferable to carry the point at a rush, with fixed bayonets, and without any firing if possible.[204]

Fort Hell proved central to the attack plan. "The Chimneys" referred to all that remained of an old house. As General de Trobriand remembered, the Confederate pickets stood beyond the ruins. The tough French general added, "The rise of ground on which were those ruins were less than a hundred yards from the fort." Union pickets therefore stood in lines not far from the abatis and other obstructions Confederates had erected. The desire for stealth in the approach and bayonets for the attacking force became obvious.[205]

Although extensive documentation exists regarding the midnight charge, the number of Sharpshooters wielding a bayonet that night cannot be discerned. Charles Ford, with his excellent 1864 diary, was unfortunately on a picket detail away from Fort Hell during the night. Also, diligent chronicler Curtis Abbott did not discuss information about Sharpshooters affixing bayonets before the attack. Generally, the Sharpshooters preferred to not use the weapon, although the value of a bayonet in the circumstances of the September 10 attack could not be denied.

Mott's second and third brigades held a role in the risky night endeavor. The Third Brigade, commanded by dependable Robert McAllister, included more veterans of the Third Corps, with some regiments having lost several companies to muster out. Mott informed McAllister of the need for limited firing from the brigade's reserve position, unless the attack force was repulsed. The importance of avoiding friendly fire wounds held prominence due to the dark that would prevail during the effort.[206]

General Hancock visited Fort Hell shortly before the assault. The leader of the Second Corps supported the effort to seize the Confederate line in the area. With the possibility of rumors leaking out to spoil the necessary element of surprise, de Trobriand waited until 10 p.m. on the 9th, two hours before opening the mayhem, to send written orders. Given verbal orders to advance, the 2nd USSS was not issued written authorization for the attack; only the two colonels leading infantrymen received such confirmation to advance at midnight. The rest of de Trobriand's troops stood "under arms, in perfect silence, without knowing what was to be done."[207]

Fort Mahone, a Confederate structure earning the Northern moniker of Fort Damnation, stood nearly a half-mile to the west of Fort Hell. With the opposing picket lines notably closer, the effort of Second Corps leaders to ensure surprise proved quite necessary. Another important aspect of the plan included providing picks and shovels to many of the advancing troops. Curtis Abbott suggested about half of the members of the three regiments moved ahead with the provided digging implements. These men, acting in the traditional role of what was called a pioneer, would improve the protective features of the new Union ground.[208]

As General Mott reported, the primary role of the 2nd USSS would be to ensure a connection between the captured Confederate skirmish line and the Union soldiers to the south around Fort Hell. De Trobriand's fine memoir specified the position of the three units that would spearhead the attack. The 20th Indiana, massed and under the direct control of Lieutenant Colonel Meikel, started out on the immediate left of Fort Hell, with the Sharpshooters to the west, the left flank of the operation. The 99th Pennsylvania lined up on the attack's right, east of the Jerusalem Plank Road.

The secrecy and planning paid off as the two infantry regiments moved forward. General de Trobriand vividly described the overwhelming effort from his troops and the positive aftermath. He called the assault,

> *the affair of a quarter of an hour. The enemy, surprised, overwhelmed by the human torrent which rushed upon him, gave way, and abandoned to us, not only the section attacked, but still more of his line, both to the right and to the left. The works were quickly turned by the companies provided with picks and shovels, and we were solidly established in the rifle-pits, which the enemy was not able to recapture from us.*[209]

Mott praised his attacking party, who "most punctually and brilliantly carried out" their orders. "Completely surprised" Confederates fled, died, or became prisoners of the Second Corps. Although the 99th Pennsylvania's contribution suffered due to the darkness and confusion, the morning deserved to be called a great success. Overall, Mott's men sustained twenty-two killed or wounded, with fifty-nine captured or missing.[210]

No USSS members lost their lives as a result of the attack, as more than eighty Confederates fell into Union hands. The Floridians and Mississippians expressed interest "to take the oath of allegiance and go North," as the provost marshal's department reported to army chief of staff Andrew Humphreys later on September 10.[211]

Curtis Abbott illustrated the advantages gained from the conquest of even a small portion of the Confederate skirmish line. Shortly after the early morning spoils accrued to the Second Corps, work parties made fine progress to improve the captured line. The Union's laborers created "a strongly intrenched picket-line, shaped like a rainbow, and extending from its right around to the wood at the left, its front within a few yards of the enemy's newly formed line of pickets."[212]

The fatal wound to a Sharpshooter after dark on the 10th was one way the Confederates could retaliate for the major surprise attackers had inflicted that morning. Pvt. William Matteson, a Pennsylvanian and another relatively new member of the 2nd USSS, died shortly after taking a bullet to the right side of his head. Company commander Ira Northup felt anguish for the Keystone Stater's demise. Northup informed his own wife, "He never spoke after being hit. I had him as far as circumstances would permit devoutly buried." The departed Sharpshooter left a large family to mourn his loss.

Northup added references to the "hot fire" kept up in the vicinity of camp, but did not detail the previous morning's successful attack north of Fort Hell. Perhaps feeling more keenly the emotional ties of family two states to the north, to say nothing of his own possible death, Northup added poignant affection to the end of his letter. "Kiss the children for me," the Pennsylvania warrior wrote. He concluded, "I send a hug and kiss to you all, and may the blessings of our Heavenly Father guide and protect us all through life that we may meet on earth, if not in Heaven."[213]

Either Side of Autumn

Although recruiting of Sharpshooter companies lacked consistent success across the war, new members of the USSS made their way south in September. Proud marksman Henry C. Leslie, bound for Company E, 2nd Sharpshooters, wrote a September 11 letter to his mother from Conscript Camp, Fairhaven, Connecticut. The patriotic home front Leslie witnessed inspired the Sharpshooter. Shortly after crossing into the Nutmeg State, Leslie experienced,

> *the kindest reception that a small company of soldiers ever met with. There was about 100 young ladies at the station besides some men and when the train stopped we boys opened the car doors and windows and told the Ladies we were Union Soldiers from Vermont and wanted to shake hands [with] them and they made a rush for the car windows and took us by the hand and bid us farewell and gave us a lot of apples and you may guess we felt pretty well about that time.*

As he wrapped up his missive, Leslie partook of the right of an American warrior, expressing great hope of receiving letters from home.[214]

Sharpshooters knowledgeable of war on the Petersburg front faced routine duties after the September 10 surprise de Trobriand unleashed north of Fort Hell. Enemy firing of greater regularity followed in the days after the attack. Charles Ford served on picket duty with his comrades, prepared for and endured inspections, and then drew rations across the days through the 13th. Dealing with some boredom at mid-month, soldierly responsibilities still called. After coming off a day of picket duty on September 17, Ford received a great reward, two letters from home.[215]

Whether posted near the Confederate skirmishers and Fort Damnation or behind the lines, Sharpshooters faced the possibility of unexpected death. The random nature of a bullet or exploding shell fostered philosophical ruminations across the Petersburg trenches. Curtis Abbott, noting the increase in danger after the September 10 attack, observed how Confederates tried to improve their chances of wounding their enemy. Due to the angles and topography, the excellent Vermont writer recorded, men passing from the rear to the picket lines faced especial danger. "Telescope rifles in the hands of the men in elevated positions some distance away," Abbott remembered, created deadly places in and around camp. The Southerners clearly worked hard to increase the size of their killing zone. Abbott also noted complaints from his comrades protected by sandbags, because close rounds impacting the protective features could end up shooting very annoying sand into their eyes.[216]

Sadly, September included the infliction of wounds and mortal injuries on USSS members, whether through a lucky Confederate round or the practiced repetition of an excellent Southern sharpshooter. On September 22, Asa Bixby, an original enlistee in Company F, 2nd USSS, died in the line of duty. Wyman White, who was cleaning his gun when he heard the fatal round strike Bixby's head, remembered his comrade as a great soldier and noble friend. Originally interred near Fort Hell, Bixby now rests not far away at Poplar Grove National Cemetery.[217]

Thanks to a chance shot, a nonfatal wound befell an excellent soldier on September 30. Allen Miller, an original enlistee in Company H, 2nd USSS, suffered the injury after not being touched by enemy fire since the beginning of his service. Curtis Abbott reflected on the random nature of military life in his memoir. His friend Miller had sternly "breasted the leaden hail" for the company's entire history. "A casual bullet passing through a crack" ended the marksman's military career during "a time of unusual quiet, and while he was behind the main works." Enduring a prolonged stay in army hospitals, Miller's discharge did not occur for eleven months. He lived until 1908.[218]

Action and Death in October

Orders arrived at Gershom Mott's headquarters at noon on October 1. Shortly thereafter, his three brigades, including both Sharpshooter regiments, started moving to support the Fifth and Ninth Corps near the vicinity of Globe Tavern. Trying to expand Union control west of the Weldon Railroad, the commands had marched into a difficult situation on September 30, known to history as the battle of Peebles's Farm or Poplar Grove Church. Mott reported that his division of about five thousand men used a newly built military railroad to move west to bolster wearied comrades. The Second Corps division served under Ninth Corps commander John Parke during the posting on the army's left.[219]

Regis de Trobriand's fine brigade arrived at a train stop along the Weldon Railroad near General Meade's location. As the army commander surveyed the scene, de Trobriand recalled the unforgiving rain. "The weather was bad," the general wrote, "rain fell in torrents; it was a most disagreeable night." After a march west Charles Ford calculated at two miles, the men were placed in reserve.[220]

Mott had orders to prepare for action early on October 2. With more component parts gone due to the mustering out process, the 1st USSS only fielded three companies (D, I, and K). The devoted soldiers stood on the left of General Pierce's skirmish line as the brigade readied their advance. The other regiment of Sharpshooters also went forward at the front of their brigade. Without taking any fatal casualties, both outfits of marksmen contributed to seizing an advanced Confederate position without major opposition. The troops then traversed more difficult, heavily wooded ground. After they advanced farther north toward the main enemy line, Sharpshooters in both regiments wrote of an enervating engagement Charles Ford classified as a "lively skirmish."[221]

The ground and Southern defenses presented a tough reality to conquer, with the Union line exposed to cannon fire and musketry. Concerns among the Northerners grew when considering the possibility of a Confederate flank attack. With a determination to perhaps return some honor to the tarnished

Second Corps name, the Union warriors held on. Mott ordered several regiments to attack, with the men facing the whirlwind for a short time. He called the force back after receiving word of army commander Meade's interest in avoiding undue risk. General Pierce reported a 4:30 p.m. order to retreat to the morning's original line, an inevitable result due to the limited tactical possibilities facing the three brigades.[222]

Captain Garrison reported only three wounded in the diminutive 1st USSS across the five-day operation. Maine marksman Michael Murphy sustained a head wound on October 2, but the bloody moment did not prove fatal, a good fate shared by the small number of wounded in the 2nd USSS. With picket duty the expectation of many marksmen during the three-day period south of their farthest advance, Sharpshooters helped construct additional fortifications. Lacking much to show for the effort, General Pierce still happily reported the "eminently satisfactory" job his brigade completed in early October.[223]

The men returned to their camps on October 6, either near Fort Hell or Fort Hays, which stood about a mile to the south. For all their hard work and suffering across the summer, the Sharpshooters and the entire Army of the Potomac seemed no closer to conquering Petersburg. Frustration grew for the 2nd Sharpshooters assigned to a reserve position below Fort Hell. Once again, Confederate ingenuity found ways to fluster the USSS. Curtis Abbott wrote of the poor protection against enemy fire they experienced while away from the main Union line to the north. Working to construct protective stockades, the men

Captain Benjamin Peck commanded the three remaining companies of the 1st USSS in the closing months of their service. Before and after his time in the USSS, Peck served in the 141st Pennsylvania Infantry. LIBRARY OF CONGRESS

found their effort did not provide the best possible defense against Confederate fire. Fortunately, the companies moved camp farther away from Fort Hell, with a fine belt of woods as a shield.[224]

Soon after their return from the early October sojourn a few miles west, the three companies in the 1st USSS gained a new leader. Benjamin Mason Peck logged stellar service in the 141st Pennsylvania Infantry for more than two years before joining the small number of his new marksmen comrades. Except for two weeks of leave at the start of December, Peck remained with his marksmen through the end of the year, then returned to his infantry company. The captain had turned twenty-six years old a few days before his temporary transfer to the Sharpshooters.[225]

On October 8, Hancock reported little activity along his extended line of troops, other than the detention of two Confederate deserters. Sharpshooter Charles Ford echoed his corps commander, suggesting "nothing of importance" occurred. The following day, the Wolverine said goodbye to some comrades in Company D, 1st USSS who were about to muster out. More warriors in green left the army two days later. Ford enjoyed the early autumn feel to the air, although the continued parceling of USSS members for fatigue duty possibly rankled. He and his comrades also received regular calls for manning the picket line.[226]

The 2nd USSS lost two members to fatal wounds through the first three weeks of the month. Wyman White again wrote of a fallen friend, William Speed, a fellow member of Company F. A native of West Concord, the Granite Stater had changed for the better because of army life, White opined. Speed's horrible temper early on abated greatly while serving as a Sharpshooter. Chance simply targeted one random soldier for death on October 10, when Speed went for water. The shot exited Speed's forehead, making him "another victim of picket fire unmerciful," White concluded. The body of the thirty-two-year-old stone mason was returned home. He rests at Maple Grove Cemetery in New Hampshire's capital city.[227]

Eight days later, another soldier in the regiment, Vermonter David Bolster, fell while serving on the picket line. Like some of his USSS companions, Bolster found original internment around Fort Hell, with final burial at Poplar Grove National Cemetery. A late enlistee, Bolster spent less than two months in the service before his fatal wound.[228]

Between the wounds to Speed and Bolster, Edwin Dutton, another member of the 2nd USSS, suffered a devastating wound to his lower left leg, just above the ankle. The Vermonter's painful fate began during an evening work detail as his entire company labored to move timber. Enduring a protracted ordeal in hospitals for the rest of the war, Dutton received a medical discharge in June 1865.[229]

Even with the removal of the bullet the day after Dutton's wound, the unfortunate member of Company H faced struggles for the rest of his life. "No fragments of bone came away then or subsequently," but, a surgeon wrote, "For about three months the discharge was profuse, offensive, and at times dark colored, after which it gradually diminished." The formation of abscesses added to Dutton's plight. At his discharge, Dutton "was in good health and able to fully extend the foot, but unable to flex it beyond a right angle," the physician recorded. Joint pain and tenderness followed the veteran into civilian life, with major impacts on Dutton's daily activities continuing. Moving to Iowa, Dutton's doctors documented his decline. Due to "disability equal to loss of the foot," the Sharpshooter eventually received a medical pension. Dutton served as a railroad engineer, but medical complications limited his ability to work and support his family. He died in January 1881, with a report suggesting, "The death of Mr. Dutton is not a surprise to anyone."[230]

Death Near Hatcher's Run

A letter with money went from William Greene to his wonderful mother on October 17. She had earlier expressed concern about the lack of funds Greene sent home, but the New Hampshire Sharpshooter tried to justify his stinginess by noting a debt of $26 to the sutler and others, an acknowledgment of Greene's penchant to borrow. The most interesting part of the letter covered a discussion of Generals Grant and Meade, men Greene labeled, "our commanding *murderers!*"[231] The reluctant soldier deplored the human toll of the generals' plans.

George Clay wrote with more optimism than Greene. Once again updating an "Absent Friend," Clay ebulliently thanked his correspondent for a new letter. The October letter continued, "I hope you will do better in regard to writing." Fall weather generally felt warm to Clay, but the 22nd seemed "very cold" to the marksman. Whatever his efforts to seek positives, war dominated Clay's reality. "There is someone getting shot every day," he lamented, specifically referencing David Bolster's unfortunate demise on the 18th.[232]

Later in the month, Captain Peck reported improved inspection outcomes for the dwindling number of 1st Regiment soldiers still in the army. The men apparently got the message after Peck recorded disappointing results about the condition of equipment and rifles earlier in October. The "much improved" status of his marksmen reflected well on the soldiers' response to Peck's previous concern about laxity in the basic task of caring for equipment.[233]

On October 24, John Johnston received his honorable discharge. A Sharpshooter from the beginning, Johnston survived all of his regiment's major engagements and seemingly countless hours on picket from Yorktown through

Petersburg. His unforgettable experience nearly wasted the brave Badger to nothing. He lost more than one-third of his body weight while in the USSS, ending his army service at only ninety-six pounds. Too weak to work, Johnston passed the next two years as an invalid. He recovered nicely, living until 1922.[234]

Actively seeking strategic advantage against the stubborn Confederates, general-in-chief Ulysses S. Grant ordered another operation west of the Weldon Railroad in late October. General Lee's army would suffer severe supply problems if Grant knocked the Southside Railroad out of action, the main goal of the latest offensive. The Second and Third Divisions of the Second Corps formed a vital part of the operation, with the small contingent of USSS marksmen once again on their way to battle.[235]

After a day of fatigue duty on October 25, Charles Ford noted the distribution of rations, prior to the march to the Weldon Railroad. Near Globe Tavern, Sharpshooters and their infantry comrades rested until early on the 27th. Before daylight, General Mott's experienced brigades followed Thomas Egan's Second Division to the west. Sharpshooter companies rested along Hatcher's Run near the Vaughn Road crossing. De Trobriand's Brigade then took a key role in the day's drama, the hunt for the western terminus of Confederate fortifications. To support the Second Corps on this day, the Fifth and Ninth Corps, to the right of de Trobriand, sought to annoy the Confederate line that had stalemated Union troops at the start of October.[236]

Egan's men led the advance for the second day of the move toward Hatcher's Run. Making good time, even with downed trees and other obstacles slowing progress, Egan engaged the enemy, successfully forcing back a line of skirmishers. Farther back, de Trobriand prepared to support Egan, with the 2nd USSS companies and the 73rd New York in the advance as skirmishers. By about noon, the brigade reached the Boydton Plank Road. "The country was absolutely covered with woods," de Trobriand remembered. The troops were more than eight miles southwest of Fort Hell.[237]

The Second Corps divisions had made fine progress across the morning. Near White Oak Road south of Hatcher's Run, Hancock's men were disconnected from supporting infantry. General quiet from Fifth and Ninth Corps lines to Hancock's right created pause in the Second Corps commander regarding what his own troops could accomplish in their somewhat isolated position. By late morning, a Fifth Corps division moved to Hancock's support. Ordered to take a defensive position, Hancock stayed put. As afternoon rolled on, Confederate troops of overflowing pluck and struggling against horrible odds along the miles of Petersburg lines since June, attempted to once again teach Second Corps men a lesson.[238]

At 2 p.m., brigade commander Pierce called on the three small but hardy companies of the 1st USSS to move forward, linking up with the 5th Michigan Infantry near an artillery position. By 3:30 p.m., major fighting could be heard to the immediate right. As Confederates lunged for Mott's line—due to the failure of the Fifth Corps to fill the gap—a difficult series of moments battered the men in green. Benjamin Peck, commanding the trio of USSS companies, remembered Confederates soon appeared in the rear of their line. "We rallied and made another stand," Peck reported, "but being unable to check the enemy's advance were compelled to fall back to the edge of the woods, where I reformed the line along a rail fence."[239]

With his Second Brigade warmly engaged, Mott took action. He called up the 17th Maine Infantry, one of de Trobriand's units, in an effort to fill the widening gap in his line. The 2nd USSS also found hot work west of their 1st Sharpshooter friends attempting to rectify a highly tense situation. As Robert McAllister, former USSS brigade commander, expertly led Mott's Third Brigade to the assistance of Egan's battered men, de Trobriand managed his men well, leading to the eventual stabilization of the entire Second Corps line.[240]

Like on so many fields across the war, immense courage from one soldier mattered greatly this day. Michigan marksman Alonzo Woodruff, a stalwart in Company I, perfectly epitomized an immortal hero. Earning a Medal of Honor, the third and last a USSS member garnered, Woodruff boldly saved comrade John Howard, who found himself in a close fight with a Confederate. As Capt. Benjamin Peck reported,

> *As the enemy passed our left flank, after both first discharging their rifles and being unable to reload, Corporal Howard ran and caught one of the enemy, who seemed to be leading that part of their line. He being overpowered, and receiving a severe wound through both legs, Sergeant Woodruff went to his assistance. Clubbing his rifle, had a desperate hand-to-hand encounter, but succeeded in getting Corporal Howard away, and both succeeded in making their escape.*[241]

"Such conduct deserves particular mention," General Mott wrote of Woodruff's deed. Those words would have rung true regardless of how many years Woodruff gave his friend Howard by saving his life. The wounded and rescued marksman in trouble at First Hatcher's Run had much time on earth ahead of him. Howard died in Kansas in January 1928 at the age of ninety-five, two-thirds of a century after the difficult afternoon that nearly took his life southwest of Petersburg.[242]

Second Lt. Samuel Shoup, a member of Company B, 2nd USSS assigned as an ambulance driver, spent time on the brigade staff during First Hatcher's Run. He received praise from General de Trobriand in his report. Shoup "remained with me in the thickest of the fight as long as his duties did not absolutely require his presence with the ambulance," de Trobriand wrote. In 1865, Shoup received brevet promotion to captain for his dedicated service as a Sharpshooter and staff officer.[243]

The ordeal of Edgar Beach, Company H, 2nd USSS, illustrated how incredibly resilient a Sharpshooter could be. Curtis Abbott incorrectly wrote that Beach sustained a mortal wound on October 27. He came very close to death in what was his third combat injury of the war. Hit in the hip, Beach remained on the field for days, suffering horribly without treatment or food. Finding himself a prisoner in early November, Beach received good care from his Confederate foes, then transferred to the hospital at Libby Prison in Richmond. Treated better than most after striking up conversations with guards who were his Masonic brothers, the Vermont marksman received parole in February 1865. He lived to the age of fifty-six, dying on December 9, 1893, back home in Chittenden County, Vermont.[244]

In the most significant loss of life in a day for the USSS since June, five marksmen fell with fatal wounds on October 27. Gregory Deyett had joined USSS comrades at the front a month before his death, while Daniel Bessy, a July recruit in the 1st Sharpshooters, rests at Harrietstown Cemetery, Lake Clear, New York. The three 2nd Regiment fatalities at First Hatcher's Run were Joseph Bradley and Charles Cilley, Company E, and Capt. William Churchill, in Company H. Like their Green Mountain comrade Bessy, both Bradley and Cilley had enlisted only a few months before. Churchill, the brave and respected leader of Company H, enlisted three years before as a sergeant, then received a wound in May 1864. A patriot of long and difficult service in the war, Churchill died in his twenty-sixth year.[245]

When adding wounded and missing, USSS casualties for the operation amounted to twenty-six. Even in their advanced position, the division under Egan sustained far fewer losses than Mott's three gallant brigades. In total, Hancock's men recorded more than one thousand casualties.[246]

The impressive stand of the two divisions became the bright spot of the action on October 27. Bungled planning, difficult terrain, and the incompetence of Gouverneur Warren, Fifth Corps commander, defined the battle along Hatcher's Run. Although General Meade hoped for a renewed offensive on the 28th, Second Corps ammunition supplies and the difficulty of the position worried General Hancock. Orders then began the withdrawal of Union pickets.

Charles Ford wrote of a night march lasting from 11 p.m. on the 27th to rest at 5 a.m. the next day. The USSS would be back in camp a few hours later.[247]

Once again away from an active operation, Sharpshooters still knew the noise and risk so common across the Petersburg front as October ended. The marksmen stood near Fort Davis on the 31st "under heavy fire," according to a scrapbook of information in the papers of discharged Michigan officer James Baker.[248]

"About a Drumstick Apiece"

Benjamin Peck recorded fine weather at the start of November. The young and last leader of the 1st USSS wrote of the happiness he felt while witnessing his determined men in green police their campsite and work to improve winter housing. Peck also noted his own effort to secure some bricks to construct a chimney to help warm his personal quarters.[249]

As time wound down for the small contingent still in the 1st USSS, death stalked Peck's command. Service on a picket line during the first day of the new month added one mortally wounded Sharpshooter to the Petersburg death toll. An enlistee from August, Friend Weeks, in the 1st Regiment's Company F, held on for more than two weeks, dying on November 17. He rests at Arlington National Cemetery.[250]

Home of the Sharpshooters for most of November, Fort Davis dominated the surrounding land south of Fort Hell. With a different type of assignment, Charles Ford assisted company officers with administrative tasks, such as payrolls, late into the evening of November 1. Also on picket early in the month, Ford noted some unfortunate Second Corps soldiers had become prisoners during the day, a reminder of war's adamant grip. Sedentary again soon after, Ford finished his updates to payrolls. He went on guard duty on the 4th, opining of the "pretty lonesome" task in his fine diary.[251]

Other Sharpshooters were suffering much more than Ford. Private Azro Shippey, Company E, plagued by diarrhea, was admitted to the Second Corps hospital at City Point on November 2. Pneumonia caused his death later in the month. The physician conducting a postmortem examination ten hours after Shippey's demise reported, "Rigor mortis very great; body very much emaciated." Shippey had a variety of health problems, including signs of notable digestive system issues, an unsurprising diagnosis for a Civil War soldier. With less than a year in the army, Shippey became another late enlistee never seeing home again. He was buried at Alexandria National Cemetery, Virginia.[252]

As the unyielding war continued, Sharpshooters pondered the looming presidential election. Buoyed by battle success elsewhere in Virginia and Georgia, President Lincoln's chances of winning another term looked good before the November 8 balloting. As the opposing candidate, George McClellan, the general Lincoln fired two years before, promised to save the Union while stuck with a platform denouncing the war as a failure. The dichotomy stands as one of the most interesting in the history of U.S. elections, one Northern voters refused to reward with victory.[253]

Captain Peck proudly counted a very strong majority for Lincoln among the troops garrisoning Fort Davis. Contrarian William Greene cast a vote for McClellan and his doomed cause. Based on data General Hancock collected, Greene was in a rather tiny group. All twenty-two voting members of the small 1st USSS supported Lincoln, as did eighty-seven of 107 in the 2nd Regiment. Thus, nearly 90 percent of voting marksmen rejected the candidacy of their former army commander, preferring the re-election of their current commander-in-chief.[254]

Political machinations did not halt the war. George Stowell, a Vermont Sharpshooter who enlisted eleven months before, sustained a fatal wound on November 11. Originally interred near Fort Hell, Stowell's remains were later moved to Poplar Grove National Cemetery.[255]

Fourteen men from Company I marched from Fort Davis to Fort Hell on November 17. Assigned as a detail from their diminutive regiment, the Wolverines found the iconic structure empty of soldiers. The band of Sharpshooters had orders to prohibit anyone from entering the fort without special authorization. They were also compelled to burn fires and make false shows of strength to deceive the Confederates, who assumed Fort Hell retained a strong force of defenders. Concerns about an enemy mining effort had vacated the fort, but no harm followed. Excellent soldier Eli Cook referred to the Confederate idea of blowing up Fort Hell as "another fizzle." The Company I soldiers returned to Fort Davis on November 24.[256]

The detail provided some men the opportunity to avoid mundane routines at camp. Work details, picket, and guard duty occupied the men as November wore on. Rainy weather brought consternation to those on duty, even on a day like November 16, when Charles Ford noted an almost eerie lack of firing from the enemy.

Many Sharpshooters felt disappointed about Thanksgiving. Ford's diary noted the lack of turkeys and fixings, which the few remaining Wolverine Sharpshooters had expected. Sarcasm reigned in other USSS comments about the day. In his memoir, Curtis Abbott recorded "the thoughtfulness and painstaking of their people at home" who had mailed "about a drumstick apiece" for the Sharpshooters. The warriors consumed the "feast" with "thankful hearts." Likewise, Pennsylvania marksman William Lytle wrote to George Crandall, a former member of the regiment, about the meal. The small number of Keystone Staters left in the USSS received treats from home, but Lytle seemed uninspired by the lack of quantity in the package of goodies.

> *For our Company of Seventeen men we received one small turkey, one pie, a half dozen Cookies, three or four water crackers and a piece of cheese. Don't you think we "poor soldiers" should be thankful to our kind friends at home who so generously donated it?*[257]

The last combat death in the 1st USSS followed the pattern of those in the dwindling companies over the previous few months, a recent enlistee from Vermont. While on picket, Charles Danforth lost his life on November 27. He had joined the Sharpshooters around Petersburg in August.[258]

The End of 1864

Starting in September, Minnesotans had been receiving discharges, marking the completion of three years in Company A, 2nd USSS. Thus, the number of men in the western-most Sharpshooter outfit declined each month through the late summer and early autumn. Forty soldiers answered the roll call at the start of August and September, but only thirty-one stood in the ranks on October 1. At the start of December, the number dropped to twenty-six.[259]

A good and young leader in Company A had risen to regimental command. James Doughty, who first enrolled in February 1862 as a second lieutenant, missed eight months as a prisoner after Second Bull Run. His leadership skills evident nonetheless, Doughty became company captain in October 1864, with promotion to major in December. He was the last commander of the USSS after the consolidation of companies.[260]

After moving from Fort Davis, late November orders positioned Mott's Division between Fort Siebert and Fort Cummings, in an east-west line from Vaughan Road to Squirrel Level Road. Fort Siebert stood slightly less than four miles southwest of Fort Davis. The Sharpshooters had some experience in the area due to their marches and fighting since the end of summer. On ground west of the Weldon Railroad, the USSS position was south of Peebles Farm by one-third of a mile.[261]

With rumors of a new campaign percolating alongside orders for men to build winter huts, sensible for the Petersburg front near year's end, frustration must have occurred in the remaining Sharpshooters late in 1864. Charles Ford noted the beginning of hut construction in fine weather on December 1, followed by a sudden half-mile march to a new camp. The marksmen then spent part of the next day constructing quarters in the excellent new location. A third consecutive day of hard work followed, with fantastic conditions for the invigorating labor. As Ford wrote, "Everybody busy hauling timber and building." With frosts occurring on some evenings, the men had great incentive to be productive in the creation of enclosed quarters that could include wood-burning stoves.[262]

While dealing with normal duties and trying to make their new spot home, orders for a march arrived in early December. Leaving behind several hundred pickets, Mott took the rest of his division, about 5,700 total soldiers, on another Weldon Railroad trek with the Fifth Corps. After losing the important rail line in September, the Confederates had a much more difficult time moving supplies north, a major threat to General Lee's army defending Petersburg. With three years of service in, Curtis Abbott, Company H, 2nd USSS, called the journey "a rapid raid of foot and cavalry" with the intent to damage the railroad farther south.[263]

"Fighting Parson" Lorenzo Barber reported on the movement of the division, which started on the morning of December 7. The rendezvous with the Fifth Corps occurred near the Gurley House, slightly east of Globe Tavern near the railroad line. Troops then moved south to "a cross-road at Hawkins' Tavern, about eighteen miles from Petersburg," Barber wrote. The men had few breaks on the trek, which concluded at about 4 p.m. Additional marching soon commenced, with the men crossing the Nottoway River, spanned by a pontoon bridge. Rain assisted the movement, Barber suggested, by decreasing dust and therefore making the enemy's detection of the assault force more difficult.[264]

Some of the marching troops had a different view of the precipitation, lamenting the misery created while walking in a late autumn rain. With six days' rations and plenty of ammunition, the rapid march likely did feel like a great burden to the troops. Conditions improved on December 8, with the march starting again at about 9 a.m. After passing Sussex Court House, the troops reached the railroad near Jarratt's Station, less than twenty miles from the North Carolina border.[265]

The reward for the long journey began on the morning of December 9, as Sharpshooters and their infantry comrades destroyed the railroad track. Curtis Abbott relished the memory in his memoir, suggesting the marksmen enjoyed the demanding job, with several grabbing a large steel beam then "as one man," pulling up. After a full day of intense work, thousands of Union troops had created piles of doomed railing. Fires then bent the rails, making them, as Abbott wrote, "unserviceable for quick repairing." Entire brigade fronts engaged in the obliteration of the railroad track appeared to work "as if by magic," Chaplain Barber observed.[266]

After destroying between fifteen to twenty miles of track, the soldiers moved back north on December 10. Ice covered nearly everything, Charles Ford observed, as the chilly Sharpshooters readied for a return to Petersburg. "The ground was slippery and the mud as deep and abundant as that in which Napoleon fought the battle of Waterloo," Barber opined. Although at a slower pace, the wearied warriors in green and blue still made good time back to camp, which was reached in the mid-afternoon of the 12th. General Meade expressed some concern about a possible Confederate attack on the returning column's southern flank, but the problem never materialized.[267]

Devoted to extolling the men in the USSS, Chaplain Barber went overboard in his description of the foray focused on railroad destruction.

> *Thus ended one of the most extensive, important, and successful infantry raids of the war, and one that must be very damaging to the enemy. . . . When the adventures of "this cruel war" shall be talked over, after peace shall have again blessed our land, the great raid on the Weldon railroad in the frost and snow of winter and in the very face of the most powerful army of the rebellion will very justly receive a prominent place in the narration.*[268]

Sick Sharpshooter Wyman White missed the adventure of tearing up Weldon Railroad track. Remaining in camp, he noted a nice visit from several former USSS members, including Major Rowell. Set for their return home in December after the expiration of terms of service, Rowell and others had spent time away in hospitals or as prisoners of war. White penned a fond remembrance of the reunion with Rowell and others, well-liked leaders who had helped USSS members endure the ordeal of the horrible war.[269]

Sharpshooters found general quiet and relaxation through the end of the year. One month after turning twenty-two years old, Llewellyn Blanchard rose to the captaincy of Company B, 2nd USSS in mid-December. Thirty-seven months after enlisting as a sergeant, Walter Wallace Smith earned his captain's commission, in which he would lead Company H, 2nd USSS for the rest of their service.[270]

In a letter home on December 16, Smith mentioned his receipt of the official notice of the promotion. He hoped for a furlough to visit home over the winter. Smith's modesty shines through in the dozens of letters he sent back to Vermont during the war, but historians should not judge the officer harshly when he emphasized his rank while signing off as "*Capt.* W. W. Smith."[271]

Multiday efforts from small groups of Sharpshooters helped comrades complete winter huts in the week after the raid on the Weldon Railroad. With poor weather on December 21, Charles Ford bemoaned a "rather dull" day. On the 22nd, the new officer took some men on a detail to division headquarters. These marksmen then went out, under the command of an infantry captain in Byron Pierce's Brigade, to man the picket line. On the following day, some Sharpshooters witnessed the execution of a soldier in the 1st Massachusetts Heavy Artillery. After the gruesome moment, Christmas Day arrived and passed without much occurring. Ford, who marvelously documented life in the USSS across each day of 1864, would muster out early in the new year.[272]

December 1864 would be the final month of existence for the 1st USSS. As the year ended, Benjamin Peck seamlessly returned to the 141st Pennsylvania as the small number of marksmen in the three remaining companies joined other organizations, including the intact 2nd Regiment. Curtis Abbott noted the enrollment of a dozen men in Company H, a few recruits in addition to the Vermonters who remained at the dissolution of the 1st Regiment. When the year ended, Maj. James Doughty and his 2nd USSS still stood with nine infantry regiments under brigade commander Regis de Trobriand.[273]

"The Past Answers for the Future"

With fewer members in the USSS at the start of 1865, historians face a dwindling number of primary sources on happenings across the weeks before the formal end of the Sharpshooter organization. Although progress in the war made a Union victory seemingly inevitable, duty remained a soldier's fate. An order from Second Corps headquarters on New Year's Day outlined what the Sharpshooters and others could expect in the first month of the war's last year.

> *The troops being now well protected against the inclemency of the season, the commanding general enjoins upon division commanders the use of every hour of favorable weather for drills and evolutions. Regular recitations in tactics and regulations should now be had, and the Articles of War should be frequently read. A systematic effort should be made by division, brigade, and regimental commanders to bring their troops to the highest practicable state of discipline.*[274]

On January 5, Capt. Walter Smith expressed thanks to his family for some new footwear and clothes, then offered general updates about happenings along the Petersburg front.

> *The boots are just the thing, couldn't have been made to fit better. The shirts are just right. . . . I have been pretty busy for the last two weeks. lots of*

writing to do making out muster rolls, returns etc. for the old men that did not reenlist. . . . We were out on Review today. It was pleasant but not so underfoot for it had snowed about two inches last night & today thawed just enough to make it muddy & slippery. We have had steady cold weather for some time. I think we will be able to stay where we are until spring. I had command of the Regt last night & most of the day today.

A week later, the young officer wrote another letter. After thanking his brother for $20, Smith hoped he would not need additional support. But that would only be possible if Uncle Sam paid the marksmen their due. Uninspired by the poor soldiers filling the ranks of regiments, Smith suggested many of the ambivalent new troops quickly desert. "Many think we will have but little more fighting," Smith mused, "but I expect to see some," hopefully not as much as the summer of 1864.[275]

The routine of skirmish duty cost no USSS lives as winter droned on. The marksmen also experienced consecutive days of drill and other regular duties. For Wolverine George Crandall, a quiet sabbath on January 23 granted time for much writing. He penned notes to several friends, as well as his brother George. Happy to hear of his brother's good health, Crandall noted his own remained strong.[276]

After passing these humdrum weeks, what Curtis Abbott called a "restful period," Sharpshooters answered the call to more active duty, a return to the swampy ground along Hatcher's Run. The early February action became the last organized combat for the USSS.[277]

Plans to attack began when Generals Grant and Meade exchanged messages about ways to best disrupt Confederate supplies moving from the end of the Weldon Railroad to the enemy camps near Petersburg. Orders had the Second Corps head west, with the Fifth Corps close behind; Warren's divisions would be eventually positioned farther north. After issuing the necessary orders, Meade informed his boss that the infantry would begin moving at 7 a.m. on February 5. General Mott prepared his three brigades for action by ensuring his soldiers carried four days of rations and fifty rounds of ammunition on their person, with another forty rounds per man in wagons.[278]

In his memoirs, General de Trobriand expressed disappointment when he learned of the Union cavalry's failure to force a crossing of Hatcher's Run before the arrival of two Second Corps divisions. After a cold trek from camp, Sharpshooters started taking enemy fire near the stream at Vaughan Road—more than three miles southeast of where the USSS had fought in late October. With the Sharpshooters acting as skirmishers, de Trobriand worked on crossing his numerous albeit small infantry regiments, a tough task due to the impediments Confederates placed in the way, mainly fallen trees.[279]

Christian Meyer lost his life in the second battle of Hatcher's Run, likely while engaged in early skirmishing. The final combat fatality in the history of the USSS, Meyer, a twenty-eight-year-old native of Germany, had enlisted in Company F, 2nd Regiment, early in the war. Meyer's remains would return to New Hampshire where the last of the 260 killed or mortally wounded Sharpshooters rests near the grave of Josiah Bartlett, a signer of the Declaration of Independence.[280] Fifty-five miles east of the general area of Meyer's mortal injury, the first three fatally wounded USSS members fell near Yorktown thirty-four months before.

Boldness among Sharpshooters became quite prominent as they advanced north of Hatcher's Run on February 5. Curtis Abbott remembered his comrade Lewis Sault, two weeks shy of his discharge, acting "most reckless" with his life, although Sault did not suffer a wound. Abbott suggested that when the Sharpshooters charged, they appeared "vieing with each other" for the most prominent role in the attack. This type of competition among soldiers bolstered the Union advance. As on so many other fields, members of the USSS set a most courageous example.[281]

Pugnacious Confederates fought hard, symbolic of General Lee's desire to protect his dwindling hopes of holding Petersburg. Later in the deadly winter day, Union troops held off multiple Confederate counterattacks. After their tactical success, soldiers in the Second and Fifth Corps held positions north of Hatcher's Run, from near Armstrong's Mill to across Vaughan Road, with the Fifth Corps holding the eastern edge of the battlefield. The following morning found the 2nd USSS in an expected place: part of a reconnaissance to ascertain Confederate positions. Along with three infantry regiments under de Trobriand, Union warriors cast aside some enemy skirmishers, and then discovered the main Southern breastworks. With no additional USSS fatalities, the regiments returned to their former position.[282]

Grant's lodgment north of Hatcher's Run offered another base from which to exert more pressure on the Confederacy as winter continued. A Pennsylvania infantry officer suggested the enemy did not concede the matter easily. The "tremendous fury" at Second Hatcher's Run made the early February offensive a difficult sojourn, especially with cold temperatures. After the intensity of the combat, the status quo reigned once again, with tough Southerners and their doomed cause not yet fought out.[283]

Time was not on the side of the Southern cause. Yet, the doomed Confederate States of America lasted two months longer than the USSS. Resting and playing ball after their last major skirmish and battle, USSS members yielded to an army bureaucracy focused on the efficiency of military organization above the distinctive history of one particular set of troops.[284]

Across the winter the number of men remaining in USSS companies had continued a gradual decline due to the mustering out of individual three-year service commitments. The adjutant general's office noted the formal disbanding of the 2nd USSS with Special Order No. 47. Those with time to serve would be transferred to regiments from the same state. The official news arrived in the camp of the marksmen soon after Second Hatcher's Run. Relatively new Sharpshooter George Leslie informed his mother, "I have not verry good news to tell you this time," as he announced the end of the regiment. Hearing of the undesired change "made most of the boys feel pretty sober," Leslie added.[285] Blunt reality unconcerned about the hopes of USSS members—a defining characteristic of the Sharpshooters' field service—once again impacted the green-clad soldiers as their elite organization formally dissolved.

Like the end of the First and Third Corps the year before, the government and army did not dishonor the USSS in the effort to consolidate regimental and battalion formations. As a counterpoint, Curtis Abbott suggested the order terminating the USSS could have waited until the official muster out of the final companies or the end of the war. Abbott felt that the government had no need to orchestrate the premature demise of the USSS. At least Abbott and his comrades transferring to the 4th Vermont received a fond welcome from the Green Mountain infantry.[286]

General Regis de Trobriand, who knew men from both USSS regiments, issued a statement as the Sharpshooters' existence as a regiment ceased. Issued on February 16, General Order No. 12 proclaimed,

> *The U.S. Sharpshooters (including the First and Second consolidated battalions), being about to be broken up as a distinct organization, in compliance with orders from the War Department, the brigadier-general commanding division will not take leave of them without acknowledging their good and efficient service during three years' service in the field. The U.S. Sharpshooters leave behind a glorious record in the Army of the Potomac, since the first operations against Yorktown in 1862, up to the last movement of the army on Hatcher's Run, and few are the battles or engagements where they did not make their mark. The brigadier-general commanding, who had them under his command during most of the campaigns of 1863 and 1864, would be the last to forget their brave deeds during that period, and he feels assured that in the different organizations to which they are to belong, severally, officers and men will show themselves worthy of their old reputation. With them the past answers for the future.*[287]

Conclusion: The Fate of Heroes

Soon after the disbandment of the USSS, a Vermont marksman accurately wrote home, "We have had a rough road to travel and have lost many brave boys."[1] Worthy of great respect from future generations for their skill with a rifle and sacrifice in the nation's deadliest war, members of the USSS crafted an immortal reputation for themselves as soldiers. Did the government succeed in developing the Sharpshooter concept into "a distinct arm of the service" for the North's best marksmen? Is the historical hype of the best marksmen of the North transcending the doldrums of infantrymen an accurate view of life in the USSS? Surviving sources point toward negative answers to these questions. Why?

Multiple reasons explain why the Sharpshooters' war experience failed to fulfill the expectations created for the marksmen. Several problems manifested themselves early in the war. First, the very high ceiling envisioned for the USSS from the moment of the first shooting tryout seemed to guarantee less than anticipated results. A journalist could easily write of the 1st USSS being the "greatest of all regiments" nine months before any Sharpshooter fired a shot at the enemy. War's pernicious grip, however, quickly smacked the green-clad soldiers into reality. The Sharpshooters had enough to do simply facing the untold rigors of Civil War combat and countless nonbattle stressors. Maintaining a "distinct" mindset in what the war became seemed impossible. The conflict's myriad dangers and horrors were not conducive to the military's hopes and objectives for a vaunted group of expert riflemen. None signed up for the USSS with visions of spending days carrying wood and building winter huts, but Sharpshooters did that each year.

Second, the hundreds of men lost to sickness offered a primary reason why Berdan's brainchild did not develop as intended. No elite military organization can lose hundreds of trained and eager volunteers before facing the enemy, and then rebound sufficiently to meet the stately vision created in the summer of 1861. Ranks of USSS companies became alarmingly small long before their worst battle losses in the spring of 1864. Disease devastated the 2nd USSS before those eight companies ever faced a Confederate in battle. Likewise, the 1st Regiment lost dozens of men to sickness and wounds in their opening campaign, the doomed effort east of Richmond.

Third, the army bureaucracy and private gun manufacturers possessed insufficient dexterity to support the USSS. Told they would slay Confederates with reckless abandon, Sharpshooters soon learned Washington authorities were not keeping up with the hopes of USSS visionaries and the soldiers themselves. How disgraced did many of the Sharpshooters feel when taking the field in April 1862 without a marksman's rifle? The issue cannot exclusively be thrown at the feet of bureaucrats who did not foresee how to make the USSS great from the beginning. Private manufacturers were simply unable to quickly outfit eighteen companies with a superior firearm.

Fourth, Hiram Berdan's unsatisfactory leadership hindered the USSS. He failed to shake his combat inexperience, could not cast aside his ego, and flopped horribly as a motivator of troops. Whether or not Berdan had the heart of a coward, he lacked the necessary leadership skills to build respect by personal example. Political decisions to place callow but connected men in important combat positions did not always fail in the Civil War. David Birney's record demonstrates a fine example of a "political general" who did quite well. Yet, Berdan was unfit for the great responsibility of leading the USSS in the field.

Berdan did possess some administrative talents. He performed his best work of the war in 1861 and early 1862 trying to turn his dream of a Sharpshooter line of service into reality. Berdan should have been given a general's star early in the war, something he hankered for, then assigned to Washington as chief of USSS recruiting. The inability of some companies to recruit successfully diminished the potential of the Sharpshooters. Berdan sitting at a desk away from action—and occasionally traveling to northern states—likely could have fixed the problem, or at least improved on the uncoordinated work that prevailed.

The laments of USSS members themselves, liberally presented in the previous pages, offer the best evidence of their disappointment in the Sharpshooter concept. One of the most fascinating moments of research for this project occurred at Bentley Historical Library, University of Michigan, a national treasure with fantastic Civil War primary sources, many available online. The 1864 diary of Charles Ford, Company I, 1st USSS, includes short descriptions of life each day of the year. Reading the diary from January 1 through December 31, one finds virtually no hint that Ford volunteered for a "distinct" service filled with brilliant shooters doing nothing but furtively killing Confederates. Those who wish to understand how the Sharpshooters essentially lived as infantrymen need only read of Ford's quest for wood, intense labor on work details, and general feeling of malaise in the army. On many occasions, other Sharpshooters echoed Ford's diary to an uncanny degree.

Grandiose claims from some historians elevate the USSS to an untenable extent. William Fox wrote that the USSS had no equal as skirmishers, a debatable notion. The 13th Pennsylvania Reserves, also armed with Sharps Rifles, brilliantly performed that role while sustaining more deaths in battle than either USSS regiment. Also, even armed with muzzleloaders, Regular Army soldiers in the front line of their commands likely doomed many Confederates thanks to their professional training and resolute work on bloody fields. Although wielding carbines of shorter range than the Sharps Rifle, cavalrymen, with the benefit of swift movement, could also be fantastic skirmishers.

Another of Fox's notions, repeated in some modern works, cannot be proven. He suggested the USSS killed more Confederates than any units throughout Union armies. I highly doubt the veracity of such a claim. Many infantry outfits engaged in heavier combat for a longer duration likely accounted for more Southern combat deaths than the USSS. The Sharpshooters did not field that many men, due to their thinned ranks and recruitment limitations. The 1st Regiment had no significant role at Antietam, a day when ten thousand Confederates fell. Moreover, the 2nd USSS did not see notable combat until August 1862. By that time, Southern blood had been filtering through the earth for many horrible months. Historians should not repeat Fox's maxim of the USSS as the best killers of Confederates. Such a notion lacks necessary historical documentation.

Antietam stands as a horribly missed opportunity to illustrate what trained men with Sharps Rifles could do. Keeping the 1st Regiment idle in Fifth Corps lines wasted the soldiers' skills as McClellan suffered twelve thousand casualties. To the north, the 2nd Sharpshooters entered the hellfire of the Cornfield with ranks frighteningly small due mainly to medical discharges. They pushed ahead with their fellow infantrymen on the right flank of a key attack with fewer than 150 men in the ranks. Lining the two USSS regiments up to fire 2,500 rounds a minute south through the Cornfield into Confederate lines at dawn stands as a major missed opportunity at Antietam. Tactical theory about how best to use the Sharpshooters never advanced as well as the warriors in green did.

The Sharpshooters' prowess with one of the best weapons of the war did much to decrease the casualties they suffered, even though they were foisted into the role of charging infantry at several deadly places. Their skirmish and picket duties saved some USSS lives but also limited their glory. Facing great danger, isolated groups of soldiers on the front line still endured far less peril than infantry. The Peninsula offers the best proof of such a notion. The 1st USSS lost only twenty-one soldiers to mortal combat injuries across three months, a toll many infantry regiments exceeded in one engagement, such as the devastation of several brigades at Gaines Mill.

Mid-1863 constituted the best period for the Sharpshooters, where they offered a marvelous example of their competence. At Chancellorsville and Gettysburg, the regiments came the closest to reaching the goal of a "distinct" line of service. The May battle demonstrated how two generals who owed their positions to politics, not military experience, Dan Sickles and David Birney, implemented a tactical vision for the USSS no West Pointer matched. Assisting with the capture of the 23rd Georgia south of Chancellorsville rightly became a central moment in Sharpshooter history. The next day, positioned to confront the Confederate horde early on, the 1st USSS undoubtedly extracted a heavy toll on a sanguinary day for both armies.

In the epic Pennsylvania brawl, Berdan's ridiculous assertion of holding off Longstreet for hours on July 2 can easily be discarded without minimizing the tremendous work of both USSS regiments during the afternoon. Sharpshooter companies resisted stoutly west of the Peach Orchard and directly east of Hood's attack. The southern flank of Longstreet's advance seemed especially ripe for the picking. The 2nd Sharpshooters could not stop the tide, but the Confederates lost time and lives as Sharps Rifles tore into Southern ranks. The delay tipped the balance in favor of the Union in the cauldron of hell along Plum Run and the Round Tops.

Yet, most of the time, the Sharpshooters' deployment failed to support their distinct status. Even well-trained marksmen with rapid-fire weapons could not work miracles. Perhaps no senior army leader possessed the acumen to organize the USSS in the most appropriate manner. Misuse by the high command regularly turned the Sharpshooters into infantry in all but name. Senior officers may have believed that the grandeur of a specialized group of soldiers with a superior rifle would be enough to ensure the Sharpshooter concept met expectations. The lack of vision about how to benefit greatly from USSS marksmanship led to unnecessary casualties while losing out on the tactical benefit of concealed expert shots at key moments.

Perhaps the exigency of war must take some of the blame. Neither Joe Hooker nor George McClellan had time to place all USSS companies north of Sharpsburg to spearhead the First Corps attack on what became the war's bloodiest field. Twenty months later, the simple necessity of the moment led the USSS to unremitting hellfire in a charge west of the Brock Road. Nearly

20 percent of Sharpshooters sustaining a mortal combat injury fell in the span of a few hours when combining the losses at Antietam and the Wilderness. All soldiers soon learn that their lives are not truly their own. Those of superior rank control the paths and possibilities of a nation's warriors.

The Sharpshooters should not have been congregated into two regiments. The best arrangement might have placed the USSS at army headquarters, with a company or small group of marksmen temporarily sent where their expert services beckoned. General Burnside implemented such a concept in early 1863, but he left the army soon after. Another possibility would have permanently integrated USSS components as skirmishers across the army's infantry brigades or divisions. The *tirailleur*, light infantry placed at the front of their commands during the Napoleonic Wars, offer one example of such a concept.[2] Divvied up USSS companies contradict the principle of concentration of force. Nonetheless, the marksmen had a better chance for higher distinction and greater impact by being parceled out.

The limitations of the USSS concept do not fall at the feet of the Sharpshooters themselves. While rejecting pontifications about the USSS, this historian stands in awe of their sacrifice. Men fell to illness by the score before the USSS took the field. Enduring the fetid Camp of Instruction and conquering their first winter turned rookies into a truly honed group ready to take on Confederates. Life in the field was never easy, especially as men dealt with concerns about their families, poor food, extreme weather, and feelings that Colonel Berdan or the army failed to prevent withering of the Sharpshooter mystique. Then there were the Confederate bullets and shells seemingly ubiquitous at times. After many years studying the perspectives of Civil War soldiers, I still cannot fathom how laborious, dangerous, disappointing, and utterly enervating their lives had been for a short period, the first half of the 1860s.

Despite all of their disappointments and the deadly nature of their existence, USSS members performed amazing feats. Whatever the limitations of their distinct service, approximately two thousand men in green survived the war's perils. The myriad ways forty USSS members filled the rest of their years offer intriguing stories.

Curtis Abbott finished his military service as a first lieutenant in the 4th Vermont Infantry, mustering out in the summer of 1865. He wrote a very interesting unpublished history of Company H, 2nd USSS. Abbott erred in some of his facts, but his keen eye and wit make the microfilm of the typed manuscript at the Vermont State Archives an invaluable study of the North's greatest marksmen. Abbott stayed in touch with several of his comrades, proving quite devoted to understanding their stories and therefore enriching history. With so many fellow Sharpshooters not surviving, Abbott, who became a lawyer after the war, might never have predicted the number of his years. He lived until the mid-1930s.[3]

Returning to Switzerland after war service that cost him his goatee and a leg, ***Rudolf Aschmann*** would write a fantastic memoir, perhaps the best published primary source from a USSS member. Written in his native German, the highly laudable work did not see English publication until 1972. After working for U.S. diplomats in Bern, Switzerland for about a decade, Aschmann generally disappears into history. He married twice, dying in 1909.[4]

After a November 1863 discharge due to Wapping Heights wounds, ***James H. Baker*** was given a sword from his Wolverine company. The gift honored Baker's courage and the confidence his men still felt for him. Devoting himself to multiple pursuits, Baker worked as a lumber buyer, a job requiring a good eye for the value of timber. He bought large tracts of land, including one hundred acres of forest in Michigan's Ingham County. Baker also served as a detective in Lansing, which brought a "strenuous life of hunting down criminals." Interested in war remembrance, Baker cared deeply for those who served the North in the 1860s. An accident while preparing for a parade caused Baker's health to fail. Six weeks short of his seventieth birthday, Baker died in 1909 in Lansing, with burial in the city's Mount Hope Cemetery.[5]

"The Fighting Parson," ***Lorenzo Barber***, oversaw all chaplains in the Second Corps later in the war, a role that included establishing burial grounds for deceased soldiers. Remembered very fondly by his marksmen comrades as "a perfect gentleman," Barber crafted a record "inferior to that of no member connected with our especial service," Charles Stevens declared. Returning to his congregation and enjoying the pursuits of a sportsman, Barber died in 1874 at his home in Troy, New York, after an accidental gunshot wound.[6]

Private turned captain ***Llewellyn Blanchard***, a bold and determined teenage enlistee, exemplified strong leadership. A Wolverine Sharpshooter from Maine, Blanchard lived much of the rest of his years in his native state. For about a decade, he worked as a bookkeeper in Bangor, then decided to attend Dartmouth Medical School in New Hampshire. Blanchard also graduated from a dental school in Pennsylvania. He established a practice in Maine but had to cut short his career due to vision problems. Employed later in real estate and insurance, Blanchard died in Dexter, Maine in October 1902, not yet sixty years old.[7]

Charles Buchanan, known to many as "Buck," enjoyed productive years after his service in New York's Company D and as the 1st Regiment's sergeant major. A clerk in the U.S. Army Quartermaster's office immediately after the war, Buchanan spent some time at Fort Snelling, Minnesota. A West Point cadet later in the decade, Buchanan did not finish his studies at the Academy. He quickly established a name for himself as a New York lawyer, eventually becoming a firm's senior partner. Buchanan also served as a trustee of Albany Law School, a bank director, and a park commissioner. His busy schedule included time as an officer in the National Guard. The learned Sharpshooter even earned a master's degree in his mid-sixties. Buchanan died in Albany on January 7, 1916, aged seventy-two. He rests at Albany Rural Cemetery.[8]

Brigham Buswell may have lived longer than any Sharpshooter. Rebounding from his combat injury on the Peninsula, Buswell later moved to Washington State. In the late 1930s, he earned $750 by living long enough to claim the buyout of his life insurance policy. The dollars undoubtedly helped the aged marksmen in his final years. After almost a century of life, Buswell died in July 1942, eighty summers after the wound that robbed him of an arm and more time in Company I. Buswell rests in Elma, Washington.[9]

Benjamin Calef became a Sixth Corps staff member after departing the USSS. Captured when parts of the command were overwhelmed at the Wilderness in May 1864, Calef would be home by the end of the year. His papers include correspondence with captured Gen. Truman Seymour, a brigade commander taken with Calef. Becoming a highly respected leader in the insurance industry, in 1880 Calef rose to manage the Boston branch of the Manhattan Life Insurance Company. He later helped organize the National Association of Life Underwriters. Dying in Boston in 1897, Calef was buried in his native town of Saco, Maine. His wife Annie lived until 1938, aged ninety-three.[10]

Jonathan Chase somehow persevered after the three Confederate bullets devastated his right foot at the Mule Shoe. With time in multiple hospitals, Chase struggled to craft a life with only one functioning foot. Transferred to the Veteran Reserve Corps, Chase served through early 1866 on light details for the military. One physician wrote, "The pensioner walks partly on the side of his foot," while another added, "the foot and leg are atrophied and there is but very little muscle left upon the limb. There is no strength in the ankle." To walk, "He is obliged to use a mechanical support on the foot and leg." With a Sharpshooter's determination, Chase became a public servant and farmer, tending fields, sugar maple groves, and cattle. Marrying a war widow, the marksman raised several children. Six months before his seventieth birthday, Chase died in his hometown of Jay, Vermont, on May 5, 1908, almost forty-four years after his Spotsylvania wounds.[11]

Minnesotan ***Joseph Dickey*** spent a short time in the 23rd Illinois Infantry late in the Civil War. He returned to Minnesota to become "a most genial and progressive citizen." Taking a job as a store clerk after resting from the rigors of military service, Dickey actively worked as a farmer in the town of Pine Island, raising large flocks of sheep. Marrying in 1869 while in his early thirties, Dickey grew interested in public service and remembering his Sharpshooter comrades. He participated in a reunion of the USSS in 1910, which took place in Minnesota. He died on July 24, 1912, at the age of seventy-four. His wife lived until 1936.[12]

Owen Evans returned to his native Indiana after departing Company A, 2nd USSS. Like so many marksmen, Evans held an interest in public service. He spent eight years as the deputy auditor of Henry County in the Hoosier State. Later moving to Arkansas, the last captain of Minnesota's USSS company died on January 29, 1904, in his seventy-eighth year.[13]

Warren Fletcher found much to do after mustering out of Company G, 2nd USSS. He moved to Clay County, Kansas, in 1865, bought 160 acres, then became involved in agricultural pursuits. Politics also beckoned, with Fletcher becoming a county clerk, register of deeds, and a state legislator. Tragically, four of Fletcher's children died young. By the late 1870s, Fletcher left his farm to pursue real estate and loan-servicing businesses. President William Henry Harrison appointed Fletcher the Clay Center postmaster in 1889. The marksman's life ended in Clay Center in 1913, with burial at Greenwood Cemetery.[14]

Benjamin Giddings ended his service with the Sharpshooters after his spring 1862 hernia and exhaustion. After resting on the family farm and a short stint as a teacher, Giddings signed up in a new infantry regiment, the 17th Vermont. The Green Mountain patriot became a captain, surviving his new outfit's very difficult ordeal in the Ninth Corps. One in eight enlistees in the regiment would be killed or mortally wounded across eleven months starting at the Wilderness. By the late 1870s, Giddings moved to California, managing the publication of a railroad magazine. He married a native of England in San Francisco in 1884. As another Sharpshooter interested in fraternal organizations; Giddings joined a Grand Army of the Republic post. In September 1926, the eighty-three-year-old Giddings died in Hayward, California, with burial at San Francisco National Cemetery.[15]

Reluctant Sharpshooter ***William Greene*** passed his last months of military service in several hospitals, returning home in poor health. He spent time with old friends and former comrades in arms before moving to the town of Haverhill in his native state. Disappointed with his prospects as a New Hampshire shoemaker, Greene headed to Dunlap, Kansas, in 1878, hoping to become a rancher. Without the means to establish such an ambitious endeavor, Greene worked in the town as a clerk. Optimistic about a better life by early 1879, tragedy struck in mid-March. Greene died later that month from the effects of a carriage accident. Only thirty-five years old, he was buried in his hometown of Raymond, New Hampshire. Greene's observant and devoted mother outlived her son by a quarter century.[16]

Truman Head gained a medical discharge in late 1863. Returning to the West Coast, he became a port inspector in San Francisco. In a Fourth of July address at French Gulch, California, in 1864, Head gave a rousing speech promoting the liberties the nation's forefathers won and the war intended to maintain a united country. A USSS veteran who interacted with Head after the war wrote to Charles Stevens, "He was always the same old California Joe, and went by no other name, except on pay rolls." Dying in his mid-sixties, the beloved "Uncle Head" rests at San Francisco National Cemetery in a plot of Grand Army of the Republic members.[17]

John Hetherington departed Company D, 1st USSS with a disability discharge in September 1864. In the two years immediately following, Hetherington's life seemed to ebb as he recuperated from three war wounds. He then hit his stride in his hometown of Cherry Valley, New York. The manager of thousands of bee hives, Hetherington became one of the greatest apiculturists of the century, a founder of the New York Bee Keepers Association, and "probably the largest honey producer in the world." In 1874, Hetherington's endeavors yielded fifty-eight thousand pounds of the sweet treat. His interest in speaking

Truman Head, immortalized in print during and after his time in the USSS, returned to California after his military service. LIBRARY OF CONGRESS

The grave of John Hetherington. AUTHOR'S PHOTO

and teaching on the topic endeared him to many in the central part of his state. Active as a Mason and member of a Presbyterian church, Hetherington garnered further encomiums. He died on the last day of 1903, with a burial at Cherry Valley Cemetery. Both of Hetherington's children lived into the 1970s.[18]

After nearly dying at Antietam, ***Silas Howard*** received a medical discharge in 1863. He assisted with the preservation of the war's story by informing some of his comrades of a Maine infantry officer's effort to correspond with Antietam veterans. Some of these Sharpshooters then sent letters that enriched our understanding of the seminal campaign of the war. The excellent collection is preserved at Dartmouth College. The historical record documents little of Howard's later life, even with many years ahead of him. His progeny spent much time on Earth, as well. His eldest daughter survived until 1977, while a granddaughter of the Green Mountain marksman lived into her nineties. She died in 2006.[19]

Discharged Sharpshooter ***John Huff*** put his accuracy skills on display at a vital time after joining George Armstrong Custer's Michigan cavalry brigade. Thanks to eyewitness testimony, Huff was credited with firing the pistol shot inflicting a mortal wound on revered Confederate cavalry leader James Ewell

Brown Stuart at Yellow Tavern on May 11, 1864. Huff had little time to relish killing the vaunted Southern horseman. The Wolverine lost his life in battle two weeks later at Haw's Shop, northeast of Richmond. The New York native, forty-four years old, rests at Willow Grove Cemetery, Armada, Michigan.[20]

A Sharpshooter who left wonderful recollections of the Peninsula and Wilderness, ***William Kent***, Company F, 1st Regiment, became a corporal in the summer of 1864 after convalescence from his May wound. Leaving the Sharpshooters after three years of service, Kent's remembrances of fallen friends may have taken an even more emotional turn after the tragic loss of an infant daughter in 1867. A lumberman for a time, Kent then worked for the Minneapolis, St. Paul & Sault Ste. Marie Railroad, rising to become Superintendent of the Commissary, Sleeping, and Parlor Cars. Thirty years after his last fight in the Wilderness, he wrote of wishing to relive moments as a soldier, possessing a drive to once again face the foe. The Sharpshooter then countered himself by suggesting the passing of three decades "might be great enough to cool the hot blood." Kent died in 1907, with burial at a family plot at Oak Hill Cemetery, Janesville, Wisconsin.[21]

George Lewis proved able to transcend a wound at Glendale and more than a month as a prisoner of war. Returning to his regiment in August, Lewis suffered as the result of his battle injury. Confined to a northern hospital for much of the autumn, Lewis promised, "I shall keep up good cheer" while the bureaucracy considered his fate. He received a medical discharge in December 1862. Returning to Wisconsin, Lewis married in 1868, worked as a butcher, and raised two children. Moving west later in life, Lewis died in 1921, aged seventy-seven. He rests at Richland Cemetery, Carpenter, South Dakota.[22]

Beginning a life of service as a Sharpshooter in his early twenties, ***George Marden*** gave history a great gift with his wonderful letters. A superb writer at a young age, Marden's communication skills helped him later. A poem read to students at his alma mater Dartmouth College in 1875 did not directly discuss the war, yet some lines educated his listeners about the difficulties a harsh world can create: "The glorious visions of ambitious youth / Are dimmed by tempering light of sober truth." Studying law for a time, Marden made journalism his calling. After serving as an editor of a West Virginia paper, Marden went home to New Hampshire to edit his native state's history of the Civil War. Moving to Massachusetts, Marden purchased two newspapers in Lowell, then held public offices in the Bay State. He died on December 19, 1906, at the age of sixty-seven. Marden rests in Lowell Cemetery.[23]

Wishing for a fresh start after his war service, ***James Matthews*** boarded a train in Portland, Maine on May 19, 1865. Destined for Chicago, Matthews joined a printer's union while employed at multiple newspapers in the Windy City. Moving east again, he found work as a book printer in Cambridge, Massachusetts. In declining health in 1874, Matthews returned to his hometown of Rockland, Maine. Leaving a wife and two children, he died that summer, only thirty-four years old, with burial at Achorn Cemetery.[24]

Jacob McClure earned higher rank months after departing his Maine company in April 1864. He became a lieutenant colonel, then briefly commanded a battalion of Maine sharpshooters. McClure found postwar work as a stone contractor, a job taking him across New England. He added to his family after the war, including four children born in 1865 or later. Soon after returning home from a business trip to Boston, McClure died on October 3, 1893, aged sixty-one, in Nashua, New Hampshire. McClure's widow, who lived another thirty years, rests beside the hero at the city's Edgewood Cemetery.[25]

Frederick Mears made the U.S. Army his career. The trainer of Sharpshooters early in their service earned the lieutenant colonelcy of the Fourth U.S. Infantry in 1888. Survived by a wife and three children, Mears died at Fort Spokane, Washington, on his fifty-sixth birthday, January 2, 1892. More than half his life was spent in the army.[26]

Although he served for a short time in the USSS, ***John Monahan***'s diaries, difficult to read in several places, offer a relatively untapped means for interested people to learn about Sharpshooter life. The Vermonter wrote several pithy phrases as he acutely observed his war-time reality. Home soon after his Chancellorsville wound, Monahan started a grocery business in Burlington, then became a lawyer and probate judge. Living in multiple Vermont municipalities, he served as the town clerk in Underhill for a third of a century. Married twice,

Jacob McClure logged devoted months of service to Maine's Company D from 1861 through April 1864. MAINE STATE ARCHIVES

Monahan left a wife and daughter when he died at age sixty-nine in October 1910 following weeks of sickness. He rests in his native city of Rutland.[27]

Cassius Peck typified the Sharpshooter mentality, with the bold action at Shepherdstown catching the eyes of many. His Medal of Honor seemed very justified to eyewitnesses and other comrades. Peck's life of service included terms in the Vermont State House and Senate. In 1897, he moved to Burlington, becoming superintendent of the Vermont State Agricultural College farm. Losing his first wife in 1901, Peck remarried four years later. In an article discussing Peck, a friend deemed the heroic Sharpshooter "a man of exceptionally good business qualities" as well as "a good citizen, worthy of trust and honor." Peck suffered three months of bad health before his death in July 1913 at the age of seventy-one.[28]

The Peninsula campaign nearly killed ***Frederick Peet***, but the brave young officer held on to life for a long time. Captured soon after his wounding, Peet spent part of July 1862 in Richmond's notorious Libby Prison. The poor food and squalid conditions started to waste away at the USSS officer. Paroled and exchanged, Peet saw further action as a member of the U.S. Marines. In addition to witnessing the famous siege of Battery Wagner near Charleston, South Carolina, Peet served on vessels that chased Confederate shipping in European waters. The cruise of nearly eighteen months ended with a return to Boston in September 1865. Peet resigned from the Marines four years later. In addition to joining veteran organizations, Peet could remember the war whenever he felt the Confederate round that remained in his shoulder from Sharpshooter service. Marrying a war widow in 1887, Peet's wife died two years later. At the age of eighty-three, Peet's life ended in Auburn, New York, on January 26, 1925. He rests at Brooklyn's Green-Wood Cemetery.[29]

Francis Peteler enjoyed many productive years after his resignation as the lieutenant colonel of the 2nd USSS in 1862. With a scientific mind and great motivation, the native of Germany invented many items that advanced the development of the railroad industry in the United States. A holder of several patents, he founded the Peteler Portable Railway Manufacturing Company, remaining a distinguished resident of Minnesota. He died in 1907, with burial at Lakewood Cemetery in Minneapolis.[30]

With his nagging Antietam wound, ***Henry A. V. Post*** never commanded troops in battle again. The colonel found a way to be fondly remembered by the Sharpshooters, even with his focus on stringent military protocol. Living in Cincinnati, then moving back to New York City, Post made a brilliant business decision by providing products and financial services to the burgeoning railroad industry. While in Ohio, he married the daughter of a Civil War general. The colonel's daughter-in-law founded the Emily Post Institute—still operated by the family. One of Post's sons died soon after setting a military aviation altitude record, while another won medals as an Olympic fencer. Colonel Post died in early 1914 in New York City, aged eighty-one. He was buried at Woodlawn Cemetery in the Bronx.[31]

Medal of Honor winner ***William Ripley*** received the promotion to colonel and the chance to lead the 10th Vermont Infantry soon after his Malvern Hill wound. He declined the offer due to his lingering injuries. Instead, the scarred Sharpshooter rose to major general in the state militia before the war ended. Ripley wrote a commendable history of his storied Green Mountain boys of the 1st Regiment. A newspaper article promoting Ripley's book stated Company F's killed and wounded amounted to 43 percent of the company's entire enrollment across the war.

Ripley became president of the Rutland County National Bank. His papers include copies of several speeches honoring veterans, a keenly felt duty to Ripley. More than thirty years after Malvern Hill, he received a letter from another excellent officer, Lewis Grant, who had led the First Vermont Brigade, which saw horrible combat, especially in the war's last year. Grant, an assistant secretary in the War Department, expressed gratitude to his old friend. In a letter noting Ripley's Medal of Honor, Grant wrote,

> *Among my official duties I have found none more pleasant than that connected with the recognition of the valorous deeds of the heroes of the War, and it gives me additional pleasure when, as in this instance, the honor is paid to one whose bravery was personally known to me and whom I esteem so highly as a friend.*[32]

New Hampshire marksman ***Joseph Rolfe***, who had become a soldier in his teens in 1861, enjoyed a very long life. Leaving his native state soon after returning home from three years in the USSS, Rolfe married in 1866. He lived in Burlington, Vermont, for seven years, then moved to Minneapolis, Minnesota. Rolfe did well in real estate and lending businesses, also serving as deputy treasurer of Hennepin County for six years. Later, he joined the board of education in Minneapolis, with three of those years as secretary. He totaled more than a quarter century as a resident of Minnesota, then moved to California. Rolfe traveled frequently, even in his later years. Married twice, Rolfe was a member of the Grand Army of the Republic. He died in June 1936, reaching the age of ninety-three. The marksman rests at Fort Rosecrans Cemetery in San Diego.[33]

Albert Sisson likely thought of his war service every waking hour for the rest of his years; the bullet hitting his leg in late July 1863 was never removed, causing much pain. Sisson worked as a butcher while raising nine children. He died in Ada, Michigan, in early 1913 as his seventieth birthday approached. He rests at Ada Cemetery.[34]

Walter Smith, the last captain of Company H, 2nd USSS, moved to Fitchburg, Massachusetts, soon after leaving the army in July 1865. He worked in the pork processing industry and joined a social lodge while suffering from chronic health problems his military service caused. He traveled north to see friends and family in Vermont during the state fair season. A newspaper eulogized Smith, who died in May 1899, as "a worthy citizen" who was "respected by all." The USSS officer rests at Fitchburg's Forest Hill Cemetery.[35]

Charles Stevens, a Company G officer who became USSS historian, remained active in his craft of shooting and in veteran groups. Very upset after the assassination of President Lincoln, Stevens conducted a highly accurate shooting demonstration in Milwaukee using a picture of assassin John Wilkes Booth as the target. Stevens worked in the newspaper and railroad industries, but a good deal of the rest of his life included the study of the USSS and interaction with his comrades. Although he embellished the Sharpshooters to some degree, Stevens's book was a labor of love for the aging marksman. He died in August 1900, with burial at Arlington National Cemetery.[36]

After being captured early in the Petersburg campaign, ***Homer Stoughton*** spent six months as a prisoner of war. Paroled in December 1864, he left the army the following month. Tragic family news struck the USSS officer, with the loss of his wife and two children. Stoughton remarried in 1869. He worked in the railroad industry in Vermont before moving to other states, including Alabama, where he managed an iron manufacturer. The colonel then made Ohio his home, working in real estate before returning to Vermont in the mid-1890s. Stoughton died in Barre, Vermont, on September 7, 1902, aged sixty-five. He rests in that city at Elmwood Cemetery.[37]

After his post-Wilderness convalescence, ***William Sweet*** returned to Company G, 1st USSS in time to muster out in September 1864. A few years later, Sweet started a new life in Le Roy, Minnesota, becoming involved in building and real estate. He became a deputy sheriff, assessor, county commissioner, village council president, and mayor. Sweet and his wife Polly also raised several children. Esteemed by his fellow residents in Le Roy, the old marksman had a hotel named in his honor. In his late eighties, Sweet died in Le Roy in 1931. Polly lived three more years. The couple rests at Le Roy Cemetery.[38]

Richard Tyler joined the Veteran Reserve Corps after losing an arm at Second Deep Bottom. Married to a Kentuckian in 1867, Tyler, whose brother served with him in Company K, 1st USSS, joined the 44th U.S. Infantry, rising to the rank of captain before his resignation in 1870. The distinguished USSS officer founded a real estate and loan company, in which he would serve as president for many years. Also practicing law, Tyler won a case at the U.S. Supreme Court. The matter involved the computation of retirement pay for members of the army. The distinguished Sharpshooter also penned an exceptional letter about Malvern Hill that survives in William Ripley's papers at Duke University. Tyler joined the Grand Army of the Republic, giving an inspiring speech in 1909 as his Washington GAR post celebrated its history. Tyler died in Pennsylvania six months later, with burial at Arlington National Cemetery.[39]

Andrew Westervelt lived life to the fullest, but he tragically had too few years after his Sharpshooter service. The man deemed "California Joe No. 2" returned west after leaving the military in 1865. Engaged in mining pursuits for a time, Westervelt greatly enjoyed the outdoors as a sportsman and hunter. Like Lorenzo Barber, Westervelt suffered a paradoxical end for a Sharpshooter, death by accidental gunshot wound. The sad incident took place in Sutter County on April 7, 1872. Forty-five years old, Westervelt was remembered as "a thoroughly honest man, and his death is greatly regretted by a large circle of friends."[40]

The excellent words of ***Wyman White*** offer much to history. The conflict proved the Sharpshooter's patriotism; military service cut White's weight from 180 to 125 pounds. Based on a short autobiographical sketch in the excellent *Civil War Diary* frequently cited herein, White's health improved after returning home in March 1865. He worked in the timber business, then cut granite for a decade. He bought a twenty-three-acre farm in Massachusetts in 1877, selling the property four years later. After working in law enforcement in Sterling, Massachusetts, for seven years, White became an insurance broker and avid gardener after purchase of a cottage in 1915. He spent much time studying the war in his later years. White died on May 4, 1923, aged eighty-one, with burial at Village Cemetery in Fitzwilliam, New Hampshire.[41]

John Wilson departed the USSS as captain when his Company B, 1st USSS mustered out in late August 1864. Considered "one of the best officers in the service," Wilson enjoyed little time on earth after his war experience. The respected "Captain Jack" remained in his native New York, becoming a state employee. Among Wilson's friends were former USSS officers, including George Hastings. Active in politics and social events in Albany, Wilson had to deal with several service-related ailments. He died on April 22, 1869, not yet thirty-four years old.[42]

Appendix

Compiling the Names of USSS Members Killed or Mortally Wounded in Action

My interest in the United States Sharpshooters began as I worked on my book, *First for the Union: Life and Death in a Civil War Army Corps from Antietam to Gettysburg.* This present volume started as a research project to find the names of those in the two USSS regiments who were killed in action (KIA) or mortally wounded (MW). As the starting point, I reviewed the total number of marksmen lost to battle in each company. A baseline was easily established from William Fox's company-level death numbers presented in his one-page histories of the Union's "300 Fighting Regiments."

Fox's data does not always align with other extant sources at the battle, company, or regimental level. New York's four USSS companies offer an example of how other sources provide an opportunity to update Fox's company-level counting. In a postwar publication, New York listed thirty-six KIA or MW Sharpshooters across the Empire State companies. Although eight lower than Fox, the state's postwar research and mine aligned exactly on the total number of USSS members dying from battle.

Second Bull Run was the first battle in which both USSS regiments had men killed. The 1st USSS, fighting Confederates across two days, lost thirteen lives from wounds, three more than Fox's total. Conversely, for the 2nd Sharpshooters, the total of five dead I found exactly matched Fox. These men fell during the August 29 engagement along the Warrenton Turnpike.

William Ripley's history of Vermont's Company F, 1st USSS, lists thirty-two KIA or MW Sharpshooters, one higher than Fox. I did not place four of Ripley's men on my list. One had an unknown fate after being taken prisoner. Another listing denotes the Sharpshooter as dying from disease in a Confederate prison, while two other listings failed to note death from battle. Even after lowering the unit's total combat fatalities to twenty-eight, the Vermonters recorded the most KIA or MW Sharpshooters from a single company.

Updating Fox's company totals proved much easier than compiling the names of each KIA or MW Sharpshooter, even though all but one USSS company has information in digital format about members lost to battle wounds. Michigan, Minnesota, New Hampshire, and Vermont published postwar rosters of their USSS companies. New York preserved cards listing details about individual marksmen, then posted the data on Ancestry.com. Maine included updates about soldiers in the state's annual adjutant general reports, an especially valuable source because the books were published during the conflict, not years later. I used Wisconsin's postwar list of KIA or MW soldiers to compare numbers with Fox. Citations for all of these very helpful and readily available sources are presented throughout my endnotes and bibliography.

Company C, 2nd USSS, posed the biggest challenge. Unlike Pennsylvania's infantry, cavalry, and artillery units, the state did not publish a roster listing the fate of its USSS members. Using helpful information at the Pennsylvania State Archives and the National Archives, I found the names of eight KIA or MW Keystone Staters—three less than Fox. The Historical Society of Pennsylvania kindly informed me of their lack of any rosters or descriptive lists for Company C. After reviewing newspapers digitally available in the quest for more names, I closed my effort to find any remaining Company C men lost in battle. Perhaps my total of eight should not trump Fox's eleven, but I lacked evidence to add more.

Finalizing my list of marksmen dying from battle injuries required consultation with other sources from the extensive yet imperfect historical record. Much evidence exists to update Fox's company totals or craft lists of marksmen falling on a certain date. Nonetheless, several examples from USSS history offer cautionary tales on exactness. We must always remember the imprecise nature of historical research, even when studying the well-documented Civil War. Historians should be prepared to balance information before them because sources sometimes conflict. Phonetic spelling and faint records can doom the quest for historical perfection.

One of the last Sharpshooters to die in combat illustrates this important point. Gregory Deyett, who enlisted in the summer of 1864, led me to add one to Fox's total of lost Wisconsin marksmen. He did not appear in the state's postwar list of KIA or MW Sharpshooters, perhaps because he joined the USSS through the authority of the state of New York. I elected to place him in the Wisconsin company because National Archives information denoted his service in Company G. Likely because of the mustering out of New York's USSS companies, the doomed Deyett logged his short period of service as a Badger marksman.

I did not count fatalities I could not confirm if a state only listed a soldier as missing in action, likely the main reason for my differences with Fox. Rosters and other data across USSS companies show certain men deemed missing after a battle later returning to their regiment or ending military service as a prisoner. Moreover, numerous FindAGrave.com entries exist with headstone pictures or other sources confirming that a missing Sharpshooter died long after the war.

The story of James Vandeburg, Company C, 1st USSS, illustrates how some digging can update the fate of certain Sharpshooters. Historian Charles Stevens listed Vandeburg as MW after a severe wound to the side at Chancellorsville. Although the state roster noted he spent a year in military hospitals, Vandeburg survived the effects of his tough day south of the Rappahannock. The brave marksman died in 1912 at the age of seventy-two.

An Ancestry.com entry for Mainer Roderick Newell classified the marksman as dying from a battle wound in December 1862. I did not count him as MW, however, because no contemporary state record or USSS member with writings I consulted noted Newell died from a combat injury. Maine was quite specific on the fate of soldiers in its annual roster lists published during the war. Controlling for me in this instance, therefore, was the state not specifying battle as the cause of Newell's death.

I also changed the historical fate of one Vermonter. The state roster listed John Meader as KIA on June 9, 1863. I doubted that specific finding, because several sources, even those diarists or letter writers usually mentioning the name of a KIA Sharpshooter, did not note the loss of Meader to Confederate fire. The mystery ended when I found a June 17 letter, published in a Vermont newspaper, that noted Meader met his demise from the effects of an accident, a nasty axe injury. Although not as glamorous an end as any USSS member would have wished, work details could be fatal assignments for Civil War soldiers.

As anyone studying nineteenth-century handwriting knows, reading some letters and documents can prove quite laborious, if not impossible. When spelling conflicts occurred between sources, I accepted published contemporary or postwar data with spelling and specific names that state governments collected. Some modern sources with spellings USSS historian Charles Stevens used were not selected as final if a state roster differed.

Colonel Berdan's report on Second Bull Run misspelled the name of the KIA captain of Company A, 1st USSS, Adolph Sennhauser. Some might prefer to accept a regimental leader's spelling of a company commander's name as final.

I adopted the spelling that matched Rudolf Aschmann's memoir because the junior officer had been a friend of Sennhauser's for many years, going back to their schooling in Switzerland.

Although sometimes incomplete, state rosters and the words of Sharpshooters themselves offer the best bet for tracking a marksman's fate. I used these most reliable sources if other authors contradicted the roster. For example, a highly commendable modern book about the battle of Shepherdstown counted Arthur Hamlin as MW on September 19, 1862. Charles Stevens made the same determination in his USSS history. However, Michigan's roster notes that Hamlin died in 1872 without saying his Shepherdstown wound caused his death. Thus, Hamlin is not counted in my tally.

Willis Colby provides another case of interest. The Granite Stater suffered a wound at Gaines Mill while also being captured. The beneficiary of a prisoner exchange later in the summer, Colby died at Fort Monroe on August 4, 1862. The state listed Colby as succumbing to disease, not wounds, so I left him off my list of battle fatalities. Perhaps the disease resulted from Colby's wound, but because the state did not list battle as his cause of death, I did not either.

A soldier dying weeks or a decade after a combat injury could have lost his life due to the wound. If the state roster said the round passing through both of Hamlin's thighs killed him ten years later, he would have been added to my list. Clearly, any wounded Sharpshooter suffered much because of his combat service. Historians are limited by the data uncovered over the course of a multiyear effort. Due to their difficult service and the importance of their victory, all members of the USSS and other Union units deserve the immortality that comes from grateful people remembering the most meaningful sacrifice imaginable.

Even for states with easily accessible data, my numbers might not be exact. Researchers and writers interested in the USSS may have some names of fallen Sharpshooters I was unable to uncover. Humility should be one of the primary tools of historical research. The perfect book will never be written. No historian can be the last word on any topic, especially one as dynamic and important as the Civil War.

Table A.1 compares my USSS company and regimental losses to Fox's total.

Table A.1. Number of Killed in Action or Mortally Wounded USSS Members by Company

1st USSS

Company	Number KIA/MW	
	Fox	Update
A	15	12
B	13	13
C	18	24
D	8	5
E	15	12
F	31	28
G	22	23
H	7	4
I	12	10
K	11	11
Total	**152**	**142**

2nd USSS

Company	Number KIA/MW	
	Fox	Update
A	11	11
B	13	13
C	11	8
D	21	19
E	24	22
F	14	14
G	12	11
H	18	18
Total	**124**	**116**

Note: The updated death toll reaches 260 for the USSS when adding Caspar Trepp and Lewis Parmelee, who fell as staff officers, rather than as members of a given company.

Notes

Preface

1. https://www.findagrave.com/memorial/192875824/robert-f-twombly; https://www.findagrave.com/memorial/151839666/silas-wright-howard.

2. William F. Fox, *Regimental Losses in the American Civil War, 1861–1865* (Albany, NY: Brandow Printing Company, 1889), 418–19.

Introduction

1. Thomas Arnold, *History of Rome: From the End of the First to the End of the Second Punic War*, vol. 3 (London: Gilbert and Rivington, 1846), 107–108; Andy Dougan, *One Shot, One Kill: A History of the Sniper* (London: William Collins, 2016), 15–21.

2. Mick Bennett, *The Story of the Rifle* (London: Cobbett Publishing, 1945), 19–23; John L. Plaster, *The History of Sniping and Sharpshooting* (Boulder, CO: Paladin Press, 2008), 25–31; John F. Luzader, *Saratoga: A Military History of the Decisive Campaign of the American Revolution* (New York: Savas Beatie, 2008), 284–85, 290–95, 408, 411.

3. Roy Marcot, *Civil War Chief of Sharpshooters Hiram Berdan: Military Commander and Firearms Inventor* (Irvine, CA: Northwood Heritage Press, 1989), 16–21; Wiley Sword, *Sharpshooter: Hiram Berdan, His Famous Sharpshooters and Their Sharps Rifles* (Lincoln, RI: Andrew Mowbray, 1988), 9–10; John H. Eicher and David J. Eicher, *Civil War High Commands* (Stanford, CA: Stanford University Press, 2001), 129.

4. *New York Herald*, May 31, 1861.

5. *Alleghenian*, June 13, 1861; *Kenosha Telegraph*, June 6, 1861; *Rutland Herald*, August 1, 1861.

6. *New York Herald*, June 18, 1861; *Raftman's Journal*, July 3, 1861; *New York Herald*, June 11, 1861; Marcot, *Civil War Chief*, 22–23.

7. *New York Sun*, May 28, 1861; *New York Times*, August 7, 1861.

8. Walter Wolcott, *Military History of Yates County, N. Y.* (Penn Yan: Express Book, 1895), 47.

9. Civil War Muster Roll Abstracts, Box 373, NYSA; Chris Schnupp, *The Long Island Company: A History of Company H, 1st Regiment of US Sharpshooters* (Kindle Edition, 2015), location 147–64.

10. *New York Herald*, July 14, 1861; a USSS recruitment ad started appearing in the *Albany Evening Journal* in October, with publication dates at least through January.

11. *New York Herald*, August 18, 1861.

12. Heinz K. Meier, ed., *Memoirs of a Swiss Officer in the American Civil War* (Bern, Switzerland: Herbert Lang, 1972), 23, 29, 31.

13. *New York Times*, August 7, 1861.

14. *Hillsdale Standard*, August 20, 1861; Adjutant General, *Record of Service of Michigan Volunteers in the Civil War, 1861–1865*, vol. 44 (Kalamazoo, MI: Ihling Bros & Everard, 1900), 123, 125, 131.

15. Meier, *Memoirs of a Swiss Officer*, 31–33; *New York Times*, September 19, 1861.

16. *Jeffersonian*, August 15, 1861.

17. Dave Grossman, *On Killing: The Psychological Cost of Learning to Kill in War and Society* (New York: Back Bay Books, 2009), xviii–xix, 177–79, 254–57, 317–18.

18. Marcot, *Civil War Chief*, 30; E. B. Quiner, *E. B. Quiner Papers: Correspondence of the Wisconsin Volunteers, 1861–1865*, vol. 2, 58.

19. Otis F. R. Waite, *New Hampshire in the Great Rebellion* (Claremont: Tracy, Chase, & Company, 1870), 567; *New York Herald*, October 24, 1861.

20. *Exeter News-Letter*, September 30, 1861.

21. *Caledonian*, September 13, 1861; Consolidated Military Service Record of Edmund Weston Jr., NA; William Y. A. Ripley, *Vermont Riflemen in the War for the Union, 1861 to 1865: A History of Company F, First United States Sharpshooters* (Rutland: Tuttle & Co., 1883), 3–7.

22. Roy Marcot Collection, MS 437, McCracken Library; Quiner, *Quiner Papers*, vol. 2, 57; *Wisconsin Daily Patriot*, July 11 and October 7, 1861; 1st U.S. Sharpshooters, Letters Sent and Order Book, NA.

23. Marcot, *Civil War Chief*, 33–34; Gerald L. Earley, *The Second United States Sharpshooters in the Civil War: A History and Roster* (Jefferson, NC: McFarland & Company, 2009), 13–15.

24. *Lamoille Newsdealer*, October 4, 1861; Homer Stoughton letter, VHS; *Caledonian*, September 27, 1861.

25. *Weekly Pioneer and Democrat*, October 25, 1861.

26. Preston Papers, BHL.

27. Adjutant General, *Record of Service*, 107–108, 118–19.

28. Company C Records, RG-19.11, Carton 152, PSA; *Potter County Journal*, December 4, 1861; https://www.findagrave.com/memorial/161016756/samuel-lattimer.

29. Company D Regimental Correspondence, MSA.

30. Darin Wipperman, *First for the Union: Life and Death in a Civil War Army Corps from Antietam to Gettysburg* (Lanham, MD: Stackpole Books, 2020), 6–7; Company D Correspondence, MSA.

31. *Annual Report of the Adjutant General of the State of Maine for the Year Ending December 31, 1861* (Augusta: Stevens & Sayward, 1862), Appendix A, 11–12; Peter Dalton, ed., *Soldiers in Green: Civil War Diaries of James Mero Matthews, 2nd U.S. Sharpshooters* (Richardson's Civil War Roundtable, 2002), 5–6.

32. Adjutant General, *Revised Roster of Vermont Volunteers and Lists of Vermonters Who Served in the Army and Navy of the United States during the War of the Rebellion, 1861–66* (Montpelier: Watchman Publishing, 1892), 608, 615–16.

33. Augustus D. Ayling, *Revised Register of the Soldiers and Sailors of New Hampshire in the War of the Rebellion, 1861–1866* (Concord: Ira C. Evans, 1895), 972; Waite, *New Hampshire*, 567–69.

34. William H. Hastings, ed., *Letters from a Sharpshooter: The Civil War Letters of Private William B. Greene, Co. G, 2nd United States Sharpshooters (Berdan's), Army of the Potomac* (Belleville, WI: Historic Publications, 1993), 3, 6, 8, 10, 16–17.

35. Mears Family Collection, USAHEC; *Weekly Pioneer and Democrat*, October 25, 1861.

36. Meier, ed., *Memoirs of a Swiss Officer*, 37.

37. Frederick Tomlinson Peet, *Personal Experiences in the Civil War* (New York: Privately printed, 1905), 15; 1st USSS, Letters Sent and Order Book, NA.

38. Ripley, *Vermont Riflemen*, 14; Quiner, *Quiner Papers*, 63.

39. Marcot, *Civil War Chief*, 43; Charles A. Stevens, *Berdan's United States Sharpshooters in the Army of the Potomac, 1861–1865* (St. Paul, MN: Price-McGill Company, 1892), 17; Frederick Tomlinson Peet, *Civil War Letters and Documents* (Newport, NY: Privately printed, 1917), 47.

40. Joseph C. Dickey and Family Papers, MNHS; Quiner, *Quiner Papers*, 61.

41. Marcot, *Civil War Chief*, 34–36.

42. 1st USSS, Order Book and Property Book, NA; *Lansing State Republican*, September 23, 1861.

43. 1st USSS, Letters Sent and Order Book, NA.

44. 2nd U.S. Sharpshooters, Regimental Letter and Order Book, NA.

45. Richard Pindell, "The Most Dangerous Set of Men, *Civil War Times Illustrated* (July/August 1993): 44; *Raftman's Journal*, October 2, 1861.

46. Ripley, *Vermont Riflemen*, 10.

47. Marcot, *Civil War Chief*, 25–28; Lt. Col. John Elting, "The United States Sharpshooters," *Military Collector & Historian* (September 1954): 60; *New York Dispatch*, October 26, 1861. Some sources do note the use of target rifles by USSS troops in battle, but such incidents seem rather rare.

48. Roy M. Marcot, *U.S. Sharpshooters: Berdan's Civil War Elite* (Mechanicsburg, PA: Stackpole Books, 2007), 33; Joel Craig, "Proposed Uniform for the 1st U.S. Sharpshooters, 1861," *Military Collector & Historian* (Summer 2001): 61; Pindell, "The Most Dangerous," 45–46.

49. Curtis Abbott, *The Third Vermont Company of the United States Sharpshooters*, 4, VSA.

50. Quiner, *Quiner Papers*, 63; Sword, *Sharpshooter*, 14; Plaster, *The History*, 152–53; Jacob Preston Papers, BHL.

51. Plaster, *The History*, 156; Elting, "The United States Sharpshooters," 61; Sword, *Sharpshooter*, 63–66; Darius Starr Papers, Rubenstein Library.

52. Henry I. Kurtz, "Berdan's Sharpshooters Most Effective Union Brigade?," *Civil War Times*, February 1863, 16; *Green Mountain Freeman*, March 17, 1862; Preston Papers, BHL; Abbott, *Third Vermont Company*, 10; Russell C. White, ed., *The Civil War Diary of Wyman S. White*, 20–21, USAHEC. This version of White's diary is an early manuscript edition of the book that would be published in 1993. The consulted manuscript was given to the USAHEC in 1979.

53. Abbott, *Third Vermont Company*, 8–9.
54. 1st USSS, Letters Sent and Order Book, NA.
55. *Wisconsin Daily Patriot*, October 10, 1861.
56. Benjamin Calef Correspondence, Rauner Library.
57. Gardner B. Clark Papers, Clements Library.
58. William Y. Ripley Papers, Box 1, Rubenstein Library.
59. Ripley, *Vermont Riflemen*, 11; Quiner, *Quiner Papers*, 62.
60. *Hillsdale Standard*, December 3, 1861.
61. *Rutland Weekly Herald*, December 19, 1861.
62. Kenneth Katta, "Conflicts in Command: An Analysis of the Leadership in the Berdan Sharpshooters in the Civil War," *Military Collector and Historian* (Summer 2001): 54–56, 58–59.
63. Company D Correspondence, MSA.
64. 1st USSS, Letters Sent and Order Book, NA; Abbott, *Third Vermont Company*, 51.
65. Sword, *Sharpshooter*, 13–14.
66. George A. Marden Letters, Rauner Library.
67. Dickey Papers, MNHS.
68. *Penn Yan Chronicle*, January 2, 1862.
69. Anna B. Campbell Papers, Rubenstein Library.
70. *New York Tribune*, January 15, 1862.
71. Stevens, *Berdan's*, 16.
72. Company C Records, PSA; https://www.hillsdalehistoricalsociety.org/letters-from-the-civil-war; https://www.findagrave.com/memorial/20607329/jerome-s-fountain.
73. Adjutant General, *Record of Service*, 120–35.
74. Ayling, *Revised Register*, 967–70, 976–982; https://www.findagrave.com/memorial/119067605/franklin-c-wadsworth.
75. William T. Savage, *A Discourse Delivered at the Funeral of Franklin C. Wadsworth, Late of Berdan's Regiment of Sharpshooters* (Concord, NH: McFarland & Jenks, 1862), 10, 13–14.
76. Byron J. Smith Civil War Letters, WHS.
77. Marden Letters, Rauner Library.
78. John Robinson Letter, Attachment 3, Donald H. Couchman Collection, USAHEC.
79. *Manchester Journal*, February 18, 1862; *Lamoille Newsdealer*, February 14, 1862.
80. Ripley Papers, Box 1, Rubenstein Library.
81. *Wisconsin Daily Patriot*, February 24, 1862.
82. Connington Letters, Box 1, Rudolph Haerle Collection, USAHEC.
83. *Lansing State Republican*, February 12, 1862.
84. Owen Evans Letters, MNHS.
85. Ripley Papers, Box 1, Rubenstein Library.
86. Ethan Rafuse, *McClellan's War: The Failure of Moderation in the Struggle for the Union* (Bloomington: Indiana University Press, 2005), 177–202; Stephen W. Sears, *George B. McClellan: The Young Napoleon* (Cambridge, MA: Da Capo Press, 1999), 147–72; Stephen W. Sears, *To the Gates of Richmond: The Peninsula Campaign* (Boston: Houghton

Mifflin, 1992), 1–24; John C. Waugh, *Lincoln and McClellan: The Troubled Partnership between a President and His General* (New York: Palgrave Macmillan, 2010), 61–83.

87. Peet, *Personal Experiences*, 16; Peet, *Civil War Letters*, 88–89.

88. 2nd USSS, Regimental Letter and Order Book, NA.

89. Preston Papers, BHL.

90. *Green Mountain Freeman*, March 17, 1862. Based on the initials given in the letter, W. W. did not survive the war. The only two possible individuals, William Wells and William Wilson, both died in 1864. See, Adjutant General, *Revised Roster*, 600–603.

Part One

1. Marden Letters, Rauner Library; White, *Civil War Diary*, 25; Abbott, *Third Vermont Company*, 12.

2. Calef Correspondence, Rauner Library; Hastings, *Letters*, 92–95.

3. Jacob Preston Papers, BHL.

4. Company D Correspondence, MSA; *Annual Report of the Adjutant General of the State of Maine for the Year Ending December 31, 1862* (Augusta, ME: Stevens & Sayward, 1863), 97.

5. Campbell Papers, Rubenstein Library.

6. Adjutant General, Regimental Service Records, RG 59-14, Box 131, Folder 9, Michiganology.org.

7. Stephen W. Sears, ed., *The Civil War Papers of George B. McClellan, Selected Correspondence, 1860–1865* (Cambridge, MA: Da Capo Press, 1992), 227–30; Abbott, *Third Vermont Company*, 14–15; Earley, *The Second United States Sharpshooters*, 36–37; Dickey Papers, MNHS.

8. Stevens, *Berdan's*, 28; Starr Papers, Rubenstein Library.

9. Ripley, *Vermont Riflemen*, 15–17; Peet, *Personal Experiences*, 17–18.

10. Russel H. Beatie, *Army of the Potomac: McClellan's First Campaign, March–May 1862* (New York: Savas Beatie, 2007), 321–25; Stevens, *Berdan's*, 32–35; Ripley Papers, Rubenstein Library; *Albany Evening Journal*, April 15, 1862.

11. U.S. War Department, *The War of the Rebellion: A Compilation of the Official Records of the Union and Confederate Armies* (Washington, D.C.: Government Printing Office, 1884), vol. 11, I, 299; Sears, *To the Gates*, 36–37; Sears, *George B. McClellan*, 174; William Marvel, *Radical Sacrifice: The Rise and Ruin of Fitz John Porter* (Chapel Hill: University of North Carolina Press, 2021), 110–15.

12. Ripley Papers, Rubenstein Library.

13. *Rutland Weekly Herald*, April 17, 1862.

14. E. S. A., ed., *Letters of Richard Tylden Auchmuty, Fifth Corps, Army of the Potomac* (Privately printed, n.d.), 41–44; https://www.findagrave.com/memorial/215975525/john-sullivan_marcy-ide; https://www.findagrave.com/memorial/11663237/david-phelps; Peet, *Civil War Letters and Documents*, 109–11.

15. Civil War Muster Roll Abstracts, Box 375, NYSA.

16. Ripley, *Vermont Riflemen*, 23; Adjutant General, *Revised Roster*, 601; https://www.findagrave.com/memorial/71923769/charles-william-peck.

17. Stevens, *Berdan's*, 42.

18. Lillie Devereux Blake Papers, MHS.
19. Ripley Papers, Rubenstein Library.
20. Sword, *Sharpshooter*, 46–49; Marcot, *U.S. Sharpshooters*, 30–31; Plaster, *The History*, 111.
21. Marden Letters, Rauner Library; *Philadelphia Public Ledger*, April 22, 1862.
22. Ripley Papers, Rubenstein Library.
23. George Lewis Papers, WHS; Stevens, *Berdan's*, 40–41.
24. Martin V. Bronson letter, Civil War Document Collection, USAHEC.
25. James I. Robertson Jr., ed., *The Civil War Letters of General Robert McAllister* (New Brunswick, NJ: Rutgers University Press, 1965), 139–40.
26. *Oswego Commercial Times*, May 9, 1862.
27. Marden Letters, Rauner Library.
28. Civil War Muster Roll Abstracts, Box 375, NYSA; Marden Letters, Rauner Library; Meier, *Memoirs of a Swiss Officer*, 59.
29. Stevens, *Berdan's*, 60–61; https://www.findagrave.com/memorial/98970146/joseph-earl-durkee.
30. E. S. A., *Letters*, 49.
31. *Cherry Valley Gazette*, April 23, 1862.
32. *Green Mountain Freeman*, May 13, 1862; Quiner, *Quiner Papers*, vol. 7, 66–67.
33. Lewis Papers, WHS; Beatie, *Army of the Potomac*, 487–95.
34. Lillie Devereux Blake Papers, MHS.
35. Jacob Bailey Letter, VHS.
36. Ripley, *Vermont Riflemen*, 28–29; Marden Letters, Rauner Library.
37. Berdan letter, Box 9, Folder 5, Civil War Documents Collection, USAHEC.
38. Peet, *Civil War Letters*, 130.
39. Sears, *Civil War Papers*, 253–56; Peet, *Personal Experiences*, 132; Ripley, *Vermont Riflemen*, 30.
40. Marden Letters, Rauner Library.
41. Peet, *Civil War Letters*, 137.
42. Sears, *To the Gates*, 103–107; William J. Cooper Jr., *Jefferson Davis, American* (Vintage Books, 2001), 409–11; Meier, *Memoirs of a Swiss Officer*, 63–66; Charles Shepard Letter (Call#45308), LVA.
43. E. S. A., *Letters*, 57–58; Board of Commissioners, *Minnesota in the Civil and Indian Wars, 1861–1865* (St. Paul, MN: Pioneer Press, 1890), 513–14; Josiah B. Chaney and Family Papers, Box 1, MNHS; Stevens, *Berdan's*, 74.
44. Rafuse, *McClellan's War*, 212–16.
45. Stevens, *Berdan's*, 83; *OR*, vol. 11, I, 698; G. Merrill Dwelle and Family Papers, MNHS; Board of Commissioners, *Minnesota*, 517–18; Brigham Buswell, "A Sharpshooter's Seven Days," *Civil War Times*, February 1996, 20.
46. Marvel, *Radical Sacrifice*, 125–29; Peet, *Personal Experiences*, 32–33; Stevens, *Berdan's*, 85–86; *OR*, vol. 11, I, 699.
47. William DeLoss Love, *Wisconsin in the War of the Rebellion* (Chicago: Church and Goodman, 1866), 384.

48. 1st USSS Folder, ANBL; Meier, *Memoirs of a Swiss Officer*, 67–68; Ripley Papers, Rubenstein Library.

49. Sears, *Civil War Papers*, 279; For a detailed account of the battle, see Robert E. L. Krick, "Prelude to the Seven Days: The Battle of Slash Church (Hanover Court House), May 27, 1862," in William J. Miller, ed., *The Peninsula Campaign of 1862: Yorktown to the Seven Days* (Campbell, CA: Savas Woodbury, 1997), 1–38.

50. *Green Mountain Freeman*, June 5, 1862; Adjutant General, *Revised Roster*, 602; Civil War Muster Roll Abstracts, Box 373, NYSA.

51. *OR*, vol. 11, I, 701; Ripley, *Vermont Riflemen*, 34–35.

52. Peet, *Civil War Letters*, 146; Marvel, *Radical Sacrifice*, 130–31.

53. Meier, *Memoirs of a Swiss Officer*, 69; Civil War Muster Roll Abstracts, Box 373, NYSA.

54. Calef Correspondence, Rauner Library; Abbott, *Third Vermont Company*, 49.

55. Campbell Papers, Rubenstein Library.

56. Abbott, *Third Vermont Company*, 20.

57. Hastings, *Letters*, 108–109.

58. *Annual Report of the Adjutant General of the State of Maine for the Year Ending December 31, 1862*, 501–503; Adjutant General, *Revised Roster*, 611–15, 620–23; Ayling, *Revised Register*, 976–82; Board of Commissioners, *Minnesota*, 511–12; Adjutant General, *Record of Service*, 107–20.

59. *Portsmouth Journal of Literature and Politics*, July 19, 1862; White, *Civil War Diary*, 40; https://www.findagrave.com/memorial/199232950/henry-mills-caldwell.

60. Benjamin Giddings Papers, VHS.

61. Walter Wallace Smith Papers, Rubenstein Library.

62. *Lansing State Republican*, June 18, 1862; Earley, *The Second United States Sharpshooters*, 50–52; Abbott, *Third Vermont Company*, 21–23; Starr Papers, Rubenstein Library.

63. 2nd USSS Regimental Letter and Order Book, NA; Hastings, *Letters*, 128–29; Ayling, *Revised Register*, 980.

64. Abbott, *Third Vermont Company*, 20; John W. Whitman, "Lorenzo Barber Was the Eagle-Eyed 'Fighting Parson' of Hiram Berdan's Famous U.S. Sharpshooters," *America's Civil War*, September 1998, 12.

65. *OR*, vol. 12, I, 169.

66. Buswell, "A Sharpshooter's Seven Days," 23; Ripley, *Vermont Riflemen*, 37; William J. Miller, "I Only Wait for the River: McClellan and His Engineers on the Chickahominy," in *The Richmond Campaign of 1862: The Peninsula and the Seven Days*, Gary W. Gallagher, ed. (Chapel Hill: University of North Carolina Press, 2000), 51–58; Sears, *To the Gates*, 151–60; Jeffry D. Wert, *A Glorious Army: Robert E. Lee's Triumph, 1862–1863* (New York: Simon & Schuster, 2011), 19–27; *OR*, vol. 11, III, 217.

67. Peet, *Personal Experiences*, 35.

68. *New York Herald*, June 20, 1862.

69. Meier, *Memoirs of a Swiss Officer*, 72; Stephen Minot Weld, *War Diary and Letters of Stephen Minot Weld* (Privately printed, Riverside Press, 1912), 110; Ripley Papers, Rubenstein Library.

70. J. H. Carr letter, USAHEC.

71. Simon Danner Letters, BHL.

72. Meier, *Memoirs of a Swiss Officer*, 71; Peet, *Civil War Letters*, 154–55.

73. Stevens, *Berdan's*, 97–98.

74. Quiner, *Quiner Papers*, vol. 7, 74–76.

75. Sears, *To the Gates*, 181–200; Brian K. Burton, *Extraordinary Circumstances: The Seven Days Battles* (Bloomington: Indiana University Press, 2001), 41–57.

76. Adjutant General, *Record of Service*, 123.

77. William Kent, "Sharpshooting with Berdan," *Civil War Times Illustrated*, May 1976, 6; Ripley, *Vermont Riflemen*, 39–41; Burton, *Extraordinary Circumstances*, 82–91.

78. Stevens, *Berdan's*, 112–13.

79. Buswell, "A Sharpshooter's Seven Days," 24–25.

80. Walter Clark, ed., *Histories of the Several Regiments and Battalions from North Carolina in the Great War, 1861–'65*, vol. 1 (Raleigh, NC: E. M. Uzzell, 1901), 367–68; Ripley, *Vermont Riflemen*, 41–42.

81. Buswell, "A Sharpshooter's Seven Days," 26–27.

82. James Fitz James Caldwell, *The History of a Brigade of South Carolinians* (Philadelphia: King & Baird, 1866), 18; Clark, *Histories*, vol. II, 25–26.

83. Marvel, *Radical Sacrifice*, 166–71.

84. Adjutant General, *Revised Roster*, 602; https://www.findagrave.com/memorial/210550941/levi-hiram-leet; James Winchell, "Wounded and a Prisoner," *Civil War Times Illustrated*, August 1965, 20–25; https://www.findagrave.com/memorial/99875650/james-winchell.

85. Isaac Bevier Letter (Call # 45071), LVA.

86. *OR*, vol. 11, II, 467.

87. Stevens, *Berdan's*, 123–31; Ripley, *Vermont Riflemen*, 44–48; Kent, "Sharpshooting," 5.

88. Burton, *Extraordinary Circumstances*, 194–229.

89. O. R. Howard Thomson and William H. Rauch, *History of the "Bucktails," Kane Rifle Regiment of the Pennsylvania Reserve Corps (13th Pennsylvania Reserves, 42nd of the Line)* (Philadelphia: Electric Printing Company, 1906), 127–29; Love, *Wisconsin in the War*, 384–85; *Wisconsin Daily Patriot*, July 18, 1862; Quiner, *Quiner Papers*, vol. 7, 76–77; https://www.findagrave.com/memorial/37617159/william-clark.

90. Quiner, *Quiner Papers*, vol. 7, 76; *Wisconsin Daily Patriot*, July 12, 1862; https://www.findagrave.com/memorial/98679654/george-lanning.

91. https://www.findagrave.com/memorial/69090190/jonas-w-shepard.

92. Thomson and Rauch, *History of the "Bucktails,"* 127, 133.

93. Peet, *Civil War Letters*, 158–62.

94. Marvel, *Radical Sacrifice*, 172–75.

95. Ripley, *Vermont Riflemen*, 52; Kent, "Sharpshooting," 44–45.

96. Kurtz, "Berdan's Sharpshooters," 17; *Cherry Valley Gazette*, July 23, 1862.

97. L. VanLoan Naiswald, *Grape and Canister: The Story of the Field Artillery of the Army of the Potomac, 1861–1865* (Mechanicsburg, PA: Stackpole Books, 1999), 94–106; Burton, *Extraordinary Circumstances*, 324–61; Sears, *To the Gates*, 321–34; Brigham Buswell, "'Blood and Feathered' at Malvern Hill," *Civil War Times*, April 1996, 26–27;

O. S. Barrett, *Reminiscences, Incidents, Battles, Marches and Camp Life of the Old 4th Michigan Infantry in the War of the Rebellion, 1861 to 1864* (Detroit: W. S. Ostler, 1888), 17.

98. Connington Letters, USAHEC.

99. https://www.cmohs.org/recipients/william-y-ripley; Volunteer Service Files, VS File # V42-VS-1862, Stack Area: 9W3: 18/22/6, Box # 147, NA.

100. Ripley Papers, Rubenstein Library.

101. Adjutant General, *Record of Service*, 155; Ayling, *Revised Register*, 968–70; *Portsmouth Journal of Literature and Politics*, July 26, 1862; https://www.findagrave.com/memorial/132951970/leroy-p-greenwood.

102. Buswell, "'Blood and Feathered,'" 30.

103. *New York Times*, July 31, 1862.

104. *OR*, vol. 11, II, 279; Marcot, *U.S. Sharpshooters*, 71–76.

105. Both the July 14 letter from Berdan and Ripley's July 21 response are in Ripley Papers, Rubenstein Library.

106. Kenneth W. Noe, *The Howling Storm: Weather, Climate, and the American Civil War* (Baton Rouge: Louisiana State University Press, 2020), 223–25; *Wisconsin Daily Patriot*, July 18, 1862.

107. *Penn Yan Chronicle*, July 17, 1862.

108. Marden Letters, Rauner Library.

109. *Livingston County Daily Press and Argus*, July 22, 1862.

110. Benjamin Franklin Cooling, *Counter-Thrust: From the Peninsula to the Antietam* (Lincoln: University of Nebraska Press, 2007), 25–26, 30; Ira M. Rutkow, *Bleeding Blue and Gray: Civil War Surgery and the Evolution of American Medicine* (New York: Random House, 2005), 122–27, 138–49; Charles E. Estabrook, ed., *Wisconsin Losses in the Civil War* (Madison: Democrat Printing, 1915), 202–203; Love, *Wisconsin in the War*, 385–86.

111. *Wisconsin Daily Patriot*, July 18, 1862.

112. Noe, *The Howling Storm*, 227–29; Stevens, *Berdan's*, 158; Quiner, *Quiner Papers*, vol. 7, 81.

113. *Wisconsin Daily Patriot*, July 24, 1862; Charles P. Shepard Letters (Call #45503), LVA.

114. Richard B. and Agnes Irwin Family Correspondence, Clements Library; Meier, *Memoirs of a Swiss Officer*, 79–82.

115. Consolidated Military Service Record of Edmund Weston Jr., NA.

116. Connington Letters, USAHEC.

117. Shepard Letters (Call #45503), LVA; Ayling, *Revised Register*, 969.

118. 1st USSS Order Book and Property Book, NA.

119. Quiner, *Quiner Papers*, vol. 7, 82.

120. Rafuse, *McClellan's War*, 240–52.

121. Amos Abbott Diary, Box 1: Folder 4, Civil War Document Collection, USAHEC.

122. Hastings, *Letters*, 134–35; Starr Papers, Rubenstein Library; Board of Commissioners, *Minnesota*, 507–508.

123. Abbott, *Third Vermont Company*, 25–26; Hastings, *Letters*, 140–41; *Mineral Point Weekly Tribune*, August 13, 1862.

124. 2nd USSS Regimental Letter and Order Book, NA; Board of Commissioners, *Minnesota*, 511.

125. Abbott, *Third Vermont Company*, 25.

126. Dickey Papers, MNHS; Darin Wipperman, *Burnside's Boys: The Union's Ninth Corps and the Civil War in the East* (Lanham, MD: Stackpole Books, 2023), 25–29.

127. Abbott Diary, USAHEC; Peter Cozzens, *General John Pope: A Life for the Nation* (Urbana: University of Illinois Press, 2000), 92–97; John J. Hennessy, *Return to Bull Run: The Campaign and Battle of Second Manassas* (New York: Simon & Schuster, 1993), 27–30.

128. William E. S. Whitman and Charles H. True, *Maine in the War for the Union* (Lewiston: Nelson Dingley, 1865), 344; Abbott, *Third Vermont Company*, 26–27.

129. Hastings, *Letters*, 142.

130. Company D Correspondence, MSA.

131. Whitman and True, *Maine in the War*, 344–45; Hennessy, *Return to Bull Run*, 42–54; *OR*, vol. 12, III, 603.

132. Abbott Diary, USAHEC; Adjutant General, *Record of Service*, 117; Adjutant General, *Revised Roster*, 621; Whitman and True, *Maine in the War*, 345. An unfortunate factual error in the original history of the USSS was repeated in a modern book about the 2nd USSS as the two authors discussed the action along the Rappahannock. Captain Henry Caldwell, Company F, was named as bringing up some men in reserve to support Lt. Col. Francis Peteler's four advanced companies on August 21. The captain had died the month before of disease. See, Stevens, *Berdan's*, 167 and Earley, *The Second United States Sharpshooters*, 58.

133. Abbott Diary, USAHEC.

134. *New York Times*, September 6, 1862; *Albany Evening Journal*, August 26, 1862; Hennessy, *Return to Bull Run*, 66–74.

135. *Penn Yan Chronicle*, September 4, 1862.

136. Quiner, *Quiner Papers*, vol. 7, 82–83.

137. *OR*, vol. 12, II, 465; Robert Tilney, *My Life in the Army: Three Years and a Half with the Fifth Army Corps* (Philadelphia: Ferris & Leach, 1912), 24.

138. Ripley, *Vermont Riflemen*, 61–62; *OR*, vol. 12, III, 646–47; Meier, *Memoirs of a Swiss Officer*, 85.

139. Hastings, Letters, 146; *OR*, vol. 12, III, 641.

140. Abbott Diary, USAHEC; Abbott, *Third Vermont Company*, 30–31.

141. Cozzens, *General John Pope*, 111–22.

142. Hennessy, *Return to Bull Run*, 145–93; *OR*, vol. 12, II, 465, 481.

143. Dalton, *Soldiers in Green*, 80; Abbott, *Third Vermont Company*, 42; Marvel, *Radical Sacrifice*, 195–204.

144. Hennessy, *Return to Bull Run*, 224–31.

145. Quiner, *Quiner Papers*, vol. 7, 82–84; Cozzens, *General John Pope*, 139–45; Hennessy, *Return to Bull Run*, 231–38; Marvel, *Radical Sacrifice*, 202–12.

146. Adjutant General, *Record of Service*, 134; E. A. Wilson, "Second Bull Run," *National Tribune*, October 19, 1905.

147. https://www.findagrave.com/memorial/119353849/william-oliver-mclean; https://www.findagrave.com/memorial/35810768/norman-d-wilson. In the state roster,

Wilson's fatal wound was recorded as occurring on August 28, but the following day seems far more likely.

148. Abbott Diary, USAHEC; Hennessy, *Return to Bull Run*, 291–94.

149. Edward L. Barnes, "The 95th New York," *National Tribune*, January 7, 1886; George G. Benedict, *Vermont in the Civil War: A History of the Part Taken by the Vermont Soldiers and Sailors in the War for the Union, 1861–5* (Burlington, VT: Free Press Association, 1886), vol. 2, 758.

150. Abbott, *Third Vermont Company*, 43–45; George F. Noyes, *The Bivouac and the Battlefield, or Campaign Sketches in Virginia and Maryland* (New York: Harper & Brothers, 1863), 129.

151. *OR*, vol. 12, II, 371; John Bell Hood, *Advance and Retreat: Personal Experiences in the United States and Confederate States Armies* (New Orleans: G. T. Beauregard, 1880), 34.

152. Board of Commissioners, *Minnesota*, 511.

153. *OR*, vol. 12, II, 367; Campbell Papers, Rubenstein Library; Stevens, *Berdan's*, 182; Marcot, *Civil War Chief*, 56; Marcot, *U.S. Sharpshooters*, 77–78.

154. Whitman and True, *Maine in the War*, 346; Board of Commissioners, *Minnesota*, 511–12; Company A Records, MNHS; Adjutant General, *Revised Roster*, 613; Ayling, *Revised Register*, 978.

155. Company D Correspondence, MSA.

156. *Portsmouth Journal of Literature and Politics*, September 13, 1862; Ayling, *Revised Register*, 982.

157. Hennessy, *Return to Bull Run*, 306–308, 317–18; Marvel, *Radical Sacrifice*, 212–13.

158. Hennessy, *Return to Bull Run*, 318; *New York Times*, September 13, 1862. The newspaper citation is for Berdan's report of the August 30 battle. The report does not appear in the *Official Records*.

159. Hennessy, *Return to Bull Run*, 318–31.

160. Ripley, *Vermont Riflemen*, 62–63; Quiner, *Quiner Papers*, vol. 7, 82.

161. J. W. Griswold, "Second Bull Run," *National Tribune*, May 31, 1894; Isaac Bevier letter (Call #45221), LVA.

162. George Lockley Diary, BHL; Eugene Arus Nash, *A History of the Forty-fourth Regiment New York Volunteer Infantry in the Civil War, 1861–1865* (Chicago: R. R. Donnelley & Sons, 1911), 99–100; *New York Times*, September 13, 1862; Quiner, *Quiner Papers*, vol. 7, 82–83; Wert, *A Glorious Army*, 96–99; James I. Robertson Jr., *Stonewall Jackson: The Man, The Soldier, The Legend* (New York: Macmillan Publishing, 1997), 570–74.

163. Ayling, *Revised Register*, 967; https://www.findagrave.com/memorial/50314423/william-p-austin.

164. Quiner, *Quiner Papers*, vol. 7, 84; Stevens, *Berdan's*, 190.

165. James Lawson Kemper Letter, LVA.

166. Meier, *Memoirs of a Swiss Officer*, 88.

167. Adjutant General, *Record of Service*, 154; https://www.findagrave.com/memorial/115148605/george-h-downing; https://www.findagrave.com/memorial/40038002/frederick-dittert.

168. https://www.findagrave.com/memorial/179007310/charles-h-brown.

169. Stevens, *Berdan's*, 189; Hennessy, *Return to Bull Run*, 439–72.
170. Abbott, *Third Vermont Company*, 45.
171. Stevens, *Berdan's*, 188–89.
172. White, *Civil War Diary*, 48–56; Starr Papers, Rubenstein Library.
173. Abbott Diary, USAHEC.
174. *Portsmouth Journal of Literature and Politics*, September 13, 1862.
175. Ripley, *Vermont Riflemen*, 64; Abbott, *Third Vermont Company*, 46.
176. Stevens, *Berdan's*, 189; *New York Times*, September 13, 1862.
177. Quiner, *Quiner Papers*, vol. 7, 84.
178. Marcot, *Civil War Chief*, 56–57; Consolidated Military Service Record of Hiram Berdan, NA.
179. Marvel, *Radical Sacrifice*, 227–33.
180. Wipperman, *First for the Union*, 1–14.
181. Benedict, *Vermont*, vol. II, 759–60.
182. Abbott Diary, USAHEC; Ayling, *Revised Register*, 976.
183. https://www.findagrave.com/memorial/39272681/horace-warner; Company C Records, PSA.
184. Dalton, *Soldiers in Green*, 84–85.
185. Robertson Jr., *Stonewall*, 588–97; Joseph L. Harsh, *Taken at the Flood: Robert E. Lee and Confederate Strategy in the Maryland Campaign of 1862* (Kent, OH: Kent State University Press, 1999), 145–67; D. Scott Hartwig, *To Antietam Creek: The Maryland Campaign of September 1862* (Baltimore: Johns Hopkins University Press, 2012), 175–89.
186. Smith Papers, Rubenstein Library.
187. Abbott, *Third Vermont Company*, 47; Wipperman, *First for the Union*, 20–22.
188. Richard Slotkin, *The Long Road to Antietam: How the Civil War Became a Revolution* (New York: Liveright Publishing, 2012), 180–90; Donald R. Jermann, *Antietam: The Lost Order* (Gretna, LA: Pelican Publishing, 2006), 145–59; Hartwig, *To Antietam Creek*, 282–99.
189. Abbott, *Third Vermont Company*, 47.
190. *OR*, vol. 51, 828. The rapid advance of the First Corps retained the wing arrangement McClellan initiated earlier in the campaign, but Sumner's two corps, the Second and Twelfth, could have reached South Mountain sooner on September 14. General Sumner did not have a high reputation in McClellan's eyes, however, likely ensuring the army commander had Hooker march much of the day to reach South Mountain.
191. John Michael Priest, *Before Antietam: The Battle for South Mountain* (Shippensburg, PA: White Mane Publishing, 1992), 255; Brian Matthew Jordan, *Unholy Sabbath: The Battle of South Mountain in History and Memory* (New York: Savas Beatie, 2012), 103–248; Hartwig, *To Antietam Creek*, 330–437; Thomas Reed, *The Original Iron Brigade* (Madison, NJ: Fairleigh Dickinson University Press, 2011), 105–108.
192. Abbott, *Third Vermont Company*, 48.
193. Dickey Papers, MNHS; Dalton, *Soldiers in Green*, 86; Stevens, *Berdan's*, 196–97.
194. Tom Clemens, ed., "A Brigade Commander's First Fight: The Letters of Colonel Walter Phelps, Jr. during the Maryland Campaign," *Civil War Regiments: A Journal of the American Civil War* 5, no. 3 (1997): 65; Wipperman, *First for the Union*, 28–31.

195. *Penn Yan Chronicle*, October 2, 1862; Stevens, *Berdan's*, 194; Ripley, *Vermont Riflemen*, 64; Quiner, *Quiner Papers*, vol. 7, 85.

196. Marcot, *U.S. Sharpshooters*, 79; *OR*, vol. 19, II, 253–54; Marcot Collection, MS 437, McCracken Library; *OR*, vol. 19, I, 38; Marvel, *Radical Sacrifice*, 234–35.

197. Marvel, *Radical Sacrifice*, 235–36.

198. Wipperman, *First for the Union*, 37; https://www.findagrave.com/memorial/193770719/charles-rand-kay.

199. Bradley M. Gottfried, *The Maps of Antietam: An Atlas of the Antietam (Sharpsburg) Campaign, Including the Battle of South Mountain, September 2–20, 1862* (El Dorado Hills: Savas Beatie, 2013), 114–18.

200. Slotkin, *The Long Road*, 216–31; Joseph Pierro, ed., *The Maryland Campaign of September 1862: Ezra A. Carman's Definitive Study of the Union and Confederate Armies at Antietam* (New York: Routledge, 2008), 184–86; George Brinton McClellan Papers, LOC. Some historians incorrectly read Hooker's note, writing that the First Corps commander deemed Lee's position formidable.

201. Rafuse, *McClellan's War*, 308–309; Wipperman, *First for the Union*, 38–41.

202. *OR*, vol. 19, I, 29–30.

203. Walter H. Hebert, *Fighting Joe Hooker* (Lincoln: University of Nebraska Press, 1999), 138; *OR*, vol. 19, I, 55; Rafuse, *McClellan's War*, 311–12.

204. *OR*, vol. 19, I, 223; Hartwig, *To Antietam Creek*, 607; Gottfried, *Maps of Antietam*, 122–25.

205. *Annual Report of the Adjutant General of the State of Maine for the Year Ending December 31, 1862*, 502; Dalton, *Soldiers in Green*, 87.

206. *OR*, vol. 19, I, 223, 235–36; Abbott, *Third Vermont Company*, 49; William Humphrey Letter, Antietam Collection, Rauner Library.

207. E. E. Stickley, "Battle of Sharpsburg," *Confederate Veteran* 22 (1914): 66.

208. Lance J. Herdegen, *The Iron Brigade in Civil War and Memory: The Black Hats from Bull Run to Appomattox and Thereafter* (El Dorado Hills: Savas Beatie, 2012), 247; Gottfried, *Maps of Antietam*, 128–29; *OR*, vol. 19, I, 218.

209. Earley, *The Second United States Sharpshooters*, 78–79.

210. Edwin Chadwick Letter, ANBL; Humphrey Letter, Rauner Library.

211. Wipperman, *First for the Union*, 48–53.

212. Stickley, "Battle of Sharpsburg," 66; 2nd Louisiana Folder, ANBL.

213. Abbott, *Third Vermont Company*, 49; *OR*, vol. 19, I, 233; Humphrey Letter, Rauner Library; Herdegen, *The Iron Brigade*, 252–73.

214. Abbott, *Third Vermont Company*, 49; Bradley M. Gottfried, ed., *Brigades of Antietam: The Union and Confederate Brigades during the 1862 Maryland Campaign* (Sharpsburg, MD: Antietam Institute, 2021), 32; https://www.findagrave.com/memorial/177834639/henry-albertson_van_zo-post.

215. Humphrey Letter, Rauner Library; Waite, *New Hampshire*, 572; Reed, *The Original Iron Brigade*, 112–13.

216. Adjutant General, *Record of Service*, 119; D. P. Craig Letter, Antietam Collection, Rauner Library.

217. Chadwick Letter, ANBL; 33rd Virginia, 21st Virginia, and 7th Wisconsin Regimental Files, ANBL.

218. Abbott, *Third Vermont Company*, 50; https://www.findagrave.com/memorial/41411969/william-harrison-benson.

219. 2nd USSS Folder, ANBL.

220. James Kent letter, Box 65: Folder 8, Civil War Document Collection, USAHEC.

221. Wipperman, *First for the Union*, 63–67; Humphrey Letter, Rauner Library; James Kent Letter, USAHEC; Harold B. Simpson, ed., *Touched with Valor: Civil War Papers and Casualty Reports of Hood's Texas Brigade* (Hillsboro, TX: Hill Junior College Press, 1964), 74; D. H. Hamilton, *History of Company M, First Texas Volunteer Infantry*, Rubenstein Library. For a new and magisterial study of the opening of the First Corps attack through Hood's counterattack, see, D. Scott Hartwig, *I Dread the Thought of the Place: The Battle of Antietam and the End of the Maryland Campaign* (Baltimore: Johns Hopkins University Press, 2023), 20–137.

222. Parmelee Family Letters, ANBL.

223. Benedict, *Vermont*, vol. II, 761; Stevens, *Berdan's*, 204; Abbott, *Third Vermont Company*, 49.

224. Parmelee Family Letters, ANBL; https://www.findagrave.com/memorial/11466380/lewis-clark-parmelee.

225. Hartwig, *I Dread the Thought of the Place*, 138–617; Harsh, *Taken at the Flood*, 423–29; 10th Louisiana Folder, ANBL; Thomas Brooks, *Lee's Foreign Legion: A History of the 10th Louisiana Infantry* (Gravenhurst, Ontario: T. W. Brooks, 1995), 33–34.

226. 33rd Virginia and 7th Wisconsin Folders, ANBL.

227. Chadwick Letter, ANBL.

228. Smith Papers, Rubenstein Library.

229. James Kent Letter, USAHEC; Clemens, "A Brigade Commander's First Fight," 66; Abbott, *Third Vermont Company*, 50.

230. Sears, *Civil War Papers*, 287–88.

231. *OR*, vol. 19, II, 331; Thomas A. McGrath, *Shepherdstown: Last Clash of the Antietam Campaign, September 19–20, 1862* (Lynchburg, VA: Schroeder Publications, 2012), 60.

232. *OR*, vol. 19, II, 344–45. Isler seems mistaken in his timing on this day, reporting an order to move ahead of the Fifth Corps at about 2 p.m. This appears far later than reality, with the men occupying the town as much as eight hours earlier.

233. Marvel, *Radical Sacrifice*, 246–47; *OR*, vol. 19, I, 339.

234. Stevens, *Berdan's*, 206–207; McGrath, *Shepherdstown*, 71–72.

235. Marvel, *Radical Sacrifice*, 247; J. B. Moore, "Sharpsburg," *Southern Historical Society Papers*, vol. 27, 213.

236. A. V. Cole, "118th PA at Shepardstown," *National Tribune*, July 14, 1910; Moore, "Sharpsburg," 214.

237. *Penn Yan Chronicle*, October 2, 1862; https://www.cmohs.org/recipients/cassius-peck; McGrath, *Shepherdstown*, 82.

238. Cassius Peck Medal of Honor File, NA.

239. *OR*, vol. 19, I, 345; https://www.findagrave.com/memorial/192750968/william-woolsey-winthrop.

240. Civil War Muster Roll Abstracts, Box 374, NYSA; Adjutant General, *Record of Service*, 143.

241. Ripley, *Vermont Riflemen*, 67–68; Quiner, *Quiner Papers*, vol. 7, 85; Cole, "118th PA at Shepardstown"; McGrath, *Shepherdstown*, 83–85; Hartwig, *I Dread the Thought of the Place*, 658–59, 665.

242. Quiner, *Quiner Papers*, vol. 7, 85.

243. Abbott, *Third Vermont Company*, 50.

244. Steven R. Stotelmyer, *Too Useful to Sacrifice: Reconsidering George B. McClellan's Generalship in the Maryland Campaign from South Mountain to Antietam* (El Dorado Hills: Savas Beatie, 2019), 215–65; Ripley, *Vermont Riflemen*, 68.

245. Calef Correspondence, Rauner Library.

246. Connington Letters, USAHEC.

247. Stevens, *Berdan's*, 211; Quiner, *Quiner Papers*, 85–86; Reed, *The Original Iron Brigade*, 117.

248. Brooks D. Simpson, "General McClellan Bodyguard: The Army of the Potomac after Antietam," in *The Antietam Campaign*, Gary W. Gallagher, ed. (Chapel Hill: University of North Carolina Press, 1999), 44–63; Wipperman, *First for the Union*, 81–85.

249. Benedict, *Vermont*, vol. II, 761; 1st USSS Order Book and Property Book, NA; Adjutant General, *Record of Service*, 107–57.

250. Quiner, *Quiner Papers*, vol. 7, 85.

251. John Monahan Diaries, VSA.

252. Civil War Muster Roll Abstracts, Boxes 373–75, NYSA.

253. Quiner, *Quiner Papers*, vol. 7, 85.

254. Ayling, *Revised Register*, 976–82.

255. 1st USSS Order Book and Property Book, NA.

256. Thomas H. Brown Civil War Letters, VHS.

257. Monahan Diaries, VSA.

258. Company D Correspondence, MSA; *Annual Report of the Adjutant General of the State of Maine for the Year Ending December 31, 1862*, 502.

259. Meier, *Memoirs of a Swiss Officer*, 95.

260. *Annual Report of the Adjutant General of the State of Maine for the Year Ending December 31, 1862*, 501, 503.

261. Love, *Wisconsin in the War*, 386–87; E. B. Quiner, *Military History of Wisconsin: A Record of the Civil and Military Patriotism of the State in the War for the Union* (Chicago: Clark & Co., 1866), 874; Stevens, *Berdan's*, 213.

262. Campbell Papers, Rubenstein Library; Bradley M. Gottfried, *The Maps of Fredericksburg: An Atlas of the Fredericksburg Campaign, Including All Cavalry Operations, September 18, 1862–January 22, 1863* (El Dorado Hills: Savas Beatie, 2018), 12–23; Stephen W. Sears, *Lincoln's Lieutenants: The High Command of the Army of the Potomac* (Boston: Mariner Books, 2018), 433–36.

263. Marden Letters, Rauner Library; A. Cassius Cross letter, LVA.

264. George C. Rable, *Fredericksburg! Fredericksburg!* (Chapel Hill: University of North Carolina Press, 2002), 59–62.

265. Stevens, *Berdan's*, 214–15; Abbott, *Third Vermont Company*, 51; Earley, *The Second United States Sharpshooters*, 95; Calef Correspondence, Rauner Library.

266. Campbell Letters, Rubenstein Library.

267. Connington Letters, USAHEC.

268. Gottfried, *Maps of Fredericksburg*, 30–39.

269. Marcot, *Civil War Chief*, 62–64.

270. *Shasta Courier*, January 3, 1863.

271. Stevens, *Berdan's*, 216–17.

272. Cross letter, LVA.

273. Smith Papers, Rubenstein Library.

274. Gottfried, *Maps of Fredericksburg*, 44–69.

275. Wipperman, *First for the Union*, 103–22; Sears, *Lincoln's Lieutenants*, 449–66.

276. *OR*, vol. 21, 414; Stevens, *Berdan's*, 222.

277. Compare the names listed in Stevens, *Berdan's*, 224, with Board of Commissioners, *Minnesota*, 511–12.

278. Ripley, *Vermont Riflemen*, 76.

279. Monahan Diaries, VSA.

280. Dalton, *Soldiers in Green*, 115–17.

281. Marcot, *Civil War Chief*, 64.

282. Ayling, *Revised Register*, 967–70, 976–82; Adjutant General, *Revised Roster*, 600–603, 611–15, 620–23; Monahan Diaries, VSA.

283. Calef Correspondence, Rauner Library.

284. Dalton, *Soldiers in Green*, 117; Marden Letters, Rauner Library.

285. *OR*, vol. 21, 973; Henry L. Bedell Diary, Box 7: Folder 9, Civil War Document Collection, USAHEC.

286. James H. Baker Collection, Clements Library; Connington Letters, USAHEC; Monahan Diaries, VSA.

287. Marden Letters, Rauner Library.

288. Meier, *Memoirs of a Swiss Officer*, 105; Ripley, *Vermont Riflemen*, 77–78; Monahan Diaries, VSA; Marden Letters, Rauner Library.

289. Connington Letters, USAHEC; Gottfried, *Maps of Fredericksburg*, 246–49.

290. Rable, *Fredericksburg!*, 412–24; Sears, *Lincoln's Lieutenants*, 480–83.

291. Brown Letters, VHS.

292. Baker Collection, Clements Libary.

293. Adjutant General, *Record of Service*, 107–59; https://www.findagrave.com/memorial/104709022/jeremiah-j-brown; https://www.findagrave.com/memorial/19729135/john-a-huff.

294. John W. Dewey Pension File, NA; https://www.findagrave.com/memorial/48273886/john-worthington-dewey.

295. Adjutant General, *Record of Service*, 145; https://www.findagrave.com/memorial/12577566/eugene-w-smith.

296. Shepard Letters (Call #45503), LVA.

297. *OR*, vol. 25, II, 20–21; Ripley, *Vermont Riflemen*, 79; Sears, *Lincoln's Lieutenants*, 488–89; Hebert, *Fighting Joe*, 171–84.

298. Stevens, *Berdan's*, 232.

299. Connington Letters, USAHEC.

300. Marcot, *Civil War Chief*, 65–70, extensively documents the charges Berdan and Trepp faced. Further information on the courts-martial can be found in Marcot, *U.S. Sharpshooters*, 86–94, and Berdan's Consolidated Military Service Record file at the National Archives.

301. Lillie Devereux Blake Papers, MHS.

302. Monahan Diaries, VSA.

303. Bedell Diary, USAHEC.

304. Calef Correspondence, Rauner Library.

305. Company D Correspondence, MSA; *Appendix D of the Annual Report of the Adjutant General of the State of Maine for the Years 1864 and 1865* (Augusta, ME: Stevens & Sayward, 1866), 831, 1255.

306. Company D Correspondence, MSA.

307. *Bellows Falls Times*, March 20, 1863.

308. Starr Papers, Rubenstein Library; Monahan Diaries, VSA; Marden Letters, Rauner Library.

309. Brown Letters, VHS.

310. Edward J. Stackpole, *Chancellorsville: Lee's Greatest Battle* (Harrisburg, PA: Stackpole Company, 1958), 1–3; Meier, *Memoirs of a Swiss Officer*, 108; Monahan Diaries, VSA; White, *Civil War Diary*, 72–73.

311. Stevens, *Berdan's*, 232–33; Adjutant General, *Record of Service*, 141.

312. White, *Civil War Diary*, 71; Stevens, *Berdan's*, 233–35; *Mineral Point Weekly Tribune*, April 23, 1863. The newspaper letter provides great detail on the games occurring on April 9.

313. *OR*, vol. 25, II, 199.

314. *Mineral Point Weekly Tribune*, April 23, 1863; Stevens, *Berdan's*, 245; Starr Papers, Rubenstein Library.

315. Hebert, *Fighting Joe*, 192–99; Stackpole, *Chancellorsville*, 113–44.

Part Two

1. *OR*, 25, I, 162 and II, 320; Stephen W. Sears, *Chancellorsville* (Boston: Houghton Mifflin, 1996), 136–71.

2. Ernest B. Furgurson, *Chancellorsville 1863: The Souls of the Brave* (New York: Vintage Books, 1993), 101–38.

3. *OR*, 25, II, 314; Wipperman, *First for the Union*, 145–50.

4. *OR*, 25, II, 315.

5. Monahan Diaries, VSA; Baker Scrapbook, Clements Library; Stevens, *Berdan's*, 246.

6. Sears, *Chancellorsville*, 193–224; Furgurson, *Chancellorsville*, 119–43; Hebert, *Fighting Joe*, 197–203.

7. *OR*, vol. 25, I, 501 and II, 324.

8. *OR*, 25, I, 408, 491; Thomas Keneally, *American Scoundrel: The Life of the Notorious Civil War General Dan Sickles* (New York: Doubleday, 2002), 265–66; Sears, *Chancellorsville*, 230–59; Furgurson, *Chancellorsville*, 138–43.

9. Sears, *Chancellorsville*, 254; *OR*, 25, I, 408; Craig L. Dunn, *Harvestfields of Death: The Twentieth Indiana Volunteers of Gettysburg* (Carmel: Guild Press of Indiana, 1999), 160; N. Sessions, "The 23d Georgia," *National Tribune*, July 10, 1884.

10. W. H. Proctor, "Stonewall Jackson and Berdan's Sharpshooters," *National Tribune*, May 8, 1884.

11. Sessions, "The 23d Georgia;" *Mineral Point Weekly Tribune*, May 23, 1863; https://www.findagrave.com/memorial/17594313/george-t-cottrell.

12. *OR*, 25, I, 501–502; H. S. Fuller, "Narrowly Escaped Prison," *Confederate Veteran*, November 1918, 473.

13. Monahan Diaries, VSA; Baker Scrapbook, Clements Library.

14. Company A Records, MNHS; https://www.findagrave.com/memorial/9798465/dudley-pike-chase.

15. *OR*, 25, I, 503; *Weekly Pioneer and Democrat*, May 22, 1863.

16. Adjutant General, *Record of Service*, 145–46, 149.

17. *Mineral Point Weekly Tribune*, May 23, 1863; Stevens, *Berdan's*, 248–53; *OR*, 25, I, 411.

18. James S. Pula, *Under the Crescent Moon with the XI Corps in the Civil War: From the Defenses of Washington to Chancellorsville, 1862–1863*, vol. 1 (El Dorado Hills: Savas Beatie, 2017), 144–92; Robertson Jr., *Stonewall*, 724–53.

19. Keneally, *American Scoundrel*, 267–68; Abbott, *Third Vermont Company*, 60–61.

20. *OR*, 25, I, 502; Wert, *A Glorious Army*, 196–97.

21. Stevens, *Berdan's*, 263–64, 276; Adjutant General, *Record of Service*, 120–35; *OR*, 25, I, 491, 502. The state's published roster also listed a Henry A. Wood as killed at Chancellorsville on May 3. I rejected this listing, a very rare error in state lists of Sharpshooters killed in action or mortally wounded. Wood's name does not appear in Michigan's original handwritten list of marksmen slain in battle, and no record of that name exists in the National Park Service database of Civil War soldiers. The listing for Wood matches the state's postwar roster data for Henry A. Hood, who was killed at Chancellorsville. The Wood listing appears to have been an error in the state's published roster.

22. Clark, *Histories*, vol. 1, 377; Sears, *Chancellorsville*, 321–23, 495; Furgurson, *Chancellorsville*, 224–26.

23. *Albany Evening Journal*, May 13, 1863.

24. Sears, *Chancellorsville*, 338–66; Sears, *Lincoln's Lieutenants*, 509–13.

25. Adjutant General, *Record of Service*, 122; E. A. Wilson, "A Sharpshooter Tells Where One Came True," *National Tribune*, September 25, 1884.

26. Abbott, *Third Vermont Company*, 61–62.

27. https://www.findagrave.com/memorial/16976170/porter-w-barker; Ayling, *Revised Register*, 969; Eicher and Eicher, *High Commands*, 564; J. S. Smith, "Gen. Whipple's Death," *National Tribune*, August 6, 1885.

28. *Mineral Point Weekly Tribune*, May 23, 1863.

29. Stevens, *Berdan's*, 269; *OR*, vol. 25, I, 503.

30. Monahan Diaries, VSA.
31. Company C records, PSA; Marden Letters, Rauner Library; Sears, *Chancellorsville*, 420–30.
32. White, *Civil War Diary*, 74; Stevens, *Berdan's*, 278.
33. *OR*, vol. 25, I, 171.
34. Smith Letters, WHS.
35. Marden Letters, Rauner Library.
36. *Shasta Courier*, October 17, 1863.
37. *Bellows Falls Times*, May 22, 1863; Adjutant General, *Revised Roster*, 623.
38. *Lansing State Republican*, May 20, 1863.
39. Company D Correspondence, MSA.
40. Marcot, *Civil War Chief*, 88–91. Marcot's review of the matter includes significant detail about Trepp's perspective and what Berdan may have done wrong at Chancellorsville. My counterpoint relies on Marcot's presentation of the issue.
41. *OR*, vol. 25, II, 464; Eicher and Eicher, *High Commands*, 261; Ripley, *Vermont Riflemen*, 107.
42. Company C Records, PSA.
43. Calef Correspondence, Rauner Library.
44. Dalton, *Soldiers in Green*, 143.
45. *OR*, 25, II, 595; Scott Bowden and Bill Ward, *Last Chance for Victory: Robert E. Lee and the Gettysburg Campaign* (El Dorado Hills: Savas Publishing Company, 2001), 1–52.
46. Marden Letters, Rauner Library.
47. *OR*, vol. 27, I, 30–35, 38; Sears, *Lincoln's Lieutenants*, 530–38.
48. Abbott, *Third Vermont Company*, 64.
49. Quiner, *Military History*, 876; *OR*, vol. 27, I, 159; Ezra J. Warner, *Generals in Blue* (Baton Rouge: Louisiana State University Press, 1992), 537–38.
50. *OR*, vol. 27, III, 58–59; Bradley M. Gottfried, *The Maps of Gettysburg* (El Dorado Hills: Savas Beatie, 2007), 6–9; David L. Ladd and Audrey J. Ladd, eds., *The Bachelder Papers: Gettysburg in Their Own Words*, vol. 1 (Dayton, OH: Morningside House, 1994), 383; Abbott, *Third Vermont Company*, 64.
51. Gottfried, *Maps of Gettysburg*, 10–15; Gary G. Lash, "'A Pathetic Story': The 141st Pennsylvania (Graham's Brigade) at Gettysburg," *Gettysburg Magazine*, no. 14, January 1996, 82; Gary Lash, "The March of the 124th New York to Gettysburg," *Gettysburg Magazine*, no. 9, July 1993, 8–9.
52. *Green Mountain Freeman*, June 23, 1863.
53. Dalton, *Soldiers in Green*, 149.
54. Ladd and Ladd, *Bachelder Papers*, I, 383.
55. Brown Letters, VHS; *Green Mountain Freeman*, June 23, 1863; https://www.findagrave.com/memorial/95548593/john-hanson-meader.
56. Dalton, *Soldiers in Green*, 152.
57. Calef Correspondence, Rauner Library.
58. Marden Letters, Rauner Library.
59. Ripley, *Vermont Riflemen*, 110–11; Abbott, *Third Vermont Company*, 64.

60. Bedell Diary, USAHEC; Thomas L. Elmore, "A Meteorological and Astronomical Chronology of the Gettysburg Campaign," *Gettysburg Magazine*, no. 13, July 1995, 8; Elmer Wallace Papers, BHL.

61. John W. Schildt, *Roads to Gettysburg* (Parsons, WV: McClain Publishing, 2003), 276–79, 324.

62. *Mineral Point Weekly Tribune*, September 2, 1863; Meier, *Memoirs of a Swiss Officer*, 115.

63. Sears, *Lincoln's Lieutenants*, 540–44.

64. Gottfried, *Maps of Gettysburg*, 36–41; Wipperman, *First for the Union*, 168–228.

65. Ripley, *Vermont Riflemen*, 112; Board of Commissioners, *Minnesota*, 508.

66. Schildt, *Roads to Gettysburg*, 408–12, 471–76; Elmore, "Meteorological and Astronomical," 11; Abbott, *Third Vermont Company*, 65.

67. The total number with the USSS at Gettysburg varies by source. The estimates in this paragraph are based on figures from John W. Busey and David G. Martin, *Regimental Strengths and Losses at Gettysburg*, 4th ed. (Hightstown, NJ: Longstreet House, 2005), 50; Company A Records, MNHS; *Mineral Point Weekly Tribune*, September 2, 1863.

68. Adjutant General, *Record of Service*, 112; Surgeon General, *The Medical and Surgical History of the War of the Rebellion*, part I, vol. 3 (Washington, D.C.: Government Printing Office, 1879), 786.

69. Bowden and Ward, *Last Chance*, 226–54; Harry W. Pfanz, *Gettysburg: The Second Day* (Chapel Hill: University of North Carolina Press, 1987), 112–14.

70. *OR*, vol. 27, I, 515; Marcot, *Civil War Chief*, 92.

71. *OR*, vol. 27, III, 617.

72. L. Y. Allen, "Berdan Sharpshooters," *National Tribune*, August 12, 1886.

73. *Dedication of the Monument to the Four New York Companies (A, B, D, and H) of the First Regiment of United States Sharpshooters (Berdan's) on the Battlefield of Gettysburg, July 2, 1889* (Albany, NY: Weed and Parsons, 1889), 19–20.

74. Pfanz, *Gettysburg*, 98–101; Benedict, *Vermont*, vol. 2, 743; *OR*, vol. 27, III, 507.

75. Roy Marcot, "Berdan's Sharpshooters at Gettysburg," *Gettysburg Magazine*, no. 1, July 1989, 37.

76. *Portland Daily Press*, October 12, 1889.

77. Hiram Berdan, "The Sharpshooters," *National Tribune*, October 14, 1886.

78. New York Monuments Commission, *Final Report on the Battlefield of Gettysburg*, vol. III (Albany, NY: J. B. Lyon, 1900), 1078–79; *Dedication of the Monument*, 43–44.

79. Marcot, *Civil War Chief*, 93–95; Marcot, "Berdan's Sharpshooters," 37, 39.

80. Stevens, *Berdan's*, 308.

81. L. J. Allen, "Berdan's Sharpshooters," *National Tribune*, December 16, 1886.

82. *OR*, vol. 27, I, 516–17,

83. Pfanz, *Gettysburg*, 101; Wiley Sword, "Lt. Col. Caspar Trepp's Colt's Revolver and the Reconnaissance to Pitzer's Woods," *Gettysburg Magazine*, no. 14, January 1996, 48–49.

84. Civil War Muster Roll Abstracts, Box 374, NYSA; Stevens, *Berdan's*, 309–10.

85. Adjutant General, *Record of Service*, 131; E. A. Wilson, "An Incident at Gettysburg," *National Tribune*, June 10, 1886.

86. https://www.findagrave.com/memorial/22341284/charles-thatcher; https://www.findagrave.com/memorial/170431570/abraham-h-cooper.

87. Adjutant General, *Revised Roster*, 603.

88. Edwin B. Coddington, *The Gettysburg Campaign: A Study in Command* (New York: Touchstone, 1997), 341–58. For an excellent book-length treatment of the kerfuffle between those supporting either Sickles or Meade, which lasted long after Meade's death in 1872, see, Richard A. Sauers, *Gettysburg: The Meade-Sickles Controversy* (Sterling, VA: Potomac Books, 2003). An article more supportive of Sickles is William Glenn Robertson, "The Peach Orchard Revisited: Daniel E. Sickles and the Third Corps on July 2, 1863," in *The Second Day at Gettysburg*, Gary W. Gallagher, ed. (Kent, OH: Kent State University Press, 1993), 33–56.

89. David B. Downs, "'His Left Was Worth a Glance': Meade and the Union Left on July 2, 1863," *Gettysburg Magazine*, no. 7, July 1992, 29–40.

90. *OR*, vol. 27, I, 515–18.

91. Morris M. Penny and J. Gary Laine, *Struggle for the Round Tops: Law's Alabama Brigade at the Battle of Gettysburg* (Shippensburg, PA: Burd Street Press, 1999), 19–29.

92. James Longstreet, *From Manassas to Appomattox* (New York: Da Capo Press, 1992), 367; Pfanz, *Gettysburg*, 144–48.

93. E. M. Law, "The Struggle for 'Round Top,'" *Battles and Leaders of the Civil War*, vol. 3 (New York: Century Co., 1888), 320–21.

94. Roger J. Greezicki, "Humbugging the Historian: A Reappraisal of Longstreet at Gettysburg," *Gettysburg Magazine*, no. 6, January 1992, 67; Longstreet, *From Manassas to Appomattox*, 367–69; Stephen W. Sears, *Gettysburg* (Boston: Houghton Mifflin, 2003), 255–65; Daniel M. Laney, "Wasted Gallantry: Hood's Texas Brigade at Gettysburg," *Gettysburg Magazine*, no. 16, January 1997, 32–38.

95. The initial line of the 2nd USSS is in three different places across as many modern maps. Compare Penny and Laine, *Struggle for the Round Tops*, 33 to Earley, *The Second United States Sharpshooters*, 120, and John J. Pullen, "Effects of Marksmanship: A Lesson from Gettysburg," *Gettysburg Magazine*, no. 2, January 1990, 57. Maps in other modern writing on the battle, such as Pfanz's solid book on July 2, do not depict Stoughton's line. Pfanz wrote of the indefinite evidence as a reason for not depicting the skirmish line on the map.

96. *OR*, vol. 27, I, 518.

97. Busey and Martin, *Regimental Strengths and Losses*, 265.

98. The two articles are Pullen, "Effects of Marksmanship," 55–60, and a fantastic published presentation. See, Tim Orr, "'On Such Slender Threads Does the Fate of Nations Depend': The Second United States Sharpshooters Defend the Union Left on July Second," 11th Biennial Gettysburg National Military Park Scholarly Seminar, Gettysburg, PA, April 2006, http://npshistory.com/series/symposia/gettysburg_seminars/11/essay5.pdf. Although Orr's article served as an excellent guide to the discussion that follows, I do not cite it at every possible footnote to avoid extensive repetition; Board of Commissioners, *Minnesota*, 508; Abbott, *Third Vermont Company*, 66. Endnote 19 in Orr's article details a sensible order of companies along the north-south axis of the 2nd Regiment's line.

99. *OR*, vol. 27, II, 404; Ladd and Ladd, *Bachelder Papers*, I, 477 and II, 860–61; Penny and Laine, *Struggle for the Round Tops*, 44–46.

100. Folder 7, Robert Coles unit history, 4th Alabama Regimental File, ADAH Digital Collections; W. F. Perry, "The Devil's Den," *Confederate Veteran*, vol. 9, 1901, 161.

101. W. C. Ward, "Incidents and Personal Experiences on the Battlefield at Gettysburg," *Confederate Veteran*, vol. 8, 1900, 347.

102. Marcot Collection, McCracken Library; Board of Commissioners, *Minnesota*, 512.

103. William C. Oates, "Gettysburg—The Battle on the Right," *Southern Historical Society Papers*, vol. 5, No. 4, October 1878, 174; Law, "The Struggle," 323–24.

104. Abbott, *Third Vermont Company*, 67.

105. *OR*, vol. 27, I, 518; White, *Civil War Diary*, 87.

106. John C. West, *A Texan in Search of a Fight* (J. S. Hill & Co., 1901), 85.

107. Penny and Laine, *Struggle for the Round Tops*, 44–51; Pullen, "Effects of Marksmanship," 56–58.

108. William Oates letter to Homer Stoughton, November 22, 1888, VHS.

109. *OR*, vol. 27, I, 509.

110. Pindell, "The Most Dangerous," 52. Some of the wounds might have been inflicted by infantrymen in Ward's Brigade, due to the proximity of Plum Run to Houck's Ridge.

111. Pfanz, *Gettysburg*, 174–200; West, *A Texan*, 85–86; Ladd and Ladd, *Bachelder Papers*, 1094–95. For an excellent discussion of the fight for Devil's Den, with plentiful maps and pictures, see Kathleen R. Georg Harrison, "'Our Principal Loss Was in This Place:' Action at the Slaughter Pen and at the South End of Houck's Ridge," *Gettysburg Magazine*, no. 1, July 1989, 45–69.

112. Benedict, *Vermont*, vol. 2, 767; Abbott, *Third Vermont Company*, 67.

113. Ladd and Ladd, *Bachelder Papers*, II, 1029; Thomas A. Desjardin, *Stand Firm Ye Boys from Maine: The 20th Maine and the Gettysburg Campaign* (New York: Oxford University Press, 1995), 50–51.

114. Gottfried, *Maps of Gettysburg*, 148–51; Elisha Coan Collection, Bowdoin College.

115. Gottfried, *Maps of Gettysburg*, 152–53; West, *A Texan*, 86.

116. https://www.gordonthorsbycivilwarnotes.com/post/the-misplaced-minnesota-sharpshooter-john-a-dolson; https://www.findagrave.com/memorial/18185232/john-o-dolson.

117. Gregory A. Coco, *Killed in Action: Eyewitness Accounts of the Last Moments of 100 Union Soldiers Who Died at Gettysburg* (Gettysburg: Thomas Publications, 1992), 36–37; https://www.findagrave.com/memorial/156662688/henry-lakeman-richards.

118. *Portsmouth Journal of Literature and Politics*, September 13, 1862.

119. Manilus Holbrook, "Berdan's Crack Shots," *National Tribune*, April 13, 1899.

120. Oates to Stoughton, VHS.

121. William C. Oates, *The War between the Union and the Confederacy and Its Lost Opportunities* (New York: Neale Publishing, 1905), 212–13.

122. New York Monuments Commission, *Final Report*, 1071; *OR*, vol. 27, I, 516.

123. Bedell Diary, USAHEC; *OR*, vol. 27, I, 515; Folder 5, 8th Alabama Regimental File, ADAH Digital Collections.

124. Stevens, *Berdan's*, 302.

125. *Mineral Point Weekly Tribune*, September 2, 1863.

126. Gottfried, *Maps of Gettysburg*, 186–93.

127. *OR*, vol. 27, II, 618; Folder 2, 9th Alabama Regimental File, ADAH Digital Collections.

128. In a letter after the war, one Bay State infantryman noted the overwhelming force of multiple brigades. Ladd and Ladd, *Bachelder Papers*, I, 193; Estabrook, *Wisconsin Losses*, 202.

129. *Mineral Point Weekly Tribune*, September 2, 1863.

130. https://www.findagrave.com/memorial/67270230/simon-k-roosa; Adjutant General, *Record of Service*, 131.

131. Pfanz, *Gettysburg*, 351–424.

132. Bowden and Ward, *Last Chance*, 423–51.

133. Wipperman, *First for the Union*, 235–39.

134. Board of Commissioners, *Minnesota*, 508, 511; A. Wright, "The 2d U.S. Sharpshooters," *National Tribune*, February 18, 1909.

135. Abbott, *Third Vermont Company*, 69.

136. Adjutant General, *Record of Service*, 128; Surgeon General, *Medical and Surgical History*, part III, vol. 2, 509. The latter source misspelled Higby's last name as Heighly. Earley, *The Second United States Sharpshooters*, 131–32; Ayling, *Revised Register*, 982; https://www.findagrave.com/memorial/60780813/george-h-white; Board of Commissioners, *Minnesota*, 511.

137. Ripley, *Vermont Riflemen*, 124.

138. Stevens, *Berdan's*, 339–40.

139. John W. Whitman, "Lorenzo Barber Was the Eagle-Eyed 'Fighting Parson' of Hiram Berdan's Famous U.S. Sharpshooters," *America's Civil War*, September 1998, 12, 16; Abbott, *Third Vermont Company*, 69.

140. Meier, *Memoirs of a Swiss Officer*, 119; White, *Civil War Diary*, 90–91; https://www.findagrave.com/memorial/242775054/j-s-kent; Board of Commissioners, *Minnesota*, 508; *Annual Report of the Adjutant General of the State of Maine for the Year Ending December 31, 1863* (Augusta, ME: Stevens & Sayward, 1863), Appendix D, 99; Dalton, *Soldiers in Green*, 163.

141. *OR*, vol. 27, I, 516.

142. Ripley, *Vermont Riflemen*, 126; Meier, *Memoirs of a Swiss Officer*, 120; *OR*, vol. 27, I, 491–92.

143. Marden Letters, Rauner Library.

144. Brown Letters, VHS.

145. Application for Correcting Military Record for John W. E. Robinson, NA; Ayling, *Revised Register*, 981.

146. Kent Masterson Brown, *Retreat from Gettysburg: Lee, Logistics, and the Pennsylvania Campaign* (Chapel Hill: University of North Carolina Press, 2005), 46–262.

147. *OR*, vol. 27, III, 519; Sears, *Lincoln's Lieutenants*, 581–82; Sears, *Gettysburg*, 471–75.

148. Eicher and Eicher, *High Commands*, 244; Stevens, *Berdan's*, 346.

149. *Penn Yan Chronicle*, July 30, 1863.

150. Longstreet, *From Manassas to Appomattox*, 429–30; Penny and Laine, *Struggle for the Round Tops*, 170; Coddington, *Gettysburg Campaign*, 565–73; Abbott, *Third Vermont Company*, 70; *Mineral Point Weekly Tribune*, September 2, 1863.

151. Sears, *Lincoln's Lieutenants*, 585–90; Marden Letters, Rauner Library; *OR*, vol. 27, I, 492 and III, 712–15.

152. Ripley, *Vermont Riflemen*, 127.

153. George Meade, *The Life and Letters of George Gordon Meade*, vol. 2 (New York: Charles Scribner's Sons, 1913), 137; Civil War Muster Roll Abstracts, Box 373, NYSA; Stevens, *Berdan's*, 352; Adjutant General, *Record of Service*, 145.

154. Dunn, *Harvestfields*, 200; *OR*, vol. 27, III, 752–53; Earley, *The Second United States Sharpshooters*, 137; *New York Herald*, August 1, 1863; Marden Letters, Rauner Library.

155. Smith Papers, Rubenstein Library.

156. Meier, *Memoirs of a Swiss Officer*, 125; Abbott, *Third Vermont Company*, 70.

157. Wallace Papers, BHL; Bedell Diary, USAHEC.

158. Brown Letters, VHS; Connington Letters, USAHEC.

159. *New York Times*, August 4, 1863.

160. Dalton, *Soldiers in Green*, 174; Abbott, *Third Vermont Company*, 70.

161. *Penn Yan Chronicle*, August 13, 1863.

162. *Annual Report of the Adjutant General*, Appendix D, 99–100; Adjutant General, *Record of Service*, 109–59; Board of Commissioners, *Minnesota*, 511–12; Ayling, *Revised Register*, 967–70, 976–82; Adjutant General, *Revised Roster*, 600–603, 611–15, 620–23.

163. Adjutant General, *Record of Service*, 121, 127; Ayling, *Revised Register*, 967, 977.

164. *Mineral Point Weekly Tribune*, November 4, 1863; https://www.findagrave.com/memorial/9622608/albert-skeals-isham.

165. Surgeon General, *Medical and Surgical History*, Part III, vol. I, 344; https://www.findagrave.com/memorial/3257301/hannibel-tichout.

166. The documents mentioned in this section are located in Berdan's Consolidated Military Service Record at the National Archives.

167. Marcot, *Civil War Chief*, 146–326.

168. Papers of Eveline Mary Pinney, VHS.

169. Connington Letters, USAHEC.

170. *Mineral Point Weekly Tribune*, September 16, 1863.

171. *Shasta Courier*, October 17, 1863.

172. Brown Letters, VHS.

173. Clark Papers, Clements Library; Stevens, *Berdan's*, 354.

174. Bedell diary, USAHEC; Dalton, *Soldiers in Green*, 183.

175. Smith Papers, Rubenstein Library.

176. *Penn Yan Chronicle*, October 8, 1863.

177. Meier, *Memoirs of a Swiss Officer*, 126–27; *OR*, vol. 29, I, 219–20; Eicher and Eicher, *High Commands*, 207–208.

178. *OR*, vol. 29, I, 310–11; Sears, *Lincoln's Lieutenants*, 598–99.
179. *Mineral Point Weekly Tribune*, November 4, 1863.
180. *OR*, vol. 29, I, 314; Regis de Trobriand, *Four Years with the Army of the Potomac*, translated by George K. Dauchy (Boston: Ticknor and Company, 1889), 541; *Mineral Point Weekly Tribune*, November 4, 1863.
181. Stevens, *Berdan's*, 360.
182. Keneally, *American Scoundrel*, 297; Clark Papers, Clements Library.
183. *Mineral Point Weekly Tribune*, November 4, 1863.
184. *OR*, vol. 29, I, 311; Abbott, *Third Vermont Company*, 71; Earley, *The Second United States Sharpshooters*, 142.
185. Connington Letters, USAHEC.
186. Pinney Papers, VHS. Clay died three days after his seventy-eighth birthday in 1918. https://www.findagrave.com/memorial/74070102/george-a-clay.
187. *OR*, vol. 29, II, 409, 412, 425–26; White, *Civil War Diary*, 104.
188. Marcot Collection, McCracken Library; *Maine Farmer*, November 19, 1863.
189. *Mineral Point Weekly Tribune*, November 25, 1863.
190. Ripley, *Vermont Riflemen*, 131–32; George Lewis, *The History of Battery E, First Regiment Rhode Island Light Artillery* (Providence: Snow & Farnham, 1892), 238.
191. Quiner, *Military History*, 877; de Trobriand, *Four Years*, 548–49; Dalton, *Soldiers in Green*, 193; Meier, *Memoirs of a Swiss Officer*, 128–29; Abbott, *Third Vermont Company*, 72–73.
192. Elaine Purdy, ed., "The Civil War Diary of Charles B. Mead," *Rutland Historical Society Quarterly* 28, no. 1 (1998): 6; Brown Letters, VHS.
193. Earley, *The Second United States Sharpshooters*, 144–45; *Portland Daily Press*, November 17, 1863.
194. Surgeon General, *Medical and Surgical History*, part II, vol. 3, 782; *Penn Yan Chronicle*, November 26, 1863.
195. Adjutant General, *Record of Service*, 132; https://www.findagrave.com/memorial/73935511/edward-j-southworth.
196. Stevens, *Berdan's*, 369–70; Connington Letters, USAHEC; Oliver Davis, *Life of David Bell Birney, Major General of United States Volunteers* (Philadelphia: King & Baird, 1867), 200.
197. Sears, *Lincoln's Lieutenants*, 601–602; *OR*, vol. 29, I, 58–61.
198. *Mineral Point Weekly Tribune*, November 25, 1863.
199. Purdy, "The Civil War Diary," 7, 9; Meier, *Memoirs of a Swiss Officer*, 132; Smith Letters, WHS; Brown Letters, VHS.
200. Abbott, *Third Vermont Company*, 73.
201. John Minor Botts, *The Great Rebellion: Its Secret History, Rise, Progress, and Disastrous Failure* (New York: Harper & Brothers, 1866), 294–95; Ripley, *Vermont Riflemen*, 134–35; de Trobriand, *Four Years*, 551–52.
202. Marden Letters, Rauner Library.
203. Company D Correspondence, MSA.
204. J. H. Stine, *History of the Army of the Potomac* (Washington, D.C.: Gibson Bros., 1893), 587–88; Lewis, *The History*, 243.

205. Meade, *Life and Letters*, vol. 2, 156–57.

206. *Green Mountain Freeman*, January 5, 1864; Marden Letters, Rauner Library. The frustrated Meade ordered an investigation of the problems in the Third Corps, which prompted French to send several messages defending his decisions and soldiers. See, *OR*, vol. 29, I, 735–49 and II, 495.

207. Ripley, *Vermont Riflemen*, 135; *OR*, vol. 29, II, 499.

208. *OR*, vol. 29, I, 750; Davis, *Birney*, 203.

209. Abbott, *Third Vermont Company*, 74; Benedict, *Vermont*, vol. II, 769.

210. Lewis, *The History*, 246; *OR*, vol. 29, I, 750.

211. *Green Mountain Freeman*, January 5, 1864; Edwin B. Houghton, *The Campaigns of the Seventeenth Maine* (Portland: Short & Loring, 1866), 142–43.

212. Connington Letters, USAHEC.

213. https://www.findagrave.com/memorial/82057136/john-wilson_irwin-chidsey.

214. Meier, *Memoirs of a Swiss Officer*, 132; Adjutant General, *Record of Service*, 125, 136, 149, 155; Civil War Muster Roll Abstracts, Boxes 373 and 374, NYSA; Adjutant General, *Revised Roster*, 602; Estabrook, *Wisconsin Losses*, 202; Purdy, "The Civil War Diary," 10, 13.

215. Stevens, *Berdan's*, 379, 384; Adjutant General, *Record of Service*, 122.

216. Abbott, *Third Vermont Company*, 73.

217. *Green Mountain Freeman*, January 5, 1864; Sears, *Lincoln's Lieutenants*, 604–605.

218. Ripley, *Vermont Riflemen*, 138; Davis, *Birney*, 203; Abbott, *Third Vermont Company*, 74; Dalton, *Soldiers in Green*, 199.

219. Meier, *Memoirs of a Swiss Officer*, 133.

220. *OR*, vol. 29, I, 751, 759; Stevens, *Berdan's*, 385–87; Civil War Muster Roll Abstracts, Box 373, NYSA; https://www.findagrave.com/memorial/70631559/alexander-joseph-dupont.

221. Whitman, "Lorenzo Barber," 18.

222. Meier, *Memoirs of a Swiss Officer*, 133–34; *Green Mountain Freeman*, January 5, 1864.

223. *OR*, vol. 29, I, 752; Meier, *Memoirs of a Swiss Officer*, 134.

224. Stevens, *Berdan's*, 387; Lillie Devereux Blake Papers, MHS.

225. Ripley, *Vermont Riflemen*, 140–41; Stevens, *Berdan's*, 387; Brown Letters, VHS.

226. *New York Times*, December 13, 1863; Approved Pension Application File for Christine Sarah Trepp (No. WC68334), NA.

227. Meade, *Life and Letters*, vol. II, 156–58.

228. Marden Letters, Rauner Library; Stevens, *Berdan's*, 391–93; Sears, *Lincoln's Lieutenants*, 605–606; Stine, *History*, 589–92; *OR*, vol. 29, II, 530–32.

229. Marden Letters, Rauner Library; White, *Civil War Diary*, 109.

230. Evans Letters, MNHS.

231. Brown Letters, VHS; Adjutant General, *Revised Roster*, 601–603.

232. Purdy, "The Civil War Diary," 8; *Wood County Reporter*, February 11, 1864; Meier, *Memoirs of a Swiss Officer*, 137.

233. Brown Letters, VHS; *Wood County Reporter*, February 11, 1864.

234. Clark Papers, Clements Library.

235. Ripley, *Vermont Riflemen*, 137.

236. Company D Correspondence, MSA.
237. Abbott, *Third Vermont Company*, 76–77.
238. Meier, *Memoirs of a Swiss Officer*, 136; Bedell Diary, USAHEC.
239. White, *Civil War Diary*, 110.
240. Davis, *Birney*, 205–206; *OR*, vol. 33, 358.
241. Charles W. Ford Diary, BHL.
242. Hastings, *Letters*, 184.
243. Elaine G. Purdy, ed., "The Final Civil War Diary of Charles B. Mead of Company F, First U.S. Sharpshooters," *Rutland Historical Society Quarterly* 32, no. 1 (2002): 4–6; Stevens, *Berdan's*, 393; *Wood County Reporter*, February 11, 1864; Houghton, *The Campaigns*, 153.
244. Ford Diary, BHL.
245. Marden Letters, Rauner Library.
246. Davis, *Birney*, 208–209.
247. Purdy, "The Final," 7; Stevens, *Berdan's*, 395–96; *Orleans Independent Standard*, March 18, 1864.
248. Meier, *Memoirs of a Swiss Officer*, 142–44; Purdy, "The Final," 8–13; Ford Diary, BHL; Dalton, *Soldiers in Green*, 208–16.
249. Wiley Sword Papers, Folder 21, USAHEC; Hastings, *Letters*, 172–201.
250. Joseph Barton letter, USAHEC.
251. H. W. Brands, *The Man Who Saved the Union: Ulysses Grant in War and Peace* (New York: Anchor Books, 2013), 288–96; John J. Hennessy, "I Dread the Spring: The Army of the Potomac Prepares for the Overland Campaign," in *The Wilderness Campaign*, Gary W. Gallagher, ed. (Chapel Hill: University of North Carolina Press, 1997), 70–85, 93–96.
252. *Shasta Courier*, April 30, 1864.
253. Sears, *Lincoln's Lieutenants*, 615–19; *OR*, vol. 33, 1038.
254. George Thornton Fleming, ed., *Life and Letters of Alexander Hays* (Pittsburgh, PA: n.p., 1919), 575, 577; Stevens, *Berdan's*, 402.
255. *Penn Yan Chronicle*, April 14, 1864.
256. 1st USSS Order Book and Property Book, NA; Meier, *Memoir of a Swiss Officer*, 138.
257. Fleming, *Life and Letters*, 583.
258. *Lansing State Republican*, March 23, 1864.
259. Company C records, PSA; Company A records, MNHS.
260. Ayling, *Revised Register*, 611–15; https://www.findagrave.com/memorial/144843490/andrew-w-berry.
261. Purdy, "The Final," 14; Meier, *Memoir of a Swiss Officer*, 146; Ripley, *Vermont Riflemen*, 143.
262. Clark Papers, Clements Library.
263. *Green Mountain Freeman*, May 10, 1864; Ford Diary, BHL.
264. Festus Spencer Letter, BHL.
265. *OR*, vol. 33, 1036.
266. Company D Correspondence, MSA; *Appendix D of the Annual Report*, 185.
267. Ford Diary, BHL.
268. *OR*, vol. 33, 1017–18.

Part Three

1. Ford Diary, BHL.

2. *OR*, vol. 36, II, 331–34.

3. Abbott, *Third Vermont Company*, 77; Stevens, *Berdan's*, 400; Purdy, "The Final," 17.

4. Fleming, *Life and Letters*, 595.

5. *Orleans Independent Standard*, June 3, 1864. Other sources suggest the USSS departed Brandy Station a bit later but still before midnight. The 1st Regiment's report timed the trek beginning at 11 p.m. See, *OR*, vol. 36, I, 485.

6. Purdy, "The Final," 17; Ripley, *Vermont Riflemen*, 143–44; Ford Diary, BHL.

7. *Orleans Independent Standard*, June 3, 1864.

8. Gordon Rhea, *The Battle of the Wilderness, May 5–6, 1864* (Baton Rouge: Louisiana State University Press, 1994), 68–69; *OR*, vol. 36, II, 374–75; Ripley, *Vermont Riflemen*, 143.

9. *OR*, vol. 36, II, 333; Rhea, *The Battle of the Wilderness*, 49–59, 94–187.

10. Abbott, *Third Vermont Company*, 78; William Kent, "A Wilderness Memory," *Civil War Times Illustrated*, March 1989, 34, 36; Davis, *Birney*, 214; *OR*, vol. 36, I, 467, 485, and II, 406–407; George W. Verrill, "The Seventeenth Maine at Gettysburg and in the Wilderness," in *War Papers Read before the Commandery of the State of Maine, Military Order of the Loyal Legion of the United States*, vol. I (Portland, ME: Thurston Print, 1898), 272–73; Francis A. Walker, *History of the Second Army Corps in the Army of the Potomac* (New York: Charles Scribner's Sons, 1886), 407–13. Walker suggested the Second Corps should have been allowed to continue its march west, with the possibility of flanking the right of Lee's army. With the Fifth Corps already engaged and a large gap between that force and Hancock, one cannot fault Grant and Meade for seeing the value of the move north for Hancock. After all, Getty's Division likely could not hold off Hill's advance east on the Plank Road.

11. Rhea, *The Battle of the Wilderness*, 187–93; George R. Agassiz, ed., *Meade's Headquarters, 1863–1865: Letters of Colonel Theodore Lyman from the Wilderness to Appomattox* (Boston: Massachusetts Historical Society, 1922), 88–89; L. A. Grant, "In the Wilderness," *National Tribune*, January 28, 1897; David M. Jordan, *Winfield Scott Hancock: A Soldier's Life* (Bloomington: Indiana University Press, 1996), 114–18; Lawrence A. Kreiser, *Defeating Lee: A History of the Second Corps, Army of the Potomac* (Bloomington: Indiana University Press, 2011), 166–67.

12. Carol Reardon, "The Other Grant: Lewis A. Grant and the Vermont Brigade in the Battle of the Wilderness," in *The Wilderness Campaign*, Gary W. Gallagher, ed. (Chapel Hill: University of North Carolina Press, 1997), 205–17; *Orleans Independent Standard*, June 3, 1864.

13. Verrill, "The Seventeenth Maine," 273, 275; Kent, "A Wilderness Memory," 37.

14. *OR*, vol. 36, II, 409–410; Clark, *Histories*, vol. 1, 594–95, 743–44; Hastings, *Letters*, 201; Purdy, "The Final," 17.

15. Adjutant General, *Revised Roster*, 602–603.

16. https://www.findagrave.com/memorial/15977067/artemas-cassius-cross; https://www.findagrave.com/memorial/17279840/william-j-domag; https://www.findagrave

com/memorial/175820353/david-w-french; *Green Mountain Freeman*, June 6, 1863; Ripley, *Vermont Riflemen*, 147.

17. Rhea, *The Battle of the Wilderness*, 202–206; Fleming, *Life and Letters*, 596–605; Kent, "A Wilderness Memory," 37; Houghton, *The Campaigns*, 167–68.

18. Earley, *The Second United States Sharpshooters*, 159; Stevens, *Berdan's*, 401.

19. Kent, "A Wilderness Memory," 38.

20. Clark, *Histories*, vol. 2, 446, and vol. 3, 75; William Kelsey McDaid, *"Four Years of Arduous Service": The History of the Branch-Lane Brigade in the Civil War*, PhD Dissertation, Michigan State University, 1987, 257–61; White, *Civil War Diary*, 119.

21. Stevens, *Berdan's*, 403; *Orleans Independent Standard*, June 3, 1864.

22. *OR*, vol. 36, II, 412.

23. Wipperman, *Burnside's Boys*, 279–86.

24. Ripley, *Vermont Riflemen*, 148–49; *OR*, vol. 36, I, 485; Abbott, *Third Vermont Company*, 78.

25. Verrill, "The Seventeenth Maine," 277; Purdy, "The Final," 18; Meier, *Memoirs of a Swiss Officer*, 148; Stevens, *Berdan's*, 403.

26. Walker, *History of the Second Army Corps*, 421; Caldwell, *The History of a Brigade*, 133.

27. Ripley, *Vermont Riflemen*, 149; Rhea, *The Battle of the Wilderness*, 292–306.

28. Ford Diary, BHL; Clark, *Histories*, vol. 3, 119; Stevens, *Berdan's*, 403.

29. Davis, *Birney*, 215–16; Verrill, "The Seventeenth Maine," 281–82.

30. Dunn, *Harvestfields*, 228–30; White, *Civil War Diary*, 120; Rhea, *The Battle of the Wilderness*, 390–98.

31. Stevens, *Berdan's*, 406–407; Adjutant General, *Revised Roster*, 614.

32. *Beloit Gazette*, July 16, 1903, and February 7, 1917. I thank Jade Schmitt Wanger for an email in which she noted James's nickname.

33. E. Morton Coulter, ed., "From Spotsylvania Courthouse to Andersonville: A Diary of Darius Starr," *Georgia Historical Quarterly* 41, no. 2 (June 1957): 181. Starr would die at the end of August at Andersonville prison in Georgia.

34. Benedict, *Vermont*, vol. 2, 770–71; https://www.findagrave.com/memorial/62452453/albert-buxton; Abbott, *Third Vermont Company*, 79–80.

35. https://www.findagrave.com/memorial/27254269/thomas-jefferson-tarbell; Adjutant General, *Revised Roster*, 611–12, 614.

36. Adjutant General, *Record of Service*, 112, 152; https://www.findagrave.com/memorial/52192198/james-j-rude; https://www.findagrave.com/memorial/19507326/franklin-w-stanwood.

37. https://www.findagrave.com/memorial/75538726/samuel-lawrence-bigelow.

38. Abbott, *Third Vermont Company*, 79; Benedict, *Vermont*, vol. 2, 770.

39. Rhea, *The Battle of the Wilderness*, 435–41; *OR*, vol. 36, II, 480–81.

40. Ripley, *Vermont Riflemen*, 153–54; *OR*, vol. 36, II, 488; *Appendix D of the Annual Report*, 186.

41. Ford Diary, BHL; *OR*, vol. 36, I, 480–81 and II, 487.

42. Stevens, *Berdan's*, 409; Meier, *Memoirs of a Swiss Officer*, 151.

43. Stevens, *Berdan's*, 409; Ford Diary, BHL; Verrill, "The Seventeenth Maine," 282.

44. *OR*, vol. 36, II, 489; Meier, *Memoirs of a Swiss Officer*, 151.

45. https://www.findagrave.com/memorial/99582344/william-wesley-sweet; Stevens, *Berdan's*, 413.

46. Abbott, *Third Vermont Company*, 79.

47. Stevens, *Berdan's*, 409–12.

48. Jordan, *Winfield Scott Hancock*, 125–26; Ford Diary, BHL.

49. Ayling, *Revised Register*, 979; https://www.findagrave.com/memorial/17387937/perrin-c-judkins; Stevens, *Berdan's*, 416–17.

50. Purdy, "The Final," 19.

51. *Orleans Independent Standard*, June 3, 1864.

52. Gordon Rhea, *The Battles for Spotsylvania Court House and the Road to Yellow Tavern, May 7–12, 1864* (Baton Rouge: Louisiana State University Press, 1997), 109–12.

53. Kreiser, *Defeating Lee*, 171–72; Ripley, *Vermont Riflemen*, 157–60; *Orleans Independent Standard*, June 3, 1864.

54. Abbott, *Third Vermont Company*, 81; Hastings, *Letters*, 203.

55. Ayling, *Revised Register*, 981.

56. Company C Morning Reports, 2nd USSS, NA; Civil War Muster Roll Abstracts, Box 375, NYSA; https://www.findagrave.com/memorial/196122429/philip-ernest_kess-sands; *New York Times*, November 7, 1864; Stevens, *Berdan's*, 534.

57. Purdy, "The Final," 19; Stevens, *Berdan's*, 423; Davis, *Birney*, 218; Earley, *The Second United States Sharpshooters*, 168–69.

58. *OR*, vol. 36, II, 636; Purdy, "The Final," 19; Ayling, *Revised Register*, 979; https://www.findagrave.com/memorial/40032940/john-f-kennedy; Adjutant General, *Record of Service*, 119–20.

59. *OR*, vol. 36, II, 630.

60. Robert K. Krick, "An Insurmountable Barrier between the Army and Ruin," in *The Spotsylvania Campaign*, Gary W. Gallagher, ed. (Chapel Hill: University of North Carolina Press, 1998), 80–85; Keith S. Bohannon, "Breastworks Are Good Things to Have on Battlefields: Confederate Engineering Operations and Field Fortifications in the Overland Campaign," in *Cold Harbor to the Crater: The End of the Overland Campaign*, Gary W. Gallagher and Caroline E. Janney, eds. (Chapel Hill: University of North Carolina Press, 2015), 113–14.

61. *OR*, vol. 36, II, 635; Rhea, *The Battles for Spotsylvania*, 223–25; Jordan, *Winfield Scott Hancock*, 128–29; Stevens, *Berdan's*, 423–24; Francis C. Barlow, "Capture of the Salient, May 12, 1864," in *The Wilderness Campaign, May–June 1864, Papers of the Military Historical Society of Massachusetts*, vol. 4 (Boston: Military Historical Society of Massachusetts, 1905), 248.

62. William Houghton, "A Staff Officer's Recollection of the Salient Angle," *National Tribune*, September 11, 1890.

63. Joseph Miner, "The Way in Which the Rebels Were Surprised," *National Tribune*, March 18, 1886; Barlow, "Capture of the Salient," 250, 252.

64. *Orleans Independent Standard*, June 10, 1864.

65. Abbott, *Third Vermont Company*, 81; Adjutant General, *Revised Roster*, 623.

66. Edwin Emery Diaries, Bowdoin College; *OR*, vol. 36, II, 656; Meier, *Memoirs of a Swiss Officer*, 156–57; Caldwell, *The History of a Brigade*, 142.

67. The size of the Mule Shoe is based on a detailed map at Rhea, *The Battles for Spotsylvania*, 267; Ripley, *Vermont Riflemen*, 162; *New York Times*, May 18, 1864; Earley, *The Second United States Sharpshooters*, 171; *OR*, vol. 36, I, 485.

68. Houghton, "A Staff Officer's Recollection"; I. G. Bradwell, "Spotsylvania May 12, 13, 1864," *Confederate Veteran*, vol. 28, 1920, 102–103; Davis, *Birney*, 220.

69. Adjutant General, *Revised Roster*, 601; https://www.findagrave.com/memorial/91348807/jonathan-e-chase; Surgeon General, *Medical and Surgical History*, Part III, vol. II, 620.

70. Purdy, "The Final," 19; Ripley, *Vermont Riflemen*, 163–64.

71. *Penn Yan Chronicle*, May 26, 1864.

72. Rhea, *The Battles for Spotsylvania*, 311–19.

73. https://www.findagrave.com/memorial/94964812/george-andrew-denniston; https://www.findagrave.com/memorial/61525241/john-alexander-denniston.

74. Stevens, *Berdan's*, 427.

75. *Orleans Independent Standard*, June 3, 1864; Ford Diary, BHL; Purdy, "The Final," 20; Hastings, *Letters*, 204.

76. Marden Letters, Rauner Library.

77. *Orleans Independent Standard*, June 3, 1864.

78. *OR*, vol. 36, II, 702; Gordon C. Rhea, *To the North Anna River: Grant and Lee, May 13–25, 1864* (Baton Rouge: Louisiana State University Press, 2000), 24–26.

79. Adjutant General, *Revised Roster*, 603; https://www.findagrave.com/memorial/17062466/henry-mattocks; *Orleans Independent Standard*, June 3, 1864.

80. Rhea, *To the North Anna*, 66–77; *OR*, vol. 36, I, 485; Ford Diary, BHL.

81. Adjutant General, *Record of Service*, 108, 119, 125; Ayling, *Revised Register*, 977; White, *Civil War Diary*, 128.

82. *Orleans Independent Standard*, June 3, 1864; Davis, *Birney*, 221; Abbott, *Third Vermont Company*, 82; Benedict, *Vermont*, vol. 2, 771; Adjutant General, *Revised Roster*, 620.

83. Ford Diary, BHL; Ripley, *Vermont Riflemen*, 165; Purdy, "The Final," 20–21.

84. Jordan, *Winfield Scott Hancock*, 132; *OR*, vol. 36, II, 866, 869.

85. *OR*, vol. 36, III, 3–9; Sears, *Lincoln's Lieutenants*, 676–77; Rhea, *To the North Anna*, 212–16, 261–63.

86. Adjutant General, *Revised Roster*, 613.

87. Ford Diary, BHL; Purdy, "The Final," 21–22; Ripley, *Vermont Riflemen*, 167–68.

88. *Orleans Independent Standard*, June 10, 1864; James W. Reagan, "More about the Fight at Brooks Crossroads," *Confederate Veteran* 18 (1910): 229–30; Abbott, *Third Vermont Company*, 83; Rhea, *To the North Anna*, 295–324.

89. James Alexander Milling, "Jim Milling and the War," downloaded at https://digitalcommons.winthrop.edu/manuscriptcollection_findingaids/610; William P. Shreve, "The Operations of the Army of the Potomac, May 13–June 2, 1864," in *The Wilderness Campaign, May–June 1864, Papers of the Military Historical Society of Massachusetts*, vol. 4 (Boston: Military Historical Society of Massachusetts, 1905), 306.

90. Hastings, *Letters*, 213; Company D Correspondence, MSA; *Appendix D of the Annual Report*, 185; https://www.findagrave.com/memorial/143358487/stephen-c-barker. Barker's brother Silas, another officer in Company D, had been discharged soon after Chancellorsville per *Annual Report of the Adjutant General*, Appendix D, 99; https://www.findagrave.com/memorial/92823625/luther-w-crane.

91. *OR*, vol. 36, I, 478–79; Earl J. Hess, *Trench Warfare under Grant and Lee: Field Fortifications in the Overland Campaign* (Chapel Hill: University of North Carolina Press, 2007), 121–24, 128–29.

92. The 20th Indiana crossed the bridge first, followed by the two USSS regiments. Dunn, *Harvestfields*, 250–51; Sears, *Lincoln's Lieutenants*, 681–83; Ford Diary, BHL.

93. Ripley, *Vermont Riflemen*, 169–70; Purdy, "The Final," 22.

94. Gordon C. Rhea, *Cold Harbor: Grant and Lee, May 26-June 3, 1864* (Baton Rouge: Louisiana State University Press, 2002), 21–39. A Ninth Corps division assisted Hancock east of Lee's lines. See, Wipperman, *Burnside's Boys*, 309–310.

95. Stevens, *Berdan's*, 438, 440; Adjutant General, *Record of Service*, 138.

96. Ford Diary, BHL; Ripley, *Vermont Riflemen*, 170; Purdy, "The Final," 23.

97. Rhea, *Cold Harbor*, 44–50; Walker, *History of the Second Army Corps*, 498–99; Kreiser, *Defeating Lee*, 181–82.

98. *OR*, vol. 36, III, 285.

99. Hastings, *Letters*, 215; William H. Shelton, "A Mansion Rich in Virginia's History," *New York Times*, August 19, 1928; T. C. Morton, "Incidents of the Skirmish at Totopotomoy Creek, Hanover County, Virginia, May 30, 1864," *Southern Historical Society Papers*, vol. 16, 1888, 47.

100. Hastings, *Letters*, 215; Ford Diary, BHL; Walker, *History of the Second Army Corps*, 500–501.

101. Stevens, *Berdan's*, 443; Civil War Muster Roll Abstracts, Boxes 374 and 375, NYSA; https://www.findagrave.com/memorial/111587608/francis-snyder.

102. *OR*, vol. 36, III, 334.

103. Abbott, *Third Vermont Company*, 84; Hastings, *Letters*, 215; *OR*, vol. 36, III, 378.

104. Civil War Muster Roll Abstracts, Box 375, NYSA; Adjutant General, *Revised Roster*, 612, 621; https://www.findagrave.com/memorial/165224984/horatio-p-bruce; https://www.findagrave.com/memorial/49224095/joseph-c-barton.

105. *OR*, vol. 36, III, 324–25; Purdy, "The Final," 24; J. D. Bloodgood, *Personal Reminiscences of the War* (New York: Hunt & Eaton, 1893), 275.

106. Ford Diary, BHL; Stevens, *Berdan's*, 442; Purdy, "The Final," 24.

107. Sears, *Lincoln's Lieutenants*, 687–89.

108. Ripley, *Vermont Riflemen*, 171; Davis, *Birney*, 224; *OR*, vol. 36, III, 441.

109. Kreiser, *Defeating Lee*, 183; Walker, *History of the Second Army Corps*, 503.

110. *OR*, vol. 36, III, 442; Kathryn Shively Meier, "I Told Him to Go On: Enduring Cold Harbor," in *Cold Harbor*, Gary W. Gallagher and Carline E. Janney, eds., 84–88.

111. Rhea, *Cold Harbor*, 287, 318–82.

112. *OR*, vol. 36, I, 485; Steven E. Sodergren, *The Army of the Potomac in the Overland and Petersburg Campaigns: Union Soldiers and Trench Warfare, 1864–1865* (Louisiana State University Press, 2017), 32–35.

113. Purdy, "The Final," 24; Stevens, *Berdan's*, 446.

114. Board of Commissioners, *Minnesota*, 511; https://www.findagrave.com/memorial/3070096/james-e-millett.

115. https://www.findagrave.com/memorial/35048592/russell-s-harding; *Appendix D of the Annual Report*, 186.

116. Ayling, *Revised Register*, 979; Hastings, *Letters*, 220; Adjutant General, *Revised Roster*, 601; https://www.findagrave.com/memorial/52825076/almon-daniel-griffin.

117. Ford Diary, BHL.

118. Hastings, *Letters*, 216–17; Ripley, *Vermont Riflemen*, 179–81.

119. Meier, "I Told Him to Go On," 89–99; Sodergren, *The Army of the Potomac*, 38–62.

120. A. Wilson Greene, *A Campaign of Giants: The Battle for Petersburg, Volume One, From Crossing the James to the Crater* (Chapel Hill: University of North Carolina Press, 2018), 42–50; Brands, *The Man*, 305–306, 308–309; Sears, *Lincoln's Lieutenants*, 696–99; *OR*, vol. 36, III, 746; Gordon C. Rhea, "Grant's Disengagement from Cold Harbor," in *Cold Harbor*, Gallagher and Janney, eds., 176–81.

121. Adjutant General, *Revised Roster*, 599.

122. Abbott, *Third Vermont Company*, 85; Purdy, "The Final," 26; Walker, *History of the Second Army Corps*, 520–23; Ripley, *Vermont Riflemen*, 182.

123. Earley, *The Second United States Sharpshooters*, 184; Hastings, *Letters*, 220; Ford Diary, BHL.

124. Greene, *A Campaign of Giants*, 107–23; Sears, *Lincoln's Lieutenants*, 699–704.

125. Hastings, *Letters*, 221.

126. *OR*, vol. 40, I, 305–306, and II, 86–87; Jordan, *Winfield Scott Hancock*, 147.

127. *OR*, vol. 40, I, 410, and II, 90–93; Abbott, *Third Vermont Company*, 86.

128. Stevens, *Berdan's*, 451; Ford Diary, BHL; Adjutant General, *Record of Service*, 127–28; https://www.findagrave.com/memorial/3072868/james-heath.

129. Stevens, *Berdan's*, 451–52.

130. Some sources list June 17 as the date of Smith's mortal injury. I accepted the date listed in Stevens's book as well as the marksman's tombstone in Albany, New York. https://www.findagrave.com/memorial/193882685/thomas-smith; Adjutant General, *Revised Roster*, 602; https://www.findagrave.com/memorial/137073456/stephen-c-james.

131. https://www.findagrave.com/memorial/57366930/ira-sanborn-blake.

132. Greene, *A Campaign of Giants*, 132–33; Dunn, *Harvestfields*, 257–58; Eicher and Eicher, *High Commands*, 223.

133. *OR*, vol. 40, II, 117, 122; Davis, *Birney*, 229.

134. Abbott, *Third Vermont Company*, 86; Greene, *A Campaign of Giants*, 148–53.

135. Stevens, *Berdan's*, 453.

136. Civil War Muster Roll Abstracts, Box 373, NYSA; Stevens, *Berdan's*, 454–55; Hastings, *Letters*, 221; Ayling, *Revised Register*, 981.

137. Purdy, "The Final," 26–27; https://www.findagrave.com/memorial/11541512/charles-b-mead.

138. Colton Family Papers, VHS.

139. Greene, *A Campaign of Giants*, 178–80, 200–201.

140. Abbott, *Third Vermont Company*, 86; https://www.findagrave.com/memorial/255860579/george-riley-tower.

141. Ripley, *Vermont Riflemen*, 187; Ford Diary, BHL.

142. Robertson Jr., *Civil War Letters*, 443–47; Greene, *Campaign of Giants*, 185–86, 201–205.

143. Robertson Jr., *Civil War Letters*, 447–48; https://www.findagrave.com/memorial/2549117/silas-f-whitcomb; https://www.findagrave.com/memorial/34947769/henry-g-eldred; Surgeon General, *Medical and Surgical History*, vol. 2, part III, 298; Adjutant General, *Revised Roster*, 612.

144. https://www.findagrave.com/memorial/134277423/henry-a-colby; https://www.findagrave.com/memorial/87358944/charles-madison-colby.

145. Ripley, *Vermont Riflemen*, 188.

146. *Penn Yan Chronicle*, July 7, 1864.

147. Marden Letters, Rauner Library; https://www.findagrave.com/memorial/14403887/edward-thomas-rowell.

148. Davis, *Birney*, 231.

149. *OR*, vol. 40, II, 156–57.

150. *Dollar Weekly Mirror*, February 4, 1865.

151. Earley, *The Second United States Sharpshooters*, 186–87; Abbott, *Third Vermont Company*, 87.

152. *Dollar Weekly Mirror*, February 4, 1865.

153. Stevens, *Berdan's*, 469; Civil War Muster Roll Abstracts, Box 374, NYSA; Adjutant General, *Revised Roster*, 620.

154. Ripley, *Vermont Riflemen*, 190.

155. https://www.findagrave.com/memorial/8107889/gorham-plummer.

156. *OR*, vol. 40, I, 388.

157. Abbott, *Third Vermont Company*, 87–88; *Caledonian*, July 22, 1864.

158. Marden Letters, Rauner Library.

159. *OR*, vol. 40, I, 221–22, and II, 468; Ripley, *Vermont Riflemen*, 191.

160. Marden Letters, Rauner Library; Hastings, *Letters*, 228; Ford Diary, BHL.

161. Crandall Family Papers, Civil War Document Collection, USAHEC.

162. Abbott, *Third Vermont Company*, 89.

163. Hastings, *Letters*, 232.

164. Ford Diary, BHL; Stevens, *Berdan's*, 472.

165. Marden Letters, Rauner Library.

166. Wallace Papers, BHL; Ford Diary, BHL.

167. Smith Papers, Rubenstein Library.

168. Marden Letters, Rauner Library.

169. *Prescott Journal*, August 6, 1864.

170. Pinney Papers, VHS.

171. Stevens, *Berdan's*, 472–73; *OR*, vol. 40, I, 399.

172. Abbott, *Third Vermont Company*, 89–90; de Trobriand, *Four Years*, 606–607; Jordan, *Winfield Scott Hancock*, 152–54; Greene, *Campaign of Giants*, 400–409.

173. Ira Northup Letters, USAHEC.

174. *OR*, vol. 40, I, 400; Civil War Muster Roll Abstracts, Box 373, NYSA; https://www.findagrave.com/memorial/9592797/adam-friedmann.

175. *OR*, vol. 40, I, 410.

176. Wipperman, *Burnside's Boys*, 343–69.

177. Ford Diary, BHL.

178. Colton Family Papers, VHS; Adjutant General, *Revised Roster*, 602.

179. Hastings, *Letters*, 242–44.

180. Stevens, *Berdan's*, 480; Ford Diary, BHL; Abbott, *Third Vermont Company*, 90.

181. Crandall Family Papers, USAHEC.

182. *OR*, vol. 42, I, 217; Walker, *History of the Second Army Corps*, 568–69; de Trobriand, *Four Years*, 627–28.

183. Ford Diary, BHL; Stevens, *Berdan's*, 480–81; Ripley, *Vermont Riflemen*, 194.

184. Walker, *History of the Second Army Corps*, 570–80; de Trobriand, *Four Years*, 630–31; Robertson Jr., *Civil War Letters*, 481–85.

185. Hastings, *Letters*, 246; *Wood County Reporter*, September 8, 1864; *OR*, vol. 42, I, 387.

186. Ripley, *Vermont Riflemen*, 195.

187. *OR*, vol. 42, I, 379, 387; Estabrook, *Wisconsin Losses*, 202; *Wood County Reporter*, September 8, 1864; Adjutant General, *Record of Service*, 139.

188. Adjutant General, *Record of Service*, 156; Surgeon General, *Medical and Surgical History*, vol. 2, part III, 227; Ripley, *Vermont Riflemen*, 196.

189. Ford Diary, BHL; Stevens, *Berdan's*, 484–85; Hastings, *Letters*, 247.

190. Civil War Muster Roll Abstracts, Boxes 373–75, NYSA; Adjutant General, *Record of Service*, 120.

191. *Wood County Reporter*, September 8, 1864.

192. Ayling, *Revised Register*, 966; Adjutant General, *Revised Roster*, 600. Michigan Companies I and K in the 1st USSS had members transfer to the 5th Michigan Infantry in December.

193. Ripley, *Vermont Riflemen*, 195–98.

194. Company D Correspondence, MSA.

195. Sears, *Lincoln's Lieutenants*, 735–36; Walker, *History of the Second Army Corps*, 587–606.

196. Adjutant General, *Record of Service*, 110, 126.

197. *OR*, vol. 42, I, 613–14.

198. Hastings, *Letters*, 250.

199. Ford Diary, BHL.

200. Stevens, *Berdan's*, 493.

201. Charles D. Merriman Papers, Clements Library.

202. Adjutant General, *Record of Service*, 118; https://www.findagrave.com/memorial/22767985/john-h-thompson.

203. Abbott, *Third Vermont Company*, 90; Dunn, *Harvestfields*, 264.

204. *OR*, vol. 42, II, 761.

205. de Trobriand, *Four Years*, 640.

206. *OR*, vol. 42, II, 762.

207. de Trobriand, *Four Years*, 641.

208. Abbott, *Third Vermont Company*, 91.

209. *OR*, vol. 42, I, 343; de Trobriand, *Four Years*, 642.

210. *OR*, vol. 42, I, 343.

211. *OR*, vol. 42, II, 770. The provost marshal reported about twenty fewer prisoners.

212. Abbott, *Third Vermont Company*, 91; *Lansing State Republican*, September 21, 1864.

213. Northup Letters, USAHEC.

214. Henry Leslie Letters, USAHEC.

215. Ford Diary, BHL.

216. Abbott, *Third Vermont Company*, 91–92; for a splendid general discussion of the difficulty and intensity of campaigning around Petersburg, see, Sodergren, *The Army of the Potomac*, 63–112, 125–45.

217. White, *Civil War Diary*, 150; https://www.findagrave.com/memorial/9593192/asa-reed-bixby.

218. Abbott, *Third Vermont Company*, 92; Adjutant General, *Revised Roster*, 622; https://www.findagrave.com/memorial/212475314/allen-p-miller.

219. *OR*, vol. 42, I, 344 and III, 13; Wipperman, *Burnside's Boys*, 375–81; Bloodgood, *Personal Reminiscences*, 295.

220. de Trobriand, *Four Years*, 651; Ford Diary, BHL.

221. Stevens, *Berdan's*, 494; *OR*, vol. 42, I, 366; Abbott, *Third Vermont Company*, 92; de Trobriand, *Four Years*, 652; Ford Diary, BHL; Hastings, *Letters*, 260.

222. *OR*, vol. 42, I, 344–45, 367; Robertson Jr., *Civil War Letters*, 511–16.

223. *OR*, vol. 42, I, 367, 388; White, *Civil War Diary*, 258.

224. *OR*, vol. 42, III, 94–95; Abbott, *Third Vermont Company*, 93.

225. David Craft, *History of the One Hundred Forty-First Regiment, Pennsylvania Volunteers, 1862–1865* (Towanda, PA: Reporter-Journal Printing, 1885), 237; Benjamin M. Peck Diaries, Newman Library; https://www.findagrave.com/memorial/99201799/benjamin-mason-peck.

226. *OR*, vol. 42, III, 121; Ford Diary, BHL.

227. White, *Civil War Diary*, 152; https://www.findagrave.com/memorial/145334979/william-farnum-speed.

228. https://www.findagrave.com/memorial/39398519/d-m-bolster; Adjutant General, *Revised Roster*, 612.

229. Abbott, *Third Vermont Company*, 93; Adjutant General, *Revised Roster*, 622.

230. Surgeon General, *Medical and Surgical History*, part III, vol. 2, 581; https://www.findagrave.com/memorial/69527447/edwin-p-dutton.

231. Hastings, *Letters*, 264–65.

232. Pinney Papers, VHS.

233. Peck Diaries, Newman Library.

234. *Baraboo Weekly*, March 16, 1922.

235. Sears, *Lincoln's Lieutenants*, 742.

236. Ford Diary, BHL; *OR*, vol. 42, I, 346; de Trobriand, *Four Years*, 659–60.

237. Walker, *History of the Second Army Corps*, 616–17; de Trobriand, *Four Years*, 660.

238. Craft, *History of the One Hundred Forty-First Regiment*, 230–31.
239. *OR*, vol. 42, I, 388–89.
240. *OR*, vol. 42, I, 359.
241. *OR*, vol. 42, I, 389.
242. *OR*, vol. 42, I, 349; Alonzo Woodruff Medal of Honor File, NA; https://www.findagrave.com/memorial/141969432/john-ward-howard.
243. *OR*, vol. 42, I, 361; Adjutant General, *Record of Service*, 117.
244. Abbott, *Third Vermont Company*, 94; https://www.findagrave.com/memorial/70533816/edgar-allen-beach.
245. Adjutant General, *Revised Roster*, 601, 612, 620; https://www.findagrave.com/memorial/153636983/daniel-e-bessy; https://www.findagrave.com/memorial/121214522/william-h-churchill.
246. *OR*, vol. 42, I, 154–55.
247. Walker, *History of the Second Army Corps*, 631–36; Ford Diary, BHL.
248. Baker Collection, Clements Library.
249. Peck Diaries, Newman Library.
250. Adjutant General, *Revised Roster*, 603; https://www.findagrave.com/memorial/41174324/friend-a-weeks.
251. Ford Diary, BHL.
252. Adjutant General, *Revised Roster*, 614; Surgeon General, *Medical and Surgical History*, part II, 191; https://www.findagrave.com/memorial/3256988/azro-a-shippy.
253. Sears, *George B. McClellan*, 374–86.
254. Peck Diaries, Newman Library; Hastings, *Letters*, 268; *OR*, vol. 42, III, 560.
255. Adjutant General, *Revised Roster*, 614; https://www.findagrave.com/memorial/76516968/george-d-stowell. The state roster's date of Stowell's wound has been accepted. The other sources list the 10th as his date of death.
256. Stevens, *Berdan's*, 497–98.
257. Ford Diary, BHL; Abbott, *Third Vermont Company*, 96; Crandall Family Papers, USAHEC.
258. Adjutant General, *Revised Roster*, 602.
259. Company A Records, MNHS.
260. Board of Commissioners, *Minnesota*, 511; *Weekly Pioneer and Democrat*, November 4, 1864.
261. *OR*, vol. 42, III, 754. For a map of the line, see, https://www.loc.gov/resource/glva01.lva00192?r=0.205,0.304,0.632,0.401,0.
262. White, *Civil War Diary*, 155; Ford Diary, BHL; de Trobriand, *Four Years*, 688.
263. *OR*, vol. 42, III, 823–24; Abbott, *Third Vermont Company*, 96.
264. *OR*, vol. 42, I, 355; Ford Diary, BHL.
265. Robertson, Jr., *Civil War Letters*, 552; de Trobriand, *Four Years*, 688–89; *OR*, vol. 42, I, 355.
266. Abbott, *Third Vermont Company*, 96; *OR*, vol. 42, I, 355–56.
267. de Trobriand, *Four Years*, 691; *OR*, vol. 42, I, 356 and III, 960; Ford Diary, BHL.
268. *OR*, vol. 42, I, 357.
269. White, *Civil War Diary*, 155–56.

270. Adjutant General, *Record of Service*, 108; Adjutant General, *Revised Roster*, 620.
271. Abbott, *Third Vermont Company*, 97; Smith Papers, Rubenstein Library.
272. Ford Diary, BHL; Adjutant General, *Record of Service*, 139.
273. Peck Diaries, Newman Library; Abbott, *Third Vermont Company*, 97–98; *OR*, vol. 42, III, 1116.
274. *OR*, vol. 46, II, 6.
275. Smith Papers, Rubenstein Library.
276. Crandall Family Papers, USAHEC.
277. White, *Civil War Diary*, 276; Abbott, *Third Vermont Company*, 98.
278. *OR*, vol. 46, I, 223–24 and II, 367–68.
279. de Trobriand, *Four Years*, 695; *OR*, vol. 46, I, 224.
280. White, *Civil War Diary*, 159; https://www.findagrave.com/memorial/216925063/c-frederic-meyer; https://www.findagrave.com/cemetery/103053/famous-memorials.
281. Abbott, *Third Vermont Company*, 98.
282. *OR*, vol. 46, I, 227–28; Craft, *History of the One Hundred Forty-First Regiment*, 235–36.
283. Sears, *Lincoln's Lieutenants*, 748; Bloodgood, *Personal Reminiscences*, 304–306.
284. Earley, *The Second United States Sharpshooters*, 205.
285. Company D Correspondence, MSA; Leslie Letters, USAHEC.
286. Abbott, *Third Vermont Company*, 99.
287. *OR*, vol. 46, II, 568.

Conclusion

1. *Rutland Weekly Herald*, March 2, 1865.
2. Theodore Ayrault Dodge, *Napoleon: A History of the Art of War, From the Beginning of the Peninsular War to the End of the Russian Campaign*, vol. 3 (Boston: Houghton Mifflin, 1907), 48–50, 148–49, 362–63.
3. Adjutant General, *Revised Roster*, 620; https://www.findagrave.com/memorial/120765773/curtis-abbott.
4. Meier, *Memoirs of a Swiss Officer*, 18–19.
5. Baker Collection and Scrapbook, Clements Library; https://www.findagrave.com/memorial/19279253/james-harvey-baker/photo.
6. Whitman, "Lorenzo Barber," 18; Stevens, *Berdan's*, 540.
7. Adjutant General, *Record of Service*, 108; https://www.findagrave.com/memorial/121166241/llewellyn-james-blanchard.
8. Stevens, *Berdan's*, 531; https://www.findagrave.com/memorial/83912952/charles-jay-buchanan.
9. https://www.findagrave.com/memorial/13194538/brigham-wallace-buswell.
10. Calef Correspondence, Rauner Library; https://www.findagrave.com/memorial/101461071/benjamin-shreve-calef.
11. Surgeon General, *Medical and Surgical History*, part III, vol. 2, 620; https://www.findagrave.com/memorial/91348807/jonathan-e-chase.
12. Dickey Papers, MNHS; https://www.findagrave.com/memorial/80184100/joseph-cortez-dickey.

13. *Indianapolis Journal*, February 3, 1904; https://www.findagrave.com/memorial/37245526/owen-evans.

14. https://www.findagrave.com/memorial/100700222/warren-h-fletcher.

15. Wipperman, *Burnside's Boys*, 402; https://www.findagrave.com/memorial/3527812/benjamin-franklin-giddings.

16. Hastings, *Letters*, 269–90; https://www.findagrave.com/memorial/131366966/william-b-greene.

17. *Shasta Courier*, July 9, 1864; Stevens, *Berdan's*, 537; https://www.findagrave.com/memorial/3529556/truman-head.

18. Stevens, *Berdan's*, 467–68; https://www.findagrave.com/memorial/233104426/john-e-hetherington.

19. https://www.findagrave.com/memorial/151839666/silas-wright-howard.

20. https://www.findagrave.com/memorial/19729135/john-a-huff; Rhea, *The Battles*, 208–209, 390.

21. William C. Kent Letter, Box 18, Folder 21, Civil War Document Collection, USAHEC; https://www.findagrave.com/memorial/15856297/william-clark-kent.

22. Lewis Papers, WHS; https://www.findagrave.com/memorial/80951870/george-h-lewis.

23. George A. Marden, *Philosophy the Guide of Life, A Poem before Phi Beta Kappa Society, Dartmouth, June 23, 1875*, 6; https://www.findagrave.com/memorial/14403761/george-augustus-marden.

24. Dalton, *Soldiers in Green*, 290–91; https://www.findagrave.com/memorial/237104612/james-m-matthews.

25. *Boston Evening Transcript*, October 4, 1893; https://www.findagrave.com/memorial/179267526/jacob-e-mcclure.

26. https://www.findagrave.com/memorial/3535656/frederick-mears.

27. Monahan Diaries, VSA; *Barre Daily Times*, October 19, 1910; https://www.findagrave.com/memorial/96684581/john-j-monahan.

28. *Middlebury Register*, July 18, 1913; *West Randolph Herald and News*, December 27, 1895.

29. Peet, *Personal Experiences*, 63–107; *New York Times*, January 27, 1925; https://www.findagrave.com/memorial/58387244/frederick-tomlinson-peet.

30. Stevens, *Berdan's*, 534; https://www.findagrave.com/memorial/42684261/francis-peteler.

31. https://www.findagrave.com/memorial/177834639/henry-albertson_van_zo-post; *New York Times*, January 27, 1914.

32. Eicher and Eicher, *High Commands*, 455; Adjutant General, *Revised Roster*, 600; *Burlington Free Press*, December 28, 1883; Stevens, *Berdan's*, 528–29; Ripley Papers, Box 2, Rubenstein Library; https://www.findagrave.com/memorial/22689/william-young_warren-ripley.

33. https://www.findagrave.com/memorial/77150834/joseph-henry-rolfe.

34. Adjutant General, *Record of Service*, 145; https://www.findagrave.com/memorial/8313535/albert-james-sisson.

35. Smith Papers, Rubenstein Library; *Vermont Phoenix*, June 9, 1899; https://www.findagrave.com/memorial/114504090/walter-wallace-smith.

36. *Daily Milwaukee News*, May 7, 1865; Stevens, *Berdan's*, 542; https://www.findagrave.com/memorial/71570919/charles-augustus-stevens.

37. Stevens, *Berdan's*, 535; *Herald and News*, May 30, 1895; *Vermont Watchman*, December 18, 1895; https://www.findagrave.com/memorial/13245227/homer-richard-stoughton.

38. https://www.findagrave.com/memorial/99582344/william-wesley-sweet.

39. *Washington Herald*, January 13 and July 20, 1909; Ripley Papers, Box 2, Rubenstein Library; Stevens, *Berdan's*, 530; https://www.findagrave.com/memorial/18813977/richard-woolsey-tyler.

40. *Shasta Courier*, April 20, 1872.

41. White, *Civil War Diary*, 161, 166; https://www.findagrave.com/memorial/55476000/wyman-s-white.

42. Stevens, *Berdan's*, 529; https://www.findagrave.com/memorial/33679266/john-wilson.

Bibliography

Manuscripts

Alabama Department of Archives and History, Montgomery, Alabama

4th Alabama Regimental File
8th Alabama Regimental File
9th Alabama Regimental File

Antietam National Battlefield Library, Sharpsburg, Maryland

1st USSS Folder
10th Louisiana Folder
2nd Louisiana Folder
2nd USSS Folder
21st Virginia Regimental Folder
33rd Virginia Regimental Folder
7th Wisconsin Regimental Folder
Edwin Chadwick Letter
Parmelee Family Letters

Bentley Historical Library, University of Michigan, Ann Arbor, Michigan

Simon Danner Letters
Charles W. Ford Diary
George Lockley Diary
Jacob Preston Papers
Festus Spencer Letter
Elmer Wallace Papers

William L. Clements Library, University of Michigan, Ann Arbor, Michigan

James H. Baker Collection and Scrapbook
Gardner B. Clark Papers
Richard B. and Agnes Irwin Family Correspondence
Charles D. Merriman Papers

Library of Congress, Washington, D.C.
George Brinton McClellan Papers

Library of Virginia, Richmond, Virginia
Isaac Bevier Letter (Call # 45071)
Isaac Bevier Letter (Call #45221)
A. Cassius Cross Letter
James Lawson Kemper Letter
Charles P. Shepard Letters (Call #45503)
Charles Shepard Letter (Call#45308)

Maine State Archives, Augusta, Maine
Company D Regimental Correspondence

McCracken Research Library, Buffalo Bill Center of The West, Cody, Wyoming
Roy Marcot Collection, MS 437

Minnesota Historical Society, St. Paul, Minnesota
Josiah B. Chaney and Family Papers
Company A Records
Joseph C. Dickey and Family Papers
G. Merrill Dwelle and Family Papers
Owen Evans Letters

Missouri Historical Society, St. Louis, Missouri
Lillie Devereux Blake Papers

Mitchell Special Collections Library, Bowdoin College, Brunswick, Maine
Elisha Coan Collection
Edwin Emery diaries

National Archives and Records Administration, Washington, D.C.
1st U.S. Sharpshooters, Letters Sent and Order Book
1st U.S. Sharpshooters, Order Book and Property Book
2nd U.S. Sharpshooters, Morning Reports, Companies B, C, F, and G
2nd U.S. Sharpshooters, Regimental Letter and Order Book
Hiram Berdan, Consolidated Military Service Record
John W. Dewey Pension File
Cassius Peck Medal of Honor File
John W. E. Robinson, Application for Correcting Military Record
Christine Sarah Trepp, Approved Pension Application File (No. WC68334)
Volunteer Service Files, VS File #V42-VS-1862, Stack Area: 9W3: 18/22/6, Box #147

Edmund Weston Jr. Consolidated Military Service Record
Alonzo Woodruff Medal of Honor File

Newman Library, Special Collections, Virginia Tech University, Blacksburg, Virginia
Benjamin M. Peck Diaries

New York State Archives, Albany, New York
Civil War Muster Roll Abstracts, Boxes 373-75

Pennsylvania State Archives, Harrisburg, Pennsylvania
Company C Records, RG-19.11, Carton 152

Rauner Special Collections Library, Dartmouth College, Hanover, New Hampshire
Antietam Collection
Benjamin Calef Correspondence
George A. Marden Letters
George A. Marden, *Philosophy the Guide of Life, A Poem before Phi Beta Kappa Society, Dartmouth, June 23, 1875*

David M. Rubenstein Rare Book and Manuscript Library, Duke University, Durham, North Carolina
Anna B. Campbell Papers
D. H. Hamilton, *History of Company M, First Texas Volunteer Infantry*
William Y. W. Ripley Papers
Walter Wallace Smith Papers
Darius Starr Papers

United States Army Heritage and Education Center, Carlisle, Pennsylvania
Amos Abbott Diary, Box 1: Folder 4, Civil War Document Collection
Joseph Barton Letter
Henry L. Bedell Diary, Box 7: Folder 9, Civil War Document Collection
Berdan Letter, Box 9: Folder 5, Civil War Document Collection
Martin V. Bronson Letter, Civil War Document Collection
J. H. Carr Letter
Connington Letters, Box 1, Rudolph Haerle Collection
Crandall Family Papers, Civil War Document Collection
Henry Leslie Letters
James Kent Letter, Civil War Document Collection
William C. Kent Letter, Civil War Document Collection
Mears Family Collection

Ira Northup Letters
John Robinson Letter, Attachment 3, Donald H. Couchman Collection
Wiley Sword Papers
Russell C. White, ed., *The Civil War Diary of Wyman S. White*

Vermont Historical Society, Barre, Vermont
Jacob Bailey Letter
Thomas H. Brown Civil War Letters
Colton Family Papers
Benjamin Giddings Papers
William Oates Letter to Homer Stoughton, November 22, 1888
Papers of Eveline Mary Pinney
Homer Stoughton Letter

Vermont State Archives and Records Administration, Middlesex, Vermont
Curtis Abbott, *The Third Vermont Company of the United States Sharpshooters*
John Monahan Diaries

Wisconsin Historical Society, Madison, Wisconsin
George Lewis Papers
Byron J. Smith Civil War Letters

Government Publications

Adjutant General. *Record of Service of Michigan Volunteers in the Civil War, 1861–1865*, vol. 44 (Kalamazoo: Ihling Bros & Everard, 1900).

Adjutant General. *Revised Roster of Vermont Volunteers and Lists of Vermonters Who Served in the Army and Navy of the United States during the War of the Rebellion, 1861–66* (Montpelier: Watchman Publishing, 1892).

Annual Report of the Adjutant General of the State of Maine for the Year Ending December 31, 1861 (Augusta: Stevens & Sayward, 1862).

Annual Report of the Adjutant General of the State of Maine for the Year Ending December 31, 1862 (Augusta: Stevens & Sayward, 1863).

Annual Report of the Adjutant General of the State of Maine for the Year Ending December 31, 1863 (Augusta: Stevens & Sayward, 1863).

Appendix D of the Annual Report of the Adjutant General of the State of Maine for the Years 1864 and 1865 (Augusta: Stevens and Sayward, 1866).

Ayling, Augustus D. *Revised Register of the Soldiers and Sailors of New Hampshire in the War of the Rebellion, 1861–1866* (Concord: Ira C. Evans, 1895).

Surgeon General. *The Medical and Surgical History of the War of the Rebellion*, 6 vols. (Washington, D.C.: Government Printing Office, 1879).

U.S. War Department. *The War of the Rebellion: A Compilation of the Official Records of the Union and Confederate Armies*, 128 vols. (Washington, D.C.: Government Printing Office, 1880–1901).

Newspapers

Albany Evening Journal
Alleghenian
Baraboo Weekly
Barre Daily Times
Bellows Falls Times
Beloit Gazette
Boston Evening Transcript
Burlington Free Press
Caledonian
Cherry Valley Gazette
Daily Milwaukee News
Dollar Weekly Mirror
Exeter News-Letter
Green Mountain Freeman
Herald and News
Hillsdale Standard
Indianapolis Journal
Jeffersonian
Kenosha Telegraph
Lamoille Newsdealer
Lansing State Republican
Livingston County Daily Press and Argus
Maine Farmer
Manchester Journal
Middlebury Register
Mineral Point Weekly Tribune
New York Dispatch
New York Herald
New York Sun
New York Times
New York Tribune
Orleans Independent Standard
Oswego Commercial Times
Penn Yan Chronicle
Philadelphia Public Ledger
Portland Daily Press
Portsmouth Journal of Literature and Politics
Potter County Journal
Prescott Journal
Raftman's Journal
Rutland Herald
Shasta Courier
Vermont Phoenix

Vermont Watchman
Washington Herald
Weekly Pioneer and Democrat
West Randolph Herald and News
Wisconsin Daily Patriot
Wood County Reporter

Websites

chroniclingamerica.loc.gov
digitalcommons.winthrop.edu/manuscriptcollection_findingaids/610
digitalmaine.com
Michiganology.org
https: //www.nps.gov/civilwar/soldiers-and-sailors-database.htm
npshistory.com/series/symposia/gettysburg_seminars
www.ancestry.com
www.cmohs.org
www.gordonthorsbycivilwarnotes.com/
www.hillsdalehistoricalsociety.org
www.findagrave.com
www.loc.gov/resource/glva01.lva00192?r=0.205,0.304,0.632,0.401,0

Books, Articles, and Dissertation

Agassiz, George R., ed. *Meade's Headquarters, 1863–1865: Letters of Colonel Theodore Lyman from the Wilderness to Appomattox* (Boston: Massachusetts Historical Society, 1922).

Allen, L. Y. "Berdan Sharpshooters." *National Tribune*, August 12, 1886.

———. "Berdan's Sharpshooters." *National Tribune*, December 16, 1886.

Arnold, Thomas. *History of Rome: From the End of the First to the End of the Second Punic War*, vol. 3 (London: Gilbert and Rivington, 1846).

Barlow, Francis C. "Capture of the Salient, May 12, 1864." In *The Wilderness Campaign, May-June 1864, Papers of the Military Historical Society of Massachusetts*, vol. 4 (Boston: Military Historical Society of Massachusetts, 1905).

Barnes, Edward L. "The 95th New York." *National Tribune*, January 7, 1886.

Barrett, O. S. *Reminiscences, Incidents, Battles, Marches and Camp Life of the Old 4th Michigan Infantry in the War of the Rebellion, 1861 to 1864* (Detroit: W. S. Ostler, 1888).

Beatie, Russel H. *Army of the Potomac: McClellan's First Campaign, March–May 1862* (New York: Savas Beatie, 2007).

Benedict, George G. *Vermont in the Civil War: A History of the Part Taken by the Vermont Soldiers and Sailors in the War for the Union, 1861–5*, 2 vols. (Burlington: Free Press Association, 1886).

Bennett, Mick. *The Story of the Rifle* (London: Cobbett Publishing, 1945).

Berdan, Hiram. "The Sharpshooters." *National Tribune*, October 14, 1886.

Bloodgood, J. D. *Personal Reminiscences of the War* (New York: Hunt & Eaton, 1893).

Board of Commissioners. *Minnesota in the Civil and Indian Wars, 1861–1865* (St. Paul: Pioneer Press, 1890).

Bohannon, Keith S. "Breastworks Are Good Things to Have on Battlefields: Confederate Engineering Operations and Field Fortifications in the Overland Campaign." In *Cold Harbor to the Crater: The End of the Overland Campaign*, Gary W. Gallagher and Caroline E. Janney, eds. (Chapel Hill: University of North Carolina Press, 2015), 109–37.

Botts, John Minor. *The Great Rebellion: Its Secret History, Rise, Progress, and Disastrous Failure* (New York: Harper & Brothers, 1866).

Bowden, Scott, and Bill Ward. *Last Chance for Victory: Robert E. Lee and the Gettysburg Campaign* (El Dorado Hills: Savas Publishing Company, 2001).

Bradwell, I. G. "Spotsylvania May 12, 13, 1864." *Confederate Veteran*, vol. 28, 1920, 102–103.

Brands, H. W. *The Man Who Saved the Union: Ulysses Grant in War and Peace* (New York: Anchor Books, 2013).

Brooks, Thomas. *Lee's Foreign Legion: A History of the 10th Louisiana Infantry* (Gravenhurst, Ontario: T. W. Brooks, 1995).

Burton, Brian K. *Extraordinary Circumstances: The Seven Days Battles* (Bloomington: Indiana University Press, 2001).

Busey, John W., and David G. Martin, *Regimental Strengths and Losses at Gettysburg*, Fourth Edition (Hightstown, NJ: Longstreet House, 2005).

Buswell, Brigham. "'Blood and Feathered' at Malvern Hill." *Civil War Times*, April 1996, 22–32, 76–77.

———. "A Sharpshooter's Seven Days." *Civil War Times*, February 1996, 20–28.

Caldwell, James Fitz James. *The History of a Brigade of South Carolinians* (Philadelphia: King & Baird, 1866).

Clark, Walter, ed. *Histories of the Several Regiments and Battalions from North Carolina in the Great War, 1861–'65*, 5 vols. (Raleigh: E. M. Uzzell, 1901).

Clemens, Tom, ed. "A Brigade Commander's First Fight: The Letters of Colonel Walter Phelps, Jr. during the Maryland Campaign." *Civil War Regiments: A Journal of the American Civil War* 5, no. 3 (1997): 59–72.

Coco, Gregory A. *Killed in Action: Eyewitness Accounts of the Last Moments of 100 Union Soldiers Who Died at Gettysburg* (Gettysburg: Thomas Publications, 1992).

Coddington, Edwin B. *The Gettysburg Campaign: A Study in Command* (New York: Touchstone, 1997).

Cole, A. V. "118th PA at Shepardstown." *National Tribune*, July 14, 1910.

Cooling, Benjamin Franklin. *Counter-Thrust: From the Peninsula to the Antietam* (Lincoln: University of Nebraska Press, 2007).

Cooper, William J., Jr. *Jefferson Davis, American* (New York: Vintage Books, 2001).

Coulter, E. Morton, ed. "From Spotsylvania Courthouse to Andersonville: A Diary of Darius Starr." *Georgia Historical Quarterly* 41, no. 2 (June 1957): 176–90.

Cozzens, Peter. *General John Pope: A Life for the Nation* (Urbana: University of Illinois Press, 2000).

Craft, David. *History of the One Hundred Forty-First Regiment, Pennsylvania Volunteers, 1862–1865* (Towanda, PA: Reporter-Journal Printing, 1885).

Craig, Joel. "Proposed Uniform for the 1st U.S. Sharpshooters, 1861." *Military Collector and Historian* (Summer 2001): 61.

Dalton, Peter, ed. *Soldiers in Green: Civil War Diaries of James Mero Matthews, 2nd U.S. Sharpshooters* (Richardson's Civil War Roundtable, 2002).

Davis, Oliver. *Life of David Bell Birney, Major General of United States Volunteers* (Philadelphia: King & Baird, 1867).

de Trobriand, Regis. *Four Years with the Army of the Potomac.* Translated by George K. Dauchy (Boston: Ticknor and Company, 1889).

Dedication of the Monument to the Four New York Companies (A, B, D, and H) of the First Regiment of United States Sharpshooters (Berdan's) on the Battlefield of Gettysburg, July 2, 1889 (Albany, NY: Weed and Parsons, 1889).

Desjardin, Thomas A. *Stand Firm Ye Boys from Maine: The 20th Maine and the Gettysburg Campaign* (New York: Oxford University Press, 1995).

Dodge, Theodore Ayrault. *Napoleon: A History of the Art of War, From the Beginning of the Peninsular War to the End of the Russian Campaign*, vol. 3 (Boston: Houghton Mifflin Company, 1907).

Dougan, Andy. *One Shot, One Kill: A History of the Sniper* (London: William Collins, 2016).

Downs, David B. "'His Left Was Worth a Glance': Meade and the Union Left on July 2, 1863." *Gettysburg Magazine*, no. 7, July 1992, 29–40.

Dunn, Craig L. *Harvestfields of Death: The Twentieth Indiana Volunteers of Gettysburg* (Carmel: Guild Press of Indiana, 1999).

E. S. A., ed. *Letters of Richard Tylden Auchmuty, Fifth Corps, Army of the Potomac* (Privately printed, n. d.).

Earley, Gerald L. *The Second United States Sharpshooters in the Civil War: A History and Roster* (Jefferson, NC: McFarland & Company, 2009).

Eicher, John H., and David J. Eicher. *Civil War High Commands* (Stanford, CA: Stanford University Press, 2001).

Elmore, Thomas L. "A Meteorological and Astronomical Chronology of the Gettysburg Campaign." *Gettysburg Magazine*, no. 13, July 1995, 7–21.

Elting, Lt. Col. John. "The United States Sharpshooters." *Military Collector and Historian* (September 1954): 57–61.

Estabrook, Charles E. ed. *Wisconsin Losses in the Civil War* (Madison: Democrat Printing, 1915).

Fleming, George Thornton, ed. *Life and Letters of Alexander Hays* (Pittsburgh, PA: n.p., 1919).

Fox, William F. *Regimental Losses in the American Civil War, 1861–1865* (Albany, NY: Brandow Printing Company, 1889).

Fuller, H. S. "Narrowly Escaped Prison." *Confederate Veteran*, November 1918, 473.

Furgurson, Ernest B. *Chancellorsville 1863: The Souls of the Brave* (New York: Vintage Books, 1993).

Gottfried, Bradley M., ed. *Brigades of Antietam: The Union and Confederate Brigades during the 1862 Maryland Campaign* (Sharpsburg, MD: Antietam Institute, 2021).

———. *The Maps of Antietam: An Atlas of the Antietam (Sharpsburg) Campaign, Including the Battle of South Mountain, September 2–20, 1862* (El Dorado Hills: Savas Beatie, 2013).

———. *The Maps of Fredericksburg: An Atlas of the Fredericksburg Campaign, Including All Cavalry Operations, September 18, 1862–January 22, 1863* (El Dorado Hills: Savas Beatie, 2018).

———. *The Maps of Gettysburg* (El Dorado Hills: Savas Beatie, 2007).

Grant, L. A. "In the Wilderness." *National Tribune*, January 28, 1897.

Greene, A. Wilson. *A Campaign of Giants: The Battle for Petersburg. From Crossing the James to the Crater*, vol. 1 (Chapel Hill: University of North Carolina Press, 2018).

Greezicki, Roger J. "Humbugging the Historian: A Reappraisal of Longstreet at Gettysburg." *Gettysburg Magazine*, no. 6, January 1992, 62–67.

Griswold, J. W. "Second Bull Run." *National Tribune*, May 31, 1894.

Grossman, Dave. *On Killing: The Psychological Cost of Learning to Kill in War and Society* (New York: Back Bay Books, 2009).

Harrison, Kathleen R. Georg. "'Our Principal Loss Was in This Place': Action at the Slaughter Pen and at the South End of Houck's Ridge." *Gettysburg Magazine*, no. 1, July 1989, 45–69.

Harsh, Joseph L. *Taken at the Flood: Robert E. Lee and Confederate Strategy in the Maryland Campaign of 1862* (Kent, OH: Kent State University Press, 1999).

Hartwig, D. Scott. *I Dread the Thought of the Place: The Battle of Antietam and the End of the Maryland Campaign* (Baltimore: Johns Hopkins University Press, 2023).

———. *To Antietam Creek: The Maryland Campaign of September 1862* (Baltimore: Johns Hopkins University Press, 2012).

Hastings, William H., ed. *Letters from a Sharpshooter: The Civil War Letters of Private William B. Greene, Co. G, 2nd United States Sharpshooters (Berdan's), Army of the Potomac* (Belleville, WI: Historic Publications, 1993).

Hebert, Walter H. *Fighting Joe Hooker* (Lincoln: University of Nebraska Press, 1999).

Hennessy, John J. "I Dread the Spring: The Army of the Potomac Prepares for the Overland Campaign." In *The Wilderness Campaign*, Gary W. Gallagher, ed. (Chapel Hill: University of North Carolina Press, 1997), 66–105.

———. *Return to Bull Run: The Campaign and Battle of Second Manassas* (New York: Simon & Schuster, 1993).

Herdegen, Lance J. *The Iron Brigade in Civil War and Memory: The Black Hats from Bull Run to Appomattox and Thereafter* (El Dorado Hills: Savas Beatie, 2012).

Hess, Earl J. *Trench Warfare Under Grant and Lee: Field Fortifications in the Overland Campaign* (Chapel Hill: University of North Carolina Press, 2007).

Hood, John Bell. *Advance and Retreat: Personal Experiences in the United States and Confederate States Armies* (New Orleans: G. T. Beauregard, 1880).

Houghton, Edwin B. *The Campaigns of the Seventeenth Maine* (Portland: Short & Loring, 1866).

Houghton, William. "A Staff Officer's Recollection of the Salient Angle." *National Tribune*, September 11, 1890.

Jermann, Donald R. *Antietam: The Lost Order* (Gretna, LA: Pelican Publishing, 2006).

Jordan, Brian Matthew. *Unholy Sabbath: The Battle of South Mountain in History and Memory* (New York: Savas Beatie, 2012).

Jordan, David M. *Winfield Scott Hancock: A Soldier's Life* (Bloomington: Indiana University Press, 1996).

Katta, Kenneth. "Conflicts in Command: An Analysis of the Leadership in the Berdan Sharpshooters in the Civil War." *Military Collector and Historian* (Summer 2001): 50–61.

Keneally, Thomas. *American Scoundrel: The Life of the Notorious Civil War General Dan Sickles* (New York: Doubleday, 2002).

Kent, William. "Sharpshooting with Berdan." *Civil War Times Illustrated*, May 1976, 4–9, 42–48.

———. "A Wilderness Memory." *Civil War Times Illustrated*, March 1989, 34, 36.

Kreiser, Lawrence A. *Defeating Lee: A History of the Second Corps, Army of the Potomac* (Bloomington: Indiana University Press, 2011).

Krick, Robert E. L. "Prelude to the Seven Days: The Battle of Slash Church (Hanover Court House), May 27, 1862." In *The Peninsula Campaign of 1862: Yorktown to the Seven Days*, William J. Miller, ed. (Campbell, CA: Savas Woodbury, 1997), 1–38.

Krick, Robert K. "An Insurmountable Barrier Between the Army and Ruin." In *The Spotsylvania Campaign*, Gary W. Gallagher, ed. (Chapel Hill: University of North Carolina Press, 1998).

Kurtz, Henry I. "Berdan's Sharpshooters Most Effective Union Brigade?" *Civil War Times*, February 1863, 14–19.

Ladd, David L., and Audrey J. Ladd, eds. *The Bachelder Papers: Gettysburg in Their Own Words*, 3 vols. (Dayton: Morningside House, 1994).

Laney, Daniel M. "Wasted Gallantry: Hood's Texas Brigade at Gettysburg." *Gettysburg Magazine*, no. 16, January 1997, 27–45.

Lash, Gary G. "A Pathetic Story: The 141st Pennsylvania (Graham's Brigade) at Gettysburg." *Gettysburg Magazine*, no. 14, January 1996, 77–101.

Lash, Gary. "The March of the 124th New York to Gettysburg." *Gettysburg Magazine*, July 1993, 5–16.

Law, E. M. "The Struggle for 'Round Top,'" *Battles and Leaders of the Civil War*, vol. 3 (New York: Century Co., 1888).

Lewis, George. *The History of Battery E, First Regiment Rhode Island Light Artillery* (Providence: Snow & Farnham, 1892).

Longstreet, James. *From Manassas to Appomattox* (New York: Da Capo Press, 1992).

Love, William DeLoss. *Wisconsin in the War of the Rebellion* (Chicago: Church and Goodman, 1866).

Luzader, John F. *Saratoga: A Military History of the Decisive Campaign of the American Revolution* (New York: Savas Beatie, 2008).

Marcot, Roy M. *U.S. Sharpshooters: Berdan's Civil War Elite* (Mechanicsburg, PA: Stackpole Books, 2007).

Marcot, Roy. "Berdan's Sharpshooters at Gettysburg." *Gettysburg Magazine*, no. 1, July 1989, 35–40.

———. *Civil War Chief of Sharpshooters Hiram Berdan: Military Commander and Firearms Inventor* (Irvine, CA: Northwood Heritage Press, 1989).

Marvel, William. *Radical Sacrifice: The Rise and Ruin of Fitz John Porter* (Chapel Hill: University of North Carolina Press, 2021).

McDaid, William Kelsey. *"Four Years of Arduous Service": The History of the Branch-Lane Brigade in the Civil War*, PhD Dissertation, Michigan State University, 1987.

McGrath, Thomas A. *Shepherdstown: Last Clash of the Antietam Campaign, September 19–20, 1862* (Lynchburg, VA: Schroeder Publications, 2012).

Meade, George, ed. *The Life and Letters of George Gordon Meade*, vol. II (New York: Charles Scribner's Sons, 1913).

Meier, Heinz K., ed. *Memoirs of a Swiss Officer in the American Civil War* (Bern, Switzerland: Herbert Lang, 1972).

Meier, Kathryn Shively. "I Told Him to Go On: Enduring Cold Harbor." In *Cold Harbor to the Crater: The End of the Overland Campaign*, Gary W. Gallagher and Caroline E. Janney, eds. (Chapel Hill: University of North Carolina Press, 2015), 73–108.

Miller, William J. "I Only Wait for the River: McClellan and His Engineers on the Chickahominy." In *The Richmond Campaign of 1862: The Peninsula and the Seven Days* Gary W. Gallagher, ed. (Chapel Hill: University of North Carolina Press, 2000).

Miner, Joseph. "The Way in Which the Rebels Were Surprised." *National Tribune*, March 18, 1886.

Moore, J. B. "Sharpsburg." *Southern Historical Society Papers* 27 (1899): 210–19.

Morton, T. C. "Incidents of the Skirmish at Totopotomoy Creek, Hanover County, Virginia, May 30, 1864." *Southern Historical Society Papers* 16 (1888): 47–56.

Naiswald, L. VanLoan. *Grape and Canister: The Story of the Field Artillery of the Army of the Potomac, 1861–1865* (Mechanicsburg, PA: Stackpole Books, 1999).

Nash, Eugene Arus. *A History of the Forty-Fourth Regiment New York Volunteer Infantry in the Civil War, 1861–1865* (Chicago: R. R. Donnelley & Sons, 1911).

New York Monuments Commission. *Final Report on the Battlefield of Gettysburg*, vol. 3 (Albany, NY: J. B. Lyon, 1900).

Noe, Kenneth W. *The Howling Storm: Weather, Climate, and the American Civil War* (Baton Rouge: Louisiana State University Press, 2020).

Noyes, George F. *The Bivouac and the Battlefield, or Campaign Sketches in Virginia and Maryland* (New York: Harper & Brothers, 1863).

Oates, William C. "Gettysburg—The Battle on the Right." *Southern Historical Society Papers* 5, no. 4 (October 1878): 172–82.

———. *The War Between the Union and the Confederacy and Its Lost Opportunities* (New York: Neale Publishing Company, 1905).

Orr, Tim. "'On Such Slender Threads Does the Fate of Nations Depend': The Second United States Sharpshooters Defend the Union Left on July Second." 11th Biennial Gettysburg National Military Park Scholarly Seminar, Gettysburg, PA, April 2006.

Peet, Frederick Tomlinson. *Civil War Letters and Documents* (Newport, NY: Privately printed, 1917).

———. *Personal Experiences in the Civil War* (New York: Privately printed, 1905).

Penny, Morris M., and J. Gary Laine. *Struggle for the Round Tops: Law's Alabama Brigade at the Battle of Gettysburg* (Shippensburg, PA: Burd Street Press, 1999).

Perry, W. F. "The Devil's Den." *Confederate Veteran* 9 (1901): 161–63.

Pfanz, Harry W. *Gettysburg: The Second Day* (Chapel Hill: University of North Carolina Press, 1987).

Pierro, Joseph, ed. *The Maryland Campaign of September 1862: Ezra A. Carman's Definitive Study of the Union and Confederate Armies at Antietam* (New York: Routledge, 2008).

Pindell, Richard. "The Most Dangerous Set of Men." *Civil War Times Illustrated* (July/August 1993): 42–53.

Plaster, John L. *The History of Sniping and Sharpshooting* (Boulder, CO: Paladin Press, 2008).

Priest, John Michael. *Before Antietam: The Battle for South Mountain* (Shippensburg, PA: White Mane Publishing, 1992).

Proctor, W. H. "Stonewall Jackson and Berdan's Sharpshooters." *National Tribune*, May 8, 1884.

Pula, James S. *Under the Crescent Moon with the XI Corps in the Civil War: From the Defenses of Washington to Chancellorsville, 1862–1863*, vol. 1 (Savas Beatie, 2017).

Pullen, John J. "Effects of Marksmanship: A Lesson from Gettysburg." *Gettysburg Magazine*, no. 2, January 1990, 55–60.

Purdy, Elaine G., ed. "The Final Civil War Diary of Charles B. Mead of Company F, First U.S. Sharpshooters." *Rutland Historical Society Quarterly* 32, no. 1 (2002): 1–32.

Purdy, Elaine, ed. "The Civil War Diary of Charles B. Mead." *Rutland Historical Society Quarterly* 28, no. 1 (1998): 1–19.

Quiner, E. B. *E. B. Quiner Papers: Correspondence of the Wisconsin Volunteers, 1861–1865* (Madison: State Historical Society of Wisconsin).

———. *Military History of Wisconsin: A Record of the Civil and Military Patriotism of the State in the War for the Union* (Chicago: Clark & Co., 1866).

Rable, George C. *Fredericksburg! Fredericksburg!* (Chapel Hill: University of North Carolina Press, 2002).

Rafuse, Ethan. *McClellan's War: The Failure of Moderation in the Struggle for the Union* (Bloomington: Indiana University Press, 2005).

Reagan, James W. "More about the Fight at Brooks Crossroads." *Confederate Veteran* 18 (1910): 228–30.

Reardon, Carol. "The Other Grant: Lewis A. Grant and the Vermont Brigade in the Battle of the Wilderness." In *The Wilderness Campaign*, Gary W. Gallagher, ed. (Chapel Hill: University of North Carolina Press, 1997), 201–35.

Reed, Thomas. *The Original Iron Brigade* (Madison, NJ: Fairleigh Dickinson University Press, 2011).

Rhea, Gordon C. "Grant's Disengagement from Cold Harbor." In *Cold Harbor to the Crater: The End of the Overland Campaign*, Gary W. Gallagher and Carline E. Janney, eds. (Chapel Hill: University of North Carolina Press, 2015), 176–209.

———. *Cold Harbor: Grant and Lee, May 26–June 3, 1864* (Baton Rouge: Louisiana State University Press, 2002).
———. *To the North Anna River: Grant and Lee, May 13–25, 1864* (Baton Rouge: Louisiana State University Press, 2000).
———. *The Battle of the Wilderness, May 5–6, 1864* (Baton Rouge: Louisiana State University Press, 1994).
———. *The Battles for Spotsylvania Court House and the Road to Yellow Tavern, May 7–12, 1864* (Baton Rouge: Louisiana State University Press, 1997).
Ripley, William Y. A. *Vermont Riflemen in the War for the Union, 1861 to 1865: A History of Company F, First United States Sharpshooters* (Rutland: Tuttle & Co., 1883).
Robertson, James I., Jr., ed. *The Civil War Letters of General Robert McAllister* (New Brunswick, NJ: Rutgers University Press, 1965).
———. *Stonewall Jackson: The Man, The Soldier, The Legend* (New York: Macmillan Publishing, 1997).
Robertson, William Glenn. "The Peach Orchard Revisited: Daniel E. Sickles and the Third Corps on July 2, 1863." In *The Second Day at Gettysburg*, Gary W. Gallagher, ed. (Kent, OH: Kent State University Press, 1993), 33–56.
Rutkow, Ira M. *Bleeding Blue and Gray: Civil War Surgery and the Evolution of American Medicine* (New York: Random House, 2005).
Sauers, Richard A. *Gettysburg: The Meade-Sickles Controversy* (Washington: Potomac Books, 2003).
Savage, William T. *A Discourse Delivered at the Funeral of Franklin C. Wadsworth, Late of Berdan's Regiment of Sharpshooters* (Concord: McFarland & Jenks, 1862).
Schildt, John W. *Roads to Gettysburg* (Parsons, WV: McClain Publishing, 2003).
Schnupp, Chris. *The Long Island Company: A History of Company H, 1st Regiment of US Sharpshooters* (Kindle Edition, 2015).
Sears, Stephen W. *Chancellorsville* (Boston: Houghton Mifflin, 1996).
———, ed. *The Civil War Papers of George B. McClellan, Selected Correspondence, 1860–1865* (Cambridge, MA: Da Capo Press, 1992).
———. *George B. McClellan: The Young Napoleon* (Cambridge, MA: Da Capo Press, 1999).
———. *Gettysburg* (Boston: Houghton Mifflin, 2003).
———. *Lincoln's Lieutenants: The High Command of the Army of the Potomac* (Boston: Mariner Books, 2018).
———. *To the Gates of Richmond: The Peninsula Campaign* (Boston: Houghton Mifflin, 1992).
Sessions, N. "The 23d Georgia." *Mineral Point Weekly Tribune*, May 23, 1863.
———. "The 23d Georgia." *National Tribune*, July 10, 1884.
Shelton, William H. "A Mansion Rich in Virginia's History." *New York Times*, August 19, 1928.
Shreve, William P. "The Operations of the Army of the Potomac, May 13–June 2, 1864." In *The Wilderness Campaign, May–June 1864, Papers of the Military Historical Society of Massachusetts*, vol. 4 (Boston: Military Historical Society of Massachusetts, 1905), 289–318.

Simpson, Brooks D. "General McClellan Bodyguard: The Army of the Potomac after Antietam." In Gary W. Gallagher, ed., *The Antietam Campaign* (Chapel Hill: University of North Carolina Press, 1999), 44–73.

Simpson, Harold B., ed. *Touched with Valor: Civil War Papers and Casualty Reports of Hood's Texas Brigade* (Hillsboro, TX: Hill Junior College Press, 1964).

Slotkin, Richard. *The Long Road to Antietam: How the Civil War Became a Revolution* (New York: Liveright Publishing, 2012).

Smith, J. S. "Gen. Whipple's Death." *National Tribune*, August 6, 1885.

Sodergren, Steven E. *The Army of the Potomac in the Overland and Petersburg Campaigns: Union Soldiers and Trench Warfare, 1864–1865* (Baton Rouge: Louisiana State University Press, 2017).

Stackpole, Edward J. *Chancellorsville: Lee's Greatest Battle* (Harrisburg, PA: Stackpole Company, 1958).

Stevens, Charles A. *Berdan's United States Sharpshooters in the Army of the Potomac, 1861–1865* (St. Paul, MN: Price-McGill Company, 1892).

Stickley, E. E. "Battle of Sharpsburg." *Confederate Veteran*, vol. 22 (1914), 66–67.

Stine, J. H. *History of the Army of the Potomac* (Washington: Gibson Bros., 1893).

Stotelmyer, Steven R. *Too Useful to Sacrifice: Reconsidering George B. McClellan's Generalship in the Maryland Campaign from South Mountain to Antietam* (El Dorado Hills: Savas Beatie, 2019).

Sword, Wiley. "Lt. Col. Caspar Trepp's Colt's Revolver and the Reconnaissance to Pitzer's Woods." *Gettysburg Magazine*, no. 14, January 1996, 46–51.

———. *Sharpshooter: Hiram Berdan, His Famous Sharpshooters and Their Sharps Rifles* (Lincoln, RI: Andrew Mowbray, 1988).

Thomson, O. R. Howard, and William H. Rauch. *History of the "Bucktails," Kane Rifle Regiment of the Pennsylvania Reserve Corps (13th Pennsylvania Reserves, 42nd of the Line)* (Philadelphia: Electric Printing Company, 1906).

Tilney, Robert. *My Life in the Army: Three Years and a Half with the Fifth Army Corps* (Philadelphia: Ferris & Leach, 1912).

Verrill, George W. "The Seventeenth Maine at Gettysburg and in the Wilderness." In *War Papers Read Before the Commandery of the State of Maine, Military Order of the Loyal Legion of the United States*, vol. 1 (Portland: Thurston Print, 1898), 260–82.

Waite, Otis F. R. *New Hampshire in the Great Rebellion* (Claremont: Tracy, Chase, & Company, 1870).

Walker, Francis A. *History of the Second Army Corps in the Army of the Potomac* (New York: Charles Scribner's Sons, 1886).

Ward, W. C. "Incidents and Personal Experiences on the Battlefield at Gettysburg." *Confederate Veteran* 8 (1900): 345–49.

Warner, Ezra J. *Generals in Blue* (Baton Rouge: Louisiana State University Press, 1992).

Waugh, John C. *Lincoln and McClellan: The Troubled Partnership Between a President and His General* (New York: Palgrave Macmillan, 2010).

Weld, Stephen Minot. *War Diary and Letters of Stephen Minot Weld* (Privately printed, Riverside Press, 1912).

Wert, Jeffry D. *A Glorious Army: Robert E. Lee's Triumph, 1862–1863* (New York: Simon & Schuster, 2011).

West, John C. *A Texan in Search of a Fight* (Waco: J. S. Hill & Co., 1901).

Whitman, John W. "Lorenzo Barber Was the Eagle-Eyed 'Fighting Parson' of Hiram Berdan's Famous U.S. Sharpshooters." *America's Civil War*, September 1998, 12–18.

Whitman, William E. S., and Charles H. True. *Maine in the War for the Union* (Lewiston: Nelson Dingley, 1865).

Wilson, E. A. "An Incident at Gettysburg." *National Tribune*, June 10, 1886.

———. "Second Bull Run." *National Tribune*, October 19, 1905.

———. "A Sharpshooter Tells Where One Came True." *National Tribune*, September 25, 1884.

Winchell, James. "Wounded and a Prisoner." *Civil War Times Illustrated*, August 1965, 20–25.

Wipperman, Darin. *Burnside's Boys: The Union's Ninth Corps and the Civil War in the East* (Lanham, MD: Stackpole Books, 2023).

———. *First for the Union: Life and Death in a Civil War Army Corps from Antietam to Gettysburg* (Lanham, MD: Stackpole Books, 2020).

Wolcott, Walter. *Military History of Yates County, N. Y.* (Penn Yan: Express Book, 1895).

Wright, A. "The 2d U.S. Sharpshooters." *National Tribune*, February 18, 1909.

Index

C